Southern Biography Series

WILLIAM J. COOPER, JR., *Editor*

FRANCISCO BOULIGNY

FRANCISCO BOULIGNY

A
BOURBON
SOLDIER
IN
SPANISH
LOUISIANA

GILBERT C. DIN

LOUISIANA STATE UNIVERSITY PRESS
BATON ROUGE AND LONDON

02 01 00 99 98 97 96 95 94 93   5 4 3 2 1

Designer: Rebecca Lloyd Lemna
Typeface: Galliard
Typesetter: G & S Typesetters, Inc.
Printer and binder: Thomson-Shore, Inc.

Library of Congress Cataloging-in-Publication Data

Din, Gilbert C.
    Francisco Bouligny : a Bourbon soldier in Spanish Louisiana /
Gilbert C. Din.
        p.   cm. — (Southern biography series)
    Includes bibliographical references and index.
    ISBN 0-8071-1795-1
    1. Bouligny, Francisco, 1736–1800. 2. Soldiers—Louisiana—
Biography. 3. Spaniards—Louisiana—Biography. 4. Louisiana—
History—To 1803. I. Title. II. Series.
F372.B78D54   1993
976.3'03'092—dc20
[B]   92-23235
                                                             CIP

The author is grateful to the Historic New Orleans Collection, Museum/
Research Center, for permission to quote from the Bouligny Papers, and to
the Howard-Tilton Memorial Library, Tulane University, for permission to
quote from the Rosemonde E. and Emile Kuntz Collection and from the
Cruzat Family Papers.

Publication of this book has been assisted by a grant from the Program for
Cultural Cooperation Between Spain's Ministry of Culture and United States
Universities.

The paper in this book meets the guidelines for permanence and durability
of the Committee on Production Guidelines for Book Longevity of the
Council on Library Resources. ∞

In memory of my father,

John Khair Din,

and for a grandson he never knew,

Alexander Matthew Din

CONTENTS

ILLUSTRATIONS

PREFACE

My first contact with Francisco Bouligny came many years ago at the Biblioteca Nacional in Madrid, where I first saw a copy of his *Memoria* of 1776. At that time I was gathering material for a dissertation on Spanish colonization efforts in Louisiana. While intrigued about his proposals and their influences, I put them aside in order to finish the work at hand. Not until 1974, when Jack D. L. Holmes was putting together a session on Spanish Louisiana for the annual meeting of the Louisiana Historical Association and suggested that I do a paper on Bouligny and the founding of New Iberia, did I get back to him. It led the next year to do research on Bouligny, the *Memoria,* and the "Bouligny affair" (as Roscoe R. Hill called Bouligny's clash with Bernardo de Gálvez in his *Descriptive Catalogue of the Documents Relating to the History of the United States in the Papeles Procedentes de Cuba)*. In 1977 the Louisiana Collection Series published what I knew about Bouligny up to that time, his encounter with Gálvez, and my translation of the *Memoria*.

I came to realize, however, that Bouligny deserved a full-length biography. In the years since the publication of the *Memoria,* even while researching other topics, I continued to collect documents and notes on him. This included four research trips to Spain and a sabbatical leave spent in Baton Rouge and New Orleans.

The result of collecting many documents over a lengthy period of time is, I hope, a biography that goes beyond most studies on colonial figures of Spanish Louisiana that do not portray their subjects in three dimensions. I have tried to tie Bouligny to his times and to show that he was a man with emotions. He was both proud and ambitious, but life was not easy for him. He lacked a personal fortune and at times a friend at court who could protect and further his career. While his family letters that undoubtedly reflected his feelings about his wife, daughter, and sons have not survived, the Spanish government has preserved records about his official duties that reveal his loyalties and occasionally even his emotions.

Equally important, however, the official records shed light on how instrumental he was in the Spanish government's altering its policy toward Louisiana in 1776. In this way, Bouligny was probably more influential than most governors of Spanish Louisiana. Also a careful examination of the affair with Gálvez casts new light on the governor, who until now has been seen only in heroic proportions. But the documents uncover a dark side of Gálvez that his admirers have hidden, avoided, or missed. I suggest that future studies of Gálvez need to view him in earthly proportions and no longer in the exalted manner of the past.

In Louisiana, it seems, Bouligny moved about easily among the different social groups. His intimate knowledge of the French language and having a French-born father no doubt helped him among French-born Louisianians. His marriage to a Louisiana Creole also facilitated developing a tie to the local Creole population. But above all, Bouligny was a Spaniard, born and raised in the Iberian nation, and his first loyalty was to his king and to his nation. Loyalty to monarchical Spain and the Catholic religion was the norm in Spanish Louisiana, and many of the French and Creole residents shared that loyalty, particularly those who worked for the Spanish government. In late 1803, when the United States acquired the province, a number of them chose to leave Louisiana and retreated with the Spaniards to Pensacola and Cuba.

It was only after 1803, with a revival of the French language in keeping government records and things French in Louisiana (perhaps the successes of Napoleon Bonaparte in Europe contributed to the Gallic revival) at a time when American influence was still negligible, that many residents began to talk and write disparagingly of the Spanish regime. That development has caused many people today to have a distorted view of what occurred during Spain's tenure of Louisiana, a distortion that is still supported by many of Louisiana's Francophiles. A part of that misinterpretation was to make Bouligny more Frenchman than Spaniard, a sentiment totally in disagreement with the real man. This biography attempts to correct that distortion and to view Bouligny and his times as they actually were.

For this study, archives on both sides of the Atlantic Ocean were consulted. They include Seville's Archivo General de Indias; Madrid's Biblioteca Nacional, which has a copy of Bouligny's 1776 *Memoria,* and the Archivo Histórico Nacional; and outside Valladolid, the Archivo General de Simancas. In New Orleans, the Historic New Orleans Collection has become the chief repository of the surviving Bouligny documents, most of which belonged to the colonel, which his children seem to have divided up among themselves. Other Bouligny documents can be found in the Rosemonde E. and Emile Kuntz Collection at Tulane University. In addition, legal documents are in the New Orleans Notarial Archives and the Louisiana Historical Center. The Parsons Collection in the Humanities Research Library at the University of Texas, Austin, contains several Bouligny documents and a copy of his 1776 *Memoria*.

I owe expressions of appreciation to many institutions and people who have helped me over the years. First and foremost is Fontaine Martin, president of the Bouligny Foundation and author of *A History of the Bouligny Family and Allied Families,* who assisted me whenever I had questions about Bouligny's relatives. Fort Lewis College provided me with a sabbatical leave, and the Fort Lewis College Faculty Development Fund gave me a research grant, as did the American Philosophical Society. Mrs. Robert Knox of the Washington State University Library provided me with a microfilm copy of the Bouligny *Memoria*. Alfred Lemmon of the Historic New Orleans Collection and Wilbur E. Meneray and his staff at Special Collections in the Howard-Tilton Library at Tulane University were helpful. Evangeline Lynch of the Louisiana Room, now Special Collections, at the Louisiana State University Library also helped in many ways.

Among historians who assisted me are G. Douglas Inglis, Light T. Cummins, Jack D. L. Holmes, Antonio Acosta y Rodríguez, Paul E. Hoffman, Ralph Lee Woodward, David J. Weber, and Eric Beerman. Ronald R. Morazán read several drafts of the Bouligny manuscript.

ABBREVIATIONS

AGI   Archivo General de Indias, Seville
  PC   Papeles Procedentes de la Isla de Cuba
  SD   Audiencia de Santo Domingo
AGS   Archivo General de Simancas, near Valladolid
  GM   Sección de Guerra Moderna
AHN   Archivo Histórico Nacional, Madrid
  Est.   Sección de Estado
AMS   Archivo Militar de Segovia
BN   Biblioteca Nacional, Madrid
          Sección de Manuscritos
  CDF   Colección de documentos varios para la historia de la Florida y tierras adjuntas
  DL   Colección de documentos sobre la Luisiana, 1767 a 1792
DSGL   Despatches of the Spanish Governors of Louisiana, 1766– 1792
exped.   *expediente* (a file of documents)
HNOC   Historic New Orleans Collection, New Orleans
  BB   Bouligny-Baldwin Family Papers, 1710–1900
  DB   d'Auberville-Bouligny Family Papers, 1618–1873
KCTU   Rosemonde E. and Emile Kuntz Collection, Howard-Tilton Memorial Library, Tulane University
leg.   *legajo* (a bundle of documents)
LHC   Louisiana Historical Center, New Orleans
MPA,   Mississippi Provincial Archives, Spanish Dominion.
SD   Mississippi State Department of Archives and History, Jackson, Miss.
NONA   New Orleans Notarial Archives, Orleans Parish Civil Courts Building, New Orleans
SMV   Lawrence Kinnaird, ed. *Spain in the Mississippi Valley, 1765– 1794*. Three parts

FRANCISCO BOULIGNY

I   SPAIN, AMERICA, AND THE RISE OF FRANCISCO BOULIGNY

G AYOSO WAS DYING. The news spread quickly through the hot and humid streets of New Orleans in July, 1799. The condition of Manuel Gayoso de Lemos, governor-general of Louisiana, had worsened. A malignant fever, probably yellow fever, which had struck Louisiana for the first time only three years before, appeared on the verge of claiming its highest-ranking victim. On the morning of July 18, a priest administered the last rites of the Catholic Church as the end neared. That same morning, Judge Advocate Nicolás María Vidal sent a terse message to Col. Francisco Bouligny, commandant of the Fixed Louisiana Regiment, informing him that preparations for the continuation of government needed to be made. Vidal acted none too soon. That evening, Gayoso lay dead in his house. The next day, Bouligny notified post commandants throughout Louisiana that since "God [had] disposed to take the life of the governor," he was now acting military governor of Louisiana and Vidal had assumed power as civil governor.[1]

Francisco Bouligny must have pondered the irony that had unexpectedly thrust him into the office of governor and given him a new opportunity when it seemed that he had none. Only two years before he had sought the coveted post of governor-general of Louisiana, and it had been denied him. Surely now the authorities in Madrid would grant him the post of proprietary governor in compensation for his many years of service and not having given it to him in 1797. As governor, Bouligny might realize the other cherished ambition that had eluded him, to be promoted to the rank of brigadier general. Those two achievements would

1. Jack D. L. Holmes, *Gayoso, The Life and Times of a Spanish Governor in the Mississippi Valley, 1789–1799* (Baton Rouge, 1965), 266; [Nicolás María Vidal] to Francisco Bouligny, New Orleans, July 18, 1799, in AGI, PC, leg. 134A; Bouligny to post commandants, New Orleans, July 19, 1799, in AGI, PC, leg. 1.

be a fitting capstone to a career that had already spanned forty-one years, thirty-seven of them in America. They would make all the years of waiting, all the years of frustration, all the years of denial, seem worthwhile. Finally, as governor-general of Louisiana and a brigadier general in His Catholic Majesty's army, Bouligny could hold his head more erect and walk the narrow streets of New Orleans with a firmer gait in the realization that he was at last the senior civil and military administrator of Spanish Louisiana. No one in the colony would stand above him. The death of Gayoso appeared to have made it all possible.

Bouligny no doubt savored the thought of becoming the top Spanish official in Louisiana. It would vindicate the twenty-one years of injustice he felt he had suffered. In 1777 and 1778, he had enjoyed the post of second military chief and lieutenant governor in charge of settlements, commerce, and Indians. That office held the potential to launch his career, and it then seemed possible that he might become governor of Louisiana while still relatively young. His abrupt removal from that post by Governor Bernardo de Gálvez, who charged but failed to prove malfeasance in office, had embittered Bouligny. He felt that Gálvez had cast a dark cloud over his subsequent career. Nevertheless, he remained in Louisiana and endured the heat and humidity, the mud and swamps, the myriad insects and dense vegetation, and the monotonous flatness of the land. Still, garrison duty in the Mississippi Delta had its compensations. He married and acquired a growing family, possessed for twenty years a large plantation worked by numerous slaves, owned an imposing house in New Orleans staffed with many servants, and gradually ascended in rank, becoming permanent colonel and commandant of the Fixed Louisiana Regiment. His status by 1799 contrasted markedly with the uncertainty he felt when he first arrived in Louisiana in July, 1769, as a thirty-two-year-old lieutenant and aide-de-camp to Gen. Alejandro O'Reilly. His was a proud achievement for a *segundón* (secondary son) of an Alicante family whose antecedents could be traced back to fifteenth-century Italy.[2]

In the late Middle Ages, the earliest known ancestor of the Bouligny family, Gian Matteo, called "Il Bolognino," lived as a soldier of fortune

---

2. Biographical information on Francisco Bouligny can be found in Gilbert C. Din, *Louisiana in 1776: A Memoria of Francisco Bouligny* (New Orleans, 1977). The sketch on Bouligny by Jack D. L. Holmes in *"Dramatis Personae* in Spanish Louisiana," *Louisiana Studies,* VI (1967), 161–69, contains serious errors.

until his death in 1460. Italy then consisted of many city-states, duchies, and principalities that feuded constantly with one another. Gian Matteo served in the mercenary band of Braccio da Monte, a renowned *condottiere*, until the former switched sides. Entrusted with the defense of a fortress in Pavia, Gian Matteo unexpectedly handed it to Francesco Sforza, duke of Milan, who subsequently took him into his family. Gian Matteo soon became the count of San Angelo Lodigiano, and he added Bolognini Attendolo (the latter name being Sforza's real surname) to his own name. He and his descendants settled down in the Milan region and married into prominent local families. Several generations later, during the Thirty Years' War, Francesco Bolognini, a cavalry captain, fell prisoner to the French, who transported him to Marseilles. Francesco elected to remain there, gallicized his name to François, and entered the import-export business of his future father-in-law. With his March 6, 1649, marriage to a local woman, Cécile Germain, whom he wed without parental consent, François began his own family line, the Bouligny. It did not, however, remain in France for long.[3]

In the wake of the establishment on the Spanish throne of the Bourbon Felipe V, grandson of Louis XIV of France in 1700, Frenchmen flocked to the Iberian peninsula to work in diverse urban occupations, become merchants, or take government service as bureaucrats and soldiers. Alicante, a port city on Spain's southeastern coast that enjoyed an extensive trade in the Mediterranean, particularly with France and North Africa, attracted Joseph and Jean Bouligny, the son and grandson of François. They were the first of this family to settle in Spain, where Jean in time became the father of Francisco.[4]

In 1710 Joseph Bouligny returned to Alicante. By then, the Boulignys had business experience as well as investments in Spain, and they now decided to explore further commercial possibilities as other Frenchmen were doing upon the termination of the War of the Spanish Succession.

3. On Bouligny's and his wife's ancestry, see Fontaine Martin, *A History of the Bouligny Family and Allied Families* (Lafayette, La., 1990). François Bouligny died in 1695 at the age of eighty-four (*ibid.,* 104).

4. Eleazar Córdova-Bello, in *Las reformas del despotismo ilustrado en América (siglo XVIII hispano-americano* (Caracas, 1975), 109n, writes, "The ascension of Felipe to the throne of Spain in 1700 was followed by immigration, on a considerable scale, by specialized French workers and technicians." A brief history of Alicante is found in *Enciclopedia de la cultura española*, Vol. 5 (Madrid, 1963), 230–33, while more is contained in Francisco Figueras Pacheco, *Compendio histórico de Alicante* (Alicante, 1957).

By 1717, their relocation in Spain had become permanent. Little is known about the family and how it fared on Spanish soil during those first years. Joseph Bouligny died in Alicante in 1734 at eighty. Eleven years before, in 1723, Joseph's twenty-seven-year-old son Jean married Marie Paret in Marseilles, daughter of French-born Dominique Paret and Françoise Vivet. Their marriage in the Gallic port city constituted only a brief return, for the Bolignys had put France behind them forever, just as Francesco had earlier forsaken Italy. Alicante, with its benign climate, arid appearance, and palm trees reminiscent of North Africa, had become the home of the Bouligny family.[5]

The thirteen children of Jean and Marie Bouligny, seven daughters and six sons, were born in Spain and grew up as Spaniards. Little is known about the Bouligny sisters beyond their marriages and children. Five of them married: Inés (born in 1730 and died before 1789) to Diego Tala, a government official; Francisca (born in 1732 and died about 1790) to Lorenzo Mabilli, a Greek diplomat; Cecilia (born in 1734 and died about 1801) to Tomás Bremond, perhaps also a government employee; María Antonia (born in 1739) to Francisco Longua; and Teresa Clara (born in 1744) to Francisco Carguet. The two sisters who did not marry were Ana (born in 1743, dead by 1758) and María de la Esperanza (born in 1752), who, motivated by the religiosity of her parents, entered the Order of Canónigas Regulares Religiosas in Alicante on August 24, 1768. She died at her convent on April 18, 1789.[6]

Among the males, one son stayed exclusively in business, and four sons served the nation in the army or government. Francisco's two oldest brothers, José (born on September 14, 1724) and Juan (baptized on March 3, 1726), took over their father's business in 1746 when he went into semiretirement until his death on March 29, 1772; their mother had preceded him in death in October, 1758. They were buried next to each other at the convent of Santo Domingo in Alicante. José and Juan retired from the business world after thirty years, in 1776, to devote themselves

5. Fontaine Martin, "The Origins of the Bouligny Family," *Bouligny Foundation Newsletter* (November, 1979); Eric Beerman, "A Genealogical Portrait of Francisco Bouligny" (Copy of typescript in possession of Gilbert C. Din).

6. Martin, *Bouligny Family*, 108, 109–12, 117–19. See also Martin, "Origins of Bouligny Family," and Beerman, "Genealogical Portrait." Cecilia Bouligny de Bremond had a son Tomás, born about 1760, who received a licenciate degree in canon law from the University of Alcala de Henares on June 15, 1782. Cecilia was then living in Madrid (AHN, Universidades, leg. 70, no. 169).

to other, probably more satisfying pursuits. Their import-export firm was then suffering badly. José remained near Alicante, living the life of a country gentleman on the family estate of Alcoraya outside Alicante, which he alone had inherited, until his death on January 20, 1802. Three of his sons also served in the army. Juan rose to the rank of brigadier general in 1810 but mistakenly sided with the French invaders of Spain in the War of Spanish Independence (1808 to 1813) after they captured him; he became a French field marshal in the war and later fled from Spain with the defeated French.[7]

Bouligny's brother Juan went job hunting in 1776 with the collapse of his and José's business. He entered the Spanish diplomatic corps the next year and achieved notable success. About 1780 he received the delicate assignment of negotiating a peace treaty with the Ottoman Empire in Constantinople. He accomplished that on September 14, 1782, including a trade agreement. The Spanish government showed its appreciation by appointing him as its minister to the Ottoman court in June, 1783. Upon his return to Madrid near the year 1796, the crown named him as an "honorario" to the Council of State. He served less than two years before dying on January 9, 1798, at seventy-one. Juan's son, José Eliodoro Bouligny y Marconie, and the latter's son, Teofilo Bouligny y Timoni, also served in the Spanish diplomatic corps.[8]

A third brother, also older than Francisco, Domingo, was born in 1728, and almost nothing is known about him. He died before 1758. Perhaps as a child Francisco had been close to him, as he would later give his first-born son the same name.[9]

Meanwhile, Francisco's two younger brothers—Lorenzo, born in 1740, and Luis, born about 1750—followed in his footsteps, pursuing army careers. Neither married. Lorenzo served in the Flanders Infantry Regiment and saw duty in New Spain from about 1769 to 1783. He eventually rose to the rank of captain before retiring to Alicante about 1790. Luis entered the Estremadura Infantry Regiment, becoming a sublieutenant in 1769 and advancing in rank slowly. He became the most widely traveled Bouligny, serving in the siege of Gibraltar against the British, and in Venezuela, Peru, and Buenos Aires. He returned to Spain in 1792. He

7. Martin, *Bouligny Family*, 108, 109, 115–26.

8. *Ibid.*, 108, 109, 116, 119–35; Juan's appointment to the Council of State is in AHN, Est., leg. 84bis. A brief obituary can be found in *Gazeta de Madrid*, February 2, 1798, X, 111.

9. Martin, *Bouligny Family*, 108, 108*n*, 109, 112, 117.

was still a captain on active duty when he died in 1793 at Ceret, France, near the Spanish border, during the war against revolutionary France (1793 to 1795).[10]

For all the Bouligny children, there was never any question of *patria*—fatherland. They identified with the adopted homeland of their father, the nation of their birth. While they probably conversed with their parents in French, among themselves they employed the language they felt most comfortable in, Spanish.[11]

The Bouligny brothers, with their ties to the nobility and several recent generations of middle-class merchants, were born at a time when Spain was recovering from the dismal decline of the seventeenth century. That age contrasted sharply with the earlier glorious era of the Catholic Kings and the first Habsburgs. Sixteenth-century Spain ruled over vast dominions in Europe, America, and Asia. Wealth from the American colonies, the Indies, poured into the Iberian peninsula, making Spain the richest and for a time the most powerful nation in Europe, the envy of its neighbors. But the talented early Habsburgs gave way to their empty-headed seventeenth-century descendants, Felipe III, Felipe IV, and finally the rachitic and feebleminded Carlos II. In the reign of Carlos II, from 1665 to 1700, Spain reached its nadir, particularly in Castile, the monarchy's center that had long sustained the nation and empire. The numerous wars of the Habsburgs sapped the country's strength and squandered its riches. The gold and silver bullion from America produced a soaring inflation that destroyed much of Spain's industry. Large quantities of bullion fled the nation to pay for cheaper goods imported from northern European countries. Widespread contraband trade in Spain and the Indies also deprived the monarchy of revenues and benefits. Similarly, the decline in the Spanish population in the seventeenth century created a manpower shortage while leaving fewer taxpayers in the productive middle and lower classes. Military defenses in Spain and in the colonies eroded and made them vulnerable to the inroads of rival nations. All these factors helped to bring on a lengthy depression. The aristocracy that had traditionally supplied leaders sank into mediocrity while its enormous wealth contrasted grotesquely with an impoverished

---

10. *Ibid.,* 108*n*, 112, 118, 119, 126.

11. The numerous letters between Bouligny and his brothers in Spain, all in Spanish and today in HNOC, clearly reflect the loyalty they held for Spain; see in particular Joseph to Francisco Bouligny, Azcovaya, Spain, September 28, 1791, in DB, HNOC.

and backward nation. In short, under the later Habsburgs, the Spanish government, economy, military establishment, and even society stagnated and appeared incapable of revival.[12]

The impetus that brought the Bouligny family to settle in Spain also provided the first French officials, who introduced the new methods that had been instituted north of the Pyrenees in the seventeenth century. France led Europe in attempting to achieve an absolutist state, especially under Louis XIV. It developed a sophisticated fiscal apparatus, specialized departments of state (ministries), and salaried intendants with wide powers in administration, finance, and the judiciary. The government directed commerce, regulated tariffs, stimulated manufacturing, and improved transport and communications. Louis magnified his status by claiming divine rights and used absolutism to build a formidable army that innovated concepts in the infantry, artillery, and cavalry. The centralizing effects, however, produced dynastic and territorial ambitions that resulted in repeated conflicts between the French Bourbons and the Spanish-Austrian Habsburgs.[13]

The new alignment between Spain and France in 1701 brought harmful as well as beneficial results. Felipe V had to fight to retain his throne in the War of the Spanish Succession (1702 to 1713), overcoming invasion from abroad and rebellion at home. The peace treaties that ended the war acknowledged the losses of the Spanish Netherlands, the Italian possessions, the island of Minorca, and most importantly, Gibraltar. Moreover, Spain conceded to England the *asiento* (a contract to introduce African slaves in the Spanish colonies) and a yearly trade ship to Puerto Belo; both served as cover for contraband activity. But on the positive side, French officials in Spain during the war tried to modernize and improve efficiency by appointing competent men to government and military posts, removing venal officeholders, producing war materiel (arms, gunpowder, artillery, and more), and centralizing authority through the use of

12. Sixteenth- and seventeenth-century Spain are satisfactorily discussed in John Huxtable Elliott, *Imperial Spain, 1469–1716* (New York, 1964), Henry Kamen, *Spain, 1469–1714: A Society of Conflict* (London, 1981), and John Lynch, *Spain Under the Habsburgs* (2nd ed.; New York, 1981). See also Henry Kamen, "The Decline of Spain: A Historical Myth?" in *Past and Present*, LXXXI (November, 1978), 24–50; and his *Spain in the Later Seventeenth Century, 1665–1700* (London, 1980).

13. The rise of French absolutism in the seventeenth century is described in detail in David Parker, *The Making of French Absolutism* (New York, 1983).

ministers and intendants. To help implement the reforms, the Bourbons utilized more people of the lower nobility (*hidalgos*) and middle classes, categories that included the Bouligny family. Overall, however, the War of the Spanish Succession was a disaster for Spain, and the government sought to recover lost lands and to strengthen itself through reforms.[14]

It was as the war ended that the Boulignys settled down on the east shore of Spain and from there witnessed Bourbon policy at work to regain the Italian possessions and safeguard bases and cities on the North African coast. From Alicante, military expeditions and trade ships sailed, and the merchant Bouligny family was no doubt involved. To satisfy the ambitions of Felipe V's second wife, Isabel Farnesio, who sought principalities for her sons to govern, Spain exercised a vigorous policy in Italy. By 1734, her son Carlos had become king of the Two Sicilies, but her younger son Felipe did not acquire duchies until 1748. With that done, thirty-five years of Spanish diplomacy, intrigue, and warfare to provide lands for Farnesio's children ended. Only then did the revitalized Spanish government devote more energy to protecting the Indies.[15]

In America, where Francisco Bouligny spent his career, Spain implemented reforms slowly. Under able men like Cardinal Alberoni, José Patiño, José del Campillo, and the marqués de la Ensenada (Cenón de Somodevilla y Bengoechea), the Spanish navy gradually recovered. Cádiz, rather than Seville, became the Spanish terminal for the fleets that sailed to America, carrying merchandise in return for bullion and other colonial products. In time, registered ships sailing alone gradually replaced the trade fleets. Patiño, in particular, revived the navy, building arsenals at El Ferrol and Cartagena in addition to Cádiz. He increased the number of ships of the line, the battleships of that age. Coast-guard vessels patrolled American waters to intercept English smugglers. They succeeded so well in reducing clandestine trade that the English commercial class clamored

14. The best work on early eighteenth-century Spain is Henry Kamen, *The War of Succession in Spain, 1700–15* (Bloomington, Ind., 1967). See W. N. Hargreaves-Mawdsley, *Eighteenth-Century Spain, 1700–1788: A Political, Diplomatic and Institutional History* (Totowa, N.J., 1979), for a discussion of reforms in Spain.

15. The era from 1716 to 1748 in Spain is adequately covered in José Luis Comellas, *Historia de España moderna y contemporanea (1474–1965)* (2nd ed.; Madrid, 1967), 303–20; he sees Spanish attention alternating between the Mediterranean and the Atlantic. The Spanish fleet that recovered Oran, a colony lost in 1708, sailed from Alicante in 1732 (Hargreaves-Mawdsley, *Eighteenth-Century Spain*, 67).

for hostilities against Spain, thus starting the War of Jenkins' Ear, known in Spain as the Guerra del Asiento, in 1739. At the outset in the Caribbean, the English sacked poorly defended Puerto Belo but failed against the Spanish bastion at Cartagena de Indias. In the war at sea, the rebuilt Spanish navy gave the English fleet as much as it got. At the conclusion of the conflict in 1748, neither Spain nor England had gained an advantage. Two years later, however, England agreed to end the *asiento* and Puerto Belo trade ship in return for an indemnity of 100,000 pounds.[16]

During the reign of the melancholic Fernando VI (1746 to 1759), Spain tried to avoid war, which had proved so destructive. Under Minister Ensenada, the nation followed a path of armed peace as it continued to build the navy and protect the colonies. After Ensenada's fall as minister in 1754, defenses deteriorated under the leadership of the Anglophile Ricardo Wall, who wanted to avoid war at all cost. Even repeated English victories over the French in the Seven Years' War (1756 to 1763) failed to budge Wall. Spanish policy changed only when Carlos III, former king of the Two Sicilies and son of Isabel Farnesio, ascended the throne in 1759. Aware that England's destruction of the French Empire and navy posed serious consequences for Spain, Carlos negotiated the Third Family Compact and rushed into the war, unprepared, in 1761. It was as one reign ended and another began that Francisco Bouligny chose the army for a career in 1758. His becoming a cadet coincided with efforts to strengthen and increase the army.[17]

16. Felipe V's reign after the War of the Spanish Succession is well discussed in Hargreaves-Mawdsley, *Eighteenth-Century Spain*, 46–83. He believes that Queen Isabel Farnesio was the actual ruler in Spain, due to Felipe's insanity. For example, he would only discuss matters of state with José Patiño while hidden behind a curtain, and he spent endless days in bed. The melancholia that afflicted Felipe was transmitted to Fernando VI, and Carlos III lived in fear that he had inherited it (*ibid.*, 100).

Much information on eighteenth-century fleets and trade is found in Geoffrey J. Walker, *Spanish Politics and Imperial Trade, 1700–1789* (Bloomington, Ind., 1979). The classic work on the Spanish navy is Cesareo Fernández Duro, *La armada española desde la unión de los reinos de Castilla y Aragón* (1895–1903; rpr. Madrid, 1973). A more concise work is José March y Labores, *Historia de la marina real española, desde el descubrimiento de las Américas hasta el combate de Trafalgar* (Madrid, 1854). See also Vicente Rodríguez Casado, "La política del reformismo de los primeros borbones en la marina de guerra española," *Anuario de estudios americanos*, XXV (1968), 601–18.

17. Hargreaves-Mawdsley, *Eighteenth-Century Spain*, 76–97; Lucio Míjares Pérez, "Programa político para América del marqués de la Ensenada," *Revista de Historia de*

Bourbon reforms in the Spanish military system were long overdue. Under Carlos III, Spain for the first time established a standing army in America. Earlier, prior to the 1560s, the inhabitants of the Caribbean, the most vulnerable region in the Spanish-American colonies, had to form their own militia units and arm themselves at their own expense. Spain used only local projects with local revenues and militia. To a large degree for defense, the government relied on the enemy's lack of New World bases, which made their long-range operations brief and hazardous. It was a hostile environment of unfamiliar waters, exotic diseases, and enervating tropical weather. Occasional attacks failed to deter Spain from abandoning this outmoded policy. After the 1560s, the crown authorized royal expenditures slowly.[18] Only the raids of Francis Drake and John Hawkins in 1585 and 1586 broke the Spaniards of their parsimony and induced them to build new fortresses at Havana, Veracruz, Puerto Rico, and Puerto Belo and to send regular soldiers from Spain. As the sixteenth century closed, the Spaniards clung to their defense system of convoys for merchant shipping and fortified key Caribbean harbors garrisoned by peninsular soldiers.[19]

Under the inept seventeenth-century Habsburgs, Spain's defenses weakened as the Dutch, French, and English empires rose to challenge Spanish claims to New World lands. Warfare escalated, and Spain's poorly defended Caribbean settlements suffered. During the century, Spain acknowledged the loss of possessions to the Dutch (1648), the English (1670), and the French (1678 to 1680) in return for their stopping support for pirates. Before the pirates were defeated, they had seized Puerto Belo in 1668, Panama in 1671, and Veracruz in 1683, and a regular French army captured Cartagena de Indias in 1697. Although the temporary loss of those four major fortresses shocked the Spaniards, the Habsburgs did

---

América (January–June, 1976), 82–130; María Dolores Gómez Molleda, "El pensamiento de Carvajal y la política internacional española del siglo XVIII," *Hispania,* XV (1955), 117–37.

18. Paul E. Hoffman, *The Spanish Crown and the Defense of the Caribbean, 1535–1585: Precedent, Patrimonialism, and Royal Parsimony* (Baton Rouge, 1980); Roland Dennis Hussey, "Spanish Reaction to Foreign Aggression in the Caribbean to About 1680," *Hispanic American Historical Review,* IX (1928), 286–89. George Earl Sanders, "The Spanish Defense of America, 1700–1763" (Ph.D. dissertation, University of Southern California, 1973), 30–77, 78–120, 122–24, contains good background information.

19. Hussey, "Spanish Reaction," 290–93.

little to modify their outdated defense methods in the Indies, and the Bourbons, who followed them in 1700, also failed to introduce innovations for the next forty years.[20]

Only with the War of Jenkins' Ear did the Bourbons reevaluate their defense policy. Before then, they continued to rely on fortresses that dominated the main colonial trade routes and commercial centers. Meanwhile, new developments in eighteenth-century warfare occurred: improved warships and the use of daring naval tactics, particularly by the English; the role of long-range artillery; and the ability of the enemy to mass numerous troops in the colonies. At the same time, the English navy became increasingly powerful while the French fleet floundered from disaster to disaster. Competent Spaniards like Patiño and Ensenada, on the other hand, acknowledged that Spain's link to the Indies depended on a strong navy, and they labored incessantly to create it. Land defenses in the Indies also needed rebuilding. The fall of Puerto Belo in 1739 pushed the government to hasten its efforts. The Spaniards soon successfully parried English thrusts at Cartagena de Indias, Santiago de Cuba, and Panama. Because of rising English interest in Central America, the Spanish government constructed forts at Omoa, Trujillo, and Matina aimed at stopping encroachment. While Spain had commenced reorganizing militia units throughout the colonies after the War of the Spanish Succession, it had not progressed far by midcentury. About the time that Francisco Bouligny entered the army in 1758, several new developments took place designed to improve defenses. Although fixed fortresses remained important, Spain shifted its emphasis to the use of greater manpower, stationing more peninsular army units in the colonies and training local troops at key locations. In the Caribbean, the main defense center moved from Cartagena de Indias to Havana, and it was to Havana that the army posted Bouligny in 1762 in the midst of the Seven Years' War.[21]

Perhaps Francisco Bouligny volunteered for service in America after Spain entered the war in 1761. Less is known about his early years than any other period in his life. He was the fourth son and the seventh child

20. *Ibid.*, 293–302.

21. Sanders, "Spanish Defense of America," 223–55; Antonio Bethancourt Massieu, *Patiño en la política internacional de Felipe V* (Valladolid, 1954); R. A. Stradling, *Europe and the Decline of Spain: A Study of the Spanish System, 1580–1720* (London, 1981), 206. See also the two studies by Juan Marchena Fernández: *Oficiales y soldados en el ejército de América* (Seville, 1983), and *La institución militar en Cartagena de Indias, 1700–1810* (Seville, 1982).

of his parents. From his birth on September 4, 1736, until his entry in the army in 1758, the only certain knowledge about Bouligny was his attendance at the Seminary of the Immaculate Conception in the neighboring town of Orihuela, a boy's school started by the local bishop only four years before. The ten-year-old lad enrolled on May 10, 1747, and completed a course in Latin grammar, receiving a diploma on March 18, 1750. Although this is the only known formal training that Bouligny acquired as a youth, it served him well, and he later put it to good use. This can be seen in the numerous letters, reports, and memoirs, mostly of an official nature, that he penned during his lifetime. The army recognized his talents, particularly in Louisiana, and kept him attached to headquarters units for most of his career. Like any bureaucratic organization, the Spanish military functioned on an endless stream of orders, records, and reports. An essential qualification for promotion to the highest positions was *saber despachar*—to know how to process paperwork. Bouligny successfully fulfilled that duty throughout his long career. In addition, his education instilled in him a lifelong interest in world affairs. Without doubt, Bouligny stood out among the best educated of the army officers in Spanish Louisiana.[22]

After earning his diploma in 1750, Bouligny most likely entered the family business for several years until it became clear that it was no longer as profitable as it had been. Jean Bouligny then inclined his fourth son, Francisco, in the direction of a military career. At the time that Bouligny entered the army in 1758, the Spanish military was introducing reforms, growing in size, and encouraging the entry of middle-class youth as officers. The army, however, showed a preference for the sons of officers. They could become cadets at age twelve, and even earlier on occasion, thus gaining years of seniority over others who entered at sixteen or twenty-one, as did Bouligny. But there were not enough sons of officers for the expanding army. Eighteenth-century Spain was basically an underdeveloped agricultural nation that suffered extremes in wealth, in-

22. Baptismal certificate of Francisco Domingo Joseph Bouligny in Libro de Baptismos, XXVIII (1735–1737), fol. 167B, Iglesia Parroquial de San Nicolás, Alicante. PC and SD in AGI contain numerous documents on the career of Francisco Bouligny. See also "Mortuaria de . . . Fran.co Bouligny," hereinafter cited as Bouligny Succession Papers, LHC, and Gilbert C. Din, "The Death and Succession of Francisco Bouligny," *Louisiana History,* XXII (1981), 314–15, for the books Bouligny owned. Bouligny's school certificate in Latin is in BB, HNOC.

fluence, and opportunity. The mostly impoverished and dispossessed lower classes made up the overwhelming majority of the population. Bourbon ministers, especially after 1750, attempted to nurture a slowly growing urban-based middle class. A tiny elite, however, dominated positions of influence and authority, and the middle class both envied and sought to join that elite. Personal contact with influential people was usually essential to obtain preferential treatment. The Bouligny family probably pulled every string at their disposal to secure an appointment for Francisco as a cadet. After presenting the proper credentials to verify his legitimacy and ties to a nobility, he entered the Zamora Infantry Regiment.[23]

Precisely where Bouligny spent the first year as a cadet is uncertain. He initially served in the company of Juan de Escalera of the Zamora regiment from March, 1758, to January, 1760. The Spanish army at that time was innovating new methods and tactics, and the Zamora regiment might have experienced the changes. Overall, Spain's army lagged far behind those of the leading European nations, France and Prussia, in military reform. Few professional schools existed in Spain for the instruction of army officers, even in the highly specialized areas of artillery and engineering. Infantry cadets generally received their training in the regiment, which was often haphazard and dependent upon the quality of the officer-teachers. The cadets obtained a smattering of knowledge in royal and military ordinances (law), the duties of each rank, command, and drill. A few officers, after completing their training as cadets, had the opportunity to study short courses in mathematics, engineering, and fortifications in specialized academies. Because of his service in America, Bouligny had no such opportunity. The government also sent selected

23. An undated statement by Juan Bouligny, but written about 1776 in Alicante, affirms that Jean Bouligny pushed Francisco in the direction of a military career (BB, HNOC). See also Martin, *Bouligny Family*, 112. On Spanish society in the eighteenth century, see two works by Antonio Domínguez Ortiz: *La sociedad española en el siglo XVIII* (Madrid, 1955), and *Sociedad y estado en el siglo XVIII español* (Barcelona, 1976); and two studies by Fernando Díaz-Plaza: *La sociedad española (desde 1500 hasta nuestros días)* (Barcelona, 1968), and *La vida española en el siglo XVIII* (Barcelona, 1946). On the nobility, see Raymond Carr, "Spain," in *The European Nobility in the Eighteenth Century*, ed. Albert Goodwin (2nd ed.; London, 1967), 43–59; and on the middle classes, Juan Manuel Herrero, "Notas sobre la ideología del burgués español del siglo XVIII," *Anuario de estudios americanos*, IX (1952), 297–326, and Vicente Rodríguez Casado, "La revolución burguesa del XVIII español," *Arbor* (January, 1951), 5–29.

officers on missions to friendly nations to study their military methods, which the Spaniards then introduced upon their return. Spanish military schools sometimes used foreign army manuals in translation. Although the crown attempted to promote the best military methods that foreign countries had to offer, especially under Carlos III, many of the traditional Spanish officers felt a repugnance for them and resisted the innovations. Throughout the eighteenth century, reforms in the Spanish military structure had only indifferent results. Bouligny, who entered the army in the midst of the new currents, probably tended to accept them more readily than the older officers. After nearly two years in the Zamora Infantry Regiment and still a cadet, Bouligny transferred to the Spanish Royal Guards, who were stationed in Madrid and served as a personal bodyguard to the king.[24]

Bouligny's transfer to the Royal Guards in 1760 was an honor inasmuch as it was an elite corps. That same year, Col. Alejandro O'Reilly returned to Spain after studying Austrian and French military tactics and began to teach those tactics to the Spanish Guards. They and the other units in Madrid learned movements that were entirely new to the Spanish army. Bouligny probably met O'Reilly at that time. When he left the Guards in January, 1762, he obtained a commission as a lieutenant—not as a sublieutenant, the first officer grade. He probably wanted a commission as quickly as possible, since his father paid for his keep. Cadets like Bouligny earned no pay, and Jean Bouligny spent approximately one thousand pesos annually for the four years that Francisco served as a cadet, a substantial sum for that age and several times the yearly income for a modest family. Life in Madrid was no doubt inviting, but as a

---

24. License from Brigadier Antonio de Idíaguez to Bouligny, Madrid, January 23, 1759, BB, HNOC. Many *hojas de servicio* (service sheets) on Bouligny's military service are in the Spanish archives. The most complete *hoja,* however, was made on the day he died, November 25, 1800, now in DB, HNOC. On the Spanish military in the eighteenth century, see Georges Desdevises du Desert, "Les institutions de l'Espagne au XVIIIe siècle," *Revue Hispanique,* LXX (1927), 354–99. The classic work on the Spanish army is Conde de Clonard, *Historia orgánica de las armas de infantería y caballería españolas desde la creación del ejército permanente hasta el día* (Madrid, 1854). Concise descriptions of European military establishments and tactics are found in R. Ernest Dupuy and Trevor N. Dupuy, *The Encyclopedia of Military History, from 3500 B.C. to the Present* (New York, 1970). A study of French military tactics that influenced the Spaniards is Robert S. Quimby, *The Background of Napoleonic Warfare: The Theory of Military Tactics in Eighteenth Century France* (New York, 1957).

twenty-five-year-old cadet dependent upon his father, Bouligny probably welcomed a commission as quickly as possible.[25]

Spain's entry in the Seven Years' War against England in 1761 presented him with the opportunity to display his mettle and earn recognition and promotion. On January 2, 1762, Ricardo Wall approved his promotion to lieutenant and his assignment to the Fixed Havana Regiment in Cuba. Spain was attempting to improve Havana's defenses in anticipation of an English attack. Bouligny was to report to the port city of Cádiz, where he would receive instructions for his transportation to Cuba. Thus ended one era in the life of Francisco Bouligny. As he left Spain in the summer of 1762 to add his contribution to the defense of the empire, he probably did not realize the new directions that service in America held for him or that he would return to Spain only once during the remainder of his life.[26]

25. Bouligny service sheet, November 25, 1800, DB, HNOC; Juan Bouligny statement, ca. 1776, BB, HNOC. An excellent description of Madrid at the time that Bouligny lived there is Charles E. Kany, *Life and Manners in Madrid, 1750–1800* (Berkeley, Calif., 1932).

26. Ricardo Wall to the marqués de Sarria, Buen Retiro, January 2, 1762, in KCTU; Bouligny's patent of promotion to lieutenant, Madrid, January 2, [1762], BB, HNOC.

2   THE CUBAN YEARS

1762–1769

I N THE SPRING of 1762, Francisco Bouligny, perhaps after
a leave to visit his family in Alicante, arrived in
Cádiz at the southern tip of Spain. From Cádiz,
he was to sail to Cuba, where he would spend the next several years.
Spain was then in the Seven Years' War, and the port city of Cádiz
teemed with commercial and military activity. At the start of the eighteenth century, Cádiz had replaced the inland port of Seville, fifty miles
up the winding Guadalquivir River, as the Spanish terminal for trade
with the American colonies. The bay of Cádiz, a deep-water Atlantic
port, now enjoyed a monopoly in that trade. Besides Spaniards, the merchant community contained numerous foreigners—Frenchmen, Italians,
and Englishmen among others—who represented countries that supplied much of the manufactured goods Spain shipped to America. Cádiz
was also Spain's main port for sending soldiers and war materiel to the
colonies, and barracks and warehouses, the latter stocked with supplies,
were everywhere.[1]

Cádiz, where Bouligny passed several months, rested on the end of
a narrow strip of land that jutted from east to west into the Atlantic
Ocean and thus protected the bay. A wall and river channel on the eastern flank guarded against an enemy attack by land, while seawalls on the
remaining three flanks sheltered the city against invasion from the water.
Soon after the war broke out, the Spaniards expected an English assault
on Cádiz. They cleared away all the small villas and gardens on the isth-

---

1. Pedro Cathalan y Hervera statement, Santa Cruz de Tenerife, June 17, 1763, BB,
HNOC. On Spanish commerce in the eighteenth century, see Antonio García-Baquero
González, *Cádiz y el Atlántico (1717–1778): (El comercio colonial español bajo el monopolio gadi-
tano)* (Seville, 1976), and Walker, *Spanish Politics*.

mus side that faced the Atlantic and built a sandy glacis. The works must have been in progress during Bouligny's residence in the city. Except for Calle Ancha (Broad Street), the streets of Cádiz were narrow and poorly paved. Almost all, however, were straight and intersected one another at right angles. Because garbage removal was primitive, the English traveler Henry Swinburne, who was there not long after Bouligny, complained of odors, filth, and nocturnal rats in the streets. In winter, Atlantic storms dumped abundant quantities of rain on the city, making it cold and humid. In contrast, the summer sun of Andalusia beat down unmercifully on Cádiz and the surrounding water.[2]

In the opening months of the war, spring of 1762, Spain prepared to send reinforcements to America for the defense of exposed Caribbean ports and cities. Although Francisco Bouligny appears mostly as a shadowy figure in the years between 1762 and 1769, it is nevertheless possible to trace his movements in that era. Bouligny's orders assigned him to the Fixed Havana Regiment, and after waiting several months for transportation, he sailed from Cádiz on July 21 for Santa Cruz de Tenerife in the Canary Islands, the usual port of call for Spanish ships headed to the Indies. The voyage took less than two weeks. Before Bouligny could depart from the Canaries, however, news from the Caribbean reported the astonishing English capture of Havana, which stopped many Spanish ships from leaving for America. Orders now instructed Bouligny to remain in Santa Cruz. There he sat out the conclusion of the war, which brought major defeats to Spanish arms.

Before the crown could prepare the defenses of Havana or Manila in the Philippines, the British had acted swiftly and conquered both, reaping large benefits in coin and goods. During its brief participation in the Seven Years' War, Spain came to share the misfortunes that France had experienced. The French, while on one hand welcoming the Spanish entry in the war, on the other quietly initiated negotiations with the English to end the conflict. Any expectation that Spain might turn the tide of battle against England had quickly faded.[3]

As Bouligny waited in Santa Cruz, perhaps enjoying the mild winter

2. A good description of Cádiz is in Henry Swinburne, *Travels Through Spain in the Years 1775 and 1776* (2nd ed.; London, 1787), I, 335–41.

3. Cathalan statement, June 17, 1763, BB, HNOC. On the Seven Years' War, see Lee Kennet, *The French Armies in the Seven Years' War* (Durham, N.C., 1968), and Charles E. Chapman, *A History of Spain* (New York, 1918), 386–87.

weather from 1762 to 1763, diplomats in Paris worked to end hostilities. The war had totally exhausted France, which sought its conclusion while the Spaniards reeled from the staggering blows they received. The latter desired above all to avoid territorial losses and to recover their most valuable possessions, but Spain soon realized that it would have to pay a price to regain Havana. It ceded Florida to England, and the French divested themselves of Louisiana, useless after the loss of Canada. Spain reluctantly accepted Louisiana west of the Mississippi River to prevent Britain from acquiring it. The east bank of the river, except for the Isle of Orleans on which New Orleans sits, passed into English hands. Louisiana was then a vast, virtually empty and undeveloped province in mid–North America. Spain sought to keep foreigners as far as possible from New Spain (Mexico) to prevent illegal trade in peacetime and conquest in wartime. The west bank of the Mississippi River appeared well suited as the Spaniards' first line of defense against Britain. The large expanse from the Mississippi across Louisiana and Texas to Mexico became a *barrera*, a barrier, to keep out encroaching foreigners enticed by the fabled riches of Mexico.[4]

Spain agreed to the peace preliminaries in November, 1762, and ratified the completed Treaty of Paris in February, 1763. But for Spain and France the peace was no more than a truce: The two members of the Family Compact sought revenge within six years. First, however, they needed to rebuild their armies and navies and restructure their defenses in America. In Madrid the members of the king's council of ministers met secretly once weekly to discuss reforms and military reorganization. They discarded the outdated Habsburg defense system of reliance upon fortifications and decreed the creation of colonial armies. Three types of military units were to exist in America: regular peninsular army units that rotated periodically between Spain and the Indies; fixed regiments and battalions of the regular army that consisted of both Spanish and colonial troops (Bouligny would serve in two such units during his military career); and disciplined militia units composed of Spanish Americans and trained by regular soldiers. While the Family Compact flourished in the

4. A useful account of the English capture of Havana is C. Martínez-Valverde, "Operaciones de ataque y defensa de La Habana en 1762," *Revista general de Marina*, CLXIV (1963), 487–503, 706–27. On the Treaty of Paris, see Zenab Asmat Rashad, *The Peace of Paris, 1763* (London, 1951), and Robert L. Gold, *Borderland Empires in Transition: The Triple Nation Transfer of Florida* (Carbondale, Ill., 1969), 13–28. See also E. Wilson Lyon, *Louisiana in French Diplomacy, 1759–1804* (1934; rpr. Norman, Okla., 1974), 13–35.

years immediately after the Seven Years' War, France appears to have influenced the Spanish court in the selection of at least some of the personnel chosen to implement reform.[5]

Spain began preparations for reorganizatoin even before the council concluded its deliberations. In the spring of 1763, it commenced its task with Cuba, Bouligny's assigned destination. Cuba, from its strategic position at the entrance to the Gulf of Mexico, had replaced Cartagena de Indias as the center of Spanish defenses in the Caribbean. Much to Spain's dismay, the British had at last penetrated the Gulf with their acquisition of East and West Florida and the forts at Pensacola and Mobile. It meant that Spanish possessions in both the Gulf and the Caribbean needed strengthening. For the task of recovering Havana from Britain and reorganizing its fortifications and military units, the crown selected Lt. Gen. Ambrosio de Funes y Villalpando, better known as the conde de Ricla, and Field Marshal Alejandro O'Reilly. They sailed from Cádiz on board the *Héctor* on April 27, 1763, heading for Santa Cruz de Tenerife, where Bouligny awaited transportation.[6]

In May, Ricla and O'Reilly arrived in the Canaries and within days left again, trying to reach Havana by mid-June. The Canaries then held many soldiers and ships waiting for the war to end before continuing to their destinations in the Indies. Not all sailed as quickly as the two generals. Bouligny remained in Santa Cruz drawing his monthly pay of thirty-two *escudos* of *vellón* (approximately twenty silver pesos) as a lieutenant. While in Santa Cruz he received charge of recruits enlisted in the Canar-

---

5. Lyle N. McAlister, "The Reorganization of the Army of New Spain, 1763–1766," *Hispanic American Historical Review,* XXXIII (1953), 8–9; Alan J. Kuethe, *Cuba, 1753–1815: Crown, Military, and Society* (Knoxville, Tenn., 1986), 25–27. Arthur S. Aiton ("Spanish Colonial Reorganization Under the Family Compact," *Hispanic American Historical Review,* XII [1932], 269–80) claims that among the Spaniards favored by the French were José de Gálvez, the conde de Floridablanca, the marqués de Croix, Alejandro O'Reilly, and the marqués de Valliere. Franco-Spanish cooperation, however, broke down when France refused to help Spain in the Falkland-Malvinas crisis of 1770–71 with Britain. See also Allan Christelow, "French Interest in the Spanish Empire During the Ministry of the Duc de Choiseul, 1759–1771," *Hispanic American Historical Review,* XXI (1941), 515–37.

6. For studies on the conde de Ricla and Alejandro O'Reilly, see Kuethe, *Cuba,* 25, 31–32, Jaime Delgado, "El Conde de Ricla, Capitán General de Cuba," *Revista de Historia de América* (January–December, 1963), 41–138, Eric Beerman, "Un bosquejo biográfico y genealógico del general Alejandro O'Reilly," *Hidalguía: La revista de genealogía, nobleza, y armas,* XXIV (March–April, 1981), 225–44, and Bibiano Torres Ramírez, *Alejandro O'Reilly en las Indias* (Seville, 1969), 18.

ies for service in Cuba. By June 17, he had orders to embark on the frigate *Corazón de Jesús,* which was leaving for the port of San Cristóbal (Havana). Either on June 17 or shortly thereafter, he and the recruits departed and reached the Pearl of the Antilles in August in the usual sailing time of six to eight weeks. On July 6, before Bouligny arrived, Ricla and O'Reilly regained possession of Havana from the English. Bouligny's presence in Cuba marked the start of a six-year sojourn, the beginning of which witnessed far-reaching military and economic reforms.[7]

It was Field Marshal Alejandro O'Reilly, subinspector general and later well known in Louisiana, who undertook the reorganization of the Cuban army and militia units. Then thirty-eight and a veteran of twenty-four years, he had wartime experience in both Italy and Portugal, had studied the Prussian and French military systems, and was regarded as a tough, no-nonsense officer. The crown had confidence in his ability to rehabilitate the island militarily. While Ricla devoted himself to rebuilding the fortifications at Havana, especially El Morro Castle and La Cabana (fortresses the English had dismantled, in addition to all the other harm they inflicted upon Spanish defenses there), and securing the cooperation of the Cuban planters for increased taxation, O'Reilly worked on the military. He began with the regular army units, including Bouligny's Fixed Havana Regiment (the Fijo), the oldest fixed (*fijo*) unit in America, established in 1719. O'Reilly disapproved of permanently rooted regiments in America and preferred to have peninsular units rotate every few years, a recommendation he made for the Fixed Havana Regiment. He cashiered more than half the Fijo's officers from service and denied promotion to others for the unit's shoddy conduct. Officers and men from other corps entered the Fijo to fill the ranks.

During the fall of 1763, Bouligny renewed his acquaintance with O'Reilly; they probably had met when the Irishman had instructed the Royal Guards in Spain in new tactics. The general now used him to drill recruits and militia pickets and train them in the use of arms and the new discipline. The Irishman favored the young lieutenant from Alicante, who served in one of the Fijo's fusilier companies. Newly arriving Spaniards enjoyed preference over men long established in the colony and those

7. Cathalan statement, June 17, 1763, and attached note of Juan Thomás de la Barrera, Havana, September 5, 1763, both in BB, HNOC; Bouligny petition to the king, New Orleans, January 7, 1794, attached to his letter to the marqués de Someruelos, New Orleans, August 8, 1799, in AGI, PC, leg. 1550; Torres Ramírez, *O'Reilly,* 17–18.

who had taken part in the defense of Havana. According to O'Reilly, the Fijo had performed poorly in the recent war, and he wanted to abolish the unit. Moreover, during the siege of Havana, sixty thousand pesos disappeared from the regiment's strongbox. The officers claimed that they took the money to protect it from the British. O'Reilly demanded that they repay the sum, and he even put up for sale the house of one officer to recover his share of the amount. Despite being favored, Bouligny remained a lieutenant during his years in Cuba. He observed firsthand the military reforms O'Reilly carried out on the island and for the rest of his life realized the need for periodic change and reorganization.[8]

The reforms Ricla and O'Reilly conducted in Cuba stand out as the start of widespread renovation in Spanish imperial administration. For the military units assigned to Havana (two infantry regiments, a dragoon regiment, and two artillery companies), the Fixed Havana Regiment, composed of four infantry battalions, stood at the center. A regular Spanish unit, the Regiment of Córdoba, was given 1,224 *plazas* (posts for soldiers), but it had many vacancies. English deserters and men from other Spanish units eventually filled many of them. In addition, O'Reilly established the Regiment of Dragoons, with 286 *plazas*. In 1764 many other soldiers arrived to serve in the Havana units. Nevertheless, attrition caused by illness, death, discharge, desertion, and imprisonment often kept the regiments at less than full strength.[9]

O'Reilly spent more time in organizing the Cuban militia, which was to represent a greater number of troops. Spain had neither the manpower nor the money to station more regular soldiers to defend its American possessions. Moreover, through discipline, which is to say training, the colonial militias were to be as fit for duty as the regular soldiers. In Havana alone O'Reilly raised 5,557 citizen soldiers, and the rest of Cuba contributed another 4,046 men. Officer commissions in the militia went to the Cuban wealthy, who sought the prestige conferred by military uniforms and the *fuero*—protection from civil legal jurisdiction and liability.[10]

8. Torres Ramírez, *O'Reilly,* 18–34; Delgado, "Conde de Ricla," 91–106; Bouligny petition to the king, New Orleans, January 7, 1794, attached to his letter to Someruelos, New Orleans, August 8, 1799, in AGI, PC, leg. 1550. See also Alexander Humboldt, *The Island of Cuba,* trans. J. S. Thrasher (New York, 1969).

9. Kuethe, *Cuba,* 33–35.

10. *Ibid.,* 37–48. On the *fuero militar,* see *Enciclopedia Espasa Calpe* (Madrid, 1964), XXIV, 1505–1506.

The yearly cost for the military units, 647,775 pesos, was staggering. O'Reilly reduced the sum to 487,453 pesos by cutting the already meager wages of the troops, but that provoked mutinies among the regular soldiers in the Córdoba, dragoon, and Fijo regiments. O'Reilly transferred the rebellious grenadiers to fusilier companies, sent other mutineers to labor in the fortifications as criminals, and had one dragoon run the gauntlet. He summoned the officers of the regiments, including the Fijo's (and Bouligny), and informed them of the government's need to economize through wage reductions. Each captain presented his company before O'Reilly and personally vowed to obey the king and accept the new pay regulations for Cuba. Their conduct pleased O'Reilly, who forgave the older officers for their past failings. The crown subsequently not only upheld O'Reilly's wage reduction but extended it to the rest of America in a royal order in October, 1764.[11]

The crown needed to increase revenues to pay for mounting expenditures. Although Mexico provided subsidies for many Caribbean possessions, including Cuba, Puerto Rico, and later Louisiana, its treasury could not bear the burden alone. Therefore, Ricla sought the cooperation of the Cuban Creole plantation owners, who had recently invested heavily in sugar production after a rise in prices. Because restrictions limited their exports, they often resorted to smuggling. In a meeting with many of the leading planters, Ricla obtained their consent for increased taxation, but implied was the assumption that the crown would relax trade restrictions. The Spanish government, however, first acted by imposing new taxes, which produced a Cuban petition begging for commercial concessions. After a time, the crown responded favorably.[12]

Beginning in 1765, Spain started to liberalize its commercial policy to encourage trade, all for the purpose of raising revenue. It lowered tariffs, abolished the Cádiz monopoly, authorized free communications between

11. Kuethe, *Cuba*, 35–36.

12. *Ibid.*, 50–71; Hugh Thomas, *Cuba, The Pursuit of Freedom* (New York, 1971), 27–41. Alan J. Kuethe ("Los Llorones Cubanos: The Socio-Military Basis of Commercial Privilege in the American Trade Under Charles IV," in *The North American Role in the Spanish Imperial Economy, 1760–1819,* ed. Jacques Barbier and Allan J. Kuethe [Manchester, England, 1984], 142–56) explains the co-optation that the Spanish government employed to obtain military cooperation from the Cuban sugar-planter class, which undertook a large share of the military defense of the island. See also Kuethe's "The Development of the Cuban Military as a Sociopolitical Elite, 1763–1783," *Hispanic American Historical Review,* LXI (1981), 695–704.

Spain, the Caribbean, and the mainland ports, and allowed intercolonial trade. In October, 1765, the government opened Cuba's commerce to eight new Spanish ports besides Cádiz, and to Santo Domingo, Puerto Rico, Trinidad, and Margarita, colonies that received the same privileges that Cuba enjoyed. Cubans could also trade in their own ships. A decree of April 23, 1768, permitted commerce between Cuba and Louisiana. It was not until 1778, however, that the government issued its major decree for free trade within the Spanish Empire, except for Mexico and Venezuela, which received it in 1789.[13]

Although Ricla and O'Reilly declared their work in Cuba completed in 1764 and sought to return to Spain, the crown kept them there for another year. In that interval O'Reilly journeyed to Puerto Rico to carry out that island's military reform, which he accomplished before returning to Europe.[14]

The Spanish government also renovated its defenses throughout the Indies. One important area was the viceroyalty of New Spain, which was then becoming Spain's most valuable colony because of its increased silver production, expanding economy, and rising population. New Spain had a symbiotic relationship with Louisiana: While Louisiana constituted the former's most remote defense against encroachment by English North America, Mexico provided it with funds and when necessary military reinforcements.

Through the first two-thirds of the eighteenth century, Spain gradually built up its armed forces in Mexico. By 1760 a number of army units already existed in the viceroyalty. Veracruz, with its important fortress of San Juan de Ulua, held an infantry battalion of 600 men (six companies), a dragoon battalion of 240 horsemen, and an artillery company of 120 men. The crown kept smaller army detachments in Mexico City, Acapulco, and

---

13. Eduardo Arcila Farías, *El siglo ilustrado en América: Reformas económicas del siglo XVIII en Nueva España* (Caracas, 1955), 94–117; Clarence H. Haring, *The Spanish Empire in America* (New York, 1952), 341–42. John Lynch (*The Spanish American Revolutions, 1808–1826* [New York, 1973], 4–8) argues that the trade reforms after 1765 were designed to bind the colonial economy closer to Spain by expanding overseas trade, increasing industrialization, providing equitable taxation, and improving communications. The crown also wanted governmental centralization for the purpose of controlling the Creoles in the colonies. See Herbert Ingram Priestly, *José de Gálvez, Visitor-General of New Spain (1765–1771)* (Berkeley, Calif., 1916), 32–37. For Bourbon reforms, see Peggy K. Liss, *Atlantic Empires: The Network of Trade and Revolution, 1713–1826* (Baltimore, 1983).

14. Kuethe, *Cuba*, 76; Torres Ramírez, *O'Reilly*, 49–94.

Isla del Carmen, and twenty-two presidios scattered across the northern regions of the viceroyalty. In all, 2,600 men made up the regular army of New Spain. In addition, urban and provincial militia units existed, but they were usually poorly trained, undermanned, and often disorganized. In the Seven Years' War, the marqués de Cruillas, the viceroy of Mexico, raised 8,500 veteran and militia soldiers in Veracruz, the most likely place to be attacked. But he believed that the defense of the viceroyalty required many more troops.[15]

In 1764 the Spanish government entrusted the task of military reorganization in Mexico to Lt. Gen. Juan de Villalba y Angulo, who received extensive powers. A Spanish infantry regiment and a dragoon regiment constituted the center of the viceroyalty's defense. The bulk of the soldiers, however, was to consist of disciplined militiamen. Villalba took with him officers and sergeants to train the civilian soldiers. Changes in planning resulted in regular army units being stationed in Veracruz, Mexico City, and Puebla. The militia units, which Villalba reorganized, included infantry regiments or battalions for the principal cities. Before leaving New Spain in 1766, Villalba's report revealed four regular units (Regiment of America, Regiment of Dragoons of Spain, Regiment of Dragoons of Mexico, and the Company of Artillery of Veracruz) totaling 2,341 men, and provincial and urban militia units numbering 13,039 men. But not all the latter units were armed and uniformed. Moreover, it was difficult to keep the militia in a state of readiness, particularly in peacetime. Although the Spaniards made extensive defense plans for New Spain, their forces there rarely achieved a state of combat readiness, for a variety of reasons.[16]

In addition to military reorganization in Cuba, Puerto Rico, and New Spain, the Spanish government gradually carried out changes in its other New World colonies: Peru, Chile, Colombia, Argentina, and else-

---

15. On New Spain (Mexico), see Lyle N. McAlister, *The "Fuero Militar" in New Spain, 1764–1800* (Gainesville, Fla., 1957), and "Reorganization," 2–7; María del Carmen Velázquez, *El estado de guerra en Nueva España, 1760–1808* (Mexico City, 1950), 24–105; and José Antonio Calderón Quijano, ed., *Los virreyes de Nueva España en el reinado de Carlos III* (Seville, 1972), Vol. I.

16. McAlister, "Reorganization," 9–32; Christon I. Archer, *The Army in Bourbon Mexico, 1760–1810* (Albuquerque, 1977), is a comprehensive study of military reform in Mexico. Additional information on the eighteenth-century Spanish army in America can be gleaned from Marchena Fernández, *Oficiales y soldados,* and Alexander De Humboldt, *Political Essay on the Kingdom of New Spain,* trans. John Black (1811; rpr. New York, 1966).

where. It gave its most immediate attention, however, to the exposed Caribbean and Gulf of Mexico possessions, which were situated closer to English North America and consequently more vulnerable. The crown worked as well to stimulate trade to raise the funds required for the expensive task of building military fortifications, stationing and rotating Spanish troops in the New World, and arming the militia units.[17]

From Havana, where Bouligny acquired his first experience in the colonial army, he witnessed the growth of Spanish military might. His years in Cuba consisted mainly of routine army duty, which eventually proved tiring. After several years, he requested a return to Spain. But the government offered him transfers to Mexico and the Canary Islands, which he rejected. The expulsion of the Jesuit Order from the Spanish colonies in 1767 produced a momentary flurry of activity. The first major excitement to come his way, however, occurred in December, 1768, when the Havana authorities learned that the French population of New Orleans had risen up in arms and expelled the Spanish governor Antonio de Ulloa. The arrival of Ulloa in Havana was followed by that of most Spanish officials and soldiers who had been stationed in Louisiana. Cuban authorities, led by Capt. Gen. Antonio María Bucareli, then waited several months for orders from Madrid before taking action against the rebel colony. In April, 1769, the Spanish government decided to suppress the rebellion and regain Louisiana. Bouligny must have welcomed the opportunity the insurrection offered because he could now participate in its reduction. Havana, the nearest colony to Louisiana containing troops, was the logical center from which to dispatch the forces to recover New Orleans.[18]

Bouligny probably had not thought of service in Louisiana before

17. Many studies deal with colonial reorganization. See in particular: Leon G. Campbell, *The Military and Society in Colonial Peru, 1750–1810* (Philadelphia, 1978); Allan J. Kuethe, *Military Reform and Society in New Granada, 1773–1808* (Gainesville, Fla., 1978); Jacques A. Barbier, *Reform and Politics in Bourbon Chile, 1755–1796* (Ottawa, 1980); Miles Wortman, "Bourbon Reforms in Central America, 1750–1786," *The Americans*, XXXII (1975), 222–38; and John Lynch, *Spanish Colonial Administration, 1782–1810: The Intendant System in the Viceroyalty of the Rio de la Plata* (New York, 1958).

18. Martin, *Bouligny Family*, 114; John Preston Moore, *Revolt in Louisiana: The Spanish Occupation, 1766–1770* (Baton Rouge, 1976), 163–64; Charles Gayarré, *History of Louisiana* (New Orleans, 1885), II, 249–65; Antonio de Ulloa to Antonio María Bucareli, Havana, December 8, 1768, in *SMV*, Pt. 1, pp. 83–84. See also Magnus Morner, ed., *The Expulsion of the Jesuits from Latin America* (New York, 1965).

his participation in the expedition to New Orleans. It was not one of the more important colonies in the Gulf of Mexico, and the Spanish government had given it little attention or money in the years after 1763. Older and more valuable possessions enjoyed priority. France, in casting off Louisiana, had regarded it as a constant drain of resources from its founding at the start of the eighteenth century. Despite the expenditure of substantial sums of money and the sending of numerous people to the colony, Louisiana's population had remained minuscule: only 2,966 whites and 4,909 slaves in 1763, according to one census. Nor had the development of the province proceeded far after six decades. The colony contained only one town, New Orleans, and settled regions were largely confined to the banks of the Mississippi River in what is today lower Louisiana, with other population clusters located at Natchitoches on the Red River and in the Missouri country in upper Louisiana. Moreover, the English acquisition of West Florida at the conclusion of the Seven Years' War gave them settlements on the Mississippi at Baton Rouge and Natchez that made Spanish defenses difficult without a considerable outlay of funds.[19]

Governor Ulloa's brief administration in Louisiana from 1766 to 1768 confronted numerous problems. The Spanish government failed to send him sufficient soldiers to back up his authority, which prompted Ulloa to decline to take formal possession of New Orleans, although he and Spanish soldiers did so at Balize (the entrance to the Mississippi River), at the mouth of the Missouri River, and at several other army posts. Despite the small number of troops, Ulloa reorganized the colony's defenses by building several new forts, since he mistrusted the British, who were across the river in West Florida. Economic conditions in Louisiana continued to deteriorate at that time because officials in New Spain and Cuba neglected to send funds for running the colony. Mexican silver was a prime necessity to stimulate Louisiana's trade and repay the merchants

19. The French era in Louisiana to 1763 is covered by Gayarré, *History,* Vols. I, II; Alcée Fortier, *A History of Louisiana* (New York, 1904), Vol. I. The early history of French Louisiana is detailed by Marcel Giraud in *A History of French Louisiana:* Vol. I, *The Reign of Louis XIV (1698–1715),* trans. Joseph C. Lambert (Baton Rouge, 1974); Vol. II, *Années de transition (1715–1717)* (Paris, 1958); Vol. III, *L'Epoque de John Law (1717–1720)* (Paris, 1966); Vol. IV, *La Louisiane après le système de Law* (Paris, 1978); Vol. V, *The Company of the Indies, 1723–1731,* trans. Brian Pearce (Baton Rouge, 1991). The French census of 1763 is in AGI, SD, leg. 2595. A census of March, 1766, gives the population as 5,595 whites and 5,940 slaves (manuscript 569, fol. 107, Museo Naval [Madrid]).

for the goods that Ulloa purchased on credit. He stopped payment for merchandise and services in February, 1768, because of the lack of money. Among the economic problems, trade declined, prices for export products fell, and a shortage of consumer goods, along with bad currency, produced inflation. Although Ulloa bore little responsibility for these difficulties, he contributed to them in another area. He upset the established Indian trade patterns of upper Louisiana by redistributing licenses, requiring prospective traders to descend to New Orleans to obtain them, stopping gifts to the Indians, and even banning traders from going to Indian villages in 1768. In these and in other ways, Ulloa earned the disapprobation of many Louisiana inhabitants.[20]

In assessing the causes for the French Creole rebellion that ousted Governor Ulloa and brought Bouligny to Louisiana, two principal reasons stand out: the small number of Spanish troops in the colony and economic instability. Because of military reorganization going on elsewhere and delays in assembling the soldiers to send to Louisiana, Spain did not have military control of the province during the Ulloa years. Spanish troops numbered fewer than a hundred, and many of them suffered from insubordination. Ulloa's efforts to induce French soldiers to enlist in the Spanish army failed. Perhaps that problem could have been overcome had economic conditions in Louisiana been favorable following Ulloa's arrival. Prior to the Spanish takeover, the colony's trade had been oriented toward France and the French West Indies. Despite a general liberalization of its commercial policy, Spain intended to confine Louisiana's trade to its empire, thus prohibiting commerce with French possessions, and to eliminate contraband wherever possible. Consequently, the colony's farmers, merchants, and speculators worried about their economic future, and every rumor of the imminent arrival of Spanish soldiers, coupled with an enforcement of trade regulations, brought louder cries of anguish and protest. A clique of determined merchants and planters in New Orleans, led by Nicolas Chauvin de Lafrénière and possibly Denis Nicolas Foucault, nurtured the discontent. They capitalized upon the loyalty of the population to the former mother country and talked of a return to French rule. The failure of Spanish colonial ad-

20. Antonio de Ulloa's administration is covered in Moore, *Revolt*, 42–142, and Vicente Rodríguez Casado, *Primeros años de dominación española en la Luisiana* (Madrid, 1942), 99–137. See also Gilbert C. Din and A. P. Nasatir, *The Imperial Osages: Spanish-Indian Diplomacy in the Mississippi Valley* (Norman, Okla., 1983), 62–67.

ministrators to provide funds to keep the colony alive financially seems to have been the major reason for uniting many of Louisiana's inhabitants.

In the fall of 1768, the conspirators learned of new commercial regulations that would radically alter Louisiana's trade; they already knew that Spanish soldiers were gathering in Havana for service in the colony. The plotters felt compelled to act immediately and staged an uprising. On October 29, the rebel faction persuaded the Superior Council of New Orleans, a governing body that represented local interests, to order the expulsion of Ulloa. Only Charles Philippe Aubry, the French governor, and Foucault, the colony's commissary, who now posed as a moderate, dissented.[21]

The next six months saw the initial euphoria of the Creole revolt give way to despair. With Lafrénière as the most public of the rebel leaders and Foucault in the background, their original intention was to restore the colony to French rule, but they delayed in sending their representatives to France. The delegates reached Paris in April, 1769, long after Spain had informed the court of events, and by then the French government valued preservation of the Family Compact more than the return of Louisiana. The dispirited delegates, confronted with an inflexible official attitude, remained in France while conditions in Louisiana rapidly deteriorated. In particular, the economy declined because of the lack of specie, inflation caused prices to soar, and contraband that had previously existed languished. Dependence made any thought of a republic, which several rebels advocated in 1769, an impossibility and similarly destroyed the idea of the creation of a bank. About the time that the delegates reached Paris, Aubry in New Orleans was writing that the Louisiana people had repented of their actions and that he believed the Spaniards could take possession peacefully if the colonials were assured of pardons, "except for the twelve who would flee quickly to avoid the punishment that their criminal conduct exposes them to."[22]

---

21. Several studies have examined the causes of the 1768 New Orleans revolt. Among them are Moore, *Revolt*, 124–64, Rodríguez Casado, *Primeros años,* 137–202, and James Winston, "The Causes and Results of the Revolution of 1768 in Louisiana," *Louisiana Historical Quarterly,* XV (1932), 181–213. Carl A. Brasseaux, in *Denis-Nicolas Foucault and the New Orleans Rebellion of 1768* (Ruston, La., 1987), has denied that Foucault was a rebel. On the military in Louisiana under Ulloa, see Gilbert C. Din, "Protecting the '*Barrera*': Spain's Defenses in Louisiana, 1763–1779," *Louisiana History,* XIX (1978), 184–92.

22. Moore, *Revolt,* 165–84, with Aubry's statement on p. 183; Rodríguez Casado, *Primeros años,* 217–63; Gayarré, *History,* II, 272–84.

It fell to Alejandro O'Reilly, now a lieutenant general and the inspector general of infantry, to restore Spanish honor by recovering Louisiana and punishing the culprits responsible for the uprising. First Secretary of State Jerónimo Grimaldi selected him because of the aggressive way he had carried out past assignments. The king issued instructions to O'Reilly on April 16, 1769. Taking with him only a few officers and equipment, O'Reilly sailed on the frigate *Palas* from Cádiz on May 5, bound for Havana. O'Reilly arrived on June 24 at that port, where he and Captain General Bucareli spent the next eleven days selecting men and equipment for the expedition to Louisiana. Many regular soldiers and militiamen, according to Bucareli, eagerly volunteered, including Francisco Bouligny. In Spain, his father had recommended him to O'Reilly, who replied that he would do whatever he could. About July 1, O'Reilly asked Captain General Bucareli for six officers; he no doubt wanted French-speaking officers on his staff. The general probably received favorable reports on Bouligny's conduct and ability, and he appointed him as his aide-de-camp. Bouligny was to prove valuable in the recovery of New Orleans. By July 6, O'Reilly had under his command a flotilla of 21 ships, 2,056 men, 46 cannon, 150,000 pesos, and abundant supplies. The regular troops came from the 1st Battalion of the Lisbon Infantry Regiment, the 1st Battalion of the Havana Fijo (possibly Bouligny's battalion), two companies of Catalan light infantry, a picket of the Dragoon Regiment of America, and 91 artillerymen, totaling 1,762 men. In addition, 294 Havana militiamen, both white and colored, joined the expedition. With this overpowering force, O'Reilly intended to leave no doubt in the minds of the French population in Louisiana that Spain was there to stay and to punish the leaders of the insurrection.[23]

23. David Ker Texada, *Alejandro O'Reilly and the New Orleans Rebels* (Lafayette, La., 1970), 26–27; O'Reilly to Bucareli, Havana, July 1, 1769, in DSGL, Bk. 1, Vol. II; "Statement showing the troops, artillery, munitions, equipment . . . ," attached to Antonio Bucareli to Julián de Arriaga, Havana, July 7, 1769, in *SMV,* Pt. 1, pp. 87–89. A diary of O'Reilly's expedition to New Orleans from July 5 to July 27 is "Relation and diary of . . . the expedition of his excellency don Alejandro O'Rrly [*sic*] since its departure from Havana . . . ," AHN, Sección de diversos, títulos y familias, Condado de Priego, leg. 2270.

An error of long standing—which perhaps began with Rodríguez Casado, *Primeros años,* 319, and is repeated in Moore, *Revolt,* 194, and elsewhere—is that O'Reilly left Spain from La Coruña toward the end of May and arrived in Havana in only four weeks, an incredibly short time. Many documents, however, in the AGI, SD, particularly leg. 2656, give proof that O'Reilly departed from Cádiz on May 5. See also Grimaldi to the conde de Fuentes, Aranjuez, June 8, 1769, in AHN, Est., leg. 3883, exped. 3.

As the flotilla left Havana harbor on July 8, 1769, Francisco Bouligny stood on the deck of O'Reilly's flagship, the *Volante*. Earlier that same day, he wrote to his father, telling him of his departure for New Orleans. At last, after five years and ten months of uneventful garrison duty on the island, opportunity beckoned. The general intended to leave a battalion of soldiers in Louisiana—he had no desire to repeat the error that had been made in Ulloa's day—and perhaps sometime during the voyage the two men discussed a captaincy for Bouligny in the unit. By that time, as he neared thirty-three, Bouligny was yearning for promotion to the head of a company. Furthermore, distinguishing himself on the expedition would add to the luster that was needed for advancement into the higher ranks of the army. His years of monotonous garrison duty in Havana must have made him ready for whatever adventures Louisiana presented. He probably did not realize as he sailed across the Gulf of Mexico in the summer of 1769 that the rest of his military career would be spent in that colony or that his life would become inextricably bound to that land. More likely, his thoughts remained fixed upon the present, hoping to find in Louisiana the opportunities that would further his career and make his fortune.[24]

24. Jean Bouligny to [Francisco Bouligny], Alicante, October 21, 1769, in BB, HNOC. See also Alcée Fortier, "Account of the Bouligny Family, Minutes of the Meeting of June 20, 1899," *Publications of the Louisiana Historical Society*, II (1900), 16–26.

3   SOLDIER, PLANTER,

     FAMILY MAN

     1769—1775

IN THE SIX YEARS beginning in 1769, Francisco Bouligny's life and career in Louisiana underwent major changes. He transferred to the Fixed Louisiana
Battalion with the rank of captain, married, purchased a plantation, and
started accumulating a modest fortune. More important, information
about Bouligny increases significantly. His first years in Louisiana, however, were not without problems. Always proud, even at times arrogant,
Bouligny had a brush with higher authority that might have seriously
damaged his career. The contretemps proved temporary, and he soon
rose to more successful achievements. His connection to Alejandro
O'Reilly helped Bouligny in the early 1770s, and that tie was cemented in
1769 when he served as the general's aide-de-camp in the recovery of
Louisiana.

Two weeks from Havana, most of O'Reilly's expedition sighted the
entrance to the Mississippi River at Balize on July 20, 1769. The general
probably had already discussed his plan of action with Bouligny, since
O'Reilly moved immediately upon arriving at the pass. He ordered his
aide-de-camp to carry a letter to the French governor Charles Philippe
Aubry in New Orleans, informing him of the Spanish expedition and
soliciting his cooperation in a peaceful transfer of Louisiana from French
to Spanish authority. Bouligny's written accounts of the next several
weeks provide much of the information about the Spanish recovery of
the colony.[1]

1. Four manuscript documents describe O'Reilly's expedition to Louisiana and Bouligny's activities in New Orleans in July and August, 1769. Two are definitely the work of

At 2 A.M. on July 21, Bouligny and twelve sailors left the flagship *Volante* and headed toward Balize in a small boat. It took more than three hours to reach the tiny island outpost, which housed a commandant and a handful of mariners and soldiers. Bouligny stopped to confer with the officer in charge. The Spanish lieutenant refused to surrender O'Reilly's letter to Aubry (it was the duty of the Balize commandant to send arriving official correspondence upriver ahead of the ships in both the French and Spanish eras), and the commandant similarly rejected Bouligny's request not to inform the city of their presence. After a brief visit, the Spanish lieutenant and his sailors continued the journey upstream, which lasted three and a half days.[2]

Bouligny got his first impressions of Louisiana as he traveled up the Mississippi. At Balize, the flatness of the horizon barely allowed him

---

Bouligny: Bouligny to O'Reilly, New Orleans, July 26, 1769, in KCTU, and [Bouligny], July 20–August 21, 1769, *ibid.*. Although these documents are not signed, internal evidence affirms that Bouligny wrote them. Two other documents were either written by Bouligny or by someone on the *Volante* who had access to Bouligny's writings. The first is "Relation and diary of all that occurred in the expedition of his excellency don Alejandro O'Rrly since its departure from Havana . . . ," AHN, Sección de diversos, títulos y familias, Condado de Priego, leg. 2270. Different versions were published by David Ker Texada, ed., "An Account of Governor Alejandro O'Reilly's Voyage from Havana to New Orleans in July, 1769," *Louisiana History,* X (1969), 370–75, and by R. E. Chandler, ed., "O'Reilly's Voyage from Havana to the Balize," *Louisiana History,* XXII (1981), 199–207. The second is "Relation of how D. Alejandro O'Reilly Pacified the city of New Orleans," New Orleans, August 30, 1769, BN, DL (published by Manuel Serrano y Saenz, ed., *Documentos históricos de la Florida y la Luisiana, siglos XVI al XVIII* [Madrid, 1912], 295–304, and R. E. Chandler, ed., "Eyewitness History: O'Reilly's Arrival in Louisiana," *Louisiana History,* XX [1979], 317–24). In the last article, Chandler refers to 27 ships and 2,700 men in O'Reilly's expedition, but Serrano y Saenz, publishing the same document, uses 21 ships and 2,100 men. The error is caused by Chandler misreading the figure *1*. Several civilian ships, usually not mentioned, also accompanied the expedition.

O'Reilly's account of the events is his letter to Julián de Arriaga, New Orleans, August 31, 1769, in BN, DL, and published in Serrano y Saenz, *Documentos,* 304–12.

2. Bouligny to O'Reilly, New Orleans, July 26, 1769, in KCTU. For accounts of O'Reilly in Louisiana, see David K. Bjork, "Alexander O'Reilly and the Spanish Occupation of Louisiana, 1769–1770," in *New Spain and the Anglo-American West: Historical Contributions Presented to Herbert Eugene Bolton,* ed. George P. Hammond (Los Angeles, 1932), I, 165–82, and his "The Establishment of Spanish Rule in the Province of Louisiana, 1762–1770" (Ph.D. dissertation, University of California, 1932); Torres Ramírez, *O'Reilly,* 99–183; David Ker Texada, "The Administration of Alejandro O'Reilly as Governor of Louisiana, 1769–1770" (Ph.D. dissertation, Louisiana State University, 1968).

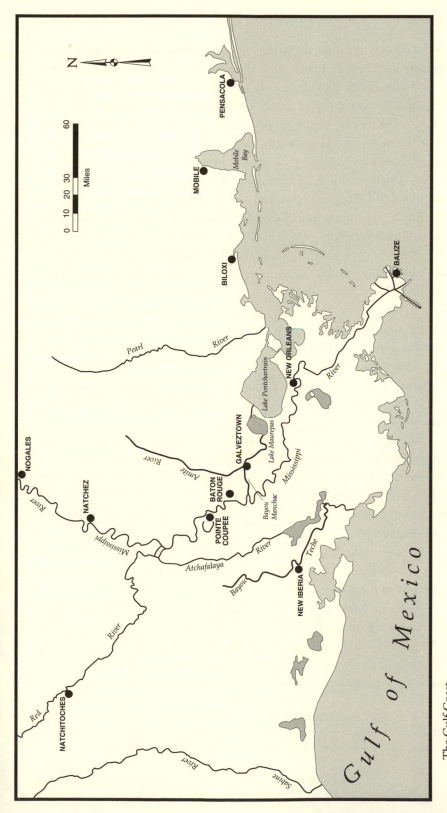

N

60
30
20
10
0
Miles

NATCHITOCHES

Red River

Sabine River

River

NOGALES

NATCHEZ

Mississippi River

River

POINTE COUPEE

Atchafalaya River

BATON ROUGE

GALVEZTOWN

Amite River

Bayou Manchac

Bayou Teche

NEW IBERIA

Pearl River

River

Lake Pontchartrain

Lake Maurepas

NEW ORLEANS

Mississippi

River

Mississippi River

BILOXI

MOBILE

Mobile Bay

PENSACOLA

BALIZE

Gulf of Mexico

The Gulf Coast
Map by John Snead

to distinguish between sky and water. As the boat progressed upriver battling a current of nearly six miles an hour, Bouligny gradually discerned the changing terrain as land and vegetation became more visible and, finally, trees appeared. Only about eighteen miles below New Orleans, in the vicinity of the English Turn, did plantations begin. As the Spanish sailors rowed laboriously against the current, they passed a number of slower-moving sloops and brigantines heading to New Orleans, most of them French and loaded with foodstuffs and wines. One captain had heard of O'Reilly's expedition and the Spanish intention to recover Louisiana. The nearly one-hundred-mile (thirty-two-league) journey to the city took Bouligny until 11 P.M. on July 24. That Monday morning, however, the men sent by the Balize commandant in a swifter pirogue reached New Orleans, and word quickly spread of the Spaniard's impending arrival. When Bouligny reached the wharf in New Orleans, he found that despite the hour, a large but silent crowd had gathered, among whom were the three Spanish officials Ulloa had left behind the year before as hostages for the Spanish debt: Juan José de Loyola (army commissary), Esteban Gayarré (comptroller), and Martín Navarro (treasurer). No doubt they had much to tell Bouligny about conditions and events in the colony; he in turn informed them of the powerful expedition at the mouth of the river.[3]

Bouligny spent the next three days in New Orleans. Despite the late hour of his arrival, he immediately went to Aubry's house to present his dispatches. The French governor had retired for the night after leaving orders to be awakened upon Bouligny's arrival. He read O'Reilly's letter twice, and Bouligny helped him with difficult passages. Aubry responded to O'Reilly's plea for assistance by declaring his readiness to turn the colony over to the Spaniards and to fight any local opposition. The next day, at 9 A.M., the governor repeated his speech to an assembly of inhabitants in the town plaza. The populace listened in silence.

An hour later, at Loyola's house, where Bouligny seems to have stayed during his visit, Aubry informed the lieutenant of the public's willingness to accept the orders of the French and Spanish sovereigns. Also, two of the former rebel leaders, Pierre Marquis and Lafrénière, had asked to accompany the aide-de-camp on his return downriver. They

---

3. Bouligny to O'Reilly, New Orleans, July 26, 1769, in KCTU. The speed of the Mississippi's current is in Abraham P. Nasatir, ed., *Spanish War Vessels on the Mississippi, 1792–1796* (New Haven, 1968), 46.

wished to beg O'Reilly for clemency. At lunch that day at Aubry's house, the Spanish officials joined the governor and several Frenchmen in toasting O'Reilly's good health. Aubry appeared relieved that the transfer of authority was going to take place peacefully. Bouligny encouraged him by revealing that this conduct would win over the Spanish general's "benign and compassionate heart."[4]

That evening, as Bouligny strolled about the city with Loyola, he noticed a few of the inhabitants staring at them suspiciously, but most of them greeted the two Spaniards in a friendly manner. On Wednesday, as the lieutenant waited for his exhausted sailors to recover from the tiring journey upstream, he again dined at the governor's house. Aubry had decided to send his senior army captain, François Demasillières, to convey his personal compliments to General O'Reilly and the harbormaster to assist the ships upriver. By then, another former conspirator, Joseph Milhet, had also joined Bouligny's party. Either on Wednesday after lunch or on Thursday, July 27, the entire group left New Orleans to meet O'Reilly at Balize.[5]

Forty hours later, Bouligny reached Balize as the *Volante* crossed the sandbar and entered the river. Most of the expedition had entered the Mississippi on July 22. Many Spanish officers from the other vessels soon gathered on O'Reilly's flagship to witness the exchange between the general and the Frenchmen. First, however, Bouligny reported the successful results of his talks with Aubry. He observed that Marquis, Lafrénière, and Milhet appeared ill at ease when they met the Spanish general. Any thought of the boisterous speeches of the year before had vanished in the presence of O'Reilly. Bouligny recorded the address by Lafrénière in which he denied that the colony had ever harbored any intention of straying from Spanish control. The Frenchman instead blamed Ulloa's demeanor and the "subversion of the privileges assured by the act of cession" for sparking the uprising. Lafrénière asked on behalf of the colony for O'Reilly's kindness and goodwill. The general reserved judgment until he had ascertained the events of the previous year. For now, he sought only to put the public at ease, since no resistance was being offered; but had it been otherwise, he would have compelled respect for the Spanish flag. He left no doubt that he intended to punish the "seditious," a word that rankled the Frenchmen. Before they returned to New Orleans,

4. Bouligny to O'Reilly, New Orleans, July 26, 1769, in KCTU.
5. *Ibid.*; Gayarré, *History,* II, 289–92.

O'Reilly invited them to dine on his ship. Bouligny did not remain with the flotilla. The general ordered him and two adjutants, Miguel Knaresbrough and Juan Bordenave, to New Orleans to prepare quarters for the Spanish troops. But that was only a cover for their real objective: to create a favorable impression "through confidences and friendly conversations" and to learn if the local population entertained thoughts of resistance. By early August, Bouligny was back in the city.[6]

The lieutenant spent two weeks in New Orleans before the expedition arrived. The city, built on a marsh, the highest part near the river giving way to swamps on the remaining sides, had a population of 3,190, of whom fewer than 2,000 were white. They occupied 468 houses within the city walls. Nearly all the dwellings were on the first four streets from the river. Many lots that are today filled in the French Quarter were then empty. O'Reilly listed six stores (perhaps general emporiums) and twelve taverns, but there were many other businesses. New Orleans' unpaved and undrained streets became muddy quagmires when it rained, and at night darkness engulfed the city. No night watch or city guard patrolled the streets. The English army officer Phillip Pittman described the Church of St. Louis as in ruinous condition in 1766. He reported that six streets ran parallel to the river and eleven perpendicular to it, giving the city sixty-six square blocks. Each side of a block was one hundred yards long and divided into twelve lots. Pittman wrote of the city: "The general plan of building in the town is with timber frames filled up with brick; and most of the houses are but of one floor, raised about eight feet from the ground, with large galleries around them, and the cellars under the floors level with the ground; it is impossible to have any subterraneous buildings, as they would be constantly full of water." Most of the houses had gardens, and the blocks at the rear and sides of town were mostly gardens, many of them with fragrant orange trees. The army barracks had formerly occupied both sides of the plaza but were now entirely destroyed. A decayed and useless stockade fronted by a small ditch enclosed the city.[7]

6. [Bouligny], July 20–August 22, 1769, KCTU; Gayarré, *History*, II, 292–95.

7. Phillip Pittman, *The Present State of the European Settlements on the Mississippi* (1770; rpr. Gainesville, Fla., 1973), 10–11, with quotation on p. 11. The cost of New Orleans' stockade, which was built in 1760, was 69,502 pesos. O'Reilly, in his letter to Arriaga, December 29, 1769 (in *SMV*, Pt. 1, p. 147), stated that the stockade was then mostly rotten and the moat filled in many places. François-Xavier Martin's *History of Louisiana*

Bouligny probably made no effort at securing quarters for the Spanish troops since it had already been decided to lodge them in the existing French barracks. They had been moved to the lower end of the city (downriver) past the Ursuline Convent. More important was ascertaining whether the inhabitants intended to resist the Spanish forces. Within the city, opposition was unlikely, but upriver in the German and Acadian coasts (river settlements) some talk of resistance went on. The Spanish officers told the would-be rebels that they risked destruction if they dared to fight.[8] The arrival of the expedition on August 17 quelled any thoughts of insurrection.

On August 15, as the flotilla neared New Orleans, Aubry descended the river to greet O'Reilly personally. Probably at that time the two men agreed to the transfer of the colony on August 18. Aubry returned to the city, and in the early morning hours of August 17 the fleet reached its destination. That day, O'Reilly left his flagship to inspect his quarters in New Orleans while the soldiers remained on board. Perhaps Bouligny reported his observations to the general at that time. Not until 5 P.M. on August 18 did the troops disembark, marching in precise formations and with great pomp and fanfare.

The French soldiers and militia had first lined up in the plaza (Jackson Square today) on the side farthest away from the levee and nearest the church. Then the Spanish troops marched out nearly two thousand strong, occupying first the two sides of the square perpendicular to the river. The last to disembark—the Havana militia, the artillerymen with fifty cannon, and ninety mounted men—filled in the remaining side of the square. Five shouts of "Long Live the King" came first from sailors on board the ships, to which the soldiers replied. Next the town bells rang out, and the Spanish ships fired their cannon, enveloping the river in thick smoke. The artillery pieces in the plaza also roared as the infantry soldiers discharged their muskets. Then, amidst thundering guns, heavy smoke, and the beating of drums, and with flags flying, Lt. Gen. Alejandro O'Reilly appeared in the square, followed by his retinue.

Was Francisco Bouligny in the general's entourage? His precise location that day is uncertain, but it is known that he witnessed the transfer

---

(1827–29; 3rd ed.; Gretna, La., 1963), 206, contains a census from that era. See also Texada, *O'Reilly*, 31.

8. [Bouligny], July 20–August 22, 1769, KCTU.

ceremonies. O'Reilly's party advanced to the center of the plaza where Governor Aubry, his council, and men of note stood waiting near a flagpole that flew the French colors. O'Reilly proceeded to inform Aubry of his mission and the orders of the two Bourbon kings for the transfer. Aubry, complying with the royal wishes, handed the keys to the city gates to O'Reilly. Then soldiers lowered the French flag and hoisted the Spanish banner. Simultaneously, several Spanish flags went up in other parts of the city, and Spanish guards replaced French sentinels at the city gates. At that point, French soldiers in the plaza shouted "Long Live the King" five times, and the Spanish troops replied three times. More discharges of both cannon and musketry followed. O'Reilly and the other dignitaries then greeted the clergy and entered the church for a Te Deum. Only after the religious services concluded and O'Reilly emerged from the church did the soldiers march to their quarters in precise formations. Thus did the formal transfer of the colony take place, and Louisiana was once more Spanish. That finished, Governor O'Reilly spent the next six and a half months punishing the rebel leaders and reorganizing Louisiana as a Spanish colony.[9]

The general first devoted himself to learning the events of the 1768 uprising and collecting evidence against the ringleaders. He moved quickly. Three days after the transfer ceremonies, O'Reilly ordered the arrest of the principal culprits. To quiet the multitude, however, that same day he issued a proclamation absolving the rest of the population—who he stated had been led by "the intrigues of ambitious, fanatical, and ill-intentioned people"—of any wrongdoing. Two days later, on August 23, O'Reilly issued a new proclamation to the public on the need to take oaths of fealty to the Spanish king. That was done in New Orleans on August 26. Post commandants administered the oath to the settlers in their districts at a later time.[10]

With those preliminaries out of the way, the trials of the rebel leaders

9. *Ibid.* Of the published accounts, Gayarré's *History,* II, 295–99, contains the most detailed description of the transfer ceremonies. O'Reilly's proclamation, New Orleans, August 21, 1769, *SMV,* Pt. 1, p. 89; and O'Reilly to Juan Gregorio Muniain, New Orleans, August 31, 1769, in *SMV,* Pt. 1, pp. 90–93.

10. Texada, *O'Reilly,* 33–35; Gayarré, *History,* II, 300–10. On O'Reilly's proclamations, see O'Reilly, New Orleans, August 21, 1769, *SMV,* Pt. 1, pp. 89–90. Bouligny (July 20–August 22, 1769, KCTU) states that the proclamation of pardons was issued on the morning of August 22, 1769.

began, lasting for two months. Since Bouligny participated in the legal proceedings as the court translator, he witnessed the hearings and signed many of the official trial documents. His account of the recovery of Louisiana ended as the trials began. On October 24, Governor O'Reilly pronounced the sentences. He condemned five men to death: Lafrénière, Jean-Baptiste Noyan, Pierre Caresse, Marquis, and Joseph Milhet. A sixth man, Joseph Villere, received the death penalty, but he had died while in confinement. Army firing squads carried out the executions the next day at 3 P.M. in the barracks area. Six other guilty men received sentences: Joseph Petit, life imprisonment; Balthasar Masan and Julien Jerome Doucet, ten years in prison; and Jean Milhet, Pierre Poupet, and Pierre Hardi de Boisblanc, six years in prison. The Spanish crown also confiscated and sold at public auction the property of the guilty, returning, however, the dowries of the widows and wives. The men sentenced to prison served only a year in Havana's Morro Castle before the king commuted their sentences. They were nevertheless barred from returning to Louisiana and were sent to French Saint Domingue. Finally, the governor expelled twenty-one persons from the colony, most of them merchants who had engaged in illegal commerce.[11]

Before the trials ended, O'Reilly embarked on the political, economic, and military reorganization of the colony, for which the crown had given him authority. He abolished the Superior Council and created a Spanish cabildo to assist in governing New Orleans. However, the bulk of the new members remained French planters. After creating the cabildo on December 1, he installed Col. Luis de Unzaga y Amezaga as governor, in charge only of New Orleans and the surrounding area until the day that O'Reilly finished his other work and departed. He imposed price controls, sent officers to inspect different parts of lower Louisiana, and with Unzaga personally journeyed to Pointe Coupee in late December and returned in early February. He raised the commandants of the two outlying districts of Natchitoches and St. Louis, called Spanish Illinois (roughly Missouri today), to lieutenant governors. He proclaimed

11. Texada, *O'Reilly*, 36–63; Rodríguez Casado, *Primeros años*, 383–402, 443–82, also has published testimony and confessions. On the sentences, see O'Reilly to Arriaga, October 27, 1769, in *SMV*, Pt. 1, pp. 105–106; and on the freeing of the prisoners, Grimaldi to Unzaga, San Ildefonso, August 25, 1770, in *SMV*, Pt. 1, pp. 181–82. People exiled from Louisiana are in "List of the persons . . . ," attached to O'Reilly to Arriaga, New Orleans, October 17, 1769, in *SMV*, Pt. 1, p. 103.

Spanish laws in effect, which he called the Code O'Reilly. He recommended to the crown that Louisiana have free trade with Havana and ports in Spain. In defense, he disapproved of most of Ulloa's innovations. He abandoned the dilapidated post the former governor had built at Isla Real Católica (at the mouth of the Mississippi) and the fort at San Luis de Natchez, opposite British Natchez. The only military posts left were Balize, Arkansas Post, Spanish Manchac, Bayou St. John, Natchitoches, and Opelousas. The bulk of the troops were to remain garrisoned in New Orleans. The general believed that dividing Louisiana's limited forces would only weaken them further, that costly fortifications were unnecessary, and that the fate of the colony, if war came, would be decided at the conference table that determined peace terms (a concept in place for many of the indefensible Caribbean islands). O'Reilly also reorganized the provincial militia for the colony, establishing units wherever there were military commandants. The general reduced the cost for administering Louisiana, the bulk of it for defense, from 150,000 to 115,322 pesos. Contrary to popular belief in the repressive conduct of the Spaniards and crown disapproval of the acts of "Bloody O'Reilly" (a nineteenth-century soubriquet for the general), most of the residents cooperated with the new rulers, and many even sought positions in government or the military. Moreover, the crown praised O'Reilly for his work and soon made him the conde de O'Reilly. Until 1776, he remained the government's chief adviser on Louisiana.[12]

Important for Louisiana and the career of Francisco Bouligny was the creation of a fixed battalion for the colony. Its origins dated from 1767 when Ulloa asked for 1,200 Spanish soldiers for the province's defense. The Spanish government, however, believed that a single battalion

12. *SMV*, Pt. 1, p. xxii; O'Reilly to Arriaga, October 17, 1769, in BN, DL. The Cabildo ordinances have been published in several places; see *SMV*, Pt. 1, pp. 108–25, and Torres Ramírez, *O'Reilly*, 187–225. On price controls, see O'Reilly, New Orleans, September, 1769, *SMV*, Pt. 1, pp. 93–94; on commerce, O'Reilly to Arriaga, New Orleans, October 17, December 10, 1769, in *SMV*, Pt. 1, pp. 103–105, 132–35. On defense policy, see O'Reilly to Arriaga, Madrid, September 30, 1770, in *SMV*, Pt. 1, pp. 183–86, and O'Reilly to Arriaga, December 29, 1769, with enclosures, in *SMV*, Pt. 1, pp. 144–52. For information on the militia and appointments, see O'Reilly, New Orleans, February 12, 1770, *SMV*, Pt. 1, pp. 158–59, Grimaldi to Unzaga, San Lorenzo, October 24, 1770, in *SMV*, Pt. 1, pp. 186–87, and Torres Ramírez, *O'Reilly*, 129–41. The cost for operating Louisiana is in O'Reilly, New Orleans, February 4, 1770, AGI, PC, leg. 1055.

(approximately 500 men) was sufficient, and by 1768 soldiers, officers, and equipment were sailing from La Coruña and Cádiz for Havana, where the entire unit was to assemble before shipment to New Orleans. About 400 sergeants, corporals, and soldiers had gathered in Cuba before the revolt occurred, and they were a part of the 2,056 troops that O'Reilly took in 1769. Bouligny was not then among the officers assigned to the Louisiana battalion. Capt. Jacinto Panis held the post of adjutant major (*ayudante mayor*) that Bouligny later acquired. In Louisiana, however, Panis joined the New Orleans militia headquarters staff, and that move allowed Bouligny to transfer to the battalion. About August, 1769, O'Reilly sent a number of recommendations to the crown for Louisiana's officers, including promotions for many of them. In response, on November 1, the crown issued patents for the officer posts in the battalion, including brevet captain and adjutant major for Bouligny. Meanwhile, in Louisiana on November 10, O'Reilly published a list of 24 officers for the battalion, a unit that contained 412 Spaniards and 100 mostly French foreigners. The general wrote of Bouligny at that time: "He is an intelligent officer in discipline and of recommendable qualities, . . . he speaks and writes French well, which here is necessary." Since Capt. Francisco Ríu, the original choice for the battalion's commandant, proved unacceptable because of his questionable conduct while in St. Louis, the government later selected Col. Francisco Estachería, then in Puerto Rico, who did not arrive in New Orleans until October, 1771. Unzaga was acting commandant until then. Several of the battalion's Spanish and French officers had served under Ulloa and had many years of seniority over Bouligny. They included, for the unit's one grenadier and seven fusilier companies, Alejandro Cousso (Coudro) as captain of grenadiers and Pedro Piernas, Fernando de Leyba, Francisco Cruzat, François Demasillières, Guido Dufossat, and Balthasar de Villiers as infantry captains. Then came Bouligny as adjutant major, and below him O'Reilly named 16 subaltern officers (lieutenants and sublieutenants). Bouligny also had his first assignment in Louisiana—to remain in New Orleans, where he spent most of his lengthy career in the colony, which gave him opportunities that officers in the detachments lacked. One of his first duties as adjutant major was assisting in compiling a report of the medical supplies at the Royal Hospital in New Orleans and at the various military posts throughout the colony. As adjutant major, Bouligny exercised the duties of sergeant major. He also participated in the training of cadets, many of whom were French Creoles.[13]

Important for a successful career was rising through the various posts in military command. For Bouligny, the next step meant becoming the head of a fusilier company. In mid-1772, Capt. Guido Dufossat retired, and the crown replaced him with Bouligny because of "his military merits and experience and other good qualities." After he took over the 5th Infantry Company, only six other captains in the battalion had seniority over him, several of whom were elderly and not serious competitors. On October 8, 1772, Bouligny received a promotion to permanent captain in recognition of his acquisition of a fusilier company. His yearly salary advanced to 744 pesos, up from 612 pesos as adjutant major.[14]

Seniority in the Spanish army was a serious matter, and the news of

13. O'Reilly, "Relation of the Officers Assigned to the Louisiana Battalion," New Orleans, November 10, 1769, BN, DL; Bouligny service sheet, August 31, 1776, AGI, SD, leg. 2661. For information on the formation of the Louisiana battalion in 1767–68, see Grimaldi to Muniain, Aranjuez, May 22, 1768, in AGI, SD, leg. 2655; O'Reilly to Bucareli, Havana, July 2, 1769, in AGI, PC, leg. 1055; Rodríguez Casado, *Primeros años,* 270–71. Recommended for sergeant major was Pascual de Ulloa, then a captain in the Immemorial King's Regiment, who had served thirty-one years, five as a senior adjutant, and was to be promoted to lieutenant colonel (O'Reilly to Muniain, Madrid, June 6, 1768, in AGI, SD, leg. 2655). The expulsion of the Jesuits also delayed in forming the battalion; see Grimaldi to Antonio de Ulloa, Aranjuez, June 25, 1768, in *SMV,* Pt. 1, pp. 54–55. Francisco Estachería, a Royal Artillery Corps lieutenant colonel in Puerto Rico, was to be promoted to colonel (Arriaga to Unzaga, Aranjuez, June 22, 1761, in AGI, PC, leg. 174A; Estachería's service sheet of December 31, 1775 is in AGI, SD, leg. 2661; see also Unzaga to Arriaga, New Orleans, October 30, 1771, in AGI, SD, leg. 2661). Bouligny's promotions to brevet captain and adjutant major, as well as promotions for other Louisiana officers, are in AGI, SD, leg. 2656. On taking a medical survey, see O'Reilly to Unzaga, New Orleans, February 15, 1770, AGI, PC, leg. 181.

14. Bouligny's patent of promotion to captain, San Lorenzo, October 8, 1772, AGI, SD, leg. 2654. Dufossat (Guy Soniat du Fossat) wrote an account of Louisiana, *A Synopsis of the History of Louisiana, from the Founding of the Colony to the End of the Year 1790,* trans. Charles T. Soniat (New Orleans, 1903). He was born in France on September 17, 1727, entered the French army in 1746, went to Louisiana about 1751, married Françoise Clodine Dreaux, and became a captain and engineer. He entered Spanish service in 1767, became a captain of engineers in 1769, and retired in 1772. Later he served on the Cabildo and owned a plantation near New Orleans. He died in 1794 (Dufossat, *Synopsis,* 3–5). On the pay for officers in Louisiana, see appendix A in Brian E. Coutts, "Martín Navarro: Treasurer, Contador, Intendant, 1766–1788: Politics and Trade in Spanish Louisiana" (Ph.D. dissertation, Louisiana State University, 1981), II, 554–56. See also Grace King, *Creole Families of New Orleans* (1921; rpr. Baton Rouge, 1971), 221–30.

Bouligny's promotion in early 1773 disturbed Capt. François Demasillières. A veteran of many years in the French army, Demasillières had been commandant at Pointe Coupee in the 1760s and at Arkansas in 1770 for a few months before being replaced, complaining vociferously when it occurred. O'Reilly, who had appointed him as Arkansas commandant, quickly became dissatisfied with Demasillières when he issued a large quantity of government supplies without authorization. Two years later, on February 25, 1772, Demasillières petitioned to retire at half pay, citing ailments. He was still in the army when he learned of Bouligny's promotion and initiated a barrage of protests. He complained to Governor Unzaga on May 10 and 25 and June 4, 1773, alleging seniority. He made such a nuisance of himself that Colonel Estachería ordered his house arrest. Obtaining no satisfaction in Louisiana, Demasillières appealed to the captain general in Havana on June 27, bewailing his arrest and proclaiming his seniority over Bouligny. He failed in his suit; the captain general denied his petition on January 21, 1774. O'Reilly had dated Bouligny's seniority as permanent captain as of 1769. Not long afterward, perhaps out of frustration, Demasillières retired from the army.[15]

Bouligny's service as adjutant major of the Louisiana battalion began with its formation in November, 1769. His duties included attending to the unit's paperwork, which included keeping the *hojas de servicio* (service sheets) for the ranks of sergeants first class, cadets, and officers, and the *Libro Maestro de Filiaciones* (the book that contained the records of the enlisted men). After Bouligny left the post, about February, 1773, to head the 5th Infantry Company, the new adjutant, Miguel Almonacid, began an examination of the *Libro* and found a number of discrepancies. Estachería first brought the errors to Governor Unzaga's attention on April 30, 1773. He instructed Estachería to continue the investigation to learn the circumstances of the mistakes.[16]

15. [Captain General] to Francisco Demasillières, Havana, August 13, 1773, January 21, 1774, both in AGI, PC, leg. 1147. See also Unzaga to the marqués de la Torre, New Orleans, September 12, 1773, *ibid.*, leg. 1145; O'Reilly to Demasillières, New Orleans, January 25, 1770, and another letter, n.d., both *ibid.*, leg. 181; Demasillières petition, New Orleans, February 25, 1772, *ibid.*, leg. 116; Unzaga to the marqués de la Torre, New Orleans, September 12, 1773, in DSGL, Bk. I, Vol. V.

16. Francisco Estachería to Unzaga, New Orleans, two letters of April 30, 1773, both in AGI, SD, leg. 2661; Unzaga to Estachería, attached to Unzaga to the conde de O'Reilly, New Orleans, May 20, 1773, *ibid.* Estachería was born about 1720 in Teruel Province, Spain. He entered the army before 1746, the year he became a sublieutenant. He fought in Italy

Adjutant Almonacid soon uncovered new errors, particularly in the *Libro Maestro* entries. Estachería, in reporting the irregularities to O'Reilly, who was still the inspector general of the infantry, was especially incensed about Bouligny's contravention of the royal ordinances by giving first-time deserters stiffer sentences than they deserved. When Almonacid contacted Bouligny about the errors, Estachería claimed that the captain responded with frivolous excuses and blamed others. Estachería also charged that Bouligny entered in the *filiaciones* the names of thirty-two soldiers who allegedly had taken an oath to the flag when in reality they had not. Although cautioned to be exact in the fulfillment of his duties, Bouligny made mistakes in the *notas* (remarks) of the records, which were necessary for giving awards for good service. The commandant singled out these errors as examples of Bouligny's carelessness and lack of zeal.[17]

Estachería summoned Bouligny to his house in May, 1773, to discuss the mistakes. The captain first inquired about the nature of Almonacid's private investigation in the barracks. Estachería denied that it was carried out furtively. It initiated an argument over the *filiaciones*. Bouligny attributed the errors to his not having a copy of the royal ordinances, an excuse Estachería dismissed because Bouligny possessed the three volumes of the ordinances. The colonel stated that his duty was to uncover the mistakes and that the captain's inattentiveness in a matter fundamental to good army service displeased him. At that point Bouligny interrupted Estachería to declare his indifference to the investigation. Angered by the reply, Estachería placed Bouligny under house arrest, suspended him from his post, and told him never to use a threatening tone of voice to him again. The colonel informed Governor Unzaga and the inspector general about Bouligny's arrest.[18]

What possessed Bouligny to behave in that extraordinary manner? Or had Estachería exaggerated? Bouligny's house arrest lasted until

---

and Austria as a volunteer; by 1760, he was a brevet lieutenant colonel. About 1763 he went to Puerto Rico, where he complained of poor health. After leaving Louisiana, he rose in rank, becoming a lieutenant general on April 21, 1792 (AMS, Estachería exped. E-1466; Archivo Histórico de Protocoles, Madrid, Protocol 22398; information provided by Eric Beerman).

17. Unzaga to O'Reilly, New Orleans, May 20, 1773, with enclosure of Estachería to O'Reilly, New Orleans, May 18, 1773, in AGI, SD, leg. 2661.

18. Estachería to O'Reilly, New Orleans, May 18, 1773, *ibid.*

April 23, 1774. Fortunately, the decision for punishment rested in Spain upon the inspector general of the infantry, Alejandro O'Reilly. No doubt Bouligny's loyal service in 1769 spared him from further humiliation. O'Reilly chose not to interpret Bouligny's misconduct as criminal, and a royal order of December 15, 1773, reinstated him, and another authorized his back pay. But the inspector general admonished him to adhere to the royal ordinances in the future.[19] Bouligny must have recognized the importance of O'Reilly's role in this affair and of having friends and protectors in high positions. But although the general helped him in 1773, Bouligny did not always have a protector, a situation he experienced several years later.[20]

Before then and only a few months after his arrival in Louisiana, Bouligny had begun his courtship of Marie Louise Le Sénéchal d'Auberville. His six years in Havana seem not to have resulted in a romantic attachment. He probably met Marie Louise through Juan José de Loyola, with whom Bouligny stayed when he first arrived in New Orleans. Loyola was then betrothed to the nineteen-year-old Creole and had secured permission from Spain to marry her. He had arrived in Louisiana in March, 1766, with Governor Ulloa. Possibly a native of Galicia in northwestern Spain, Loyola agreed in La Coruña in 1765 to serve in Louisiana as the *comisario de guerra* for two thousand pesos per year, a salary well above those of Esteban Gayarré and Martín Navarro, his companions at the *contaduría principal* (main accounting house) of Galicia, who were offered only twelve hundred and six hundred pesos, respectively. Loyola's illness in 1768, perhaps an affliction in a leg, and later the rebellion postponed the marriage. Although his health improved in the spring and summer of 1769, he suddenly worsened and died on September 2. Bouligny may have served as the executor of Loyola's estate, and if he had not known Marie Louise earlier, he became acquainted with her then. Romance followed almost immediately, and on February 25, 1770, he petitioned the government for permission to marry her. Possibly her mother helped in arranging the match.[21]

19. Conde de O'Reilly to Arriaga, Madrid, December 13, 1773; Royal order to the governor of Louisiana, Madrid, December 15, 1773; Unzaga to Arriaga, New Orleans, May 30, 1774, all *ibid*.

20. Texada, "Administration of O'Reilly," 237.

21. On Loyola's illness, see Loyola to Bucareli, New Orleans, April 20, 1769, in *SMV*, Pt. 1, pp. 84–86. Documents in AHN, Est., leg. 3883, exped. 2, indicate that Loyola was

The family that Bouligny sought to enter through marriage could trace its ancestry to Guillaume Le Sénéchal in fifteenth-century Normandy. Several generations later, Marie Louise's paternal grandfather, Louis Charles Le Sénéchal, followed a naval career. His only son, Vincent Guillaume Le Sénéchal, sieur d'Auberville, was born on October 25, 1713, at the port city of Brest and began his naval career at age fifteen. After nearly twenty years of service, he accepted the position of *commissaire ordonnateur* in charge of finances and supplies in Louisiana, where he arrived in 1748. The following year, after signing the marriage contract on March 15, he married a seventeen-year-old widow, Marie Françoise Petit de Coulange de Levillier, whose father, Pierre Louis Petit, sieur de Coulange, had been killed fighting the Chickasaws in 1736. Françoise, who usually omitted her first given name, was born on September 23, 1732, and had first married about November 19, 1746, when the marriage contract had been drawn up. She was then fourteen, and her husband, Jean Baptiste Boucher de Monbrun, sieur de Saint Laurent, was forty-six. He died at the Illinois post a year after their marriage. From the d'Auberville–Petit de Coulange union came two daughters—Marie Louise, born on May 1, 1750, and Céleste Elisabeth, born on June 7, 1752.[22]

In 1760, three years after her second husband's death on March 14, 1757, and in the midst of the Seven Years' War, Françoise left New Orleans for Paris with her two young daughters. Because of hostilities, they journeyed first to Spain and overland from there. At the parish church of Meudon, near Versailles, the twenty-eight-year-old widow married her third husband, Jean Pierre Robert Gérard, chevalier de Vilemont, on

---

well on July 11, 1769, thirteen days before Bouligny arrived in New Orleans. On the recruitment of Loyola, see Coutts, "Martín Navarro," I, 17. On what might have been the cause of Loyola's illness, see Loyola to Ulloa, New Orleans, May 29, 1766, in AGI, PC, leg. 82, and Gayarré to Grimaldi, New Orleans, April 1, 1770, in AGI, SD, leg. 2543. Bouligny's petition to marry, New Orleans, February 25, 1770, is in his *expediente matrimonial*, AMS (information supplied by Eric Beerman). The *expediente* contains documents on his application to marry, including mention of Loyola's request to wed Marie Louise. See also Martin, *Bouligny Family,* 162–63.

22. Martin, *Bouligny Family,* 20–63. Genealogical accounts of the Petit de Coulange family are in DB, HNOC; see also a sketch of the Petit de Livilliers de Coulange family, Marie Louise's mother, in Stanley Clisby Arthur and George Campbell Huchet de Kernion, eds., *Old Families of Louisiana* (1931; rpr. Baton Rouge, 1971), 234–37. Marie Françoise Petit de Coulange was born on September 23, 1732, in New Orleans (baptismal certificate, DB, HNOC).

June 17, 1761. Vilemont had served in Louisiana as an infantry captain between 1750 and 1758 and possibly had become acquainted with his future wife at that time. Following the French cession of Louisiana to Spain, he met the marqués de Grimaldi, the Spanish ambassador in Paris, who was impressed by Vilemont's knowledge of the colony. When Grimaldi became the first secretary in the Spanish government, he summoned Vilemont to Spain in early 1764 to be his chief adviser on Louisiana. The Spaniards at that time knew virtually nothing about their new acquisition. In 1764 Vilemont wrote several memoirs on Louisiana, about French troops, Indians, commerce, and religious affairs. He also advised Grimaldi on the kinds of supplies Louisiana needed. For his services, the crown appointed Vilemont to the post of second military chief in Louisiana with the rank of lieutenant colonel of cavalry on June 11, 1765, with a salary of one thousand pesos per year.

In 1764 and 1765, the government waited for shipments from France of Indian presents and flour to arrive in northwestern Spain. At the port of El Ferrol, the crown was outfitting the ship *La Liebre* with supplies, soldiers, and officials, among them Loyola, to send to Louisiana for the colony's transfer. In the second half of June, 1765, Vilemont and other personnel left Madrid for El Ferrol to board *La Liebre*. Delays in receiving the flour, contrary winds, and a corsair lurking off the coast prevented the ship from sailing until September 5, 1765. After a stop in Santo Domingo, where a number of soldiers deserted, the ship reached Havana on November 20. Vilemont, Governor Ulloa, who was picked up in Cuba, the soldiers, and the supplies departed for New Orleans on January 17, 1766, on board the *Volante* and the *El Rey de Prusia*. No doubt by then Vilemont had become well acquainted with Loyola, his traveling companion for more than six months.[23]

Vilemont's wife, stepdaughter Marie Louise, and two-year-old son

---

23. Martin, *Bouligny Family,* 74. The marriage contract of Vilemont and Madame d'Auberville, Paris, June 15, 1761, and their marriage certificate of June 17, 1761, are in DB, HNOC, with another marriage contract in BB, HNOC. On Vilemont in France and Spain and his memoirs of 1764, see Lyon, *French Diplomacy,* 41–42, who confuses the son, Louis, with the father, Jean Pierre Robert Gérard de Vilemont; the Spanish documents in AHN, Est., leg. 3883, do not. See also Grimaldi to Ulloa, Madrid, July 3, 1765, in SMV, Pt. 1, pp. 2–3; numerous documents in AGI, SD, leg. 2542, are on the sailing of *La Liebre;* and Marc de Villiers du Terrage, *The Last Years of French Louisiana,* ed. Carl A. Brasseaux and Glenn R. Conrad, trans. Hosea Phillips (Lafayette, La., 1982), 259. Moore (*Revolt,* 20) erroneously states that Vilemont commanded *El Rey de Prusia.*

Carlos, as he was known in Spanish documents, had returned to Louisiana earlier. Their ship, *Angelique,* departed from France in September, 1764, and arrived in Louisiana in December. They left behind Céleste Elisabeth, who was then sick with smallpox and died in Paris on November 10, 1764.[24]

Over the next two years in Louisiana, Lieutenant Colonel Vilemont, who assumed charge of the New Orleans militia, tried to protect the interests of his wife and stepdaughter. Their plantation, left to them by Le Sénéchal d'Auberville, had been purchased by Claude Joseph Villars Dubreuil (the younger). He had acquired it on credit for eighty thousand livres in 1758, but then failed to pay. Villars and his wife, Jeanne Catherine La Boulaye, mortgaged the new acquisition and other holdings as security for the debt but nonetheless evaded payment. Vilemont filed numerous petitions in the Superior Council to compel collection from Villars, but that institution had become powerless to enforce its decisions. The lieutenant colonel did not live to see the debt paid.[25]

On August 11, 1768, in a fight with Etienne de Vaugine, which might have been a duel, Vilemont received a sword wound in the stomach, followed by blows rained upon him after he was down, that left him seriously disabled. He never recovered from the injuries and died on October 10, 1769, only a month after Loyola's demise. Now widowed for a third time, Mme Vilemont felt it imperative for her daughter, Marie Louise, and her two young sons by Vilemont, Carlos and Luis (Louis Joseph Gérard de Vilemont, who was born in New Orleans on Sep-

---

24. Mortuary extract, Church of St. Nicolas des Champs, Paris, dated July 11, 1764, but made in 1765, DB, HNOC; Martin, *Bouligny Family,* 85–86; Carl A. Brasseaux, ed., *A Comparative View of French Louisiana, 1699 and 1762: The Journals of Pierre Le Moyne d'Iberville and Jean-Jacques-Blaise d'Abbadie* (Lafayette, La., 1979), 135.

25. Many documents in KCTU are on the Claude Joseph Villars Dubreuil debt to Petit de Coulange-d'Auberville, beginning with July 10, 1766; see in particular Procès-verbal of a meeting of relatives and friends of Marie Louise Dauberville, New Orleans, August 5, 1766, and another of February 1, 1768; Superior Council decisions, New Orleans, August 23, November 10, 1766, May 2, July 11, September 3, 1767, March 9, April 13, 1768, all in KCTU. Martin, *Bouligny Family,* 164–68; *Bouligny Foundation Newsletter* (September, 1982). The Superior Council's lack of power is mentioned in O'Reilly to Arriaga, New Orleans, October 17, 1769, in *SMV,* Pt. 1, p. 99: "For many years past there has been the greatest disorder in the administration of justice in this province. Even when suits between parties have been adjudicated by the council, the decisions have not been carried out. This has increased my tasks, but the public welcomes this work."

tember 22, 1767), to have a protector in the Spanish regime. On November 10, 1769, she petitioned General O'Reilly for the appointment of a new guardian (curator) for Marie Louise. Perhaps that action led to her engagement and later marriage. Bouligny recognized the advantage of marrying into a family that possessed some money and prominence in Louisiana.[26]

To obtain official permission to marry, Bouligny furnished Marie Louise's baptismal certificate and a statement that she was of the right social position to marry an officer, and declared her dowry to be 54,000 livres (10,800 pesos), the sum owed by Villars. On February 25, 1770, with the proper documentation and Governor Unzaga's approval, Bouligny made his formal application to wed. O'Reilly, who was still in New Orleans, probably gave his blessings. In Spain, Bouligny's family joyously greeted the news and wished "Frasquito" (his family name) and his bride-to-be happiness. The Spanish Council of War granted Bouligny permission to marry on August 17, with a royal order issued to that effect a week later. O'Reilly, then back in Spain, sent his best wishes to Bouligny and conveyed his compliments to the bride after the December 29, 1770, wedding in New Orleans' St. Louis Church.[27]

Both before and after the marriage, Bouligny did what he could to help Marie Louise's family in collecting the money Villars owed them. In late January, 1770, Governor Unzaga approved the seizure of Villars' property to liquidate debts of 32,470 livres (6,494 pesos). Vilemont's widow claimed that Luis Villars owed her large sums and that her second husband had lent Claude Joseph Villars Dubreuil 28,000 livres, for which the latter had mortgaged 28 slaves. She petitioned that the slaves be for-

26. Ulloa to Grimaldi, New Orleans, August 18, 1768, in AGI, SD, leg. 2542; Vilemont's burial certificate, New Orleans, October 10, 1769, DB, HNOC; *Bouligny Foundation Newsletter* (September, 1982). Madame Vilemont's petition for a curator for her minor daughter Marie d'Auberville is in LHC, Spanish Judicial Records, File 10555, November 10, 1769. See also Laura L. Porteous, "Index to the Spanish Judicial Records of Louisiana," *Louisiana Historical Quarterly*, VI (1923), 156; St. Louis Cathedral Book of Baptisms, VI (1767–1771), 59; and Earl C. Woods and Charles E. Nolan, eds., *Sacramental Records of the Roman Catholic Church of the Archdiocese of New Orleans*, Vol. II, *1751–1771* (New Orleans, 1988), 93, where the entry is listed under DeVilemont.

27. Bouligny matrimonial *expediente*, AMS; Muniain to Grimaldi, San Ildefonso, August 19, 1770, in AGI, SD, leg. 2543. The marriage contract of Bouligny and Maria Luisa Le Sénéchal d'Auberville, New Orleans, December 22, 1770, is in LHC, Spanish Judicial Records, Doc. 141, File 10812.

feited. Her assertion that she was in financial need was probably correct, since her husband's salary was suspended at the time of his injury in 1768 and she was not receiving a widow's pension. On November 22, 1770, Governor Unzaga ordered the attachment of additional Villars properties; however, it does not appear that any of them were taken in 1770. Two years before, armed men had blocked an attempt to seize assets belonging to Villars. In 1771, Bouligny petitioned Governor Unzaga, alleging that Villars had not paid Marie Louise for the d'Auberville property, which was now in ruins, and asking for the payment of 31,270 livres (6,254 pesos). Probably in response, Unzaga ordered an inventory of the Villars properties. In the fall of 1771, the inventory showed that Villars owned a house on Royal Street, a lot on Conde Street, twelve lots at the end of Royal Street, furniture, and a plantation located one league above New Orleans containing buildings, slaves, livestock, bricks, and lumber. In 1772, the Vilemont family finally succeeded in recovering the d'Auberville plantation. Because of its damaged condition, other Villars holdings were liquidated to compensate the Vilemonts. Villars' indebtedness, however, exceeded his assets. Consequently, in September, 1773, Françoise Petit received only 3,353 pesos, not the 5,600 owed to her, and Marie Louise obtained 3,846 pesos instead of 6,494. When the Villars properties were auctioned off, Bouligny bought the plantation above New Orleans.[28]

Francisco Bouligny's first acquisition of property in Louisiana, however, had occurred a few months after his arrival in the colony. He bought several slaves in late 1769 or early 1770 from the Spanish government's sale of property confiscated from the convicted rebels. He soon disposed of three bondsmen; the buying and selling of slaves was a favorite pastime of many of the better-off residents of Louisiana. In January, 1770, Bouligny sold a female slave named Thevya to Pedro Gálvez for 260 pesos and Losia to Captain Serrantes of the Havana regiment for 200 pesos. Both Gálvez and Serrantes were part of the O'Reilly expedition and were then returning to Cuba. Three years later, in October, 1773, they still had not paid Bouligny, which prompted him to give power of

28. Françoise Petit de Coulange petition to Unzaga, New Orleans, December 30, 1770; Procès-verbal of seizure of Villars Dubreuil property by order of Governor Unzaga, New Orleans, January 26–27, 1770; petition of Françoise Petit de Coulange, New Orleans, November 22, 1770; Bouligny to [Unzaga], 1771; Unzaga, November 22, 1770, all in KCTU. See also Laura L. Porteous, "Index to the Spanish Judicial Records," *Louisiana Historical Quarterly*, IX (1926), 345–51; Martin, *Bouligny Family*, 92–95.

attorney to Juan Clavería in Havana to recover the sums owed him. On February 10, 1770, Bouligny sold to General O'Reilly the thirty-five-year-old slave Héctor, who had been purchased from the widow of Nicolas Chauvin Lafrénière for 200 pesos.[29]

In March, 1772, Bouligny sank additional roots in the colony by buying the Villars plantation called Barataria and a number of slaves. (His first land acquisition of 16 arpents [1 arpent is approximately 192 feet] of front by 40 deep on the Iberville coast on August 24, 1771, was purely for speculation.) The Villars plantation, also measuring 16 arpents of front on the Mississippi by 40 arpents deep, was located a league upriver on the opposite bank from New Orleans in a region also called Barataria. It had a house, a sawmill, a warehouse, carpentry and blacksmith shops, 24 slave cabins, 2 furnaces, 25 sheep, 3 pairs of oxen, and assorted other holdings. It cost 2,080 pesos. Purchased separately from the land were the plantation slaves, approximately 22 of them, including children, for 4,513 pesos. The plantation's chief purpose was the production of lumber and staves. It also had a large canal that began 2 arpents from the Mississippi and connected with a bayou that led to Lake Barataria.[30]

When Bouligny purchased the Villars slaves on March 12, he agreed not to alienate Francisco, a twenty-six-year-old mulatto carpenter, and to sell him in two years to his relatives, who sought to free him. Bouligny emancipated Francisco in March, 1774, for 380 pesos, although the sum was not paid until January 16, 1779. Bouligny appears not to have pressed Francisco and Mariana Lebrau, his wife, for the money during that time.[31] Over the years, the Spaniard continued to buy, sell, and emancipate slaves.

Bouligny acquired a family, not just a wife. His mother-in-law and her two young sons from her marriage to Vilemont lived with him and Marie Louise. Because of Vilemont's service to the crown, his son Carlos was permitted to become a cadet in the Louisiana battalion at only age eight, and Bouligny no doubt looked after him. His own family soon

---

29. Andrés Almonester Notary, March 20–December 31, 1770, fols. 57–58, NONA; Juan B. Garic Acts, Vol. IV, January–December, 1773, fols. 299v–300, NONA.

30. Almonester Notary, January–December, 1772, fols. 89–90, 131–32; Porteous, "Index to Spanish Judicial Records" (1926), 546–47.

31. Almonester Notary, January–December, 1772, fols. 115–116v, and January–December 31, 1774, fols. 69–71; Leonardo Mazange Notary, Vol. I, January–December, 1779, fols. 36–36v, NONA. See also Kimberly S. Hanger, "Avenues to Freedom Open to New Orleans' Black Population, 1769–1779," *Louisiana History,* XXXI (1990), 260–61.

began. His first child, María Luisa Josefina, called "Pepa," a name which her father bestowed and which stuck, was born on July 28, 1771. A son, Carlos José Domingo, followed on August 22, 1773. A third child, Luis Etienne Remy, came on October 2, 1774. He lived for less than two years, dying in 1776; he was buried on September 6. The growing brood soon required additional space. Where Bouligny and his new family lived immediately after his marriage is not known; possibly it was initially with his mother-in-law. In April, 1773, a year after acquiring the plantation, Bouligny purchased a substantial house in New Orleans, which he retained for a number of years.[32]

He bought the lot and house from Magdalena Brazilliers and Enriques Deprez. The house had been Governor Ulloa's residence and was adjacent to the river. It was probably one of the more desirable locations in New Orleans, since the ground was higher and the open space next to the Mississippi allowed more breezes in the summer. The lot measured ninety-three feet of front on Levee (now Decatur) Street by two hundred feet deep on St. Louis Street. The house, one floor set on a nine-foot brick base (which actually served as a cellar), extended for eighty-five feet on Levee Street and sixty-four feet on St. Louis Street. It had an unspecified number of rooms and chimneys, with a gallery made of brick pillars. The style of construction, quite common in New Orleans, was brick between posts, called *colombage*. Behind the principal residence stood another structure, fifty-seven feet long by eighteen feet wide, that contained several rooms, including a kitchen. It probably housed the slaves. Moreover, in the rear were a twenty-six-foot-square wooden stable, a well made of bricks, and latrines. Of the sixteen-hundred-peso price for the lot and buildings, which averaged four times the cost of a modest home, Bouligny immediately paid half, obliging himself to pay four hundred pesos more in August and the balance in a year. However, it was not until October 11, 1774, that the debt was canceled, having been satisfied in full.[33]

Almost at the same time that he purchased his New Orleans residence where he lived for nineteen years, Bouligny faced a lawsuit from Claude Joseph Villars Dubreuil's nephews over his recently acquired

---

32. Woods and Nolan, eds., *Sacramental Records,* II, 29; *ibid.,* Vol. III, *1772–1773* (New Orleans, 1989), 34; Martin, *Bouligny Family,* 172–74.

33. Garic Acts, Vol. IV, January–December, 1773, fols. 133v–137; Bouligny petition to the governor general [Unzaga], [New Orleans], April 30, 1773, AGI, PC, leg. 187A.

plantation. Several of them, Lt. Jacobo Dubreuil, Sublt. Raimundo Dubreuil, and Lt. Luis Villars Dubreuil, were then serving in the Louisiana battalion. They and their minor brother, Alejandro Dubreuil, claimed in May, 1773, that their deceased grandfather (also named Claude Joseph Villars Dubreuil) had reserved one arpent of land on the plantation, through which ran a canal that allowed them to reach their fourteen leagues of lands in the interior. Their grandfather, they asserted, while choosing not to include that reservation in his will, had nevertheless intended to benefit all his heirs equally by leaving the passage on the canal unobstructed. In the sale to Bouligny, the heirs agreed that the plantation would contain all sixteen arpents of front, including the canal, and they claimed that they planned to purchase back the one arpent from the proceeds of the plantation's sale. On that one arpent of land they would put up buildings of their choice, leaving a public road thirty-six feet wide that followed the canal.

In replying to the claims of the Villars nephews in July, Bouligny stated that he owned sixteen arpents of front and that the alleged one-arpent reservation lacked foundation. Moreover, he charged that Alejandro Dubreuil had placed on that arpent adjacent to the canal a free black, Carlota, who was selling liquor to his slaves contrary to the terms of sale. Bouligny presented witnesses to substantiate his arguments. On August 12, Governor Unzaga's verdict favored Bouligny. Six days later, however, the nephews and Bouligny reached an out-of-court settlement. Bouligny and the other creditors of their uncle Claude Joseph Villars Dubreuil would pay the nephews two hundred pesos; the brothers had the right to remove the bricks, wood, and other construction materials they had used on the one arpent they claimed; and they, their heirs, and other persons who needed the canal would continue to enjoy free passage on it. Finally, the former slave Carlota had to find new premises to live in.[34]

The successful settlement of several problems by 1774 cleared the way for Bouligny's journey to Europe the next year. For some time he had been planning the trip, originally to collect property belonging to his wife in France, later to attend to family and business affairs in Spain. His request for a year's leave, dated May 1, 1772, was approved by O'Reilly on

---

34. Porteous, "Index to Spanish Judicial Records" (1926), 546–52; Doc. 269, May 10, 1773, Box 30, LHC. Partially correct information on the Dubreuil de Villars family is in Arthur and Huchet de Kernion, *Old Families,* 107–108.

September 13, with a royal order to that effect ten days later. Before Bouligny could depart, however, he suffered house arrest in 1773 that lasted until April, 1774. By that time, he was involved in the acquisition of property and had young children, which perhaps delayed his leaving.[35]

In early 1775, Bouligny renewed his preparations to leave Louisiana. On the back of his royal license to marry, he wrote in French to "Ma chere Mouson" (Marie Louise) that if he did not survive his journey, she should present the license to Treasurer Navarro to receive a widow's pension. He borrowed fifteen hundred pesos from fellow captain Fernando de Leyba, which he promised to repay in February, 1776, and for which he pledged his New Orleans house. Delays postponed his journey for three months. On May 6, he informed Navarro of the accounting office of his imminent departure. Six days later he left New Orleans and was in Havana by May 31. There he spent a week or two, perhaps visiting familiar places and friends. About mid-June, he sailed on a ship bound for Cádiz, Spain.[36]

Thirteen years had passed since Bouligny last saw the Iberian peninsula. Half that time had been passed quietly in Cuba, but the final six years in Louisiana had changed his life considerably. At thirty-nine, he was a firmly established family man seeking the acquisition of property. But as well as his personal life was progressing, his professional career needed rejuvenation. After seventeen years of army service, he was still in the junior ranks. Although Bouligny might have harbored inner thoughts of pushing his career forward while in Spain, it is known that he had plans for advancing his private fortune, which he attempted to do upon arriving in Cádiz.

35. Bouligny petition with marginal notations, New Orleans, May 1, 1772, AGI, SD, leg. 2661; Arriaga to the governor of Louisiana, Aranjuez, September 23, 1772, in AGI, PC, leg. 174A.

36. [Bouligny] to Mouson [Marie Louise], [New Orleans], April 3, 1775, in BB, HNOC; Garic Acts, Vol. VI, January–December, 1775, fols. 29–30v. The Leyba debt was canceled on January 27, 1777. Martín Navarro, New Orleans, May 15, 1775, AGI, PC, leg. 566; Unzaga to de la Torre, New Orleans, May 12, 1775, in AGI, PC, leg. 1146; [de la Torre] to Unzaga, Havana, May 31, 1775, in AGI, PC, leg. 1147; Unzaga to Arriaga, New Orleans, February 14, 1775, with petition of Petit de Coulange, widow of Vilemont, in AGI, SD, leg. 2661.

4 SPAIN AND THE *MEMORIA*
1775–1776

IN THE SUMMER of 1775, Francisco Bouligny crossed the Atlantic Ocean on a second occasion, returning to Spain after an absence of thirteen years. During that time Spain had enjoyed peace in its American colonies, although there were problems with the Arab states of North Africa. The Spanish crown under Carlos III continued its policies of reform in government, economics, and the military, striving to strengthen its possessions but not doing so with the speed and success that it wanted. The Family Compact had dissolved in the wake of France's failure to support Spain's objections to the English seizure of the Malvina (Falkland) Islands in 1770. The Spaniards withdrew their claims to the islands rather than risk war alone. In the important North American viceroyalty of New Spain, the government continued to shore up its defenses against aggressive European rivals and warring natives. It commenced the occupation of upper California in 1769, erecting presidios and Franciscan missions against a possible Russian challenge from Alaska. In 1772, after an inspection tour by the marqués de Rubí, the crown, in a new *reglamento,* reorganized the military garrisons that stretched from Sonora to Texas against marauding Indians such as the Apaches and Comanches. For East Texas, however, it meant the abandonment of the posts at Los Adaes and Orcoquisacs, as the acquisition of Louisiana had made them redundant. Meanwhile, the crown pushed its building program, adding to the fortifications of the Caribbean colonies.[1]

Louisiana, however, had experienced little growth since Bouligny's arrival in 1769. O'Reilly's reorganization had reduced its subsidy to

---

1. For this time era, see Carlos E. Castañeda, *The Passing of the Missions, 1762–1782,* Vol. IV of *Our Catholic Heritage in Texas, 1519–1936* (Austin, 1936–50); Herbert Eugene Bolton, *Texas in the Middle Eighteenth Century* (Berkeley, Calif., 1915).

115,000 pesos, money that was essential for stimulating commerce. Although he permitted the colony to trade with Spain and Cuba, both of those regions consumed few of Louisiana's products. For the most part, the province slumbered along economically in the early 1770s, and Governor Luis de Unzaga won the approval of the French planters by allowing smuggling to flourish with the neighboring English in West Florida. He probably had little choice. Trade was vital, and criticism of Spain's shortsighted commercial policy mounted as more people believed that the Mississippi Valley's potential for development was infinite if it received the proper incentives. Bouligny soon revealed in Spain that he too had become a convert for change in Louisiana.[2]

About mid-August, 1775, the captain arrived in Cádiz, the same port from which he had sailed many years before. His first activity was to present a proposal to introduce slaves in Louisiana to the agents of the Compañía Gaditana de Negros that had an *asiento* (monopoly contract) to supply the Spanish Caribbean with slaves. Bouligny appears to have been thinking of a slave contract while in Louisiana as a way of helping to develop the colony and make money. A slave-supplying contract was potentially lucrative. The Compañía Gaditana, however, was not enjoying such success, in part because it was a recent innovation. Foreign nations had long furnished the Spaniards with bondsmen. Formed on June 14, 1765, the company first received a ten-year contract to supply 3,500 slaves for Cuba, New Granada (Colombia), Panama, Honduras, Campeche, Cumaná, Santo Domingo, Trinidad, Margarita, Santa María, and Puerto Rico. But the company immediately ran into problems of insufficient capital that led to its reorganization in 1766. In the seven years between 1765 and 1772, it introduced 13,149 slaves but sold only 11,700, incurring a loss of 298,916 pesos. Its total financial indebtedness, however, rose to over a million pesos as it borrowed money heavily. By 1775, when Bouligny arrived in Spain with his proposal, the company's creditors were hounding it for payment. Unknown to him, his prospects for success were bleak.[3]

The captain's proposal of August 22 contained five articles to provide Louisiana with unassimilated black slaves (*bozales*), who would spur de-

2. A brief description of Louisiana under Governor Unzaga is in John Walton Caughey, *Bernardo de Gálvez in Louisiana, 1776–1783* (Berkeley, Calif., 1934), 43–57, and Din, *Louisiana in 1776*, 5–10.

3. Bibiano Torres Ramírez, *La compañía gaditana de negros* (Seville, 1973), 15–102.

velopment. He offered to introduce at least one hundred bondsmen annually at the same price the company sold them in Havana and to accept Louisiana produce in payment. In addition, he obligated himself to introduce all the slaves the province needed, but presumably at a higher price. Bouligny would reimburse the company directors ten pesos for each slave landed in Louisiana. He pledged as security for his operations his real estate holdings in and adjacent to New Orleans, including one hundred Creole slaves, all estimated to be worth at least fifty thousand pesos.[4]

When the company directors in Cádiz received Bouligny's proposal, they referred him to Juan José de Goicoa, an associate and their court lawyer. Goicoa was in Madrid, and rather than wait in Cádiz, Bouligny journeyed there for an answer. As the proposal represented competition and the company was teetering on the edge of insolvency, Goicoa opposed it. He raised the specter of illegal trade with foreign colonies, complained that an annual trade of one hundred slaves was insufficient for the company to keep an office in New Orleans, and argued that the firm could not afford to send slaves to Louisiana without assurances of their purchase. Goicoa counterproposed that if Louisiana required slaves, it should obtain them from the company in Havana. But as he observed, no one from Louisiana had yet asked the company for them. Goicoa's answer constituted a rebuff. Bouligny abandoned the idea of an *asiento* for himself and stayed on in Madrid.[5]

It was then late September or October, 1775, and Bouligny was not without connections in Madrid. Two of his sisters, Inés and Cecilia, lived there. Possibly Inés, who had a son Juan Tala y Bouligny, put him up during his stay in the Spanish capital. He also saw his thirteen-year-old brother-in-law, Carlos de Vilemont, who through his mother had obtained permission to study in Spain. He was attending the Real Seminario de Nobles (Royal Seminary of Nobles) in Madrid, which was located in the northwest corner of the city near the Puerta de San Bernardo and not far from the Spanish Guards' barracks where Bouligny had served. The school specialized in teaching Latin, philosophy, mathemat-

4. Francisco Bouligny, "Articles by which dn. Fran.co Bouligny obligates himself to provide African blacks (*bozales*) to the City of New Orleans and Province of Louisiana," Cádiz, August 22, 1775, in AGI, SD, leg. 2586.

5. Juan José de Goicoa to Marcos Ximeno, Madrid, June 2, 1776, in AGI, SD, leg. 2586.

ics, and religion. Vilemont had left New Orleans the previous January in the company of his cousin, thirty-three-year-old militia lieutenant Carlos de Grand-Pré.[6]

Besides escorting young Vilemont, Grand-Pré had jouneyed to Spain for personal reasons. He had transferred from the New Orleans militia to the Spanish Brussels Regiment as a regular army lieutenant. But upon his arrival in Spain, he learned of the retirement of Captain Demasillières—Bouligny's old rival—and petitioned the crown for the vacancy, with a promotion to captain. On July 15, 1775, the government approved the petition and conferred upon him the 7th Company of the Louisiana battalion. His total time in the Brussels regiment as a regular lieutenant amounted to one and a half months. Perhaps Grand-Pré stayed in Spain long enough to see Bouligny and relayed to him his extraordinary good fortune in achieving a captaincy so quickly. The friendship between Grand-Pré and Bouligny was well established. Grand-Pré's father had looked after the financial interests of Bouligny's wife until his death, and Grand-Pré himself and his mother, Marie Louise's grandaunt, were witnesses at the Bouligny-d'Auberville wedding in 1770. The relationship between the two men grew closer, and Grand-Pré became the godfather of Bouligny's first child, Pepa. Immediately after his promotion, Grand-Pré returned to Louisiana, cutting short his sojourn in Spain. He missed becoming better acquainted with the major events then under way there.[7]

Bouligny, however, saw firsthand some of the changes occurring in Spain. Talk of reforms by the enlightened despot Carlos III and his ministers filled the kingdom, and a number of projects were already under way. Since Bouligny had traveled over the deplorable coach roads from Cádiz to Madrid, he probably observed the colonization efforts at Sierra Morena, the region that separates the higher tablelands (*meseta*) of New

6. Unzaga to [the captain general], New Orleans, January 2, 1775, in DSGL, Bk. I, Vol. IV; "Justifications of Nobility of the Seminarist Don Carlos Villemont," AHN, Universidades, leg. 672; Antonio Ponz, *Viage de España* (1772–94; rpr. Madrid, 1972), V, 183. On Inés Bouligny de Tala, see Martin, *Bouligny Family*, 108, 109, 112, 117.

7. Unzaga to [the captain general], New Orleans, January 11, 1775, in DSGL, Bk. I, Vol. IV; Patent to Carlos de Grand-Pré, Madrid, July 15, 1775, AGI, SD, leg. 2654; On the Grand-Pré-Bouligny tie, a personal communication to the author from Fontaine Martin, New Orleans, May 26, 1987, and Martin, *Bouligny Family*, 14–15, 86, 164, 172. Grand-Pré was in Paris in 1764 and attended Céleste Elisabeth d'Auberville's funeral.

Castile from the lower coastal plain of Andalusia. The government used thousands of German settlers to establish a number of towns and villages, including one called La Luisiana, and the Sierra Morena colonization project was only one of several schemes to populate vacant rural areas. Land and agricultural reforms were important parts of royal policy. Government physiocrats believed that genuine wealth sprang from the soil and that inefficiency characterized most of the 70 percent of the national domain owned by the aristocracy and clergy.[8]

In addition to agricultural reforms, Carlos III undertook many other projects to revitalize Spain. He tried to improve communications through a system of better roads and canals. He attempted to raise the quality of education with curricular reform and new schools. The government promoted the dissemination of scientific knowledge from foreign sources. It created museums, libraries, and botanical gardens. Enlightened despotism was encouraged by officials known as *golillas,* who came from the middle ranks of society and increasingly replaced nobles in government. They introduced progressive French ideas and customs that often clashed with the traditionalism of the aristocracy, the Church, and the lower classes. Part of the new customs could be seen from the 1760s in the adoption of the French costume by many in the middle and upper classes, government officials, and army personnel. It consisted of a long-skirted coat with collar or short cape, a long waistcoat, tight-fitting knee breeches, a cravat, a three-cornered hat, and a wig. The traditional Spanish costume, a long cloak, a hair net, and a floppy broad-brimmed hat (*chambergo*), predominated in provincial towns and the countryside. The few major cities reflected the innovating trends far more than the rural areas, which remained isolated, uneducated, and overwhelmingly traditional.[9]

Madrid, where Bouligny spent much of his stay in Spain, felt the

8. Cayetano Alcázar, *Las colonias alemanas de Sierra Morena (notas para su estudio)* (Madrid, 1930); William J. Callahan, *Church, Politics, and Society in Spain, 1750–1874* (Cambridge, Mass., 1984).

9. On the reforms of Carlos III, see in particular Anthony H. Hull, *Charles III and the Revival of Spain* (Washington, D.C., 1981); Richard Herr, *The Eighteenth-Century Revolution in Spain* (Princeton, 1958); Antonio Ferrer del Río, *Historia del reinado de Carlos III en España* (Madrid, 1856); Vicente Rodríguez Casado, *La política y los políticos en el reinado de Carlos III* (Madrid, 1962); and David R. Ringrose, *Transportation and Economic Stagnation in Spain, 1750–1850* (Durham, N.C., 1970).

effects of modernization in the 1760s and 1770s. Before midcentury, the city failed to rank among the leading European capitals. Its population of about 150,000 lived crowded in buildings that lined the narrow, twisted, and often dirty streets. These cobblestoned thoroughfares sloped from the outside to the center, where a stream of polluted water usually ran. The age-old practice of discarding soiled water from apartment windows continued, often to the discomfort of passersby below. Pigs, dogs, and other animals roamed freely through the streets. But from the 1760s projects for improving the city began. The architects and engineers of Carlos III erected massive ornamental gates (*puertas*) in the walls around the city and built new fountains within it. Also, the Paseo del Prado, a broad and straight avenue running north and south, was under construction on the eastern flank of the city. Nearby, the wooded Retiro Park became fashionable for outings.[10]

Lacking industry, Madrid was a governmental city that teemed with bureaucrats, military personnel, and office seekers. In the 1760s, the government began the annual publication of a book listing office vacancies in Spain and the colonies. Petitioners and job hunters crowded the villa's inns, taverns, cafés, and government waiting rooms. Bouligny joined the hordes of favor seekers and, perhaps influenced by the bureaucratic climate of Madrid, penned several petitions over the next few months.[11]

When the captain left Madrid to visit his family in Alicante is unclear, and it is possible that he did not. His hometown was one of several principal ports on Spain's southeastern coast. Although possessing fewer than twenty thousand inhabitants, it had a significant commerce with Mediterranean and Atlantic ports in northern Europe. The English traveler Henry Swinburne, who was in Alicante in December, 1775, left behind a description of the port city at that time. He wrote in the deprecatory manner typical of foreign visitors in Spain:

> It has neither buildings nor streets to recommend it to notice; though the houses in general are solidly built with flat roofs, covered with cement; their walls are plastered, and every thing is white as the soil of the adjacent country . . . the dust flies about in whirlwinds; if it rains, there is no possibility of making one's way through the streets without boots, the *Callemayor* being the only paved

10. Kany, *Life and Manners,* 8–46, 176–79; Ponz, *Viage,* II, 4–6, V, VI.
11. Antonio Domínguez Ortiz, *Hechos y figuras del siglo XVIII español* (Madrid, 1973), 217.

street in the whole town. In the hot months, this place is a very furnace. . . . In such mild winter weather as we have felt here, it is impossible not to be delighted with the climate, and the beauties of situation that the port of Alicant affords. . . . Behind the castle-hill [at the rear of the town] is a plain some leagues in circumference, called *Las huertas,* the gardens of Alicant lying along the seashore, surrounded on three sides by very lofty mountains. It is a very beautiful vale, thickly studded with villages, villas, farms, and plantations of all kinds of fruit-trees.[12]

From Alicante, much to his chagrin, Bouligny's brothers and sisters greeted him with a lawsuit. When his father, Jean, died in 1772, he left only a modest inheritance to his eleven surviving offspring. The sons and daughters present in Spain divided it among themselves, including Francisco's share. They justified their behavior by charging that their father had lavished thousands of pesos on Francisco while he was a cadet. But they did more. When Frasquito returned to Spain appearing like a man of substance, they sought to recover the remainder of the money that their father had expended on him as a cadet, which his share of the inheritance had not covered. Francisco resisted, declaring that he had been a minor and that their father had borne the expenses out of his own free will. The legal maneuver appears not to have gone far. Perhaps, however, it led to Bouligny's effort to pull his two older brothers, José and Juan, out of the economic doldrums that their business was then experiencing in Alicante.[13]

Having failed to secure a slave-supplying contract for himself, he probably suggested that José and Juan Bouligny, together with another Alicante merchant, Miguel Kearney, gain an *asiento* for themselves. On March 12, 1776, in Alicante the three men drafted their petition, stating that Louisiana needed *bozales* to cultivate the province's fields. The three partners proposed to supply them to the planters on credit and to receive the colony's produce as payment. The monopoly company had thus far not supplied Louisiana, and it neither extended credit nor took produce. The three partners submitted themselves to the same terms that the company enjoyed and for the time period that the crown might assign.[14]

12. Swinburne, *Travels,* II, 172–74.

13. An unsigned and undated document on Francisco Bouligny's alleged debt to his brothers and sisters, *ca.* 1776, BB, HNOC.

14. Juan and José Bouligny and Miguel Kearney, Alicante, March 12, 1776, AGI, SD, leg. 2586.

After receiving the petition, the government consulted the Compañía Gaditana's agent Goicoa at court. He informed the government about Bouligny's proposal of the previous August and continued with the argument that the company could supply Louisiana if there was a need. In ten years, however, the province had not requested slaves from the company's Havana office; on the contrary, Louisiana merchants had tried to sell slaves in Cuba. Moreover, Goicoa brought up the possibility of illegal trade, particularly as the British were in neighboring West Florida, and that contraband slaves, once introduced in Louisiana, could then be shipped to other Spanish colonies. But Goicoa's opinion was not the final voice heard, as the government continued to study the proposal.[15]

Soon after disembarking in Cádiz in August, 1775, Bouligny must have learned about O'Reilly's ill-fated expedition against Algiers. It had resulted from Spain's loss of prestige in European eyes when it backed down in the Malvinas crisis (1770 to 1771) with Britain and from recent difficulties with North African states. The Arab governments had long committed acts of piracy and raided the Spanish coast. In 1774, Morocco assaulted Spain's North African outpost of Melilla almost immediately after signing a peace treaty. Carlos III chose to chastize the Algerians for their support of Morocco. Lt. Gen. Alejandro O'Reilly, of the hawkish Aragonese faction at court, volunteered to direct the expedition against Algiers with no more than twenty thousand men.

Almost at the same time that Bouligny left Havana for Spain in the summer of 1775, O'Reilly completed gathering his troops and ships in Cartagena on the Spanish southeastern coast. He sailed in June and arrived off the Algerian coast by early July. Although the general had handled the expedition to New Orleans brilliantly, on this occasion he blundered completely. Without coastal reconnaissance, knowledge of the enemy's strength, or the element of surprise, the Spanish landing on the beach near Algiers on July 8 produced hundreds if not thousands of casualties. After the debacle, in which a number of officers who later served in Louisiana participated, the survivors limped back to Alicante. Carlos III attempted to shield O'Reilly from the wrath of the Spanish

15. Juan José de Goicoa to Marcos Ximeno, Madrid, June 2, 1776; Statement by Marcos Ximeno, Tomás Ortiz de Landazuri, and Manuel Lanz de Casafond, Madrid, April 8, 1777; "The Junta of the General Contract (*Asiento*) of Slaves," Madrid, April 8, 1777; all in AGI, SD, leg. 2586.

public, and the count retired to Puerto de Santa María, across the bay from Cádiz, where he lived in semiexile and disgrace for many years. He kept the post of inspector general of the infantry until 1777.[16]

Although he corresponded amicably several times with O'Reilly, there is no evidence that Bouligny saw the count during his sixteen months in Spain. The career of the Irishman had become tarnished, and Bouligny also disagreed with the general's economic policy for Louisiana. By the time the captain left the kingdom, he had established a new relationship with a higher government official, and he relied upon him for protection. Communications between Bouligny and O'Reilly seem to have ceased for the most part.

Bouligny's presence in Madrid is known in January, 1776, and again in March. In January, Dr. Pablo de Ganosse attended to the ailing captain, who was suffering from "a convulsive effect in the chest, with some symptom of nephritic colic." The sickness had begun in the fall of 1775 with the onset of cold weather. The physician prescribed a regimen of medications and ordered him to take the "native airs," presumably those of his birthplace, for a lengthy convalescence before he hazarded a journey. Perhaps at that time Bouligny visited Alicante, but if he did, he returned to Madrid by mid-March, as he submitted petitions to the crown about then.[17]

Bouligny procured a statement from Dr. Ganosse to support his request for a year's extension to his leave. The court granted his petition on April 16, 1776, but only for six months. Also, sometime before March, 1776, perhaps as early as the fall of 1775, Bouligny solicited a promotion to lieutenant colonel. Possibly he wanted to duplicate Grand-Pré's recent success in acquiring a promotion with such ease. The court sent the request to Inspector General O'Reilly, but he failed to respond at that time or to a royal order of March 4, 1776. Not until July, 1777, when the crown inquired again, did the general give his approval. The Ministry of War issued a patent of promotion to brevet lieutenant colonel

16. There is no agreement on Spanish casualties in O'Reilly's expedition. For accounts of the events, see Fernández Duro, *Armada española,* VII, 165–76; the supplement to the *Gazeta de Madrid* of July 18, 1775, in W. N. Hargreaves-Mawdsley, ed., *Spain Under the Bourbons, 1700–1833: A Collection of Documents* (Columbia, S.C., 1973), 148–49; Hull, *Charles III,* 188; Sir Charles Petrie, *King Charles III of Spain: An Enlightened Despot* (New York, 1971), 157–60.

17. Certificate of Dr. Pablo de Ganosse, Madrid, March 15, 1776, AGI, SD, leg. 2661.

on August 3, 1777. The delay in securing the promotion later hurt him in seniority.[18]

Besides involvement in his own activities, Bouligny must have been aware of the momentous events occurring in the Ministry of the Indies in early 1776. On January 28, the minister Julián de Arriaga died, and on February 2, José de Gálvez replaced him, starting an eleven-year stewardship. An activist and former inspector general in New Spain, Gálvez in his first year as minister authorized the establishment of the commandancy general of the Internal Provinces for northern Mexico and erected the viceroyalty of the Río de la Plata (Argentina, Uruguay, Paraguay, and Bolivia). He endorsed the appointment of Gen. Pedro de Cevallos, who had wisely declined the Algerian campaign, to lead the largest armada ever sent across the Atlantic, with the goal of defeating the Portuguese in the Banda Oriental (Uruguay) and establishing a new viceroyalty. The expedition left Cádiz in November, 1776, and the next year scored an impressive victory that was desperately needed after O'Reilly's disaster.[19]

Minister Gálvez clearly revealed his desire to reinvigorate the Indies against foreign threats. One of his main concerns was North America, where English colonials had rebelled against Britain in 1775. In February, 1776, he sent secret orders to Caribbean officials to gather intelligence on the rebellion. Through 1776, high government authorities debated policy and reexamined defenses in Spanish possessions adjacent to the English.

18. Bouligny's unsigned and undated petition, AGI, SD, leg. 2661; José de Gálvez to the governor of Louisiana, Aranjuez, April 18, 1776, in AGI, PC, leg. 174B; [José de Gálvez?] to O'Reilly, El Pardo, March 4, 1776, in AGI, SD, leg. 2534; O'Reilly to José de Gálvez, [Puerto de Santa María], July 18, 1777, in AGI, SD, leg. 2534; Patent of promotion for Bouligny to brevet lieutenant colonel, San Ildefonso, August 3, 1777, AGI, SD, leg. 2534. Two Spanish officers in Louisiana then enjoyed seniority over Bouligny, Pedro Piernas and Fernando de Leyba. In July, 1777, O'Reilly admitted only to Piernas, who had been promoted to brevet lieutenant colonel in mid-1775 and always remained senior to Bouligny. Leyba, who served as commandant at Arkansas and later at St. Louis until his death in 1780, was promoted to that rank in 1779.

19. Royal patent appointing José de Gálvez as Secretario del Estado y del Despacho Universal de Indias, AGI, PC, leg. 569. There is no complete biography of José de Gálvez. Two studies of his work in New Spain are Priestley, *Gálvez,* especially pp. 1–11, and Luis Navarro García, *José de Gálvez y la Comandancia General de las Provincias Internas* (Seville, 1964), 131–208. See also Isidoro Vázquez de Acuña, "El Ministro de Indias don José de Gálvez, Marqués de Sonora," *Revista de Indias,* XIX (1959), 449–71, and Dauril Alden, "The Undeclared War of 1773–1777: Climax of Luso-Spanish Platine Rivalry," *Hispanic American Historical Review,* XLI (1961), 55–74.

They worried that the conflict could spread beyond the British colonies to engulf Spanish America.[20]

In addition to responding favorably to Louisiana governor Unzaga's entreaties for more arms and soldiers, Gálvez made two significant appointments for the colony in 1776. In the first, the Louisiana battalion needed a replacement for Colonel Estachería, who had returned to the peninsula in 1774 to restore his health and who helped O'Reilly in planning the Algerian expedition. Perhaps as a reward, O'Reilly gave him command of a regiment in the Balaeric Islands and promotion to brigadier general. In May, 1776, O'Reilly recommended for his replacement the minister of the Indies' nephew, Bernardo de Gálvez, and a patent to that effect was issued on May 22.[21]

Was it a politically motivated appointment by the recently disgraced O'Reilly, who was attempting to ingratiate himself to the new minister? Or was it due to José de Gálvez's notorious penchant for nepotism? The recent activities of the younger Gálvez included returning from France after studying French military tactics and learning that language, participating on O'Reilly's ill-fated expedition, and serving at the Avila Military Academy. Only recently advanced to brevet lieutenant colonel, the thirty-year-old Bernardo gained command of the Louisiana battalion with a promotion to full colonel, bypassing two lower ranks where less privileged officers, including Bouligny, toiled for years.[22]

But there was more. In the second appointment, made in July, Uncle José named Bernardo as interim governor of Louisiana to replace Unzaga, who won elevation to the captaincy general of Venezuela. The new governor left Spain within a month or two, as he was in Cuba by

20. On Governor Unzaga's preoccupation with events in the English Atlantic colonies, see Din, "Protecting '*Barrera*,'" 199–202; on Spanish efforts to gain information about the English North American colonies, see Light Townsend Cummins, "Spanish Agents in North America During the Revolution" (Ph.D. dissertation, Tulane University, 1977).

21. O'Reilly to [José de Gálvez?], Puerto de Santa María, May 7, 1776, in AGI, PC, leg. 2586; Patent of promotion to colonel for Bernardo de Gálvez, Aranjuez, May 22, 1776, AG, SD, leg. 2654. Estachería petitioned for a one-year leave to improve his health on August 10, 1773 (AGI, SD, leg. 2661); a royal order to the governor of Louisiana approved it on January 5, 1774 (AGI, PC, leg. 569; Royal order to the governor of Louisiana, Madrid, April 9, 1776, AGI, SD, leg. 2661).

22. Caughey, *Gálvez*, 61–69; Winston De Ville, ed., *Yo Solo, The Battle Journal of Bernardo de Gálvez During the American Revolution* (New Orleans, 1978), x–xii.

October and landed in New Orleans on December 6, 1776. Whether the minister of the Indies selected Louisiana for his nephew because of the possibility of warfare erupting there is not known, but certainly North America was looming larger in the thinking of the Spanish government.[23]

In the spring of 1776, José de Gálvez wanted reliable information on Louisiana. Despite a dozen years of Spanish ownership, the province remained largely unknown and neglected. Spain's expenditure on it had been minimal, but its importance now soared as it constituted the empire's first line of defense in North America. Writing to Louisiana for data on conditions required time, and the minister wanted it quickly. Gálvez came to disagree with O'Reilly's narrow strictures for Louisiana's trade, where the general still exercised influence over economics. On June 23, 1774, and March 8, 1775, Governor Unzaga had written to Arriaga to complain about commercial restrictions and smuggling. Arriaga deferred the letters to O'Reilly, who ignored the problem. In November, 1774, the Irishman stubbornly insisted that free trade with Spain and Cuba was sufficient for Louisiana's trade and to stop contraband, clearly revealing his abysmal ignorance about the colony. He did not respond to the second letter until April 2, 1776, and he reiterated his earlier decision. While José de Gálvez sent a royal order to Louisiana, repeating the contents of O'Reilly's judgment, it probably made him reconsider policy for the colony, where he assigned his nephew a few weeks later.[24]

By April or May, the minister learned of Bouligny's presence in the capital, which coincided with the appointment of Bernardo de Gálvez as military commandant of Louisiana, and induced the captain to write a report about the province. He probably learned of his presence when Gálvez was considering the slave-supplying project of José and Juan Bouligny and Kearney; possibly Francisco appeared at court to assist it. Thus, about May, 1776, Bouligny began composing his *Memoria*. It became the first lengthy document about the colony to be written by a

23. Royal order to the governor of Louisiana, Madrid, July 19, 1776, AGI, PC, leg. 174B; Marqués de la Torre to José de Gálvez, Havana, November 24, 1776, in AGI, SD, leg. 2656; Cummins, "Spanish Agents," 130.

24. Unzaga to Arriaga, New Orleans, October 18, 1773, June 23, 1774, March 8, 1775; Royal orders to the governor of Louisiana, San Lorenzo, November 18, 1774, and Aranjuez, May 8, 1776; O'Reilly's notations, Puerto de Santa María, November 14, 1774, April 2, 1776; all in AGI, SD, leg. 2586.

Spaniard. During its composition, Bouligny consulted with Gálvez on several occasions as royal orders, anticipating the *Memoria*'s completion, began flowing to Louisiana.[25]

Bouligny remained in Madrid while drafting the *Memoria*. He probably recognized that his report might advance his career and even result in an *asiento* for his brothers. In writing the *Memoria,* however, he had to rely upon his memory and the experiences gained from a six-year residence in Louisiana. He is not known to have traveled extensively about the province, but by talking to officers, planters, traders, and hunters, he had become intimately acquainted with it. Living in the only town in the colony exposed him to its economy and trade. As a plantation owner, he knew the land's natural resources and what the soil produced. But in addition to describing the province, Bouligny wanted the government to promote its development. Therefore, he wrote enthusiastically and even overoptimistically about Louisiana.

The *Memoria* was a meticulously crafted composition that wove together several themes. Bouligny began it with a general description of Louisiana. He continued with discussions of its natural resources, exports, and potential. He devoted two chapters to its inhabitants and two more to its commerce. In the four concluding chapters, Bouligny endeavored to convince Minister Gálvez to achieve Louisiana's potential through new settlements, improved defenses, closer Indian relations, an *asiento* for more black laborers, and new imposts to ease the crown's financial burden.[26]

Bouligny focused on lower Louisiana. He emphasized the importance of waterways, since they constituted the only viable form of transportation in the colony: All the plantations and farms were situated on them. He pointed out the threat from the British in neighboring West

25. There are several copies of Bouligny's *Memoria:* at the Biblioteca Nacional, Madrid, Sección de Manuscritos (this copy has several pages missing); at the Washington State University Library, Pullman, Washington; in the Parsons Collection, Humanities Research Library, University of Texas, Austin; and probably the original copy in BB, HNOC. Fortier published an abridged version of it in *History,* II, 25–55. The complete memoir is translated in Din, *Louisiana in 1776,* 41–93.

26. Bouligny's account of Louisiana can be compared with several other contemporary descriptions. See Pittman, *European Settlements,* Thomas Hutchins, *An Historical Narrative and Topographical Description of Louisiana and West-Florida* (1784; rpr. Gainesville, Fla., 1968), and Bernard Romans, *A Concise Natural History of East and West Florida* (1775; rpr. Gainesville, Fla., 1962).

Florida. They could reach their settlements on the Mississippi by traveling from Pensacola, their principal garrison, via Lakes Borgne, Pontchartrain, and Maurepas, the Amite River, and Bayou Manchac, a route that bypassed New Orleans and most Spanish observation. For security reasons, Bouligny advocated settling loyal families on the abundant vacant lands in lower Louisiana to check the British and protect New Orleans.[27]

In detailing Louisiana's natural resources and agriculture, Bouligny singled out cypress and oak trees, which were excellent for ship construction, shingles, staves, and lumber in general. Once the forests were cleared, the land could be placed under cultivation. Louisiana farmers already produced a substantial amount of indigo and corn; a small amount of cotton, rice, vegetable wax; some sugarcane and vegetables; and beef from the Opelousas and Attakapas herds. Hunters provided furs, skins, and animal fats. Bouligny praised the quality of Natchitoches tobacco, which could also be grown in Attakapas and Opelousas. The French, he claimed, valued the colony's tobacco, and its cultivation could provide the planters with the capital needed to grow other crops. Bouligny suggested flax and hemp, silk (because of the presence of mulberry trees), and wheat in the upper reaches of the province, which could eventually supply all of the Spanish Caribbean. He ranked agriculture first because the land could support numerous families, a dense population would defend it against intruders, and according to physiocratic theory, it represented true wealth.[28]

Bouligny estimated Louisiana's white inhabitants between ten thousand and fifteen thousand, while there were only three thousand to four thousand slaves, an estimate that perhaps purposely understated the black population. He praised the fertility of Creole women and the industriousness of the men, all of whom lived in an earthly paradise. Creole males, skilled artisans and diligent planters alike, exhibited elegant manners. Bouligny classified the white men as planters, merchants, and laborers, with most of his compliments reserved for the first two categories; the third wasted part of their time indulging in the vices of the tavern. He mistakenly, or possibly intentionally, minimized the harshness of slavery, claiming that it existed in name only. He idealized the lot of

27. Din, *Louisiana in 1776*, 43–46.
28. *Ibid.*, 47–54.

blacks and compared their condition favorably to the poor of Europe. Only their bare feet, he averred, attested to their servitude.[29]

Commerce constituted an important ingredient in the *Memoria*. The restrictions the crown imposed on Louisiana had caused it to decline since Spain assumed possession. The legal trade with the Iberian peninsula amounted to a pittance of 15,000 pesos; with Havana, 50,000 pesos; and from naval contracts, perhaps 12,000 pesos. Nevertheless, merchants and planters flouted the law, stocking their storehouses with smuggled goods. But its illegal nature induced fears of punishment, and a number of inhabitants fled to British West Florida. Their departure depressed property values in Louisiana, while they climbed in adjoining English lands.[30]

Bouligny separated himself from O'Reilly's mercantilist policies that had resulted in the British capturing the bulk of Louisiana's trade. It amounted to all but 15,000 pesos of the colony's 600,000-peso annual commerce that came from the Spanish subsidy (120,000), indigo (180,000), peltries (200,000), and lumber (100,000). He did not include minor exports such as rice, salted meat, bear oil, and mules. He complained about English boats and floating warehouses loaded with contraband goods on the Mississippi. Moreover, the absence of restrictions and imposts in British West Florida expedited settlement. Bouligny warned against the rapid growth of British Manchac, which could prove detrimental to Louisiana, the Gulf of Mexico, and even the viceroyalty of New Spain.[31]

The Indians occupied a significant place in the *Memoria*. The Spaniards had neglected them, in comparison to the British, who had larger numbers of natives on their lands. Bouligny believed that Indian friendship was vital for Louisiana's defense. He praised the British post of superintendent general of Indians, whose duties included holding periodic congresses with the tribes, punishing native wrongdoers, and manipulating commerce to retain their loyalty.[32]

In the concluding chapters of the *Memoria* Bouligny recommended changes for Louisiana. In the important area of commerce, he advocated

29. *Ibid.,* 55—58.
30. *Ibid.,* 59—61.
31. *Ibid.,* 62—64.
32. *Ibid.,* 65—68.

a modified version of free trade, one open to Spaniards, Cubans, and Louisianians alike, the latter carrying their own exports in their locally built ships. The vessels would bring Spanish families to settle in Louisiana. He also urged allowing merchants from Cádiz and elsewhere to establish offices in New Orleans. With proper encouragement, Bouligny predicted, a phenomenal growth would occur in the Mississippi Valley, eventually redounding in a benefit of more than thirty million pesos for Spain. The enlarged population would be useful in raising a sizable army, which could send reinforcements to other Gulf cities when danger threatened.[33]

Bouligny recommended the establishment of a superintendent general in charge of Indian affairs and new settlements, modeling it in part on the British post. He argued that Louisiana's gigantic size necessitated good relations with the Indians to enlist their support in defense. The superintendent, with the assistance of subdelegates, would provide information on the natives' hunting, warriors, and lands, and the trade goods they required. Every two to three years he was to hold a congress with the tribes to make peace treaties, distribute gifts, hear complaints, and render justice.[34]

But in addition to watchdogging Indian affairs, the superintendent general should be entrusted with new settlements. Bouligny recommended establishing newly arrived families in clusters of fifty, each cluster having a blacksmith, carpenter, and artisans skilled in woodworking. Each family would receive land measuring 560 feet of riverfront (200 varas, or about 3 arpents) by 6,720 feet deep (about 35 arpents). The local head of each settlement would keep accounts of all the aid given to the families, who would gradually reimburse the government. Bouligny urged the settlement of discharged soldiers, French Canadians, and Spaniards knowledgeable in working flax and hemp. He also advocated the building of ships by the new immigrants, bringing teachers to staff schools in the settlements, and two to three years of military service for the sons of immigrants, who could later work as day laborers, rowers, and hunters.[35]

33. *Ibid.,* 70–77.

34. *Ibid.,* 78–81. On the British post of superintendent general of Indians, see the study of that office by John Richard Alden, *John Stuart and the Southern Colonial Frontier: A Study of Indian Relations, War, Trade, and Land Problems in the Southern Wilderness, 1754–1775* (Ann Arbor, Mich., 1944).

35. Din, *Louisiana in 1776,* 81–85.

Bouligny believed that Louisiana's security demanded better defenses. He proposed constructing a powerful frigate on the Mississippi with thirty to forty cannon of thirty-six-pound caliber to act as a floating battery, reestablishing two former French artillery implacements at the English Turn, and strengthening the forts at Bayou St. John and Spanish Manchac. He advocated erecting new forts at Pointe Coupee, Arkansas, and farther upriver. Moreover, New Orleans was to be protected with a brick wall and the garrison enlarged as Louisiana's population expanded.[36]

Bouligny argued that most of his proposals required only minimal royal expenditures. By allowing an *asiento* that introduced two thousand to three thousand slaves yearly, in which the *asentistas* paid forty pesos per slave for the privilege, the crown would derive a financial benefit after an initial investment. Furthermore, to defray immigration costs, Bouligny proposed modest taxes on skins and other items agreeable to the colonials. The captain also recommended the creation of an economic society for Louisiana, similar to those then starting in Spain, that promoted development. One such society had been established in Madrid in 1775.[37]

By mid-August, Bouligny had completed his work, and he wrote a cover letter to Minister Gálvez on August 15, 1776, probably the day he presented the *Memoria*. The captain's information and recommendations must have intrigued Gálvez. Later that month, he invited Bouligny to court, then at San Ildefonso (La Granja), the Spanish Versailles, in the Guadarrama Mountains. Conversations with the minister progressed well, and with Gálvez's encouragement, Bouligny wrote out recommendations for instructions to send to the recently appointed governor of Louisiana. In addition, Gálvez let Bouligny know that he would be appointed to the new post of lieutenant governor of Louisiana and that, most incredibly, he could describe his own duties.[38]

On September 1, having written an earlier draft, Bouligny penned a final version of his recommendations for the Louisiana governor's instructions, which he submitted to the minister. In it he advised an in-

36. *Ibid.*, 86–88. On the Spanish military in Louisiana during Governor Unzaga's administration, see Din, "Protecting '*Barrera*,'" 194–202.

37. Din, *Louisiana in 1776*, 89–93.

38. Bouligny's cover letter to José de Gálvez, Madrid, August 15, 1776, is in AGI, SD, leg. 2586, but without the memoir; [Bouligny], "Confidential instructions which the Governor of . . . Louisiana should observe," [La Granja], [late August, 1776], KCTU.

spection trip to Pointe Coupee, Natchitoches, and Attakapas to reconnoiter settlement sites and learn the crops most suited to each area.
Another inspection trip to Balize, via Bayou St. John and Lakes Borgne
and Barataria, to map the shores should extend westward on the Gulf to
Espiritu Santo Bay. Information on the regions north of Pointe Coupee,
Arkansas and Illinois, up the Missouri and Mississippi rivers, including
the English regions, should also be gathered. A census of New Orleans
and the rest of the province should be compiled, using data provided by
the post commandants. Thereafter, each new governor was to make a
census. A yearly summary would list the subsidy and government expenditures. Supplemental instructions included making Louisiana a barrier
for New Spain, improving relations with the Indians and supplying them
with yearly gifts, and developing the colony's economy. Bouligny gave
himself the title Director of Indians, New Settlements, and Commerce
to carry out assignments in those three areas. The governor-general, who
would serve as his superintendent, was to be consulted on these and
other matters. He would be immediately over the director. Bouligny suggested using the house of the paymaster and treasurer (Martín Navarro),
located next to the governor's residence, where, he claimed, there was
ample room. The director was to visit the settlements, listen to complaints, promote agricultural development, and establish an Economic
Society of the Friends of the Nation, similar to the one in Madrid, which
he appears to have joined while he was there. He also recommended
establishing a consulate in New Orleans, similar to the one in Bilbao,
Spain, for merchants and ship outfitters and for the rapid resolution of
disputes. He advised that the governor should appoint able and impartial
persons as Cabildo councilmen who would be erect in conduct, particularly in naming ordinary *alcaldes*. Bouligny assigned himself the task of
personally carrying to New Orleans the regulations for beginning the
economic society and consulate.[39]

Other duties for the governor included watching over the conduct
of slaves. Runaways should be punished severely. But owners who failed
to treat the bondsmen humanely had to sell them. Bouligny discouraged
black assemblies and nocturnal dances, either in New Orleans or on plan-

39. [Bouligny], "Memorandum regarding the instructions for the Governor-General
of Louisiana," La Granja, September 1, 1776, KCTU. See also R. J. Shafer, *The Economic
Societies in the Spanish World, 1763–1821* (Syracuse, N.Y., 1958).

tations. He advocated deporting free mulatto women who cohabited with white men, but only after warning them. He also cautioned against letting blacks marry freely, a point that masters appeared indifferent about but blacks believed the only legal marriages. Bouligny advised allowing Vicar General Dagobert to remedy this problem.[40]

Finally, Bouligny recommended a number of assorted points. The governor was to impose peace and harmony between Spaniards and Frenchmen (which suggested that problems existed between the two groups), limit the ambitions of Father Cirilo de Barcelona, and curb excessive military exercises demanded by some post commandants. In addition, the governor should encourage the growing of tobacco, set prices for its purchase and the costs for shipping it to Veracruz, and take precautions to avoid abuses in this business. Besides these recommendations, Bouligny wrote two shorter papers on Louisiana's economy early in September.[41]

On September 4, he discussed the trade goods that might be sent to Louisiana. For products that Spain did not then manufacture, he contacted the former Louisiana resident Jean Lafitte, then living in Bordeaux, France, to send samples to Spain. According to Bouligny, Louisiana could consume annually 10,000 fusils in the Indian and hunting trades if they were of excellent quality and priced at from 35 to 40 *reales;* 30,000 blankets or canvas coverings; more than 30,000 pieces of Limbourg cloth of 28 to 30 *varas* in length; large quantities of crude linen shirts and trousers for field work; ironmongery (axes, machetes, hoes, nails); thread stockings; the ordinary wines of Cataluña and Valencia for the common people and blacks; 8,000 to 10,000 *quintales* of gunpowder of the French variety; soap in the same amount; and foodstuffs consisting of figs, almonds, sausages, tuna, sardines, cod, and the like, if they were fresh. But items that had little demand included men's hats, as agricultural workers wore only handkerchiefs; women's silks, taffetas, or Valencian ribbons; and most Spanish wines for the lower classes and blacks, who imbibed cheap *tafia* or cane *aguardiente*. Bouligny cautioned against introducing Creole slaves from the French Caribbean islands because of their viciousness. He continued to advocate the use of *bozales*. Spain should also send to New Orleans sails and rigging for building

40. [Bouligny], "Memorandum regarding the instructions," KCTU.
41. *Ibid.*

ships. Finally, smaller ships of 300 and 400 tons, with cargoes valued at 30,000 to 40,000 pesos, should be employed in the trade instead of larger ships with more valuable cargoes.[42]

Two days later, Bouligny submitted a new report. Gálvez wanted to use tobacco as a catalyst to stimulate Louisiana's development, and the captain endorsed the idea because it might result in a slave *asiento*. He believed that within a half-dozen years the colony could produce 24 *cargas* (loads of 300 pounds each) of tobacco if 6,000 black or white laborers entered Louisiana to work in that industry. At that time Natchitoches had only about 400 workers, and the New Orleans areas could furnish only 200 more. The new settlers in Louisiana would achieve greater production. Bouligny believed that Mexico would accept Pointe Coupee tobacco and that France would buy that of Natchitoches, Opelousas, and Attakapas. He argued on behalf of the slave project that he had earlier presented for Louisiana's development. If the crown declined to advance 80,000 to 100,000 pesos that the company for blacks (presumably that of his brothers) needed, for which the company would pay 10 percent interest, then a Madrid guild might advance the sum. Either way, blacks were needed to increase the province's tobacco production.[43]

In late September, Bouligny left La Granja to return to Madrid, where he arrived by early October. While at court, he had talked enthusiastically about Louisiana's need for slaves to promote its rapid development. On returning to Madrid, he met on October 4 with government officials overseeing the slave trade who were considering the petition of his brothers and Kearney. He harbored hopes of success because on October 11, the junta ruled against the Companía Gaditana's claim of a monopoly in Louisiana. That temporarily kept alive his brothers' proposal. In Alicante, however, José Bouligny pessimistically concluded that the *asiento* would not be granted.[44]

---

42. Bouligny to José de Gálvez, San Ildefonso, September 4, 1776, in AGI, SD, leg. 2586. On the merchant Jean Lafitte, see Margaret Fisher Dalrymple, ed., *The Merchant of Manchac: The Letterbooks of John Fitzpatrick, 1768–1790* (Baton Rouge, 1978), 77n. Lafitte received permission to leave New Orleans for France in 1775 (Julián de Arriaga to the governor of Louisiana, Aranjuez, April 9, 1775, in AGI, PC, leg. 569). Bouligny wrote a letter to Lafitte from San Ildefonso on September 12, 1776 (copy in AGI, SD, leg. 2586).

43. Bouligny to José de Gálvez, San Ildefonso, September 6, 1776, in AGI, SD, leg. 2586.

44. Bouligny to José de Gálvez, [Madrid], [October 3, 1776], in AGI, SD, leg. 2661; José de Gálvez to Marcos Ximénes, San Ildefonso, October 11, 1776, *ibid.*, leg. 2586. The

In the next two months, Bouligny continued to reside in Madrid, not far from the court, which had moved to El Escorial. In early October, the crown extended his stay until the end of the month. But since Minister Gálvez delayed in formulating the instructions for the Louisiana governor, he postponed Bouligny's departure for several more weeks. On November 25, 1776, the minister completed the instructions, which consisted of thirty-six articles. They owed their inspiration to Bouligny's *Memoria,* recommendations, comments on tobacco, and conversations with Gálvez.[45]

Increasing Louisiana's population retained its importance in the instructions. The government permitted Spanish subjects and foreign Catholics who were not English, Dutch, or potential enemies to settle there. The immigrants were to take an oath of allegiance, receive lands, and be treated equally with other subjects. The crown pardoned any inhabitants guilty of smuggling but warned them against repeating the offense. Gálvez left open the possibility of sending Spaniards to augment Louisiana's population.[46]

Commerce accounted for a number of articles in the instructions. The crown encouraged the inhabitants to build their own ships, employing the excellent native woods, and prohibited them from using foreign vessels. The governor was to foster tobacco production in Natchitoches, Opelousas, and Attakapas, sending samples to the viceroy of New Spain and learning the costs of production and freight. He was to promote agricultural pursuits, especially in hemp and cotton, settle new families, and reduce export and import duties on primary agricultural materials. In silk production, Gálvez permitted only the export of raw silk to Spain for processing, under a 2 percent tariff. Nitrates suitable for gunpowder manufacture were to be sought out in upper Louisiana and the quality and cost of sending them to New Spain determined.[47]

---

slave project was denied on February 1, 1777; see other documents in the *expediente* of José and Juan Bouligny and Miguel Kearney, all *ibid.,* leg. 2586; José Bouligny to Francisco Bouligny, Alicante, September 3, 1776, in BB, HNOC.

45. Royal order to O'Reilly, San Ildefonso, October 3, 1776, AGI, SD, leg. 2661; José de Gálvez to the governor of Louisiana, San Lorenzo, November 25, 1776, with a copy of the royal instructions to the governor of Louisiana of the same date, in AGI, PC, leg. 174B. Bouligny kept a copy of the instructions for himself, which is now in KCTU.

46. José de Gálvez to the governor of Louisiana, San Lorenzo, November 25, 1776, AGI, PC, leg. 174B.

47. *Ibid.*

In Indian relations, the governor was to attract the tribes of Louisiana and those living on British lands to the friendship of the Spanish crown. He was to hold periodic congresses with them, distribute gifts, and use the natives to enhance the province's security.[48]

In article 17, Gálvez created the office of lieutenant governor, charged with settlements, commerce, and Indian friendship, and he named Bouligny to fill it temporarily. In those important areas, Gálvez counseled the new governor to work closely with the lieutenant governor, who was to be his immediate subaltern, to obtain the quickest possible results. To pay for expenses incurred to achieve those three objectives, the minister raised Louisiana's subsidy by forty thousand pesos.[49]

A number of articles in the instructions probably stemmed from Bouligny's conversations with Gálvez. They could have come only from someone well acquainted with the province. Among them: Militia commandants should not be arbitrary in dealing with the men in their command, punishing some severely while ignoring the misconduct of others. Roads and levees were to be kept in good repair, particularly during flood season. The manufacturers of bricks outside the city walls were to move away from New Orleans and cease making holes in the ground that filled up with water. Also, the governor was to clear away the trees, brush, and debris from the stockade that encircled New Orleans.[50]

Blacks received more attention in the instructions than did the Indians. Masters, owing them humanity and justice, were to avoid excessive punishment and not instill a feeling of desperation that produced uprisings and flight. If they fled, slaves were to be pursued, but the governor was to publish a pardon to get them to return to their owners. Anyone who sold the blacks liquor, guns, or gunpowder and was paid in stolen goods was to be castigated severely. Gálvez prohibited nocturnal dances

48. *Ibid.*

49. *Ibid.* José de Gálvez instructed the viceroy of New Spain on November 25, 1776, to increase the subsidy for Louisiana by 40,000 pesos (AGI, PC, leg. 569).

50. Royal instructions to the governor of Louisiana, November 25, 1776, AGI, PC, leg. 174B. Article 5 of the instructions advised a reconnaissance of coastal Louisiana. On November 27, 1777, Governor Gálvez ordered Captain Luis Landry to carry it out on the schooner *El Señor de la Yedra*. Landry left New Orleans on December 17, 1777. On October 24, 1778, Gálvez reported him missing and feared that he and his crew were dead. It proved to be true. (Gálvez instructions, New Orleans, November 27, 1777, and Gálvez to José de Gálvez, New Orleans, October 24, 1778, both in AGI, SD, leg. 2662).

and assemblies by blacks in New Orleans and the countryside. The governor was to stop the abominable practice of black Catholics refusing to marry in the Church. Free female mulattoes who persisted in living dishonestly faced deportation to Haiti. The instructions, however, failed to mention anything about the introduction of slaves or an *asiento*.[51]

Still other instructions to the governor were clearly attributable to Bouligny. He was to make a census of the province, conduct yearly inspection tours, make a customs schedule, administer justice fairly with the help of the judge advocate, select people of substance to serve on the Cabildo, supervise the conduct of priests, repair royal buildings, and stop counterfeiting and the flight of Spanish coins from the province. However, not attributable to Bouligny was the order for the governor to learn the true nature of the recent revolt of the English colonials in North America and to obtain information about the British on the Mississippi.[52]

While the instructions to the Louisiana governor were secret, Bouligny knew their contents, including his appointment as lieutenant governor. He also knew that he was the inspiration for the royal instructions. It must have pleased him immensely to realize the confidence that the minister of the Indies had placed in him, naming him as the governor's immediate subaltern with a budget of forty thousand pesos, one-fourth of the total sum assigned to Louisiana. Bouligny could not have anticipated the success he enjoyed at the end of 1776.

Long before Bouligny crossed the Atlantic to return home to Louisiana, change for the colony was already under way. On July 24, 1776, Minister Gálvez dispatched secret instructions permitting Louisiana to send its produce and lumber to the French Caribbean islands. Gálvez, who belonged to the pro-French faction at court, favored closer relations with France and redirecting Louisiana's commerce away from Britain. It was part of the government's liberalization of commerce in the Caribbean that culminated in free trade within the empire in 1778.[53]

51. Royal instructions to the governor of Louisiana, November 25, 1776, AGI, PC, leg. 174B.

52. *Ibid.*

53. José de Gálvez to the governor of Louisiana, San Ildefonso, July 24, 1776, repeated on September 28, 1776, both *ibid.;* José de Gálvez to the governor of Louisiana, San Ildefonso, September 28, 1776, *ibid.,* leg. 569; Gálvez to José de Gálvez, New Orleans, January 21, 1777, in AGI, SD, leg. 2547.

For now, however, in early December, 1776, the crown prepared Bouligny's return to New Orleans. It authorized him to embark in Cádiz with two servants—José García Fernández, of Asturias, and his seventeen-year-old nephew, Juan Tala y Bouligny, who settled down in Louisiana. Tala, son of his oldest sister, Inés, was the only Bouligny relative to do so. In addition, young Carlos de Vilemont, accompanied by his servant Manuel Albarez, returned with his brother-in-law. By December, 1776, now fourteen, Vilemont had been away from home for nearly two years, and the purpose of his trip to Europe to master the Spanish language had been accomplished. Bouligny used the power-of-attorney he held from his mother-in-law to request the boy's release. On December 5, the crown consented to Vilemont's withdrawal from the Real Seminario de Nobles. Sometime prior to leaving Spain, Bouligny learned the distressing news that his second son, Remy, had died in New Orleans.[54]

Bouligny sailed with his party from Cádiz about the end of December. His absence from Louisiana can be judged an unexpected success. While he had failed to gain an *asiento,* he returned to Louisiana as the second-ranking official in the colony, charged with settlements, commerce, and Indians. The crown, through José de Gálvez, was committed to assisting Louisiana's development. Part of it was Bouligny's doing, but much of it was due to the rebellion of the English North American colonies. Relations between the Spaniards and the British had again become strained. The possibility of war had existed since the conclusion of the last conflict in 1763. Now, however, Spain's Gulf colonies posed the greatest concern. Soon Louisiana began to stir with activity aimed at strengthening it through development and preparing it for hostilities. In the two years before war came, Francisco Bouligny experienced both triumph and despair as lieutenant governor of Louisiana.

54. Bouligny petition for the withdrawal of Vilemont, Madrid, December 3, 1776, with royal order approving it, December 5, 1776, both in AGI, SD, leg. 2661. Bouligny offered to take with him to Louisiana his brother José's second son José, called "Pepe"; his brother declined the offer (Martin, *Bouligny Family,* 177n).

5

LIEUTENANT GOVERNOR OF
LOUISIANA
1777—1779

FOLLOWING A WINTRY Atlantic crossing, Francisco Bouligny and his party arrived in Havana by early
March, 1777, and departed on board the sloop of
Captain Juan Ronquillo on March 14. They reached New Orleans at the
beginning of April. Bouligny had been absent from Louisiana and his
family for nearly two years. On April 2 and 11, 1777, Governor Bernardo
de Gálvez sent notices to post commandants of Bouligny's appointment
as lieutenant governor in charge of settlements, commerce, and Indians;
as Gálvez's immediate subaltern; and, in the April 11 announcements in
French, as second military chief of the colony. Naming Bouligny second
military chief exceeded Minister José de Gálvez's instructions. The governor seemed unaware of his error, and Bouligny believed later that secret instructions had enlarged his position. His post as lieutenant governor meant a fifteen-hundred-peso emolument, which, together with his
army salary, made him one of the best-paid officials in the colony. The
next fourteen months, before disagreements with Governor Gálvez arose,
was the proudest time Bouligny had experienced thus far in Louisiana.[1]

1. José Bouligny to Francisco Bouligny, Alicante, May 24, 1777, in BD, HNOC;
"Royal Dispatch of Political and Military Lieutenant Governor in favor of Dn. Fran.co
Bouligni," San Lorenzo, November 25, 1776, AGI, PC, leg. 566. Bernardo de Gálvez sent
letters in Spanish to Spanish commandants announcing Bouligny's appointment on April 2,
which I have not found in the Spanish archives. Bouligny reproduced a copy of the an-
nouncement in his June 3, 1778, letter to Gálvez (AGI, PC, leg. 2358). Copies of Gálvez's
April 11, 1777, letters in French to post commandants are in AGI, PC, leg. 1. Bouligny began
receiving pay as lieutenant governor as of April 2, 1777; see his pay record (asiento), New
Orleans, April 3, 1777, AGI, PC, leg. 538A. On June 4, 1777, Bouligny was a witness at the

His personal life also proceeded well despite the death of Remy the previous September. His other two children, Pepa and Domingo, had grown in his absence, and a new son, Francisco José, better known as Ursino, was born on November 8 of the following year. Upon the captain's and young Vilemont's arrival in Louisiana in 1777, they received the salaries that had been suspended during their leaves. The month following Bouligny's return, he and Carlos Grifon purchased thirteen male and eleven female slaves, confiscated from the English ship *Peggy,* for 2,450 pesos on six months' credit. In September, 1777, Bouligny added to his plantation above New Orleans the adjoining landholding, four arpents of front by forty deep, from the widow Françoise Lareche. He paid only 320 pesos because Mme Lareche wanted assistance in her declining years. She reserved until her death the use of one square arpent of land containing a house and the right to use another cabin. Bouligny pledged to furnish his slaves to assist her in the upkeep of the land and buildings.[2]

The conditions that confronted the Spaniards and Bouligny in Louisiana had changed since his departure in 1775. Tensions with the British in West Florida had mounted because of the rebellion in their North American colonies. American rebels appeared in New Orleans in 1776 requesting assistance, and Governor Unzaga helped them, a policy the Spanish government endorsed, much to the displeasure of British officials. Britain augmented its soldiers in West Florida, and that in turn discomforted Unzaga; only the understrength Louisiana battalion stood watch on the extensive Mississippi frontier. In late 1775, Unzaga lamented to his immediate superior, the captain general of Cuba, his few troops, inexperienced militia, dilapidated forts, and instructions to retreat toward Mexico if attacked by superior forces. After José de Gálvez became minister of the Indies, Spain and Cuba dispatched fresh gunpowder, mountings for cannon, artillery shots, rifle bullets, and other war materiel to Louisiana. But improvements came slowly, and the Spaniards risked compromising themselves by assisting the American rebels. The British, who usually kept more soldiers and warships on the Gulf Coast

Jean Livaudais and Gathe Duffosat marriage, where he was listed as "second chief of the colony." Woods and Nolan, eds., *Sacramental Records,* III, 118–19.

2. Almonester Notary, Acts of 1777, fols. 330v–31; Garic Acts, Vol. VIII, January–December, 1777, fols. 344–46.

than the Spaniards, occasionally behaved outrageously. When Bernardo de Gálvez assumed the governorship on January 1, 1777, he was determined to avoid humiliation and to protect Spanish rights.[3]

Bouligny personally brought to Louisiana the November 25, 1776, instructions. The governor had an inkling of the new policies by the individual orders that had arrived in the second half of 1776 on opening trade with the French to undermine the English. Two French commissioners for commerce, Joseph Dubreuil de Villars and Charles-Philippe Favre D'Aunoy, had established themselves in New Orleans in February, 1777, observing the Anglo-American conflict and expediting the influx of arms. Only two weeks after Bouligny's return to New Orleans, the first brush with the British on the Mississippi occurred. The recent instructions from Spain strengthened Gálvez's resolve to resist British arrogance.[4]

While Minister Gálvez sought to curb illegal British commerce, Governor Gálvez contemplated the right moment to act, more worried about the angry reaction of French planters if he did (perhaps mindful of Ulloa's fate) than about the British, when an incident provided him with the proper excuse. The British armed schooner *West Florida* captured three small Spanish boats loaded with tar on Lake Pontchartrain, and that prompted the Louisiana inhabitants to grumble about the ungrateful British. Armed with public opinion, Gálvez retaliated. On the night of April 17, he seized eleven ships, mostly floating warehouses tied to the Spanish bank, engaged in smuggling. The next day, April 18, he issued a proclamation expelling British merchants residing on Spanish territory within fifteen days. The reorientation of trade toward the French had commenced. Capt. Thomas Lloyd of the British frigate *Atalanta,* then on the Mississippi, protested the seizures. But Lloyd had already annoyed Gálvez for firing on the Spanish ship *María* and the French vessel *Margarita* and boarding the first ship below New Orleans, alleg-

3. José de Gálvez to the governor of Louisiana, San Lorenzo, October 23, 1776, in AGI, PC, leg. 174B; Unzaga to the marqués de la Torre, New Orleans, December 21, 1775, *ibid.*, leg. 1146. On Spanish aid to the Americans, see Caughey, *Gálvez,* 85–88.

4. Proof that Bouligny carried the November 25, 1776, instructions is in José de Gálvez to the governor of Louisiana, Madrid, December 13, 1776: "Instruction of His Majesty which is sent to you with the captain of battalion of that Province Dn. Francisco Bouligni" (AGI, PC, leg. 174B). See also Cummins, "Spanish Agents," 177–223, for Gálvez's dealings with the British.

ing that they harbored rebels. The river in that region was Spanish on both banks, and the British enjoyed only a right of navigation. It produced an exchange of letters between the governor and Lloyd that lasted three weeks.[5]

While Lloyd's ship was anchored at New Orleans, menacing the city with the guns of a frigate and a sloop, Gálvez urgently requested army and navy support from Cuba. The governor parried Lloyd's demands, capitulating neither to him nor to two other British representatives, who arrived in August to retrieve the captured goods. Before assistance came, Gálvez began construction of two armed launches to protect the river. He judged them superior to ships because they could each mount a heavier cannon and, equipped with oars and sails, were more maneuverable. That was the start of purely Louisiana vessels on the Mississippi to protect the colony. While the crown authorized a frigate and a packet to be stationed in Cuba for New Orleans' use, the governor returned them to Havana despite the fact that in September, 1777, the British corsair *Florida* fired several shots at and boarded the Spanish mail packet *Príncipe de Asturias*.[6]

When Minister Gálvez learned of the April incident involving Lloyd, he authorized raising the Fixed Louisiana Battalion to a regiment by bringing the first battalion to full strength and creating a second battalion of seven hundred men. The task of recruiting the new soldiers, including married men with families, fell to Matías de Gálvez, Bernardo's

5. José de Gálvez sent a royal order on September 15, 1776, instructing the Louisiana governor "to persecute with greatest vigor frauds in the illicit trade that injures the just rights of the Royal Treasury and to oust them from the Province" (AGI, SD, leg. 2547). Bernardo de Gálvez replied that he would carry out the orders to annihilate the frauds (New Orleans, March 21, 1777, *ibid.*). See Bernardo de Gálvez to the marqués de la Torre, New Orleans, May 6, 1777, in AGI, PC, leg. 1146; de la Torre to José de Gálvez, Havana, May 25, 1777, in AGI, SD, leg. 2661; Gayarré, *History,* III, 106; and John Walton Caughey, "Bernardo de Gálvez and the English Smugglers," *Hispanic American Historical Review,* XII (1932), 46–58.

6. Bernardo de Gálvez to de la Torre, New Orleans, May 6, 1777; Royal order to [the governor of Louisiana], [n.p.], August 15, 1777; de la Torre to José de Gálvez, Havana, May 25, 1777; Bernardo de Gálvez to Juan Baptista de Bonet, New Orleans, December 12, 1777, all in AGI, SD, leg. 2661; Bernardo de Gálvez to José de Gálvez, New Orleans, June 2, 1777, in BN, DL; José de Gálvez to Bernardo de Gálvez, [n.p.], October 14, 1777, in AGI, PC, leg. 174B; Bernardo de Gálvez to José de Gálvez, New Orleans, September 15, 1777, in AGI, SD, leg. 2547; Cummins, "Spanish Agents," 195–200.

father, in the Canary Islands. To enlist additional men, Governor Gálvez sent a recruiting team to Mexico in late 1777. In the new battalion, meritorious junior officers would be promoted, and others could purchase the posts of captain, lieutenant, and sublieutenant.[7]

Through 1777 and 1778, Gálvez was busy dealing with the American rebels, standing up to the British in West Florida, promoting friendly relations with the Indians, and implementing the November 25 royal instructions. The latter included supervising the meat supply in New Orleans, issuing a pardon to persons who left Louisiana because of smuggling activities, hiring new secretaries, attracting settlers to Louisiana, and promoting agriculture. In July, 1777, the *Volante* entered the Mississippi with the colony's subsidy, including forty thousand pesos to expedite development. Although charged with the care of settlements, commerce, and Indian relations and named the governor's immediate subaltern, Bouligny's duties lacked clear definition. Gálvez assigned him to a variety of chores, including taking charge of New Orleans in the summer of 1777 when the governor journeyed to Pointe Coupee to meet with Indians. But he did not employ Bouligny in conformance with the royal orders, and many of the documents explaining the lieutenant governor's activities in 1777 and 1778 are no longer extant.[8]

Bouligny's star was still in the ascendancy in December, 1777, when he learned of his promotion to brevet lieutenant colonel. He wrote to José de Gálvez, thanking him ecstatically: "I did not need the patent evidence of protection that you have deemed worthy to dispense on this latest occasion for me to recognize my debt and obligation [to you]. . . . My rank of lieutenant colonel increases my satisfaction but it cannot increase my gratitude . . . my burning zeal for His Majesty's service will not be the only proof of my eternal gratitude but also the intense desire that I have to always conserve your protection." Bernardo de Gálvez also

7. José de Gálvez to Bernardo de Gálvez, San Ildefonso, two letters of August 15, 1777, one of them reserved, both in AGI, PC, leg. 174B; Royal order to Matías de Gálvez, San Ildefonso, August 15, 1777, AGI, SD, leg. 2661. On the recruitment, transfer, and settlement of the Canary Islanders in Louisiana, see Gilbert C. Din, *The Canary Islanders of Louisiana* (Baton Rouge, 1988), 13–83, and "The Canary Islander Settlements of Louisiana: An Overview," *Louisiana History*, XXVII (1986), 353–73.

8. Bernardo de Gálvez to José de Gálvez, New Orleans, July 10, August 9, December 11, 1777, all in AGI, SD, leg. 2547. See also de la Torre to José de Gálvez, Havana, May 25, 1777, *ibid.*, leg. 2661.

thought well enough of Bouligny in December, 1777, to put on his service sheet, "fit for promotion."⁹

Perhaps Bouligny's first official task after returning to Louisiana was to compile a census of the province. Governor Gálvez had begun the 1777 tally when he assigned Bouligny to complete it. By April 24, he was at work and finished it on May 12. The census placed Louisiana'a population at 17,926, consisting of 8,381 whites, 9,009 slaves, and 536 free blacks. Slaves were more than twice as numerous as Bouligny had stated in his *Memoria*. New Orleans' population numbered 3,202. He probably aided in compiling the 1778 New Orleans census that revealed only 3,059 inhabitants, which might not have been accurate. New Orleans was then experiencing renewed economic activity, including a building boom, and demand for housing had driven rents up.¹⁰

On November 25, 1777, Governor Gálvez gave Bouligny supervision of tobacco activities in the colony. Increasing output was important because it would bring badly needed earnings to Louisiana. Tobacco had been grown in the province since the French era, and on May 21, 1776, a royal order directed the Louisiana governor to encourage its growth. By the fall of 1776, the Natchitoches planters had agreed to produce more tobacco. On April 13, 1777, Gálvez announced to the New Orleans public that the colony's subsidy had been increased by 40,000 pesos and that the government encouraged the cultivation of tobacco in Louisiana. Bouligny probably worked with Gálvez and the planters to draw up the rules governing packing tobacco into rolls or bundles and their sale in the colony. On June 15, Gálvez issued a seventeen-point regulation on the tobacco trade. By the fall of 1777, the first shipment of 29,488 rolls to New Spain was made, for which the governor asked 60,000 pesos. Because of expenses, Viceroy Bucareli reduced the sum to 50,000 pesos. By 1778, it was evident that Louisiana could not then produce the 500,000 pounds that Mexico expected. The next year, Louisiana dispatched only 138,808 pounds. Documents for Bouligny's activities in tobacco adminis-

9. Bouligny to José de Gálvez, New Orleans, December 28, 1777, *ibid.*, leg. 2534; Bouligny service sheet, New Orleans, December 31, 1777, *ibid.*, leg. 2662.

10. Document fragment, "No. 12 Recensement," April, 1777, AGI, PC, leg. 188A; 1777 census, New Orleans, May 12, 1777, *ibid.*, legs. 2351, 191. The June, 1778, New Orleans census is in *SMV,* Pt. 1, p. 290. New or totally rebuilt houses in New Orleans were one in 1774, two in 1775, three in 1776, fifteen in 1777, and eleven to March, 1778 (Bernardo de Gálvez to José de Gálvez, New Orleans, March 11, 1778, in AGI, SD, leg. 2547). On rent increases, see Bernardo de Gálvez to José de Gálvez, New Orleans, June 22, 1778, in AGI, SD, leg. 2547.

tration are scarce, and only indirectly is it known that he operated a to-bacco warehouse and occasionally kept tobacco rolls and bundles under the gallery of his house on Levee Street.[11]

On November 21, 1777, Governor Gálvez proclaimed new laws for Louisiana's trade with the French Caribbean based on a royal order of the previous March 10 designed to promote agricultural development, permitting planters to accept money, bills of exchange, or slaves (except mulatto or quadroon bondsmen) in return for their produce. The Spanish government had decided against a slave *asiento* for Louisiana.[12]

Ironically, in October, 1777, Governor Gálvez received an inquiry from the minister of the Indies about Bouligny's property holdings in Louisiana. The governor delayed answering until July 10, 1778, when he informed the minister that Bouligny owned eighty slaves. But Gálvez advised strongly against a slave *asiento* that profited only four people (three Boulignys and Kearney) and made blacks expensive. He further considered the lieutenant governor's involvement in commerce improper. He was no doubt correct in his opposition to a slave contract, but Bouligny had given up aspirations of securing one nearly three years before. In addition, the government had authorized the French to supply slaves. Gálvez's answer showed that in July, 1778, relations between the governor and Bouligny were rapidly deteriorating.[13]

11. Pamphlets of tobacco prices are in French in AGI, PC, legs. 190, 1232; in Spanish, in AGI, SD, leg. 2633, and published in *SMV*, Pt. 1, pp. 237–38; Bucareli to José de Gálvez, Mexico City, May 27, 1778, in *SMV*, Pt. 1, pp. 279–80; Bernardo de Gálvez proclamation, New Orleans, April 13, 1777, KCTU; Laura L. Porteous, "Index to the Spanish Judicial Records of Louisiana," *Louisiana Historical Quarterly*, XVIII (1935), 728–46. Gálvez notified Mr. Dutisne and Carlos de Grand-Pré on November 25, 1777: "On matters pertaining to tobacco, you will communicate directly with Francisco Bouligny, Lieutenant Governor of this province, to whom you will send all news on this point, and observe the orders that this official sends you" (AGI, PC, leg. 1). See also Brian E. Coutts, "Boom and Bust: The Rise and Fall of the Tobacco Industry in Spanish Louisiana, 1770–1790," *The Americas*, XLII (1985–86), 289–309.

12. Bernardo de Gálvez, "Proclamation Concerning Louisiana Commerce," New Orleans, November 21, 1777, *SMV*, Pt. 1, pp. 242–43. See also royal orders of José de Gálvez to the governor of Louisiana, [n.p.], July 24, September 28, 1776, AGI, PC, leg. 569. An earlier order on the reorientation of trade is dated in Madrid, July 8, 1776, and published in Marc de Villiers du Terrage, *Les dernières années de la Louisiane française* (Paris, 1903), 353–54.

13. José de Gálvez to the governor of Louisiana, Aranjuez, May 13, 1777, in AGI, PC, leg. 174B; Bernardo de Gálvez to José de Gálvez, New Orleans, October 24, 1777, July 10, 1778, both in AGI, SD, leg. 2586, exped. 9.

Earlier in the year, however, Bouligny had cooperated harmoniously with the governor. As the second-ranking official in the colony, he had been selected to present Gálvez with the Royal Order of Carlos III in a small informal ceremony. Bouligny revealed his optimism when on February 15 he wrote to his friend Balthazar de Villiers, the Arkansas Post commandant, declaring that Gálvez was making himself more loved by everyone and that through his mediation the colony could expect many favors from the court. A new battalion was being formed, which created opportunities for promotion, and Bouligny had the responsibility of settling the Spanish families coming to Louisiana. Having heard about possible settlement sites on the Mississippi's right bank along the Ouachita, Arkansas, White, and St. Francis rivers, the lieutenant governor asked de Villiers' opinion of them, particularly on the Arkansas.[14]

The spirit of cooperation between Bouligny and Gálvez withered in the aftermath of the March, 1778, arrival of the James Willing expedition in New Orleans. The American rebel Willing and his men had descended the Mississippi on the barge *Rattletrap,* plundering Tory plantations in West Florida in February and March, 1778. The rebels then disposed of their loot in New Orleans, where Gálvez had also welcomed British refugees fleeing before the Americans. While outwardly neutral (he returned British property seized on Spanish soil and where Spain owned both banks of the Mississippi, and he protected and aided the rebels in spite of British protests), Gálvez found the presence of Willing irritating until he departed in the fall.[15]

In the midst of British threats to recover the seized booty and take the Americans prisoner, a clash of personalities between Bouligny and Gálvez became evident on April 11 when the latter queried the lieutenant governor about defensive measures. Gálvez alleged that he had government approval to permit all of Willing's activities, thus undercutting the arguments of the more cautious Bouligny. The governor, however, refused to show him the court orders, if they existed, because they were not part of Bouligny's duties. At that time, hostile British action seemed possible, since two frigates were coming up the Mississippi and a third

14. Bouligny to Balthazar de Villiers, New Orleans, February 15, 1778, in AGI, PC, leg. 2358; Archbishop of Seville to Bouligny, [n.p.], November 19, 1777, in KCTU.

15. John Walton Caughey, "Willing's Expedition down the Mississippi, 1778," *Louisiana Historical Quarterly,* XV (1932), 5–36; see also Robert V. Haynes, *The Natchez District and the American Revolution* (Jackson, Miss., 1976).

ship of thirty-two guns was reported at the river's mouth. Bouligny worried about the governor's seeming lack of concern and a disposition to risk a fight with the British. Gálvez reflected that same attitude in his April 12 letter to his uncle. If New Orleans fell because of its weak defenses, the governor told Bouligny, he would resist in the countryside with the rural population. The skeptical lieutenant governor, however, did not believe that a fight in the wilderness would be easy, and he offered to counter all of Gálvez's arguments. Bouligny strongly advised employing all their resources in advance. If the British had harmful intentions, they would not give the Spaniards time to prepare. He counseled warning Havana of Louisiana's critical situation and requesting two frigates. He asked that Gálvez outline Bouligny's duties as lieutenant governor and immediate subaltern, which he claimed were equivalent to those of "king's lieutenant." Bouligny implored Gálvez not to take amiss his letter that was "dictated by the sincerest and truest friendship." The governor's defeat of the British would cover Gálvez with "immortal glory." Bouligny professed zeal, esteem, and veneration for him and stated that his proposals were fitting for the crisis.[16]

The next day, April 12, Bouligny expressed dismay over the governor's "lukewarm" and "indifferent" attitude toward him. That day, Gálvez again sounded out the lieutenant governor about the situation they faced. Bouligny mistrusted the British, who were capable of a surprise attack, and he reiterated the need to put all their forces, including slaves, on alert, post more sentinels along the river, prepare war materiel, and watch the English frigates closely. He preferred placing veteran captain Manuel Pérez at the head of the battalion instead of the inexperienced adjutant, Lt. Jacobo Dubreuil. The Spanish brigantine *Santa Teresa* and Willing's *Rebecca* should be made ready and the gunboat launched immediately. More artillery should be placed on the river, including the opposite side of the Mississippi.[17]

On April 13, Gálvez initiated a correspondence with Capt. Joseph Nunn of the frigate *Hound,* anchored near New Orleans, who was making demands on the governor. The Spaniards were convinced that the

---

16. Bouligny to Bernardo de Gálvez, New Orleans, April 12, 1778, in AGI, PC, leg. 2358; Bernardo de Gálvez to José de Gálvez, reserved, New Orleans, April 12, 1778, in AGI, SD, leg. 2596.

17. Bouligny to Bernardo de Gálvez, New Orleans, April 13, 1778, in AGI, PC, leg. 2358.

British wanted a fight. Only then did Gálvez double the patrols and guards and put more batteries about New Orleans. Perhaps Bouligny's suggestions propelled him into taking action.[18]

The lieutenant governor proposed further precautionary measures on April 14: stationing more men and pirogues on the river to observe the English, informing the Mexican viceroy of their situation, and notifying post commandants upriver to be vigilant. Worried about Gálvez's ego, Bouligny stressed that his recommendations did not detract from the governor's reputation; the glory would belong to Gálvez alone. In his final sentence, Bouligny told him: "There are occasions when it is necessary to be exact, firm, and severe, and today it is indispensable."[19]

That same day, the governor urgently requested from Cuba troops, artillerymen, and three or four warships to reinforce his two hundred regular soldiers in New Orleans. He intended to prolong negotiations with the English, prepare the militia, and increase the armament on the *Santa Teresa*. He also put a newly constructed armed launch on the water, stationed pirogues to watch the British frigates, and distributed gunpowder throughout the city. The next afternoon, the mail ship *El Postillón de México* departed hurriedly for Havana with letters for the captain general. On that same day, April 15, Gálvez published a *bando* requiring oaths of neutrality from the foreigners in New Orleans. The English refugees took it on April 16, the Americans on April 17.[20]

Because most of the letters of Gálvez are missing, his thoughts about Bouligny are uncertain. But there were reasons for his displeasure with the lieutenant governor. Bouligny had contradicted Gálvez about what course of action to pursue, and his post cut into the governor's authority. Bouligny was the only official in Louisiana to have personally advised the minister of the Indies, and his appointment as lieutenant governor was made in Spain without Gálvez's consent or knowledge. In addition to a difference in temperament between the two men, the governor resented any diminution of his authority and was disinclined to accept advice.

18. "General Diary," April 11–13, [1778], MPA, SD, with the original in AGI, PC, leg. 2351; Caughey, *Gálvez*, 121–23. A study based extensively on British documents of the same events is J. Barton Starr, *Tories, Dons, and Rebels: The American Revolution in British West Florida* (Gainesville, Fla., 1976).

19. Bouligny to Bernardo de Gálvez, New Orleans, April 14, 1778, in AGI, PC, leg. 2358.

20. Gálvez to Diego José Navarro, confidential, New Orleans, April 14, 1778, in *SMV*, Pt. 1, pp. 265–66; "General Diary," April 14–17, (1778), MPA, SD.

Moreover, on November 2, 1777, Gálvez had secretly and without official permission married Felicité de St. Maxent, daughter of the wealthy and ambitious merchant Gilbert Antoine de St. Maxent. That relationship led Gálvez toward favoritism, since St. Maxent recognized the commercial potential of Bouligny's office of lieutenant governor.[21]

Tension between the Spaniards and the British continued unabated throughout April because of the British warships and new seizures of Spanish boats on Lake Pontchartrain. British soldiers and loyalists recovered West Florida from the American rebels in the spring of 1778 and imposed a blockade on the Mississippi adjacent to their outposts. Gálvez, meanwhile, continued exchanging letters with Captain Nunn, and on April 27, he dispatched a second ship to Havana with appeals for help. About that time, the royal sloop *Nuestra Señora del Carmen* arrived with Louisiana's subsidy, and the governor hurriedly took precautionary measures to ensure that the British warships did not seize the money. In early May, the frigates departed, and the Spaniards breathed more easily. The royal sloop left for Havana on May 16 with correspondence requesting assistance.[22]

The last letters proved unnecessary, since word arrived six days later that the royal packet *San Carlos* and the private frigate *La Luisiana* had reached Balize with two hundred troops, artillerymen, and officers from Havana. Soon the government brigantine *El Renombrado* joined them. In early June, the ships and soldiers arrived in New Orleans and doubled the Spanish forces.[23]

21. Bernardo de Gálvez's hostility toward Bouligny is seen in documents cited below. Gálvez has generally been described in Louisiana in heroic dimensions, except for the favoritism exhibited toward his father-in-law. His character, however, is more complex than that usually described. For Spanish studies on Gálvez, see José Rodulfo Boeta, *Bernardo de Gálvez* (Madrid, 1977), and Guillermo Porras Muñoz, *Bernardo de Gálvez* (Madrid, 1952). The Gálvez–St. Maxent marriage certificate is in the St. Louis Cathedral (New Orleans) Book of Marriages (1777), fol. 15. See also Eric Beerman, "The French Ancestors of Felicité de St. Maxent," *Revue de Louisiane/Louisiana Review,* VI (1977), 69–75. Gálvez's wife was the widow of Jean-Baptiste Destrehan and had a child, Adelaide, from that marriage.

22. Bernardo de Gálvez to José de Gálvez, New Orleans, April 24, 1778, in AGI, SD, leg. 2547; Bernardo de Gálvez to Diego José Navarro, confidential, New Orleans, April 27, 1778, in *SMV,* Pt. 1, pp. 269–70; "General Diary," April 21–May 8, [1778], MPA, SD; Bernardo de Gálvez to Diego José Navarro, reserved, New Orleans, May 16, 1778, AGI, PC, leg. 1232.

23. "General Diary," May 22–June 3, [1778], MPA, SD; Bernardo de Gálvez to José de Gálvez, New Orleans, June 9, 1778, in AGI, SD, leg. 2547.

The vessels, however, brought higher-ranking officers, who ended Bouligny's role as second military chief. By early June, despite Gálvez's assurance that he harbored no animosity toward Bouligny, the governor wanted to remove him as second in military command. Gálvez seized the opportunity to revise the chain of command to run to the two Havana officers, Bvt. Col. Manuel González and Lt. Col. Blas Martín Romeo; to Pedro Piernas of the Louisiana battalion, who had a year of seniority as lieutenant colonel over the lieutenant governor; and finally to Bouligny. Gálvez convened a council of officers with the rank of captain and above, which upheld the principle of seniority. Bouligny was lieutenant governor with responsibility only in the areas of settlement, commerce, and Indian affairs. The inclusion of two officers from Havana marked the only time that temporarily assigned officers in Louisiana became part of the colony's chain of command.[24]

But besides these officers, a new battalion official also outranked Bouligny. The battalion had been without a sergeant major since its formation in 1769, despite pleas from Governor Unzaga. The governor needed a replacement, usually the ranking battalion officer, whenever he was absent from New Orleans. The need increased with Bernardo de Gálvez's dual appointment as governor and battalion colonel. In May, 1777, O'Reilly belatedly proposed for sergeant major Capt. Esteban Miró y Rodríguez of the Lisbon Regiment. He spoke French well, had served in Mexico as adjutant major of the Crown Regiment, and was then attending the Avila Military Academy, where Governor Gálvez had met him. On May 25, 1777, the government named Miró sergeant major of the Louisiana battalion and promoted him to brevet lieutenant colonel. Although Bouligny was several years older, Miró had two months of seniority in rank. On completing his course of study, Miró visited his elderly parents on leave. Delays prevented him from sailing from Cádiz until March 14, 1778, and he arrived in New Orleans on June 7 with the last of the Havana reinforcements.[25]

<hr />

24. J. Horace Nunemaker, ed., "The Bouligny Affair in Louisiana," *Hispanic American Historical Review*, XXV (1945), 346–48; Bouligny to Bernardo de Gálvez, New Orleans, June 3, 1778, in AGI, PC, leg. 2358.

25. O'Reilly to José de Gálvez, Puerto de Santa María, May 13, 1777, AGI, SD, leg. 2534; Two patents to Miró of brevet lieutenant colonel and sergeant major, Aranjuez, May 25, 1777, *ibid.*; Miró petition, [n.d.], with Governor Gálvez's marginal notation, July 11, 1778, *ibid.*, leg. 2654; Miró to José de Gálvez, New Orleans, June 18, 1778, *ibid.*, leg. 2534. For

Upon learning of the new chain of command, Bouligny heatedly protested his demotion, arguing that he had been exercising the function of second military chief for fourteen months. Moreover, his post as lieutenant governor outranked those of Miró and the two Havana officers. Bouligny believed that he should be named as king's lieutenant, military commander in New Orleans. He mustered all the arguments he could think of: Minister Gálvez's orders of November 25, 1776; Governor Gálvez's proclamations of April 2 and 11, 1777, which he repeated to the governor; and sympathy—his demotion would damage his reputation. While Bouligny professed love and esteem for the governor and recognized his many favors, he expected the court, not Gálvez, to decide this issue.[26]

On June 3, 1778, Bouligny petitioned José de Gálvez, his protector in Spain, for the post of king's lieutenant, and he pleaded with the minister's brother, Miguel de Gálvez, who held a number of court offices and diplomatic posts, to intercede on his behalf. Bouligny argued that the office of king's lieutenant was clearly defined and that of lieutenant governor was controversial since its functions and place in Louisiana had not been clarified. Bouligny sought no further compensation beyond his salary as lieutenant governor and brevet lieutenant colonel of 2,244 pesos. Because Governor Gálvez had not removed him from settling families, Bouligny proposed to work diligently to fulfill that function. He entrusted the governor to forward the letters to his uncles José and Miguel under his cover letter, expecting an impartial decision. Over the next several months, Bouligny waited for the court to decide, not suspecting that Gálvez never forwarded the letters.[27]

On June 4, the governor tried to reassure "amigo Bouligny" that despite not being named king's lieutenant, he would not lose prestige in the colony. Bouligny refused to comprehend that the post of king's lieutenant was different from that of lieutenant governor, and although Gál-

a biography on Miró, see Caroline Maude Burson, *The Stewardship of Don Esteban Miró* (New Orleans, 1940).

26. "General Diary," May 22–June 3, [1778], MPA, SD; Two letters of Bouligny to Bernardo de Gálvez, New Orleans, June 3, 1778, both in AGI, PC, leg. 2358.

27. Bouligny to Bernardo de Gálvez, New Orleans, June 3, 1778; Bouligny to José de Gálvez, New Orleans, June 3, 1778; Bouligny to Miguel de Gálvez, New Orleans, June 3, 1778, all in AGI, PC, leg. 2358.

vez would obligingly refer the question to the court, he was certain that
Bouligny would fail to win the appointment. The governor considered
both the new sergeant major Miró and Bouligny his friends, but he drew
the distinction that Bouligny would be aggrieved if he lost his case while
Miró was indifferent and "content just to be at my side." That statement
made it clear that Gálvez expected obedience.[28]

By late June, 1778, Bouligny retained only a vestige of his former
authority, settling newly arrived families. The first Spaniards to come to
Louisiana were the hemp and flax experts from Granada, who reached
the province in late March, 1778, on board the *Santa Teresa*. Delays postponed their settlement, possibly because of Willing's raid. When Governor Gálvez sounded out Bouligny on the Granadinos' settlement and
experiments, the lieutenant governor recommended Ouachita as an excellent site but too distant and exposed to Osage Indian raids. Attakapas
and Opelousas, however, had good lands that were both near and safe.
But before settling the workers, he advised reconnoitering the region to
ascertain its suitability. The task of these laborers, however, was to teach
the growing of hemp and flax, not permanent settlement.[29]

In mid-1778, Bouligny continued to gather information on settlement sites for the Spanish immigrants, but he stubbornly maintained a
preference for Ouachita, a hundred leagues away. In an August 4 report,
he dwelt at length on the Ouachita River valley because of its fertile
lands, healthful climate, and plentiful game. Indians, he now claimed,
constituted no threat, although they occasionally hunted there. He believed that eventually a thousand families could be established to form a
massive bulwark to guard both Louisiana and Mexico. Bouligny urged
the governor to induce the viceroy of Mexico and the captain general of
Cuba to send discharged soldiers to Louisiana. The four-hundred-peso
to five-hundred-peso cost to settle each family could be recovered when
it achieved prosperity. But because of rumors of Indian attack and British
warships—the Spaniards held councils of war on June 28 and July 15—
Bouligny advised sending the immigrant families to either Attakapas or
Opelousas in southwestern Louisiana. The few individuals there with
cattle herds and extensive landholdings should be moved farther west, to
the Calcasieu and Vermillion rivers. Bouligny mentioned a royal order,

28. Bernardo de Gálvez to Bouligny, New Orleans, June 4, 1778, AGI, PC, leg. 2358.
29. Bouligny to Bernardo de Gálvez, New Orleans, June 23, 1778, *ibid.*

which Gálvez alleged he had received but did not show him, that prohibited settlement on the Ouachita. Its existence, however, is questionable; the governor was opposed to establishing the immigrant families in Ouachita.[30]

In the next three months, little disagreement occurred as Bouligny waited for the new settlers to arrive. The governor let the matter of authority lie dormant until October 21 when he wrote to post commandants to return secretly to him the April, 1777, announcements that proclaimed Bouligny lieutenant governor as well as any other correspondence they might have received from him. Most of the letters returned to Gálvez seem to have been destroyed. When the first ship bringing Canary Islander recruits and families arrived on November 1, Bouligny revived the question of authority, since he felt it slipping from his grasp. The governor wanted to strip Bouligny of power completely, but he had to act cautiously.[31]

Gálvez, in arrogating to himself most authority on settlements, wanted to locate the Canary Islander families on waterways near New Orleans to bolster its security and facilitate commerce. Many of the Canarian soldiers had families too large for them to support with their meager military pay, and the governor chose to employ them as settlers. When Gálvez announced a trip to reconnoiter settlement sites at Lafourche des Chetimachas (modern Donaldsonville, Louisiana) and Bayou Manchac and entrusted interim command to Colonel González, Bouligny insisted on a new council of officers to reexamine the post of second in military command, to which Gálvez acceded. The officers reread the royal instructions that stated that Bouligny was only lieutenant governor, provoking him to demand indignantly why then had he been proclaimed second military chief. Rather than admit error, Gálvez accused him of sending out the April notices. That unfounded charge cut Bouligny to the quick, and losing composure, he lashed out disrespectfully that Gálvez had impugned his honor. The governor then abruptly terminated the meeting.

30. Bouligny to Bernardo de Gálvez, New Orleans, August 4, 1778, *ibid.*, and published in Gilbert C. Din, ed., "Francisco Bouligny's 1778 Plans for Settlement in Louisiana," *Southern Studies*, XVI (1977), 211–24.

31. Examples of Bernardo de Gálvez's October 21, 1778, orders to post commandants are in AGI, PC, leg. 1. See Nunemaker, ed., "Bouligny Affair," 339–63, which publishes many documents. Although Nunemaker reveals many aspects of the so-called Bouligny affair, he did not have access to documents other than those in AGI, PC, leg. 1.

The next day, November 12, as he departed from New Orleans, Gálvez unexpectedly permitted Bouligny to settle the Malagueños in Ouachita.[32]

With Gálvez absent, Bouligny consoled himself by taking his post as lieutenant governor seriously. On November 16, he asked for an office in Government House, which he needed for taking charge of the Malagueños and developing a plan for their settlement. The next day, he tried to assume charge of the forty thousand pesos assigned to development, and actually received one thousand pesos from Treasurer Bernardo Otero. But, startled by his requests, Enrique Atayde, whom the governor had left in charge in Government House, personally informed Bouligny at home that he had no authority to recognize the lieutenant colonel's demands. Gálvez later contended that he had instructed Atayde to assist Bouligny.[33]

Stymied in his efforts, Bouligny soon requested from González copies of the papers of a French ship that had just arrived from Haiti with slaves. Until then, Bouligny had not exercised jurisdiction over commerce or Indian affairs, but with Gálvez away, the lieutenant governor believed that he had responsibility in those areas, while González had charge of purely military affairs. The colonel, however, answered discreetly that jurisdiction belonged to the Treasury and the governor and that it would be better to await Gálvez's return before taking any measures. This new rebuff emphasized Bouligny's impotence even in the areas mandated by the royal orders. He would not learn what authority he retained until the governor's return.[34]

While waiting, Bouligny received a November 22 letter from Gálvez on Bayou Manchac that again questioned the wisdom of settling the Malagueños in Ouachita. He cited distance, exposure to Indians, added costs, and the settlers' difficulty selling their produce in New Orleans. At the same time, he glowingly described the confluence of Bayou Manchac and the Amite River, where he proposed to establish the Villa de Gálvez

32. Nunemaker, ed., "Bouligny Affair," 349–63. [Bernardo de Gálvez] to Bouligny, New Orleans, November 12, 1778; Bouligny to Bernardo de Gálvez, New Orleans, December 3, 1778, both in AGI, PC, leg. 2358.

33. Bouligny to Enrique Atayde, New Orleans, November 16, 1778; Bouligny to Bernardo Otero, New Orleans, November 16, 1778, both in AGI, PC, leg. 2358. Bouligny, in his December 3, 1778, letter to Bernardo de Gálvez, wanted Atayde fired (ibid.).

34. Bouligny to Manuel González, New Orleans, November 18, 19, 1778; González to Bouligny, New Orleans, November 19, 20, 1778; Bernardo de Gálvez to Bouligny, Villa de Gálvez, November 22, 1778, all ibid.

and a fort. The governor, however, failed to budge Bouligny. In a lengthy reply, he steadfastly praised the Ouachita prairies, the abundant game, the ease of settlement, and the proximity of Natchitoches, Pointe Coupee, and Rapides (modern Alexandria). Bouligny used the opportunity to deplore the swamps and thick forests of the Manchac-Amite site the governor favored for military reasons. The Spanish immigrants, the lieutenant governor argued, deserved a settlement site more propitious than one fraught with hardship. His words were prophetic; the Galveztown settlement struggled long against hardships before ultimately failing.[35]

Bouligny also complained that the accusation that Gálvez had hurled at him in the council of officers was "nothing less than a crime so contrary to my principles of honesty, and to the true honor that have always shined in all my actions" and that his reputation was now so tarnished that even his friends avoided him. Moreover, he believed the present disagreements and Gálvez's opposition inopportune for settling the Malagueños in Ouachita. Bouligny also concluded that later royal orders had rescinded his commission. But since the governor denied it, Bouligny requested a copy of his appointment in order for him to fulfill his duties completely, and he asked to be acknowledged as lieutenant governor "in the Cabildo with all due formality."[36]

In early December, Gálvez returned to New Orleans. No doubt Bouligny's recent activities at Government House had angered him, and he refused to have Bouligny proclaimed as lieutenant governor in the Cabildo or to give him authority. Moreover, Gálvez denied that any other orders had arrived from Spain that enhanced Bouligny's duties. A bitter disappointment must have engulfed the lieutenant governor, and on December 10 he petitioned the crown, via the governor, for permission to resign on the grounds of poor health. Perhaps that act made Gálvez recognize that he had overstepped himself and that he had to let Bouligny salvage his bruised dignity. Gálvez had not yet reported to his uncle José his dealings with the lieutenant governor or concocted an explanation of why he had stripped Bouligny of authority. It seemed preferable to allow

---

35. Bernardo de Gálvez to Bouligny, Villa de Gálvez, November 22, 1778; Bouligny to Bernardo de Gálvez, New Orleans, December 3, 1778, both *ibid.* On the difficulties of the Canary Islanders at Galveztown, see Din, *Canary Islanders,* 28–45. A biased account of what happened at Galveztown is V. M. Scramuzza, "Galveztown: A Spanish Settlement of Colonial Louisiana," *Louisiana Historical Quarterly,* XIII (1930), 553–609.

36. Bouligny to Bernardo de Gálvez, New Orleans, December 3, 1778, in AGI, PC, leg. 2358.

him to settle the Malagueños while Gálvez devised an excuse for the lieutenant governor's removal. As an example of the disappearance of goodwill, at year's end the governor wrote in Bouligny's service sheet, "good in his post," not the higher accolade of 1777, "fit for promotion," and "average" in ability, not "good" as in the 1776 record. Bouligny, however, stubbornly clung to his pride. On November 28, 1778, when he sold two slaves for twelve hundred pesos to Juan Bormon Livaudais, he referred to himself as "governor of this *plaza*," a title identical to king's lieutenant.[37]

By December 23, Gálvez had accepted Bouligny's decision to settle the Malagueños on Bayou Teche in the Attakapas. He employed the excuse that only a small number of these Spaniards had arrived and that soldiers to protect them could not be spared. Gálvez allowed an equal number of Irishmen, Frenchmen, or Germans to join the Spaniards. He gave Bouligny command of the Attakapas and Opelousas district as lieutenant governor—but not in a manner akin to the lieutenant governors O'Reilly established in Natchitoches and St. Louis—to settle the immigrants and hear and judge cases on appeal from the local commandant. Gálvez assigned a corporal and four soldiers to accompany the lieutenant governor. The commission seemed to revive Bouligny, and he plunged energetically into his work. He hired officials, artisans, rowers, and slaves; obtained goods from the merchant St. Maxent, who was also supplying the four Canary Islander settlements then in formation about New Orleans; rented boats; and engaged Flammand (François Grevemberg), an Attakapas resident, to assist in the settlement. Probably no group of immigrants received as much assistance in settlement as the Malagueños. Bouligny also employed his nineteen-year-old nephew Juan Tala as storekeeper, his first job in Louisiana since arriving almost two years before. Bouligny personally bought more than thirty slaves to take with him as hired workers.[38]

37. Bouligny to the king, New Orleans, December 10, 1778; [Bernardo de Gálvez to Bouligny], New Orleans, December 11, 1778, both *ibid.*; Bouligny service sheets of August 31, 1776, and December 31, 1778, AGI, SD, legs. 2661, 2662, respectively; Almonester Notary, May 9–December 31, 1778, fols. 429v–431v.

38. Bernardo de Gálvez to Bouligny, New Orleans, December 23, 1778; Bouligny to Bernardo de Gálvez, New Orleans, January 8, 1779, both in AGI, PC, leg. 2358. A list of goods for the Malagueños from that legajo is published in Mathé Allain, "Bouligny's Account of the Founding of New Iberia," *Attakapas Gazette,* XIV (1979), 81–82. See also Gilbert C. Din, "Lieutenant Colonel Francisco Bouligny and the Malagueño Settlement at New Iberia, 1779," *Louisiana History,* XVII (1976), 187–202.

Southwestern Louisiana was then a cattle region and already had a number of scattered residents—Frenchmen, Acadians, blacks, and Indians. Many speculators, among them retired French officers, possessed extensive land grants, and they were trying to obtain more. The hemp and flax workers were then on the plantation of Alexandre DeClouet, commandant of the Attakapas-Opelousas district (in present St. Martin Parish), conducting experiments with little success.[39]

Taking only four families and several bachelors, totaling twenty Malagueños, Bouligny set out in the middle of winter with his officials, hired men, and slaves. He seemed anxious to carry out his first major commission since arriving in Louisiana in 1769. His party departed from New Orleans about January 26 and was in the Tunica village on February 4, at Lafourche des Chetimachas the next day, and one league from the Atchafalaya two days later. The travelers reached the Teche on February 11 after a rain-soaked journey that one soldier described as "fifteen days of Purgatory." Two days later, they encountered DeClouet, who was to assist them in the settlement.

By February 18, Bouligny was examining possible sites and contemplating giving each family six arpents of front on the left bank for farming and the same amount on the other bank for a common pasture. Already he had named the fledgling settlement New Iberia. Gálvez was pleased with Bouligny's leadership, writing to him on February 22, "You should not doubt as to what depends on me as I will contribute to the success of the commission you are charged with." On March 4, the governor sent him four more families, twenty-four persons.[40]

39. Glenn R. Conrad, "Some Observations on the Founding of New Iberia," *Attakapas Gazette,* XXII (1987), 41–46, which contains a description of the Attakapas area in 1779; Bernardo de Gálvez to Bouligny, New Orleans, April 26, 1779, in AGI, PC, leg. 2358. The Granadinos petitioned to leave Louisiana in 1780 but did not do so until after the war; documents about them are scattered in AGI, PC and SD. See also Maurine Bergerie, *They Tasted Bayou Water: A Brief History of Iberia Parish* (New Orleans, 1962), which contains several documents and lists of Malagueños who settled in New Iberia, and Glenn R. Conrad, *New Iberia, Essays on the Town and Its People* (Lafayette, La., 1979).

40. Bouligny to Bernardo de Gálvez, New Orleans, January 26, 1779; Bouligny to Bernardo de Gálvez, Los Tunicas, February 4, 1779; Bouligny to Bernardo de Gálvez, one league from Chafalaya, February 7, 1779; [Bernardo de Gálvez] to Bouligny, New Orleans, February 22 and March 4, 1779, all in AGI, PC, leg. 600; Bouligny to Bernardo de Gálvez, New Iberia, February 18, 1779, *ibid.,* leg. 2358; Louis Judice to the governor, Lafourche des Chetimachas, February 7, 1779, *ibid.,* leg. 192.

The journey of these latest Malagueños to New Iberia took eighteen days. By March 22, when they arrived, some progress had been achieved in New Iberia. But several of the settlers who had come with Bouligny were suffering from *sarna* (mange) or *galico,* and he asked Gálvez to consult Dr. Robert Dow in New Orleans for a remedy. New Iberia's beautiful location twelve leagues up the Teche (present Charenton, Louisiana) delighted Bouligny. The site was suitable for settling two hundred families, although he intended to place only twenty-five there. He learned more about the area's numerous bayous and rivers to improve communications with New Orleans and to export the local produce. He also planted flax and hemp, but to no avail, since the seed was old. Bouligny purchased oxen, cows, horses, pigs, and chickens to distribute to the families. He was hoping for a crop of corn, rice, and tobacco that year. The slaves had built a hut for each immigrant family, two provisional warehouses, and cabins for the officials and soldiers; plowed twelve to fifteen arpents of land; made a quantity of cypress lumber; and performed other tasks. With all this activity, New Iberia appeared to have gotten off to a sound start.[41]

The spring rains of lower Louisiana, however, soon negated the promising beginnings. After Easter the Teche rose more than a foot each day until the huts were under six to eight feet of water. The flood forced Bouligny to relocate New Iberia, and only then did he discover that the high ground on the Teche already had owners. He consequently purchased land from Joseph Prevost *dit* Colette seven to eight leagues farther up the bayou for four hundred pesos. It was on the west bank and consisted of thirty arpents of front by eighty deep. Again Bouligny described the location (at New Iberia's present site) as excellent, with good waters, a two-league meadow, easy access to other settlements, and a nearby lake (Spanish Lake) rich in fish and game. By April 21, temporary housing sheltered the families. This time the slaves planted only corn, rice, and other foodstuffs in order for the Malagueños to achieve self-sufficiency as quickly as possible.[42]

Bouligny wanted New Iberia to develop rapidly by attracting mer-

---

41. Bouligny to Bernardo de Gálvez, New Iberia, March 17, 1779, *ibid.*, leg. 2358; Bouligny to Bernardo de Gálvez, New Iberia, March 22, 23, 1779, both *ibid.*, leg. 600.

42. Bouligny to Bernardo de Gálvez, New Iberia, April 21, 1779; Bernardo de Gálvez to Bouligny, New Orleans, April 26, 1779, both *ibid.*, leg. 2358.

chants and artisans. It was earmarked as a future town in southwestern Louisiana. A step forward in its development was the visit of the first priest, Father Grumeau, who on Ascension Day held a high mass and later blessed the ground for a cemetery. The people of the region flocked to the settlement to celebrate with the Malagueño families.[43]

While Bouligny worked at New Iberia's establishment, he received an inquiry into his financial status from New Orleans. He had left the city owing 14,000 pesos, 3,000 of it to Gálvez. In May the governor questioned Bouligny's solvency. The lieutenant governor replied that the large debt came from buying slaves, the poor conduct of his plantation overseer, and sending 1,000 pesos in indigo to support young Luis de Vilemont in France. Nevertheless, Bouligny's anticipated earnings for 1779 were substantial: 2,000 pesos from his salary, 2,000 to 3,000 pesos from his lumber mill and plantation, and 3,500 to 4,000 pesos from the wages of his thirty-two slaves in New Iberia. That year alone he planned to pay his creditors 8,000 or 9,000 pesos, which would reduce his debt significantly. As for his family's living expenses, Bouligny had provided them with money prior to his leaving New Orleans, his mother-in-law had an income, and foodstuffs and other assistance from the plantation would allow them to subsist for a year without more help from him, as his wife had informed him. Gálvez was nevertheless concerned about his 3,000 pesos, since he had requested a transfer and was putting his financial affairs in order. If he left, the loan would have to be repaid at once.[44]

The summer of 1779 brought slow development to New Iberia. Bouligny spent part of his time promoting the exploration of the area. At his behest, Flammand undertook several voyages to discover routes and passes down the Teche and out to sea. The exploration provided knowledge for the first time of the waterways in southwestern Louisiana. In late July, upon the death of Fernando Ibáñez, Bouligny recommended a medical doctor for New Iberia. A Dr. Vellon lived in the Attakapas region, whom the lieutenant governor proposed to employ for 200 pesos annually. The small Malagueño community felt Ibáñez's death deeply; he had been a leader among them, encouraging and consoling them, serving as an example. Bouligny asked Gálvez to grant the widow and her three

43. Bouligny to Bernardo de Gálvez, New Iberia, May 16, 1779, *ibid.*, leg. 600.
44. Bouligny to Bernardo de Gálvez, New Iberia, June 6, 1779; [Bernardo de Gálvez] to Bouligny, New Orleans, June 26, 1779, both *ibid.*, leg. 2358.

small children a munificent pension of 500 pesos annually. The governor referred the matter to court, allowing the family a small sum in the interim.[45]

In late July, Bouligny wrote several letters to Gálvez that revealed problems at the settlement. Many of the Malagueños were still living in temporary huts. Bouligny proposed hiring Acadians to build the houses, which were to be twenty-eight by fifteen feet with a nine-foot height, a gallery in front, and raised off the ground. He employed Louis Loisel of Opelousas to help in keeping the accounts, which had become complicated. Bouligny confided in a private letter to Gálvez that DeClouet, the local commandant, had undermined the lieutenant governor with rumors and false stories. Bouligny declared that he had done nothing to incur the ire of DeClouet and had refused to listen to numerous complaints from the inhabitants about the commandant. Rather, he had tried in vain to befriend DeClouet. Bouligny accused the commandant of setting exorbitant prices for local purchases, particularly livestock, and creating obstacles to the acquisition of land. Many people had extensive concessions, which they held solely for speculation. Hoping that his past disagreements with Gálvez were vanishing, the lieutenant governor closed his private letter: "Sooner or later I will find in you a firm protector and true friend. . . . Your letter [of June 26] begins to verify my hopes. . . . Finish opening your arms . . . to a true friendship from someone, who not only esteems and venerates you, but who sincerely and truly loves you and in whose heart no event can eradicate the gratitude that he will profess to you eternally."[46]

In August, communications between Bouligny and Gálvez virtually ceased as war with Britain approached. Negotiations between Spain and Britain had reached an impasse in the spring of 1779. The French, who had entered the conflict on the side of the American rebels in 1778, kept pressuring the Spaniards to join them. José de Gálvez sent a warning of the forthcoming war to Louisiana on May 18 and the actual declaration

45. Bouligny to Bernardo de Gálvez, New Iberia, July 28, 1779; [Bernardo de Gálvez to Bouligny], [n.p.], [n.d.], both *ibid.*, leg. 600. On exploration, see Bouligny to Bernardo de Gálvez, New Iberia, June 20, 30, July 9, 1779, all *ibid.*, leg. 2358; and Bouligny to Bernardo de Gálvez, July 3, 10, 1779, both *ibid.*, leg. 600. Two diaries on exploration are *ibid.*, leg. 2358.

46. Bouligny to Bernardo de Gálvez, New Iberia, July 27, 1779, Bernardo de Gálvez to Bouligny, New Orleans, October 11, 1779, both *ibid.*, leg. 2358; Bouligny to Bernardo de Gálvez, New Iberia, July 28, 29, 1779, both *ibid.*, leg. 600.

on June 21. Captain General Diego José Navarro of Cuba, also aware of the impending rupture, asked Governor Gálvez for a war plan and prepared to send a battalion to New Orleans in late July. The recovery of East and West Florida was a prime objective in the coming struggle. In New Orleans, Governor Gálvez contemplated war measures as he learned in August of the declaration. He gathered as many men as he could, put New Orleans on the best defense possible, and warned the commandants upriver to prepare their forces. Gálvez intended to attack the British posts on the Mississippi, employing surprise if possible. A hurricane on August 18 temporarily delayed his departure, but before the end of the month, Gálvez moved upriver with his army of soldiers, militiamen, and civilians, totaling 667 men.[47]

Although Gálvez notified the post commandants of the declaration of war, he pointedly omitted informing Bouligny, who learned about it from DeClouet. It saddened Bouligny to realize that Gálvez still harbored animosity toward him. The New Iberia residents, however, wanted to do their share in the war. By August 25, Bouligny, labeling himself the first volunteer, had fifteen Malagueños ready to follow him in battle, and, as he wrote to Gálvez, "My greatest satisfaction will be to die at your side." As a soldier, Bouligny understood that he could not linger behind but needed to demonstrate his valor under enemy fire. Moreover, success on the battlefield often brought rewards. While the war had come when Bouligny was forty-three, he was determined to prove his valor. Without faltering, he gathered up his five soldiers, two discharged veterans, two deserters, two Malagueños, one militiaman, two Americans, two volunteers (of whom one was Juan Tala), and twenty-five slaves. They departed for the Mississippi, traveling with DeClouet's detachment. By the afternoon of September 3, Bouligny reported to Gálvez at Plaquemine, incorporated the New Iberians into the Spanish army, and took charge of his own 5th Company. Astonishingly, the governor found fault with Bouligny's abandonment of New Iberia but accepted it as a wartime exigency.[48]

47. On events immediately preceding the outbreak of war, see Caughey, *Gálvez*, 149–53; Diego José Navarro to Bernardo de Gálvez, Havana, August 17, 1779, in AGI, PC, leg. 1.

48. Bouligny to Bernardo de Gálvez, New Iberia, August 25, and Casa de Campaña, September 3, 1779, with attached "List of the People who left New Iberia and have arrived here with the detachment of Mr. DeClouet"; [Bernardo de Gálvez] to Bouligny, [n.p.], [n.d.], all in AGI, PC, leg. 600.

The war ended Bouligny's rule as lieutenant governor, altering priorities in Louisiana. He was needed as an army officer, and development of the colony would have to wait. Bouligny also learned that despite his efforts to convert Gálvez into a genuine friend, the governor desired only to dispossess him of authority, which he at last succeeded in doing. Now, however, Bouligny, like other ambitious officers, welcomed the war for the opportunities it presented. But he must have looked back at the past two years with immense disappointment. His tenure as lieutenant governor, begun so auspiciously in Spain, had foundered upon the rock of Gálvez's intransigent opposition. With a more reasonable governor, Bouligny might have emerged as a dominant figure in Louisiana by 1779. Gálvez, however, had his own concepts of leadership and of the men he wanted around him. Bouligny, with his pride and ego, did not fit in the Gálvez mold. The governor, nevertheless, had yet to explain to Spain why he had canceled the lieutenant governor's commission. Bouligny's unequal struggle with Gálvez, who soon had promotions and honors heaped upon him by his uncle José, continued for several more years.

6

WAR AND THE END OF THE BOULIGNY-GÁLVEZ AFFAIR

HOSTILITIES AGAINST BRITAIN at last existed. Spain had waited since the end of the Seven Years' War to seek revenge for losses in that conflict. War might have been averted had diplomatic efforts to recover Gibraltar from England not failed in early 1779. Spain then joined France in an alliance, refraining from establishing formal ties with the North American rebels. Spanish ministers worried that helping English colonials achieve independent might prove counterproductive, since Spain had many colonials of its own. Wartime objectives consisted of recovering Gibraltar and Minorca in Europe and cleaning out the English in the Floridas, near Bernardo de Gálvez's province of Louisiana, and in Central America, where Matías de Gálvez was now captain general. No doubt Minister José de Gálvez had an important role in determining priorities. Louisiana and the Gulf of Mexico soon emerged as an active theater of war.[1]

Four days after Francisco Bouligny's arrival on the Mississippi from New Iberia, Governor Gálvez attacked the British at Manchac. The earliest encounter, however, had occurred not twenty miles away several days earlier at Galveztown, where Commandant Francisco Collell began

---

1. On Spanish diplomacy before entering the war, see Samuel Flagg Bemis, *The Diplomacy of the American Revolution* (1935; rpr. Bloomington, Ind., 1975), 41–45, 55–57, 75–87; J. F. Yela Utrilla, *España ante la independencia de los Estados Unidos* (Lerida, Spain, 1925), I. On Matías de Gálvez in Central America, see Troy S. Floyd, *The Anglo-Spanish Struggle for Mosquitia* (Albuquerque, 1967), 128–62. Gálvez, a colonel, reached Guatemala in early 1779; was named captain general on April 5, 1779; was appointed viceroy of New Spain in March, 1783; and died in Mexico City on November 3, 1784. For British policy in West Florida, see Robin F. A. Fabel, "West Florida and British Strategy in the American Revolution," in *Eighteenth Century Florida and the Revolutionary South,* ed. Samuel Proctor (Gainesville, Fla., 1978), 49–67.

seizing enemy boats on the Amite River. British Lt. Col. Alexander Dickson, who was apprised of the Spanish army advancing up the Mississippi and of activity on the Amite, withdrew the bulk of his troops from Fort Bute at Manchac to Baton Rouge on September 3. Four days later, having isolated Manchac, the Spaniards attacked at dawn, killing one enemy soldier, taking twenty prisoners, but allowing six Britons to escape.

Gálvez soon moved his army to assault the Baton Rouge fort, which was girdled by a sizable ditch and held by 550 regular and irregular troops with thirteen cannon. He bombarded the fort from an unexpected quarter on September 21 and forced its capitulation later that day. The Spanish forces took 375 soldiers prisoner but released the civilians and slaves. Gálvez insisted, however, that the enemy also surrender Fort Panmure at Natchez, the remaining British garrison on the river. Capt. Juan Delavillebeuvre took possession of Fort Panmure on October 5. Carlos de Grand-Pré, commandant for several years at Pointe Coupee, also seized the British post at Thompson Creek on the Mississippi, opposite his. Bouligny stayed in Baton Rouge after the fighting ended and returned with the army and prisoners to New Orleans. In October, when the Spanish soldiers arrived, they paraded through the city streets as the citizens joyously celebrated their victory over the enemy. A solemn Te Deum in the St. Louis Church culminated the festivities. Bouligny had participated in both the battles of Manchac and Baton Rouge, using twenty-seven of his slaves at Baton Rouge in many ways, including carrying munitions to the artillery emplacement. While the army listed the river campaign in his service record, he did not receive a promotion, as did many others whom Governor Gálvez chose to favor.[2]

Rather than praise Bouligny, Gálvez reviewed the New Iberia accounts and accomplishments. He called on the lieutenant colonel to explain his expenditures, no doubt astonishing him that in the midst of war

2. Caughey, *Gálvez*, 154–61; Bouligny service sheet, June 30, 1793, AGI, PC, leg. 161A; Bouligny petition for promotion. New Orleans, July 26, 1784, BB, HNOC. See also Bettie Jones Conover, "British West Florida's Mississippi Frontier Posts, 1763–1779," *Alabama Review*, XXIX (1976), 177–207, which puts the total British force on the Mississippi on September 1, 1779, excluding officers, at 457. Printed articles of the capitulation at Baton Rouge, dated September 21, 1779, are in AGI, PC, leg. 83. A convenient short study of the war in West Florida is Albert W. Haarmann, "The Spanish Conquest of British West Florida, 1779–1781," *Florida Historical Quarterly*, XXXIX (1960), 107–34.

Pastel drawing of Francisco Domingo
Joseph Bouligny, *ca.* 1770s.
Courtesy the Historic New Orleans
Collection, Museum/Research Center,
Acc. No. 1980.255.1

Pastel drawing of Marie Louise Le
Sénéchal d'Auberville de Bouligny,
wife of Francisco Bouligny, *ca.* 1770s.

Courtesy the Historic New Orleans
Collection, Museum/Research Center,
Acc. No. 1980.255.2

Painting of Domingo Bouligny,
son of Francisco Bouligny.
Courtesy Mrs. Felix H. Lapeyre (Marie
Thérèse Villeré)

Oil painting of Luis Bouligny, son of
Francisco Bouligny.
Courtesy Mrs. Patricia Lynch Carter

Pastel drawing of Carlos de
Vilemont, brother-in-law of
Francisco Bouligny.
Courtesy A. Howard Stebbins III

and planning for the assault on Mobile, the next Spanish objective on the Gulf, Gálvez took time to dwell on that subject. But unknown to Bouligny, while he had been on Bayou Teche, the governor tried to justify his reduction of the powers of the lieutenant governor.

In place of the friendship that Bouligny fervently sought, Gálvez revealed in a biting letter of March 2, 1779, to his uncle José that not only Bouligny but the councilors of the New Orleans Cabildo exhibited ingratitude toward Spain. Bouligny was filled with "erroneous ideas," and Gálvez promised to send the minister "documents that prove the illegal nature of his [Bouligny's] conduct and make you [José de Gálvez] see that the said official has no other intention than his own interests." As for the Cabildo members, Gálvez lacked proof for his charges but knew of their disaffection for Spain. Several had participated in the 1768 uprising and still maintained a rebellious spirit and hatred for Spain. For two years, the governor claimed, he had been laboring in vain to procure their allegiance. Only these few men in all the province failed to appreciate the blessings of their benevolent monarch Carlos III. Gálvez vowed to learn more about their seditious ways, after which he would take the necessary measures to deal with them.[3]

The governor probably spent the next several weeks contemplating arguments to use against Bouligny. On March 26, he sent out questionnaires to the army officers González, Miró, Panis, Piernas, Francisco Cruzat, Manuel de Navas, Martín Pérez Mozún, Delavillebeuvre, and Hilario Ramírez Estenoz, and to Navarro, a civilian Treasury official, all of whom had attended one or both of the officers' meetings that discussed the issue of second in military command. The questionnaire contained four issues: (1) that on the arrival of the reinforcements from Havana, at Bouligny's insistence, the leading chiefs and captains met at Gálvez's house to discuss whether the lieutenant governor should be regarded as the king's lieutenant and second in military command; (2) that in the "infinite arguments" with Bouligny, Gálvez behaved "reasonably, gently, and prudently," while Bouligny complained immoderately; (3) that despite the first meeting, Bouligny insisted upon a second, where he importuned the officers for a favorable decision, acted disrespectfully, and demanded to know why he had been proclaimed the second military chief if the royal orders did not so state it; and (4) that Gálvez had con-

3. Bernardo de Gálvez to José de Gálvez, reserved, New Orleans, March 2, 1779, in AGI, PC, leg. 2662.

tinually disapproved of a settlement at Ouachita while Bouligny refused to relinquish the idea. The questionnaire held the answers that Gálvez wanted, and the officers, aware of the delicate nature of their replies, did not disappoint him.[4]

But how serious were Bouligny's "erroneous ideas" of wanting to be named second military chief after Gálvez had actually done it, insisting on Ouachita as a settlement site, and showing disrespect to Gálvez? Moreover, an argument could be made against Gálvez for refusing to fulfill the royal instructions of November 25, 1776, about the lieutenant governor without sufficient cause. Gálvez must have realized the flimsiness of his reasoning because he bundled up the officials' replies without sending them to Spain. He needed new charges against Bouligny before he could write to José about the matter.

In Spain, on June 25, 1779, Minister Gálvez acknowledged the receipt of his nephew's March 2 letter about Bouligny and the New Orleans Cabildo. The minister and the king awaited a full explanation from the governor. But since Governor Gálvez did not send the promised information, on August 30, the king inquired about "the true reports and complaints . . . of the irregular procedures . . . of Captain Bouligny" and Governor Gálvez's failure to contain or reduce him to captain. The minister ordered the governor to investigate and substantiate the charges against Bouligny. Gálvez was to suspend Bouligny as lieutenant governor if he found just motives for doing so. When this order arrived in Louisiana at the end of 1779, Gálvez had the authorization he needed for terminating Bouligny's commission, although he still lacked a valid reason.[5]

Gálvez waited until returning to New Orleans from the Mississippi River expedition before dealing with Bouligny. On October 11, 1779, the governor examined Bouligny's last letters from New Iberia and checked the accounts. In answer to a Gálvez question on building houses for the Malagueños, Bouligny replied that he needed 11,000 pesos more. That led the governor on October 26 to add up the costs thus far, which totaled 31,150 pesos. He then inquired how much additional money was needed and how long it would take to finish settling the families. It

4. Nunemaker, ed., "Bouligny Affair," 347–63, contains Gálvez's questionnaire and the replies (originals in AGI, PC, leg. 1).

5. José de Gálvez to the governor of Louisiana, Aranjuez and San Ildefonso, June 25, reserved, August 30, 1779, both in AGI, PC, leg. 174A.

should be noted that the settlement of the Canary Islanders in Galvez-town, St. Bernard, and Valenzuela was also taking longer than expected.[6]

Bouligny's lengthy reply two days later outlined his problems at New Iberia, his costs, and his proposals for concluding the settlement. Important in the expenditures were the generous contracts made in Spain with the Malagueños that pledged assistance until their first harvest. For the families without housing, Bouligny suggested giving them 200 to 300 pesos to build their own dwellings. Until January 17, 1780, when the contract of the slaves expired, they would help the families gather the harvest, build houses, and bring lumber from the first site to New Iberia. The cost for the seventy-five blacks, discounting two months for the twenty-seven who had served on the Mississippi expedition, would be 15,000 to 16,000 pesos, of which only 5,200 pesos had been paid. He wanted to mark out lots in the town for one hundred settlers, who were to be mainly artisans to help in its development. Bouligny's house on Bayou Teche, on Colette's former plantation, could serve as the residence for the district commandant. The settlement did not require a church, since there was one three leagues away, but a priest was needed. Bouligny planned to suspend aid soon to the Malagueños, except for the Ibáñez family. He proposed charging them only what each family had received in money, goods, and animals, plus 150 pesos for the slaves' assistance. Of the 31,150-peso cost thus far, St. Maxent had received 5,000 pesos for goods, of which 3,000 had not been spent. Bouligny awaited Gálvez's wishes to execute them promptly.[7]

Five days later, Gálvez replied, "[Your letter] has put me in the perplexity of not knowing what to say to you," since the families were still without houses. Moreover, Gálvez had heard a rumor that the Attakapas residents did the planting, and he wondered how the slaves had been employed. "Until you remove me from this doubt," he added, "I will remain with the greatest unrest."[8]

Bouligny immediately denied that the Attakapas residents did the planting. He had asked two local farmers to teach the Malagueños to

6. Bernardo de Gálvez to Bouligny, New Orleans, October 11, 1779, in AGI, PC, leg. 2358; Bouligny to Bernardo de Gálvez, New Orleans, October 12, 1779; Bernardo de Gálvez to Bouligny, New Orleans, October 11, 26, 1779, all *ibid.*, leg. 600.

7. Bouligny to Bernardo de Gálvez, New Orleans, October 28, 1779, *ibid.*, leg. 600. See also Bernardo de Gálvez to Bouligny, New Orleans, July 30, 1779, in BN, DL.

8. [Bernardo de Gálvez] to Bouligny, New Orleans, November 2, 1779, in AGI, PC, leg. 600.

plow, and he had employed several Acadians, who volunteered to work. They plowed thirty arpents. Bouligny again blamed the royal contract for the Malagueños refusing to toil diligently and preferring to live on government assistance. He had to compel them to work. As for the use of the slaves, he replied with a lengthy list of their activities: transporting the families and goods from the first to the second site; plowing, planting, and caring for sixty-five arpents of corn, twenty-five of rice, four to six of potatoes, and thirty-five of corn at the first location; tending to the tobacco that Colette planted; building two sixty-foot sheds to house the families; constructing houses for the blacksmith, several of the families (Artado, Prados, Migas, Ibáñez, and Vidal), the Germans, the soldiers, Flammand, and Henderson; building a warehouse for the manufacture of bricks; erecting a corral and tending to the animals; making and transporting lumber; building carts; and engaging in many smaller tasks. Henderson and Flammand (whom Bouligny left in charge during his absence) had instructions to oversee the slaves who stayed in New Iberia. Bouligny concluded his explanation with his willingness to return to the settlement with the slaves he had with him to complete the work in the next two months.[9]

On November 6, Gálvez, pointing out the shortage of officers in the regiment and citing Bouligny's August 25 letter, ordered the lieutenant colonel to take charge of his company. Gálvez appointed the Cabildo councilor (*regidor*) Nicolas Forstall commandant of New Iberia. He instructed Bouligny to make a formal transfer to Forstall, accompany him back to New Iberia, and provide an accounting of expenses for the settlement within a month.[10]

Since Forstall could not leave New Orleans immediately, Bouligny offered to take the slaves. But the one-month deadline was insufficient for traveling to New Iberia and making an accounting. The governor then ordered him to complete the work in the shortest time possible. Forstall was in New Iberia by December 23, and a week later Bouligny turned over to him 1,048 reales in money, 2,959 reales in goods, and command of the settlement. Having concluded his work, Bouligny returned to New Orleans by early January. At that time, Gálvez, armed with José's August 30 letter, ordered the accounting house to suspend Bouligny's extra pay as lieutenant governor and to bar him from further involvement

9. Bouligny to Bernardo de Gálvez, New Orleans, November 3, 1779, *ibid*.
10. [Bernardo de Gálvez] to Bouligny, New Orleans, November 6, 1779, *ibid*.

in settlements, commerce, and Indian affairs. Because the expedition for the assault on British-held Mobile was about to depart, Bouligny failed to finish the accounting of his expenses at New Iberia.[11]

The safety of New Orleans in the war hinged upon the assault on Mobile, a dependency of Pensacola. While Gálvez preferred seizing Pensacola, the center of British power in West Florida, he lacked the forces to do so. On January 11, 1780, the governor reviewed his troops prior to embarkation. They totaled 754, including 141 men from the Louisiana Regiment, 323 white militiamen, 107 free blacks and mulattoes, and 24 slaves. The fleet to transport them consisted of two frigates, four settees, four brigantines, one packet, and one galliot. By January 18, the ships were at the mouth of the Mississippi, but they were not fully across the sandbar and into the Gulf until February 4. Six days later, bad weather forced the expedition into Mobile Bay, where several ships went aground in the shallow waters. Bouligny was in command of the *San Francisco de Paula,* which saved itself from stranding and ferried a large number of officers, soldiers, and supplies from the grounded ships to shore. Only the frigate *Volante* was lost. Despite the inauspicious start, the Spaniards pressed forward with their attack on Fort Charlotte at the rear of Mobile Bay. After setting up a battery at the entrance to the bay and with the arrival of reinforcements from Havana, Gálvez moved to Dog River, fewer than ten miles from Mobile, on February 26. Two days later, he set up camp about a mile from the town, and the next day his patrols came under enemy fire.[12]

11. Bouligny to Bernardo de Gálvez, New Orleans and New Iberia, November 9, December 23, 1779, respectively; [Bernardo de Gálvez] to Bouligny, New Orleans, November 10, 23, 1779, all *ibid.*; Nicolas Forstall, Account, "November 10, 1779, to the end of December, 1784," New Iberia, AGI, PC, leg. 576; [Bernardo de Gálvez] to Juan Ventura Morales, New Orleans, January 12(?), 1780, in AGI, PC, leg. 83; Bernardo de Gálvez, "Instructions that Dn. Martín Navarro . . . Principal Accountant of the Army and Royal Treasury . . . should observe," New Orleans, January 8, 1780, AGI, PC, leg. 82. Bernardo de Gálvez's instructions to Forstall of November 15, 1779, are in AGI, PC, leg. 192. Forstall had problems in New Iberia; see [Piernas?] to [Bernardo de Gálvez], New Orleans, September 19, 1780, in AGI, PC, leg. 193A. Gálvez did not issue a patent to Forstall as commandant of New Iberia and Attakapas until April 6, 1785 (AGI, PC, leg. 11). Juan St. Marc Darby, who had been serving as interim commandant, was named on April 1, 1787, to replace Forstall (AGI, PC, leg. 200).

12. Caughey, *Gálvez,* 174–77; Starr, *Tories,* 168–69. Bouligny petition to the king, New Orleans, July 26, 1784, BB, HNOC. Gálvez's diary on Mobile, "Diary that I,

On March 1, Gálvez called upon the services of Bouligny to take a message to Capt. Elias Durnford, commander of Fort Charlotte, pointing out the futility of resistance. He was also to observe the condition of the fort and its defenders. The lieutenant colonel went with a drummer carrying a flag of truce. Durnford later described the arrival of the Spanish officer: "The Flag was brought in Person by an old acquaintance, Colonel Bolyny, who sent me a polite card wishing for the pleasure of an interview if possible, and Profession of Friendship, although we were National enemies, on which I sent Mr. Barde to conduct him into the Fort with the customary ceremony, where he dined and continued until near five o'clock, drinking a cheerful glass to the healths of our Kings and Friends." At the meeting, Bouligny emphasized the large Spanish force of 2,500 men and denied any losses because of the ships that had run aground. Durnford, however, claimed a superior position. Honor forbade him from surrendering without resistance. After the talk stalemated, Bouligny returned to the Spanish encampment to report.[13]

Over the next several days, while Gálvez continued to exchange notes with Durnford, he prepared the artillery for the bombardment of Fort Charlotte. An intercepted enemy letter revealed that the English might try to relieve the fort, and Gálvez sent out more patrols. On March 10, the British opened up a lively fire against the Spanish troops working to set up an artillery emplacement, forcing them to stop until nightfall. Two days later, the battery in place, Gálvez commenced shelling Fort Charlotte with eight 18-pounders and one 24-pounder, doing more damage than he received. That evening, after the fort sustained breaches in the walls, Durnford proposed a truce to negotiate terms of surrender. On the morning of March 14, the Spaniards entered Fort Charlotte, Bouligny probably leading his men as they marched in. In the fighting, he had command of the pickets and the Louisiana grenadiers, participating in all the sallies and protecting the trench for the three

---

Dn. Bernardo de Gálvez, Brigadier of the Royal Army and Governor of the Province of Louisiana, and charged by His Majesty with the Expedition against Pensacola and Mobile, formed of the events that occur in it," Mobile, March 18, 1780, is in AGS, GM, leg. 6912.

13. William Beer, ed., "The Surrender of Fort Charlotte, Mobile, 1780," *American Historical Review*, I (1896), 696–99; see also Gálvez's diary regarding Mobile (AGS, GM, leg. 6912), and Peter J. Hamilton, *Colonial Mobile: An Historical Study* (Rev. ed.; Boston, 1910), 314–15.

consecutive nights that the siege lasted. The Spaniards took prisoner 134 whites and 51 blacks. British casualties numbered only 1 dead and 11 wounded, while the Spaniards lost 7 dead, 9 wounded, and 2 deserters. The capitulation came barely in time. Gen. John Campbell, military commander at Pensacola, was reported in the Tensa area, thirty miles away, with 1,100 men, artillery, and Indian allies.[14]

The Spaniards immediately strengthened their defenses and welcomed the reinforcements that arrived from New Orleans. The threat from Campbell vanished when he learned of Fort Charlotte's fall, and he beat a hasty retreat to Pensacola. The English in West Florida, reduced to a single stronghold, fell back on the defensive, except for threatening The Village (La Aldea), an outpost on the opposite (eastern) shore from Mobile, on several occasions and attacking unsuccessfully in January, 1781. After Mobile's fall, Gálvez preferred to move rapidly against Pensacola, but he lacked both the ships and the men to assault the well-defended fortifications. Disappointed, he left a reduced garrison in Mobile and sent the Louisiana soldiers, including Bouligny, and militiamen back to New Orleans.[15]

Between the fall of Mobile and the final offensive against Pensacola, Bouligny waited in New Orleans. During this time, he probably advised purchasing the captaincy of the third company in the regiment's second battalion for Carlos de Vilemont for the substantial sum of 4,000 pesos. Only shortly before, Vilemont had been mistakenly promoted to sublieutenant twice, first on November 14, 1779, and again on February 17, 1780, this time as a reward for his participation on the Mississippi campaign. Bouligny was in New Orleans on August 24, 1780, when another hurricane, more serious than the one the year before, swept through lower Louisiana, causing at least ten deaths and inflicting harm upon crops, ships, and buildings, including the barracks, hospital, and many warehouses. The losses in the city alone were estimated at 600,000 pesos. Bouligny's house near the river sustained 4,000 pesos in damages as the

---

14. Caughey, *Gálvez*, 178–86; Starr, *Tories*, 170–74. See also William S. Coker and Hazel P. Coker, *The Siege of Mobile, 1780, in Maps, with Data on Troop Strength, Military Units, Ships, Casualties, and Prisoners of War Including a Brief History of Fort Charlotte (Conde)* (Pensacola, 1982).

15. Caughey, *Gálvez*, 187–95. "Relation of the dead, wounded, and prisoners in the attack of the detachment of The Village on January 7, 1781" is in AGS, GM, leg. 6912. Fifteen men died on each side.

wind tore at the roof and rain soaked the interior. Bouligny lost many of his papers in the calamity. The damages prevented him from reducing his debt significantly, as he had planned.[16]

While temporarily in New Orleans after the capture of Mobile, on June 5, 1780, Gálvez replied to his uncle about Bouligny's irregular conduct. Openly dissembling, he wrote: "Upon a pretext, I ordered the said officer to come to [New Orleans] to render his accounts, which are, without doubt, the most solid proof of his irregular management and disorderly proceedings." Gálvez promised to proceed on this matter after the war. For the present, he accused Bouligny of poor record keeping, about which Gálvez had known nothing when he complained about the lieutenant colonel in his March 2, 1779, letter and when he composed the questionnaire. Moreover, neither at this time nor later did Gálvez elaborate on the alleged misconduct of the members of the New Orleans Cabildo. If the governor wanted to remove Bouligny to replace him with his father-in-law, the merchant St. Maxent, he succeeded in part the next year.[17]

Meanwhile, planning for the attack on Pensacola continued. The campaign was more difficult than the earlier expeditions. Gálvez believed that Pensacola held 1,302 regular soldiers, 600 civilians and hunters, 300 sailors, 300 armed blacks, and an unspecified number of Indian auxiliaries. In addition, Pensacola Bay was guarded by artillery at Red Cliffs (Barrancas Coloradas) near the entry to the bay and by a frigate or two

16. Bernardo de Gálvez set the price for officer posts in the second battalion at 4,000 pesos for captain, 2,000 for lieutenant, and 1,000 for sublieutenant; [Gálvez] to Martín Navarro, [n.p., n.d.] (AGI, PC, leg. 83). Earlier, O'Reilly had set prices at 3,000, 1,500, and 800 pesos, respectively, for the three ranks (O'Reilly to José de Gálvez, Puerto de Santa Maria, May 7, 1779, *ibid.*, leg. 2662). Not all posts were to be sold, as several were reserved for deserving officers. Vilemont's purchase is noted in a dispatch from El Pardo, March, 1781 (AGI, SD, leg. 2655). Vilemont's patents of promotion to sublieutenant are San Lorenzo, November 14, 1779, and El Pardo, February 17, 1780 (both in AGI, SD, leg. 2654). Martín Navarro reported hurricane winds as beginning at 10:30 A.M. on August 24, 1780, and lasting to 7:00 P.M. Calm then prevailed to midnight, when the winds began again and lasted until 3:00 A.M. The waters on Lake Pontchartrain rose ten feet (Martín Navarro to José de Gálvez, New Orleans, August 29, 1780, in AGI, SD, leg. 2586).

17. Bernardo de Gálvez to José de Gálvez, New Orleans, June 5, 1780, in AGI, SD, leg. 2547. On Bernardo de Gálvez favoring his father-in-law, see Arthur Preston Whitaker, ed. and trans., *Documents Relating to the Commercial Policy of Spain in the Floridas, with Incidental Reference to Louisiana* (Deland, Fla., 1931), xxviii–xxix.

within the bay itself. After a brief stay in New Orleans in the summer of 1780, Gálvez departed for Cuba to secure the necessary troops, ships, and supplies from Capt. Gen. Diego José Navarro.[18]

Gálvez was in Havana by August 2, 1780, and a council of war soon agreed to support him. The military expedition sailed for Pensacola on October 16 with 3,829 men and 164 officers. Two days out of Havana, an autumn hurricane scattered the fleet throughout the Gulf of Mexico, and a dejected Gálvez returned to Cuba to prepare again. As winter was ending in late February, the Louisiana governor once more sailed for Pensacola with five warships and more than twenty transports but only 1,315 men; additional troops were to come from New Orleans and Mobile. Unbeknown to Gálvez, his uncle had relieved Lt. Gen. Victorio de Navia y Osorio of command of the Army of Operations on February 21, 1781, and appointed Bernardo to head it with the rank of field marshal.[19]

The Gálvez fleet arrived off Santa Rosa Island, at the entrance to Pensacola Bay, on March 9, and that night the general disembarked his troops on the island. After the frigate *San Ramón* ran aground trying to enter the bay on March 11, the navy refused to try again. A week elapsed before Gálvez, who had direct command of four Louisiana vessels (the brigantine *Galveztown*, the sloop *Valenzuela*, and two armed launches), led them safely across the channel into the bay despite enemy fire from Red Cliffs. The next day, all the ships except the *San Ramón* entered the bay, sustaining only minor damage from enemy fire. Reinforcements from Mobile arrived on March 22 and from New Orleans the next day, giving Gálvez an additional 3,857 troops. Bouligny, on board the *San Francisco de Paula* and in charge of the Louisiana grenadiers, had left New Orleans shortly after February 21. A roster of Louisiana officers made at the time of their departure showed Bouligny at their head.[20]

18. Bernardo de Gálvez to Diego José Navarro, Mobile, March 20, 1780, in AGI, PC, leg. 1232. Estimates of British strength at Pensacola vary. Albert W. Haarmann ("The Siege of Pensacola: An Order of Battle," *Florida Historical Quarterly*, XLIV [1966], 193) places it at 2,000 men; Starr (*Tories*, 192) puts it at between 1,735 and 1,835 men.

19. Caughey, *Gálvez*, 192–98; Everett C. Wilkie, Jr., "New Light on Gálvez's First Attempt to Attack Pensacola," *Florida Historical Quarterly*, LXII (1983), 194–99; José de Gálvez to the intendant of Louisiana, El Pardo, February 12, 1781, in AGI, PC, leg. 603B.

20. F. de Borja Medina Rojas, *José de Ezpeleta, Gobernador de la Mobila, 1780–1781* (Seville, 1980), 676n; William S. Coker and Hazel P. Coker, *The Siege of Pensacola, 1781, in Maps, with Data on Troop Strength, Military Units, Ships, Casualties, and Related Statistics* (Pensa-

On March 23, leaving 200 men on Santa Rosa Island, the remaining Spaniards crossed the bay to the mainland, west of Pensacola. In the next six weeks, despite bad weather and repeated moves to new encampments, Gálvez inched his troops closer to the English positions, particularly the Queen's Redoubt, which was on low-lying Gage Hill overlooking Pensacola. Fort George, the main stronghold, was on lower ground and nearer the town. The Prince of Wales Redoubt was in the center and connected the flanking British posts to each other. On April 19, Spanish and French reinforcements arrived from Havana, bringing 1,600 Spanish and 725 French soldiers and 1,504 sailors. That gave Gálvez a total of 7,686 men under his command. Indian skirmishing and enemy artillery fire hampered the encroaching Spaniards, forcing them to dig trenches to protect themselves and their cannon. Bouligny served in the forward positions, which frequently came under enemy fire. His activities are known in the last phase of the campaign. Francisco de Saavedra noted in his diary for April 26:

Slightly after 3:00 P.M., five companies of grenadiers and chasseurs headed by Mr. Bouligni, captain of the [Louisiana] Fixo, went out to assist the engineers who were to lay out the trench which was to be opened that night. Soon after this operation began, they were attacked by 200 English troops and numerous Indians. [The latter] were within a woods which was on their right with the intent to cut off a company that was very advanced; our men perceived their movement, and some groups were sent with two campaign cannons that forced the Indians to retreat to the English troops, who slowly losing ground, fell back to their half-moon, which commenced a lively artillery fire. Our men, seeing their sally frustrated and that it was getting dark, retired, leaving markers where the trench should be opened.[21]

---

cola, 1981), 109; [Piernas] to Martín Navarro, New Orleans, February 21, 1781, in AGI, PC, leg. 83.

21. A detailed description of Pensacola's defenses is in Stanley Faye, "British and Spanish Fortifications of Pensacola, 1781–1821," *Florida Historical Quarterly*, XX (1942), 277–92. Francisco de Saavedra, Diario (MS in the Colegio de Jesuitas, Málaga, Spain; copy of Francisco Morales Padrón's copy provided by Jack D. L. Holmes). Bernardo de Gálvez's diary (*Diario de las operaciones contra la plaza de Penzacola, 1781* [2nd ed.; Madrid, 1959], 53–55) states, in an entry for the night of April 26–27, that two attempts were made by the Spanish engineers, the first frustrated by an Indian attack and the second by the proximity of dawn and a rainstorm. Eight hundred grenadiers and chasseurs supported the engineers. Other diaries of the Pensacola siege are: "Diario de Panzacola. Diario de lo mas particular

Over the next twelve days, Bouligny, who served in the brigade of Brig. Gen. Jerónimo Girón, rotated his men from the front line to the rear about every other day to eat, rest, and get dry from the drenching rains. The front lines constituted hazardous duty because the enemy might counterattack at any time, as they did on May 4, when Bouligny was absent. The British moved out at 7 A.M. after a cannonade, striking an unprepared Spanish position from the rear. They seized four cannon and inflicted thirty-eight casualties. A determined Gálvez ordered an attack by Girón's unit of seven hundred grenadiers, including Bouligny, on May 7. But the governor postponed it, believing that the enemy had been alerted. The next morning, the usual bombardment began at dawn. About 9 A.M., a Spanish shell burst outside the open door of a powder magazine in the Queen's Redoubt, producing an explosion that destroyed the stronghold, killed seventy-six men outright, and wounded twenty-four more. The Spaniards at first did not realize what had happened but then prepared to move forward.[22]

At that point, Bouligny requested Gálvez's permission to lead one of the columns seizing the redoubt. The first Spanish assault failed, but about 10 A.M. Bouligny and his grenadiers entered the burning fort with flames and exploding bombs all about them. His men threw several enemy mortars into the moat while he personally hauled down the British flag that flew over the redoubt. The Spaniards quickly set up their own artillery pieces, which poured shells on the adjoining Prince of Wales Redoubt, causing many casualties. With the Spaniards on the high ground inflicting mounting losses and with no hope of relief, General Campbell, commandant of Fort George, asked for terms of surrender. After the fighting ended, Bouligny personally presented Gálvez with the captured Union Jack.[23]

---

ocurrido desde el día de nuestra salida del puerto de la Havana," *Archivo del General Miranda, 1750–1785,* I (Caracas, 1929), 150–79, translated by Donald E. Worcester and published as "Miranda's Diary of the Siege of Pensacola, 1781," *Florida Historical Quarterly,* XXIX (1951), 163–95; and James A. Padgett, ed., "Bernardo de Gálvez's Siege of Pensacola in 1781 (as Related in Robert Farmer's Journal)," *Louisiana Historical Quarterly,* XXVI (1943), 311–29.

22. On the British losses suffered at Queen's Redoubt, Gálvez stated (*Diario,* 65) that they numbered 105, while a British report listed 76 dead and 24 wounded, many of whom died (Starr, *Tories,* 209–10).

23. Bouligny petition to the king, New Orleans, July 24, 1784, BB, HNOC; Caughey, *Gálvez,* 209–10.

The next day, Campbell gave up all of West Florida and obtained protection for the noncombatants, the return of slaves to their owners, and the release of the prisoners of war. On May 10, the British marched out of Fort George with military honors. The fighting had produced 90 British dead, 46 wounded, and 953 prisoners, while the Spaniards lost 96 dead and 202 wounded. The victors also reaped a war bounty of nearly 200 large and small cannon, 298 barrels of gunpowder, more than 2,000 fusils, and large quantities of other military equipment. Gálvez sent the prisoners to Havana on June 1, and they departed from there for New York on June 30. Since Gálvez did not keep the bulk of the Spanish forces at Pensacola, Bouligny and the other Louisiana men soon returned to New Orleans. By midsummer, he was home from his last excursion outside the Mississippi Valley.[24]

Bouligny's military services during the war failed to earn him promotion, gaining only entries in his service record for the Mississippi, Mobile, and Pensacola campaigns and pay as lieutenant colonel, despite his brevet rank, for Pensacola. Miró, the most recent arrival and the senior officer in the Louisiana regiment under Gálvez, fared best, as he was aide-de-camp to the governor during the war. Examples of Gálvez's generosity toward others were the rewards for the Mississippi campaign when Miró advanced to permanent lieutenant colonel, Piernas to sergeant major, and Alejandro Cousso, Francisco Xavier de Cruzat, and Carlos de Grand-Pré to brevet lieutenant colonel. Lower-ranking Louisiana regimental and militia officers, sergeants, and cadets also did well: eight advanced to captain, thirteen to lieutenant, and nineteen to sublieutenant. All of this was in addition to the promotions gained by officers in other army units. Looking back in 1794 on his wartime services, Bouligny wryly observed that he had failed to earn one promotion for three campaigns, while almost all the other officers of his rank gained an advancement for participating on a single campaign.[25]

24. Miró to Cagigal, New Orleans, November 2, 1782, in AGI, PC, leg. 1304; Caughey, *Gálvez*, 211–12.

25. Bouligny service sheet, November 25, 1800, BB, HNOC; Royal patents to Bouligny, San Ildefonso and El Pardo, August 23, 1781, and March 11, 1782, respectively, AGI, SD, leg. 2655; Jac Nachbin, ed., "Spain's Report of the War with the British in Louisiana," *Louisiana Historical Quarterly*, XV (1932), 479–80; Bouligny petition to the king, New Orleans, enclosed in Bouligny to the marqués de Someruelos, New Orleans, August 8, 1799, in AGI, PC, leg. 1550. Miró's promotions came quickly; his patents for permanent lieutenant colonel and colonel of the regiment are El Pardo, February 17, 1780, and February 8,

Bouligny nevertheless advanced in seniority in the Louisiana regiment because of the deaths of two men who were listed ahead of him on December 31, 1778. On June 28, 1780, Fernando de Leyba, lieutenant governor of upper Louisiana, died a month after he had successfully defended St. Louis from a British and Indian attack. Also, the demise of Alejandro Cousso on May 12, 1781, made Bouligny captain of grenadiers in the 1st Battalion, an advancement in the chain of command, although he had exercised that function at both Mobile and Pensacola because of Cousso's illness.[26]

By March 1, 1782, when Esteban Miró became acting governor of Louisiana and Pedro Piernas took over as acting commandant of the Louisiana regiment, Bouligny assumed the post of acting sergeant major. He was then the third-ranking officer in the regiment. Gálvez left Louisiana in August, 1781, to continue the war against Britain. Earlier that year he was made captain general of Louisiana (which was separated from Cuba's jurisdiction) and the Floridas, including those areas still to be conquered. After a stay in Havana, he spent the last year of the war in Guarico (Cap François), Haiti, planning a joint Spanish-French invasion of Jamaica that never materialized. After a brief return to Havana at the end of the war, he departed in 1783 for Spain where in July of the next year he was appointed captain general of Cuba. This reunited Louisiana, the Floridas, and Cuba under the same man, but the two separate political jurisdictions continued. The general also received the title of conde de Gálvez from Carlos III. On his return to the Caribbean in early 1785, Gálvez learned that his father, the viceroy of Mexico for the past two years, had died. Knowing that his father was sick, Gálvez had received a promise in Spain to succeed him as viceroy, which he did in June.[27]

1782, respectively (both in AGI, SD, leg. 2654). Bouligny's private letter to the captain general of Cuba contains his feelings on being passed over for promotion (Bouligny to Luis de Las Casas, New Orleans, January 7, 1794, in AGI, PC, leg. 1396).

26. John Francis McDermott, "The Myth of the 'Imbecile Governor': Captain Fernando de Leyba and the Defense of St. Louis in 1780," in *The Spanish in the Mississippi Valley, 1762–1804,* ed. John Francis McDermott (Urbana, Ill., 1974), 314–63. On Cousso's death, see Patent to Bouligny for captain of grenadiers, Aranjuez, May 12, 1782, AGI, PC, leg. 2535, which also contains Bernardo de Gálvez's proposing Bouligny to that post and O'Reilly's approval.

27. Patent to Bouligny as sergeant major and another to Piernas to command the regiment are El Pardo, March 11, 1782, in AGI, SD, leg. 2655. Bouligny wrote to Bernardo de Gálvez on September 17, 1782, thanking him for the post of sergeant major (BB,

The permanent departure of Gálvez from Louisiana in 1781 had brought a sigh of relief from many of the colony's officers. The presence of a governor who with the help of his powerful uncle had risen with lightning speed from colonel to lieutenant general; captain general of Louisiana, the Floridas, and Cuba; and finally viceroy of Mexico left them in awe. He had soared far beyond their own modest expectations, but they realized the influential connections he possessed at court had made it possible. But more disappointing, only those closest to Gálvez— and in the Louisiana regiment chiefly Miró—benefited from participation in the war. The highest promotions went to officers from other army units. Nevertheless, a camaraderie existed among many of the leading Louisiana military and civilian officials. They often spent their evenings at Government House genially chatting over games of cards while their wives and children met at one of the homes to gossip and play. In the small New Orleans community, they all knew each other. Moreover, Bouligny, a Spaniard married to a Creole, had a foot in both social camps.[28]

Bouligny must have enjoyed his brief tenure as acting governor in the fall of 1782. In June, the war not yet ended, Miró led reinforcements from New Orleans to Natchez to defend it against a possible attack from the loyalist band of James Colbert, who refused to honor Campbell's surrender at Pensacola of British West Florida. Colbert seized boats on the Mississippi and unsuccessfully attacked Fort Charles III at Arkansas Post. About October 3, regimental commandant Piernas journeyed upstream to relieve Miró, and Bouligny temporarily assumed command until the governor returned on October 27. Perhaps the recovery of status to a leading regimental officer helped to improve his self-image. But what Bouligny felt about his clash with Gálvez emerged when Juan Ventura Morales of the accounting office sought a reconciliation of the New Iberia expenditures of 1779.[29]

HNOC). Duvon Clough Corbitt, "The Administrative System in the Floridas," *Tequesta*, I (1942), 43. Miró claimed to have become acting governor of Louisiana on February 26, 1782 (Miró to Juan Manuel de Cagigal, New Orleans, February 28, 1782, in AGI, PC, leg. 1304), while Martín Navarro gives the date as March 1 (Navarro to Bernardo de Gálvez, New Orleans, March 26, 1782, in AGI, PC, leg. 83).

28. The more relaxed atmosphere in Louisiana after Bernardo de Gálvez's departure can be seen in numerous documents by Louisiana officials in AGI, PC, legs. 9A, 9B.

29. Bouligny to Cagigal, New Orleans, October 4, 1782, in AGI, PC, leg. 31; Miró to Cagigal, New Orleans, November 2, 1782, *ibid.*, leg. 1304. On Colbert, see Gilbert C. Din,

Gálvez returned to New Orleans after the capture of Pensacola and on July 16 instructed Martín Navarro to audit Bouligny's accounts of New Iberia to make a final settlement. If there was any difficulty, Juan Ventura Morales had his correspondence with Bouligny to assist him. Once a settlement was reached, a certified copy was to be sent by the "*via reservada*" (confidential route) to the minister of the Indies, as the governor had been directed.[30]

With these instructions Navarro initiated the auditing of accounts in 1781, but he was obliged to put them aside. Two years later, Morales resumed the task, examining the expenses made from December 23, 1778, to December 30, 1779, when Bouligny ceased his command at New Iberia. Morales meticulously compiled a list of all the discrepancies in the accounts. Confronted with Morales' unreconciled figures, Bouligny first attempted to answer the queries with the information he had available and then appealed to Gálvez in Havana on May 5, 1783, since he was still the governor of Louisiana.[31]

The lieutenant colonel found it impossible to respond in detail to all of Morales' questions because the records in his home had been destroyed in the 1780 hurricane. His memory failed him as well, since he had studiously attempted "to eradicate all the events of an affair which has caused me so much bitter unpleasantness." But Bouligny sought a decision from Gálvez, since he had served under the governor's immediate orders and believed that he could never make another judge understand the circumstances. The passage of time, the loss of documents, and poor health all combined to render the task impossible. Bouligny continued with his appeal: "With the confidence and certainty I have that you cannot fault me for lack of zeal, vigilance, and integrity, I deserve that you order an end to these accounts. I humbly ask and implore your protection and favor in order that the vestiges of a sorrow, which so

---

"Loyalist Resistance After Pensacola: The Case of James Colbert," in *Anglo-Spanish Confrontation on the Gulf Coast During the American Revolution,* ed. William S. Coker and Robert R. Rea (Pensacola, 1982), 158–76, and "Arkansas Post During the American Revolution," *Arkansas Historical Quarterly,* XL (1981), 3–30.

30. Bernardo de Gálvez to Martín Navarro, New Orleans, July 16, 1781, in AGI, PC, leg. 606; Navarro to José de Gálvez, New Orleans, July 20, 1781, in AGI, SD, leg. 2609.

31. "General Summary formed by Dn. Juan Ventura Morales," New Orleans, March 7, 1783, AGI, PC, leg. 1304; Bouligny to Bernardo de Gálvez, New Orleans, May 5, 1783, *ibid.,* leg. 1393.

many times has brought me to the threshold of death, may be forever obliterated."[32]

Gálvez replied on July 12 that the matter would end according to the order he was sending to Morales and that Bouligny must accept it; otherwise, he had to answer the queries with all the required formality. In Gálvez's exchange of letters with Morales, the governor dismissed a few expenses but stood fast on others, plus the exploration costs, which Bouligny should repay if the court—to which the lieutenant colonel should appeal—rejected the expenditure as legitimate.[33]

Delays then came while Morales attended to the office of accountant of the army, which he temporarily filled after the death of Bernardo Otero, and while Bouligny was in Natchez from June, 1785, to March, 1786. Gálvez too had been busy with other matters, particularly his trip to Spain and his brief sojourn as captain general of Cuba. It was only on July 11, 1785, in Mexico City that he again reviewed the New Iberia accounts and asked Louisiana officials for a resolution. In response, on July 12, 1786, Navarro reminded Bouligny to provide the missing information to put to rest the final accounting. The lieutenant colonel then labored on his figures until October 8, 1786, when he presented Navarro with a receipt from Juan Tala for 181 reales, statements of how other sums of money had been spent, a list of the goods lost in the 1779 spring floods, munitions consumed, and other explanations.[34]

After Navarro received Bouligny's statements and following Gálvez's 1783 recommendation that an appeal should be made to Spain, he sent them to the minister of the Indies. At that time, the Louisiana Treasury, literally bankrupt because of the lack of funds, was also attempting to end aid to the Canary Islander settlements. On February 27, 1787, José de Gálvez judged that Bouligny had to pay the New Iberia explo-

---

32. Bouligny to Bernardo de Gálvez, New Orleans, May 5, 1783, *ibid.*, leg. 1393.

33. Bernardo de Gálvez to Bouligny, Havana, July 12, 1783, *ibid*. As early as July 30, 1779, Bernardo de Gálvez had informed Bouligny that the exploration expenses at New Iberia were not a part of the settlement costs (BN, DL).

34. [Martín Navarro] to Bouligny, New Orleans, July 12, 1786, in AGI, PC, leg. 603A, which has Bernardo de Gálvez's letter of July 11, 1785; Bouligny to Navarro, New Orleans, October 8, 1786, *ibid*. On October 8, 1786, Morales replied to Navarro about New Iberia expense accounts the latter had sent him that Gálvez had left unfinished; Morales offered to close the accounts if Navarro gave him 193 reales (*ibid.*, leg. 606). However, there were other expenses.

ration costs of 364 pesos. The minister's decision made it patent, as had been clear for several years, that Bouligny had lost his protector at court. By the summer of 1787, he seems to have paid the sum. That act brought an end to his New Iberia experience and his affair with Bernardo de Gálvez. Although Bouligny lived for more than twenty years after he left New Iberia, there is no evidence that he visited it again. The settlement struggled on for many years, first under Forstall and later under Jean Baptiste Darby, before its existence was assured. Despite its problems, perhaps Bouligny had the satisfaction of knowing that New Iberia was a far more successful settlement than Galveztown, whose site on the Amite River the governor had personally selected.[35]

Bouligny's contact with Gálvez was limited after Gálvez left Louisiana. In the fall of 1785, after Gálvez had become the viceroy of New Spain, he surrendered the post of Louisiana governor and head of the Louisiana regiment to Miró and Piernas, respectively. Although he retained the captaincy general of Louisiana and the Floridas, which seemed to have become his personal property, as the departing governor, Gálvez furnished the Louisiana officials who had served under him recommendations for their services. Bouligny was in Natchez when they arrived, and Miró, who had become a close friend, wrote a personal note alerting him that Gálvez's recommendation for Bouligny was not as favorable as those for the other officers. Attempting to console him, Miró urged Bouligny not to become melancholy and said that they would have a good chat when he returned to New Orleans. Gálvez's note to Bouligny read: "*Amigo,* Bouligni: The King having deigned to confer on you the post of Lieutenant Colonel of your Regiment due to the promotion to its command of Pedro Piernas, I direct to the Governor of that Plaza (New Orleans) Esteban Miró the corresponding despatch on this grace, which I much celebrate. I congratulate you [and] as I am desirous of repeating it, . . . I will always gladly contribute whenever I have an opportunity." Gálvez added in a postscript his compliments to the ladies (Marie Louise and Mme Vilemont) and "a thousand kisses to Josefina."[36]

35. Navarro to the marqués de Sonora (José de Gálvez), New Orleans, October 31, 1786, in BN, DL; Navarro's letterbook (in AGI, PC, leg. 633) contains a copy of the royal order of February 27, 1787, stating that Bouligny had to pay 2,912 reales. The exploration expenses are in "Account of the expenses caused by the three voyages made by Juan Bau.ta Grevemberg . . . ," (BN, DL).

36. [Miró] to Bouligny, [New Orleans, 1785], in AGI, PC, leg. 117B; Corbitt, "Administrative System," 43; Bernardo de Gálvez to Bouligny, Mexico City, October 24, 1785, in

Thus in this seemingly disarming way that showed the Gálvez charm, Bouligny received what was probably his last direct communication from the former governor. As Gálvez rose in rank and position, his affair with Bouligny diminished in significance. Nevertheless, despite his profession of friendship, Gálvez did nothing to help Bouligny's career. He gained the post of regimental lieutenant colonel because of seniority, not because of the viceroy's benevolence.

A year and a half after Bouligny received the recommendation, almost at the same time that the final conclusion of the New Iberia accounts was made in Spain, news arrived in New Orleans of the demise of Bernardo de Gálvez on November 30, 1786, in Mexico City. While Bouligny had struggled in Louisiana to overcome the damage inflicted on his reputation, Gálvez's meteoric career played itself out, ten years after its phenomenal rise had begun. His death, however, brought no consolation. The harm to Bouligny had been done. Although the memory of his experience as lieutenant governor under Gálvez haunted him for years, Bouligny strove in the 1780s to vindicate his honor and to serve to the best of his ability. In doing so, he soon found himself at the center of another important event in the history of Spanish Louisiana.[37]

KCTU. Some time in 1785, Marie Louise Bouligny wrote a letter of congratulations to Bernardo de Gálvez on his appointment as viceroy; he in turn sent her a thank-you note (Gálvez to Madame d'Auberville Bouligny, [Mexico City], September 25, 1785, in BB, HNOC). Possibly her husband did not feel like congratulating Gálvez.

37. On Bouligny's bitterness, see his letter to Las Casas, New Orleans, January 7, 1794, in AGI, PC, leg. 1394.

7

ACTING GOVERNOR BOULIGNY CONFRONTS THE *CIMARRÓN* MENACE

AT THE CONCLUSION of the war against Britain at age forty-seven, Francisco Bouligny still toiled as a brevet lieutenant colonel, since he had not risen in rank since 1777. His connections in Spain had failed to shelter him, and abandoning political aspirations, he devoted himself to his army duties. He was the sergeant major in the Fixed Louisiana Regiment, third-ranking officer after Pedro Piernas, the acting commandant, and Governor Miró, the real commandant. Bouligny got along well with both his superiors. More importantly, he no longer suffered from the humiliation that he had experienced at the hands of Gálvez. As sergeant major, Bouligny was a fixture at regimental headquarters in New Orleans. His permanent assignment in the provincial capital permitted him to enjoy comforts and opportunities that none of the commandants stationed at the remote posts possessed.

The end of the war should have ushered in an era of stability in Louisiana that would have allowed it to develop unhindered. That, however, did not happen. Instead the province exchanged the menace of the British in West Florida for controversy and possible aggression from the newly independent United States. The conclusion of the war left the boundary of West Florida confused because Britain negotiated different terms with Spain and the United States. The British recognized Spanish ownership of both East and West Florida, although without fixed boundaries. But with the American delegates to the peace conference intent on deriving the best territorial advantages, Britain ceded to the United States the east bank of the Mississippi to the thirty-first parallel, including lands the Spaniards had conquered in the war. However, if by some unexplained reason Britain retained West Florida, then the boundary was to be 32° 26' north latitude, approximately at the mouth of the Yazoo River on the Mississippi.[1]

Spain continued to occupy West Florida and claimed lands as far north as the mouths of the Ohio and Tennessee rivers and as far east as the Appalachian Mountains. The Spaniards felt more certain about the east bank of the Mississippi River up to the Yazoo River—in other words, West Florida. The terms of the Anglo-American treaty, however, baffled the Spaniards. They failed to understand how Britain could give away, and the United States accept, territory occupied by a third nation. They felt confident, nonetheless, that their minister to the United States in 1785, Diego Gardoqui, would secure a satisfactory boundary settlement or at the very least West Florida. Meanwhile, by the royal order of June 26, 1784, they officially prohibited the entry of Americans in West Florida and closed navigation of the Mississippi to them. British residents of West Florida received eighteen months to depart, later extended by four months. For the Spaniards, the postwar era meant restructuring control of their North American possessions to deal with the new problems at hand, particularly their relations with the Southern Indians: Creeks, Choctaws, and Chickasaws.[2]

Bouligny's first duties as sergeant major dated from August, 1782, when he replaced the acting sergeant major Tomás de Acosta, a junior officer. The post involved army paperwork, since he kept the *libretas* (booklets) of the enlisted men in the regiment, which contained information on their service and conduct, and prepared the *estados* (statements of troop strength). He kept track of soldiers in the companies—deaths, discharges, pay records, and funds for the soldiers' mess (*rancho*). Offi-

1. Arthur Preston Whitaker, *The Spanish American Frontier, 1783–1795: The Westward Movement and the Spanish Retreat in the Mississippi Valley* (1927; rpr. Glouster, Mass., 1962); Samuel Flagg Bemis, *Pinckney's Treaty: America's Advantage from Europe's Distress, 1783–1800* (1926; rev. ed., New Haven, 1960), 1–148.

2. José de Gálvez to the governor of Louisiana, Aranjuez, June 26, 1784, in AGI, PC, leg. 2360; Petition of Harris Alexander and eleven others, New Orleans, March 1, 1785, and the conde de Gálvez to Miró, Havana, April 15, 1785, both *ibid.*, leg. 11. The Spanish government's instructions to Diego Gardoqui of October 2, 1784, are in AHN, Est., leg. 3885, exped. 21. See also José de Gálvez to Gardoqui of the same day, in AHN, Est., leg. 3894, exped. 1. Gardoqui waited in Havana from January, 1785, for Bernardo de Gálvez to return from Spain; he received instructions from Gálvez on April 28, 1785 (AHN, Est., leg. 3885, exped. 6).

cers above the rank of lieutenant participated in councils of war, and Bouligny presided over a council that investigated the killing of a corporal by Lt. Carlos de Reggio. Bouligny had learned much about processing paperwork since his run-in with Estachería nine years earlier. By December, 1782, he was informing Nicolas DeLassize, the junior officer who prepared the *estados,* that as "they are the most authentic documents it is necessary that they are made up with complete accuracy." Other duties of Bouligny included personnel assignments to the detachments, troop details in New Orleans, and the dispatch of arms, supplies, and money to the outposts. The 1st Battalion had detachments at Balize, Galveztown, Bayou St. John, Manchac, Baton Rouge, Natchez, Arkansas, and St. Louis.[3]

In October, 1782, Bouligny briefly acted as governor, the first time he had exercised that post since 1777. His major preoccupation during his twenty-four-day tenure was safeguarding Galveztown against the possibility of an Indian attack. The dispatch of a few soldiers and the knowledge that the Indians had never assaulted a fort or settlement in lower Louisiana precluded taking greater measures.[4]

An important function of the Louisiana officers was keeping up the strength of the regiment, which now also had West Florida to protect. With the war ended in 1783, the Spaniards withdrew units not assigned to Louisiana or West Florida. The Louisiana 2nd Battalion replaced soldiers of the Príncipe and España regiments in Pensacola and Mobile while the Fixed Havana and Navarra regiments in New Orleans also prepared to leave. Bouligny reported on September 25, 1783, that the Fixed Louisiana Regiment lacked 190 men, although Gálvez had attempted to bring it to full strength by sending new troops from Cuba and allowing soldiers from other units to transfer to the regiment. Gálvez did this shortly before departing from Cuba for Spain, where he reported at length on conditions in the Gulf of Mexico, leaving Juan Manuel de Cagigal as acting captain general. The two Louisiana battalions were

3. Piernas to Nicolas DeLassize, New Orleans, August 27, 1782, and Bouligny to DeLassize, New Orleans, December 18, 1782, both in AGI, PC, leg. 126; Miró to José de Ezpeleta, New Orleans, August 8, 1784, *ibid.,* leg. 1394. DeLassize, a militiaman, was acting sergeant major in 1782; he died in February, 1789, as adjutant of the New Orleans militia (Miró to Ezpeleta, New Orleans, February 12, 1789, *ibid.*).

4. Bouligny to Juan Manuel de Cagigal, New Orleans, October 3, 1782, and Miró to Cagigal, New Orleans, November 2, 1782, both *ibid.,* leg. 1304.

authorized 1,377 *plazas* (slots), and on May 1, 1784, they still needed 199 men. Discharge, death, desertion, and imprisonment constantly sapped the strength of the regiment, and it needed new men to keep up its full allotment; local recruitment yielded few soldiers. Service in the army was long (eight years), pay low, discipline often harsh, and assignments frequently tedious. In recognition of the difficulty of enlisting men locally, on August 20, 1784, the minister of the Indies sent a royal order announcing that a recruiting team under Lt. Juan de San Saudens (Saint Saudens) had been established in Pamplona, Spain, to enlist men for the Louisiana regiment.[5]

In addition to being the sergeant major, Bouligny acted as the regimental lieutenant colonel, or second in command, entrusted with the 1st Battalion. In 1783 and 1784, the regiment's 2nd Battalion transferred to Pensacola and Mobile. The governor of Pensacola and commandant of the 2nd Battalion, Col. Arturo O'Neill, at one point attempted to break his subordination to the Louisiana governor by reporting directly to the captain general in Havana. Miró protested O'Neill's misconduct, and Gálvez upheld him as in charge of both Louisiana and West Florida. In an emergency, the Pensacola commandant could correspond directly with Havana, but the New Orleans governor was still his immediate superior. In 1799, Bouligny encountered the same subordination from the Pensacola commandant when he was acting governor.[6]

In the late spring of 1784, circumstances gave Bouligny an opportunity to demonstrate his executive ability. In May and June, 1784, Governor Miró and Intendant Martín Navarro journeyed to Pensacola and Mobile to hold congresses with the natives. Soon after the war, the Spaniards, recognizing the importance of the natives, tried to gain the friend-

5. Miró to the conde de Gálvez, New Orleans, August 20, 1783, *ibid.,* leg. 2; Bouligny, "Notice of the Reduction that this Regiment has on this date," New Orleans, September 25, 1783, *ibid.,* leg. 1377; Miró to Ezpeleta, New Orleans, July 4, 20, August 20, 1783, all *ibid.,* leg. 1377; Bouligny, "Relation of the Strength of the Louisiana Regiment," New Orleans, May 1, 1784, *ibid.,* leg. 10; Bernardo de Gálvez to Miró, Havana, March 1, 1785, with a copy of José de Gálvez's royal order enclosed, *ibid.,* leg. 11. AGI, PC, leg. 117A, contains a number of Bouligny letters as sergeant major to the commandant of Arkansas Post Jacobo Dubreuil.

6. Conde de Gálvez to Arturo O'Neill, Havana, May 1, 1785, *ibid.,* leg. 11. For a biographical sketch of O'Neill, see Eric Beerman, "Arturo O'Neill: First Governor of West Florida During the Second Spanish Period," *Florida Historical Quarterly,* LX (1981), 29–41. On Bouligny's 1799 problem as acting governor, see Chapter 11.

ship of and control over the Southern Indians. Friendly natives and their lands would serve as a barrier to keep the Americans as far away from Spanish territories as possible. It should be remembered that Bouligny had advocated improved relations and periodic congresses with the Indians in his *Memoria* of 1776. But supplying them with trade goods, particularly arms and gunpowder, was essential for their cooperation. However, it quickly became evident that Spain could not furnish the goods the Indians wanted, and the trade was turned over to British firms, first to Mather and Strother, later to Panton, Leslie and Company. Because regimental commandant Piernas was also absent from New Orleans, Bouligny received charge of the province in early May, 1784. This time he would fill that office for two and a half months.[7]

Bouligny substituted for the governor at a time when *cimarrones* (escaped slaves) plagued lower Louisiana. Runaway bondsmen had long infested Louisiana, but they had become numerous during the recent war despite a hostile environment. Since they were surrounded by swamps, marshes, bayous, and dense forests, there was little likelihood of successful flight. What, then, impelled them to attempt the impossible? The reason seems to have been inhumane treatment by their owners, reflected in the abusive French Code Noir that Louisiana employed until 1769. Although O'Reilly introduced Spanish slave laws, French slaveholders continued much as before.[8]

In September, 1782, the first tentative measures against the runaways were taken, but the problem grew worse through 1783. A Cabildo junta on April 29, 1784, attracted a large planter crowd that drew up new regulations for the conduct of slaves and punishment for their misconduct. Two days later, Governor Miró issued a *bando* for their behavior based on Cabildo regulations. Upon leaving for the Indian congresses on May 5, Miró charged the Cabildo with maintaining good order and left

7. William S. Coker and Thomas D. Watson, *Indian Traders of the Southeastern Spanish Borderlands: Paton, Leslie & Company and John Forbes & Company* (Pensacola, 1986), 58–63. On Bouligny's 1776 recommendations to hold Indian congresses, see Din, *Louisiana in 1776*, 65–68.

8. See Jo Ann Carrigan's commentary on blacks and runaways in Alcée Fortier, *History*, II, 378–91, and Juan José Andreu Ocariz, *Movimientos rebeldes de los esclavos negros durante el dominio español en Luisiana* (Zaragoza, Spain, 1977). On the brutality of the French slave code, see Joe Gray Taylor, *Negro Slavery in Louisiana* (Baton Rouge, 1963), and James Thomas McGowan, "Creation of a Slave Society: Louisiana Plantations in the Eighteenth Century" (Ph.D. dissertation, University of Rochester, 1976).

Bouligny as military governor and Francisco María de Reggio, a Cabildo magistrate (*alcalde ordinario*), as civil governor. It thus fell upon Bouligny to deal with the *cimarrón* question and the murderous San Malo band. The Cabildo, which represented many of the plantation and slave owners, exerted enormous pressure on Bouligny to secure their ends.[9]

May, 1784, was filled with Cabildo demands for vigorous action. On May 18, Bouligny met with the officials of the New Orleans militia, and he entrusted command of that body to Henriques Depres. Gilbert Antoine de St. Maxent, the nominal militia commandant, had been under house arrest since March 9, accused of smuggling and suspended as lieutenant governor to supply the Indians. Gálvez's grand design for his father-in-law in the potentially lucrative Indian trade had thus ended dismally. The militia would assist regular soldiers in expeditions against the runaways. On May 20, with the capture of the fugitive Pierre, who belonged to Guido Dufossat, Bouligny learned that the San Malo band of twenty to twenty-five men had taken refuge in the inhospitable "Land of Gaillarde," between the Mississippi and Lake Borgne. Bouligny immediately ordered Capt. Gilberto Guillemard, the New Orleans militia adjutant major, to head an expedition to that area to capture several runaways whose hideout had been revealed. By May 21, Bouligny reported to Miró that the expedition had failed but that the San Malo band was now confined to the Gaillarde area. He proposed to defeat it by launching a major expedition against it.[10]

If the governor approved, Bouligny suggested a two-hundred-peso reward and emancipation for the slave who killed San Malo. He also proposed rewards for apprehending three other members of the band—Michel, Philippe, and Etienne. Knowledge of the band's killing of five American inhabitants from Bay St. Louis drove the Cabildo to near hys-

9. Actas del Cabildo, September 20, 27, 1782 (Microfilm of WPA typescripts in Spanish in New Orleans Public Library), II, fols. 135–36, 136–38. The Cabildo band of April 30, 1784, is *ibid.*, II, fols. 207–209, while Miró's band of May 1, 1784, is in AGI, PC, leg. 3A. On Miró's departure from New Orleans, see Actas del Cabildo, May 14, 1784, II, fols. 209–10, and Bouligny to Jacobo Dubreuil, New Orleans, May 6, 1784, in AGI, PC, leg. 10.

10. Bouligny to Miró, New Orleans, May 18–21, 1784, in AGI, PC, leg. 10. Bernardo de Gálvez ordered his father-in-law, St. Maxent, suspended from his posts and placed under city arrest, and imposed an embargo on his goods and papers; Juan Ventura Morales received charge of Indian affairs (Bernardo de Gálvez to Miró, Madrid, December 27, 1783, *ibid.*, leg. 9B). For San Malo, see Gilbert C. Din, "*Cimarrones* and the San Malo Band in Spanish Louisiana," *Louisiana History*, XXI (1980), 237–62, and Burson, *Miró*, 113–18.

teria. It claimed that runaways had never before had the temerity to shed white blood. The Cabildo asserted, probably with considerable exaggeration, that plantations had been abandoned and that fields lay uncultivated. Besides murdering the Bay St. Louis whites, the band at different times had killed four Englishmen and several black retainers. The Cabildo nervously alleged that the runaways were attempting to stage a general slave insurrection and petitioned Bouligny to send a massive expedition to apprehend the San Malo band. Miró, however, rejected the increased expenditures that a major expedition entailed, but he neither felt the pressure nor experienced the emotional state of the Cabildo and the whites of lower Louisiana. Nevertheless, he permitted Bouligny to be guided by circumstance, thus not ruling out a costly expedition.[11]

Bouligny continued with plans for a massive strike against the fugitives, which the Cabildo urged because of the killings of whites and blacks. Since all of lower Louisiana appeared to be swarming with runaways, Bouligny sent out a number of small detachments to apprehend them. They seized two dozen *cimarrones* by June 3. The large expedition of approximately one hundred men departed on June 2 under Captain Guillemard to the Land of Gaillarde. There they broke up into smaller units and followed the waterways that penetrated the forbidding region of swamps and marshes. Bouligny also dispatched groups into other areas where *cimarrones* were thought to be, to set ambushes. He issued circular letters to the planters to double the guards on their storehouses and pirogues and send out loyal slaves to search the forests that runaways frequented.[12]

Success seemed to be at hand when Lt. Pierre DeMarigny's party in the Land of Gaillarde caught four runaways sent by San Malo to steal food and spy on the militia patrols. One of the four fugitives was Bastien, a spy recruited by Miró, who revealed the whereabouts of San Malo. Excited by the news, DeMarigny paused only long enough to pen Bouligny a note on his good fortune before rushing on to capture the *cimarrón* ringleader in the vicinity of Lake Borgne. His men, however, fired prematurely when they sighted the cabins of the hideout, wounding one

11. Bouligny to Miró, New Orleans, May 18–21 and June 19, 1784, in AGI, PC, leg. 10; Miró to Bouligny, Pensacola, May 28, [1784], *ibid.,* leg. 3A; Actas del Cabildo, May 28, 1784, II, fols. 213–15.

12. Bouligny to Miró, New Orleans, June 13, 1784, in AGI, PC, leg. 10. The Cabildo demanded action again on June 4 (Actas del Cabildo, June 4, 1784, II, fols. 215–17).

runaway and permitting the others to escape. Upon learning of De-Marigny's bungling, Bouligny was furious at him for wanting the sole honor for capturing the San Malo band and ordered DeMarigny removed from the command of his party. Nevertheless, Bouligny left Guillemard in that area, certain that the *cimarrones* were still there.[13]

Only three days later came the apprehension of San Malo and the greater part of his band. Capt. Baptista Hugon found the trail of the fugitives and informed Guillemard, who sent five pirogues filled with soldiers and militiamen. They came upon the encampment of the runaways and this time succeeded in capturing nearly all the *cimarrones,* including San Malo. Guillemard led a triumphal parade of pirogues up the Mississippi, past plantations that cheered the expedition's success, and reached New Orleans on June 12. A large multitude awaited their arrival, including the auxiliary bishop of Cuba, Cirilo de Barcelona, who watched from a balcony on Bouligny's riverfront house. Bouligny and his family were probably also there. The Cabildo insisted on swift punishment for the fugitives, most of whom were guilty only of running away.[14]

In recognition of the brutal treatment of slaves, Bouligny sent the planters a circular letter to improve their conduct. As he explained in a message to Governor Miró on June 14: "I . . . recommend[ed] to [the planters] to always conserve and uphold on their plantations the most exact policy of treating their blacks with kindness and humanity which they are obliged to do. I have much advocated the preservation [of the slaves] because I know there are some [planters] who deserve to be severely censured in this matter." Bouligny here acknowledged that slavery in Louisiana was harsher than "existing in name only," as he had written in his *Memoria* eight years earlier.[15]

In New Orleans, Reggio, as chief magistrate, received the captured *cimarrones* and quickly tried those who had murdered whites. His chief witness was San Malo, who developed gangrene after being shot during his capture. Repentant for his misdeeds, he implicated in the murders

13. Bouligny to Miró, New Orleans, June 9, 14, 1784, both in AGI, PC, leg. 10. Miró was also angry at DeMarigny; he ordered Bouligny to investigate his conduct and arrest him if it was warranted ([Miró] to Bouligny, Mobile, June 23, 1784, *ibid.,* leg. 117A).

14. Bouligny to Miró, New Orleans, two letters of June 14, 1784, *ibid.,* leg. 10; Actas del Cabildo, June 11, 1784, II, fols. 217–19; Burson, *Miró,* 116.

15. Bouligny to Miró, New Orleans, June 14, 1784, in AGI, PC, leg. 10.

Joly Coeur (the "Knight of the Axe"), Henry, and Michel, all of whom eventually confessed. Within a week of their jailing in New Orleans, Reggio concluded his investigation and sentenced the culprits. San Malo, his three accomplices, and his companion, the free woman Cecilia Canoy (whose only crime was consorting with fugitives), all received death sentences. The hangings were carried out on June 19, except for Cecilia, who claimed to be pregnant, in the Plaza de Armas before a large crowd. The other fugitives received punishment of two hundred or three hundred lashes, branding on the cheek with an *M* (for *maroon*), carrying a twelve-pound shackle for three months, or banishment from Louisiana. A number of female fugitives were also punished with flogging, branding, and shackles. Bouligny claimed that a total of 120 slaves had been apprehended.[16]

Once the prisoners were in Reggio's hands, Bouligny surrendered responsibility. He was present, however, when San Malo testified, and he was impressed by his qualities as a leader, his natural eloquence, and his able group. Bouligny wrote down much of the testimony of San Malo. It is the only record that provides an insight into his personality.[17]

Bouligny also stayed out of the dispute that arose between Reggio and Barcelona, the auxiliary bishop. The quarrel stemmed from Reggio's sentence of two hundred lashes for Batista, a runaway slave who belonged to the Capuchins. Barcelona had claimed a privilege (*fuero*) for Batista, thus intending to put the slave beyond Reggio's jurisdiction. The magistrate, however, rejected the contention and regarded himself as competent to punish Batista. Barcelona then took revenge by refusing to hear the confessions of the condemned at the gallows, alleging that their spiritual needs had been attended to in prison. The callous attitude of the bishop and clergy shocked the New Orleans populace. The Cabildo

---

16. Bouligny to Miró, New Orleans, June 19, 1784, *ibid.;* "Criminal proceedings against fugitive slaves for shooting at arresting expedition and for running away from their owners," LHC, Judicial Records for the Spanish Cabildo, March 12, 1783, fols. 196–98. Reggio's unfairness in wanting to execute Cecilia Canoy for merely being San Malo's woman is seen in "Suspension of the death sentence imposed on Cecilia, based on report by the surgeons," LHC, Spanish Judicial Records, March 12, 1783, fols. 199–200). Miró perhaps intervened in time to save her life; see Miró to Bernardo de Gálvez, New Orleans, October 1, 1784, in AGI, PC, leg. 3A, and Gálvez to Miró, Havana, April 16, 1785, in AGI, PC, leg. 11.

17. Bouligny to Miró, New Orleans, June 19, 1784, in AGI, PC, leg. 10.

protested Barcelona's outrageous behavior to the crown through the bishop of Cuba, Barcelona's superior. The Cuban bishop, however, returned the protest, stating that he was not the proper channel to the crown. More than a year later, Gálvez censured the Cabildo for its disrespect of Barcelona. Perhaps Gálvez remembered with appreciation that Barcelona had officiated at the governor's small and informal wedding in 1777, which was held without the required royal approval.[18]

While not involved in the church-state controversy, both Bouligny and Miró had learned through experience about Reggio's contentious personality. In June, 1784, the magistrate occupied the room in Government House, used by the Spanish school of New Orleans, to interrogate the runaways. On July 9, after the investigation had ended, Bouligny gave Reggio Miró's order of July 5 to evacuate the room, since school had been suspended while he used it. Miró's problem with Reggio commenced the previous February over disrespect shown to Barcelona. It was not Reggio's only failing. On September 13, Miró upbraided him for being disrespectful to the governor too. Reggio waited nearly a month before replying, suggesting that perhaps both of them were wrong, and he pledged to be subordinate when he was ordered by the governor's tribunal. But he insisted that in other cases he was the colony's highest magistrate. That assertion probably failed to impress Miró, the chief civil and military administrator in Louisiana.[19]

On July 5, the governor wrote to Bouligny from Mobile approving the apprehension of so many runaways and the sentences imposed on those who had been tried. He would dole out punishment to the rest of

18. Bouligny reported the church-state controversy in his letters to Miró, New Orleans, June 19, 22, and July 9, 1784 (*ibid.*); additional documents are in AGI, PC, leg. 1375. See also Actas del Cabildo, June 25, 1784, II, fol. 219, with enclosures; Cirilo de Barcelona to Francisco María de Reggio, June 19, 1784, in Actas de Cabildo, II, fol. 220; Reggio to Barcelona, June 19, 1784, in Actas de Cabildo, II, fol. 221; Reggio to the Cabildo, June 25, July 1, 1784, in Actas de Cabildo, II, fols. 221–25, and III, fol. 1, respectively, with enclosures; New Orleans Cabildo to the king, June 26, 1784, in Actas de Cabildo, III, fols. 1–2; the Bishop of Cuba to the New Orleans Cabildo, October 4, 1784, in Actas de Cabildo, III, fol. 24; Bernardo de Gálvez to Miró, Mexico City, December 24, 1785, in AGI, PC, leg. 2360.

19. Barcelona to Miró, New Orleans, February 12, 1784, in AGI, PC, leg. 2360; Bouligny to Reggio, New Orleans, July 9, 1784, *ibid.*, leg. 10; [Miró] to Reggio, [New Orleans], September 13, 1784, *ibid.*, leg. 10; Reggio to Miró, New Orleans, October 10, 1784, *ibid.*, leg. 11. Reggio died in New Orleans on October 5, 1787.

them on his return to New Orleans. He mildly scolded Bouligny for failing to help Bishop Barcelona, who had complained to Gálvez. But Miró was not upset with Bouligny. He concluded his letter: "Friend, he who governs is exposed to being right in what is essential, and you have acted with total correctness and prudence. It is only in a friendly way that I tell you what I feel about the above-mentioned point, all of which does not diminish the affection that I profess for you and for all your family. I offer myself, with my Céleste [Miró's wife], to be at your disposal."[20]

Despite approving Bouligny's conduct in the *cimarrón* crisis, when Governor Miró returned to New Orleans, he raised questions on August 23, which Bouligny replied to on the following day. Miró had been in opposition to heavy expenditures, but the planters had agreed to defray all the costs for the expeditions. Bouligny was satisfied with the measures, which captured numerous runaways, including three ringleaders. He had worked in concert with the planters, informing them of police measures and costs and charging them with vigilance. He had also kept in touch with the Cabildo about his actions. His efforts, carried out within the parameters of Miró's orders, met "with the most happy and complete success." Although the Cabildo and the planters failed to satisfy immediately all the costs for the expeditions, the reduction of the *cimarrón* danger and punishment for the murderers of whites helped to soothe the nervous planters. Nevertheless, the runaway problem in Louisiana would last as long as slavery endured.[21]

On June 14, after Guillemard's return to New Orleans with the captured *cimarrones,* Bouligny named the officers and men of the expeditions who were worthy of receiving a royal reward: militia captain Guillemard; Lieutenant DeMarigny, who had improved his conduct; SubLts. Nicolas Olivier, Pedro Olivier, Felix Trudeau, Francisco Dutillet, and Carlos de Villiers; Sgt2c. Angel Ruiz, a corporal, and twenty grenadiers; cadets Pedro Larronde and Luis Lalande; and captain of mulattoes Baptista Hugon.[22]

But Miró set aside the recommendations and made his own. He praised Bouligny, Guillemard, Nicolas Olivier and his slave Bastien, and Sergeant Ruiz. He recommended that Olivier be given the rank of sub-

20. Miró to Bouligny, Mobile, July 5, 1784, *ibid.,* leg. 11.
21. Bouligny to Miró, New Orleans, August 24, 1784, *ibid.,* leg. 10.
22. Bouligny to Miró, New Orleans, June 14, 1784, *ibid.*

lieutenant in the army with half pay, and Ruiz, who was already being promoted to sergeant first class, be given a pay increase. All the military personnel on the expeditions were to have an entry made in their service record listing their participation as a military campaign; it included Bouligny. The crown accepted Miró's recommendations.[23]

Bouligny, however, used the opportunity to initiate on July 26 a petition for promotion to the rank of colonel. To create a more attractive appearance at court, he had the petition printed. In supporting his request, Bouligny cited his wartime service on the Mississippi, at Mobile, at Pensacola, and his recent accomplishments, particularly the crushing of the *cimarrón* menace. It was the first of several attempts to win advancement. Miró received the petition and wrote his endorsement. He affirmed as true Bouligny's heroism at Baton Rouge and Pensacola, which he had personally witnessed. As for the *cimarrones,* the governor wrote, "[Bouligny] put in practice with much haste, activity, and accuracy the dispositions I left him in charge of, and he achieved them as he states. . . . He is an officer of talent, valor, and much application, for which I believe him meritorious of the grace that he solicites from your Majesty's piety."[24]

Bouligny's petition probably followed the usual routing—to Cuba, where it remained for months awaiting the arrival of the new captain general of that island, Gálvez, who probably ignored it during his stay there from February 4 to May 15, 1785. His replacement forwarded it to Spain for a decision. But there was little likelihood that the crown would advance Bouligny to colonel ahead of Piernas or to the same rank as the governor in a system that relied heavily on seniority. Nevertheless, the army and its chiefs had been remiss in failing to promote the leading figures in the Louisiana regiment during the war, principally Bouligny and Piernas.

Only when Gálvez returned to Havana and was soon raised to viceroy to succeed his dead father did promotions go to the top Louisiana officers. The promotions, however, were due to seniority, not royal recognition of meritorious service. Gálvez gave up his posts of governor of Louisiana (he was no longer referred to as captain general of Louisiana and West Florida) and captain general of Cuba, but he still retained su-

23. Miró to Gálvez, New Orleans, July 13, 1784, *ibid.,* leg. 3A.

24. Bouligny petition to the king, New Orleans, July 26, 1784, KCTU; [Miró's] statement on Bouligny's petition to the king, [New Orleans], August 1, 1784, AGI, PC, leg. 117A.

perior authority over the two provinces. Therefore, on April 22, 1785, he recommended that Miró become the proprietary governor of Louisiana, Piernas the colonel of the regiment, Bouligny the lieutenant colonel, and Enrique White the sergeant major—this on the basis of seniority. In Cuba, Ezpeleta became the captain general. By July 13, the patents were filled out, and the promotions were soon dispatched to Gálvez in Mexico to forward to Louisiana. In this manner Bouligny achieved the rank of permanent lieutenant colonel.[25]

While he failed to receive royal recognition for his services as acting governor during the *cimarrón* threat, Bouligny nevertheless enjoyed the appreciation of his fellow officers, particularly that of Governor Miró. The next year, Miró showed his confidence in Bouligny by appointing him as the commandant of Natchez during a crisis that shook the tranquillity of the Spaniards in the Mississippi Valley.

25. José de Gálvez to the conde de Gálvez, Madrid, July 20, 1785 (AGI, PC, leg. 1375), mentions Gálvez's proposals of April 22, 1785. Bouligny's patent of promotion of July 13, 1785, to lieutenant colonel is in AGI, PC, leg. 570A, and AGI, SD, leg. 2655. By December 1, 1785, Miró had the patents in New Orleans; see his note, New Orleans, December 1, 1785, AGI, PC, leg. 198A.

BOULIGNY'S EXPERIENCE AS acting governor in 1784 revealed his competence to handle that office. The *cimarrón* problem had earned him praise and improved his self-image. He soon proved his ability again as commandant of the Natchez district, a region that became a lightning rod for Spanish troubles on the Mississippi. The 1785 crisis over Natchez was the start of many years of difficulties with the United States. Cognizant that two battalions of the Fixed Louisiana Regiment were inadequate to guard both Louisiana and West Florida against foreign aggression, on June 24, 1785, Gálvez, now viceroy of New Spain, urged his uncle to increase the regiment to three battalions. By November 17, the crown had approved the creation of the third battalion, which was to be stationed in Pensacola and its dependencies, Mobile, and, after 1787, San Marcos de Apalache. Meanwhile, the 2nd Battalion returned to New Orleans to assist the 1st Battalion in guarding the Mississippi River.[1]

The most persistent threat to Spanish Louisiana grew immediately after the war when Americans began crossing the Appalachian Mountains in large numbers. Some of them continued down the rivers to the Mississippi and to West Florida despite the illegality of such movements. Miró allowed Catholics, agricultural laborers, and mechanics to settle there if they took an oath of fidelity; those who refused were to be forced out. Still, their influx into Spanish territory, coupled with the Anglo-Americans who already resided there, worried Spanish officials. Where Spain owned both banks, the government closed the Mississippi River to outsiders in June, 1784. Nearly a year later, on March 18, 1785, Miró

---

1. Marqués de Sonora (José de Gálvez) to the conde de Gálvez, San Lorenzo, November 17, 1785 (AGI, PC, leg. 1375), mentions the conde's June 24, 1785, proposal for a third battalion.

consulted Gálvez, who had recently returned to Cuba from Spain, about the foreign settlers. Gálvez believed that allowing Americans to settle on Spanish lands was dangerous, since it "would be to gather up enemies in our territory." Evicting them by ship via Balize was an extravagance the Treasury could ill afford, and forcing them to return upriver was an impossibility. He ended by advising Miró to consult Spain on this dilemma. Officially, Gálvez was against the Anglo-Americans remaining on Spanish soil if they refused to take up arms against Britain in case of war; nevertheless, he permitted them to stay.[2]

In the Natchez district, a few Americans favored U.S. control, as the 1783 U.S.-British treaty had stipulated. One of them was the outspoken George Rapalje, whom Governor Miró advised Bvt. Lt. Col. Felipe Treviño, commandant of Fort Panmure and the Natchez district, to put under surveillance in late 1784 or early 1785. Rapalje had entered the district illegally in 1781 after the Spanish conquest and had refused to take the oath of allegiance despite receiving lands and other benefits from the Spaniards. Treviño arrested Rapalje on February 6, 1785, after James Elliot, another Natchez resident, accused him of plotting rebellion with forty-nine cohorts, hiding eight hundred pounds of gunpowder, and seeking the assistance of the Choctaw and Chickasaw Indians. Treviño took testimony from witnesses and sent his findings and the accused to New Orleans about March 4. The Elliot charges, if true, were serious, but Treviño failed to uncover proof of Rapalje's guilt. To get at the truth, on March 19 Miró entrusted Bouligny with investigating the testimony to determine Rapalje's culpability.[3]

Bouligny consumed nearly a month poring over the conflicting and often puzzling evidence before rendering a judgment. He rejected the testimony of Sutton Banks and Parker Caradine, who did not agree with Elliot on all points and were probably eager to please Spanish authorities. All suspicions about Rapalje had originated with Elliot, a man Treviño had enlisted to spy on Rapalje and was hostile to him. Nor was there positive evidence about the forty-nine conspirators, the gunpowder, or the Indian auxiliaries. Convinced that the accusations were

2. Piernas to Miró, Natchez, May 31, 1783; Miró to Felipe Treviño, New Orleans, September 15, 1783; Treviño to Miró, Natchez, October 17, 1783, all *ibid.*, leg. 9B; Conde de Gálvez to Miró, Havana, April 23, 1785, in AGI, PC, leg. 11.

3. Burson, *Miró,* 24–25; Laura L. Porteous, "Index to the Spanish Judicial Records," *Louisiana Historical Quarterly,* XXVII (1944), 916–17.

false, Bouligny declared, "This rebellion, I say and affirm, has never existed and if it has existed it has only been in Rapalje's mouth and in Elliot's imagination."[4]

Bouligny knew that the Natchez residents debated the boundary question and which nation was the rightful owner of that area. As he stated, the Anglo-Americans from an early age were addicted to reading newspapers (a "degenerate custom") and often sat around a table imbibing tea or wine and arguing affairs. As an exponent of Carlos III's enlightened despotism, Bouligny deplored their behavior but did not regard it as tantamount to rebellion. Nevertheless, he believed that Rapalje was guilty of insolent and seditious speeches, was a threat to public order, and deserved exemplary punishment as a lesson to others "to restrain their conversations within the limits of respect and veneration . . . for the authority of those who govern them."[5]

Following procedure, Miró forwarded the documents on the Rapalje case to Gálvez in Mexico for a definitive finding. There, on July 9, the jurist Félix del Rey gave his judgment. He found that both Treviño and Bouligny had erred in using military procedure for Rapalje, who as a civilian could have been tried in Natchez. Moreover, Treviño was derelict for not investigating thoroughly the charges against the accused. Rey could not find proof of rebellion, but like Bouligny, he considered Rapalje guilty of loose speech, poor conduct, and illegal entry in Spanish territory. He decreed that Rapalje should be expelled from Louisiana with his wife and child to an American port. Gálvez, however, ordered a new investigation of the American. Because of that and new events in Natchez, not until April, 1786, did the Rapalje family leave Louisiana, borrowing three hundred pesos to do so.[6]

Following his opinion on the Rapalje investigation, Bouligny put Natchez affairs aside. But events in the United States brought the first serious foreign threat to Louisiana. In February, 1785, the state of Georgia, which had refused to cede its claims to lands extending to the Mississippi River, which it based on the U.S. treaty with Britain of 1783, acted on the petition of Thomas Green to create Bourbon County, which included the Natchez district. Green, a sixty-one-year-old former resident

4. Porteous, "Index to Spanish Judicial Records" (1944), 917–19, with quotation on p. 919.

5. Ibid., 919–22, with quotation on p. 922.

6. Ibid., 922–26.

of Natchez who had settled there with numerous relatives in 1782, had upset officials when he sought to befriend the Indians with medals. He fled from Natchez the next year rather than face Spanish charges. Disgruntled and vengeful, he persuaded the Georgia legislature to create Bourbon County and to name him, Nicholas Long, William Davenport, and Nathaniel Christmas justices of the peace for the county. These four men adopted the title of commissioner and assumed military rank. Two of them claimed additional authority when they reached Natchez. It was probably the volatile Green who unleashed rumors of 2,500 American soldiers marching westward to seize Natchez from the Spaniards.[7]

When the first stories of American troops reached New Orleans about May 30, they had escalated to alarming proportions. As reports poured in, Governor Miró waited nervously until June 11 before asking the captain general of Cuba for military assistance, and three days later he explained his straits to Gálvez. Louisiana's forces were minuscule: 323 soldiers in New Orleans (many of them raw recruits) of 625 in the 1st Battalion and a militia force of 500 whites and 200 blacks. Fort Panmure in Natchez was the only fortress on the Mississippi capable of resistance. The governor had heard of American plans to occupy the Natchez district for months, but they seemed unfounded, since the Spanish minister Gardoqui was traveling to New York to resolve the boundary dispute between the two nations. As often happened in a crisis, Miró summoned a council of war. It met at 8 P.M. on June 15 to discuss the crisis. Bouligny attended and the next day gave his opinion on questions the governor posed.[8]

Bouligny believed that the Americans coming to Natchez must have known that the provincial governor lacked the authority to surrender territory and that the approach of American troops represented hostile intentions. Not a moment should be lost in readying the heavy artillery, Louisiana's best defense. The galley at Balize should be brought upriver,

7. The problem of Bourbon County as the Spaniards saw it is examined in Gilbert C. Din, "War Clouds on the Mississippi: Spain's 1785 Crisis in West Florida," *Florida Historical Quarterly*, LX (1981), 51–76; many documents are in Edmund C. Burnett, ed., "Papers Relating to Bourbon County, Georgia, 1785–1786," *American Historical Review*, XV (1909–10), 66–111, 293–353.

8. Council of War, governor's house, June 15, 1785, AGI, PC, leg. 2360. In August, 1785, 121 recruits arrived from Havana on the ship *El Carmen* ([Miró] to Petely, [New Orleans], August 11, 1785, *ibid.*, leg. 11).

the two gunboats outfitted, and other boats capable of mounting heavy guns constructed. He advised building a fort above Natchez (perhaps he had in mind Nogales) containing twenty cannon, some of them of heavy caliber. Bouligny regarded Louisiana as a barrier and a safeguard for Mexico, Spain's most valuable colony in the late eighteenth century. Defense was important, since the Americans, already twenty thousand strong on the banks of the Ohio, were capable of launching an invasion that could catch Louisiana unprepared. It was necessary to be vigilant, give immediate warning of danger, and meet the enemy when he appeared. Finally, Bouligny advised keeping in uniform the soldiers about to be released and supplementing them with discharged veterans, who lived throughout the province.[9]

Because the members of the council of war agreed unanimously with Miró in taking measures and because rumors kept arriving, the governor continued preparations to defend Louisiana. He asked Pensacola for a hundred troops under Piernas (who was there replacing the absent O'Neill) and Carlos de Vilemont (who as a captain in the 2nd Battalion had transferred there in October, 1783), and Mexico for a thousand soldiers with munitions, artillery, and other war materials. Privately, he also requested that Gálvez not send any officer senior to him, perhaps remembering the scheme that had stripped Bouligny of authority in 1778. To represent him in Natchez during the crisis, Miró replaced Treviño with Bouligny as commandant. The latter was to arrest the Anglo-Americans Tacitus Gaillard, Richard Ellis, and Sutton Banks for issuing a public notice advocating the independence of the district. Miró doubtlessly selected Bouligny because of his knowledge of English, his experience, and his reliability. Furthermore, Bouligny, along with the merchant David Hodge, was a proxy for the British residents of Natchez, who were departing and leaving property. He was obviously respected among the loyalists. Miró recognized that discretion was needed in handling the foreign population of sixteen hundred in Natchez. He must have puzzled over what court policies were then in effect, and he needed time, until August at least, to have the gunboats ready, the Havana reinforcements

9. Opinion of Francisco Bouligny, New Orleans, June 16, 1785, in Burnett, ed., "Bourbon County," 87–89. The opinions of other council members are scattered; three of them are Nicolas d'Aunoy to Miró, New Orleans, June 16, 1785, and Juan Alvarez to Miró, New Orleans, June 16, 1785, both in AGI, PC, leg. 11, and Grand-Pré to Miró, New Orleans, June 16, 1785, in AGI, PC, leg. 117B.

present, and new instructions. Miró remained filled with consternation until June 20, when Charles Steen arrived from St. Louis with furs and reported no hostile troops on the Mississippi or Ohio rivers. It eased the governor's worries but did not end the crisis.[10]

Meanwhile Green, the first of the Bourbon County commissioners, reached Natchez on June 9. He publicly announced his authority to take charge of Bourbon County, dispensed commissions of justice of the peace, and asked Treviño to surrender the fort and district. He permitted the commandant to forward copies of his credentials to Governor Miró in New Orleans. But to his surprise, Green encountered local opposition, even from his own family; they denounced him as untrustworthy and captious. Several others favored an independent status for Natchez, if Spain approved. In New Orleans, Miró demanded that Green come down to the city with the originals of his documents, and privately he rejoiced over the delays that gave him time to obtain military aid.[11]

For the next eight months, Bouligny was absent from New Orleans on his new commission, and the activity buoyed his spirits. His enthusiasm and desire to do well are reflected in the more than 160 letters he wrote to Governor Miró from Natchez. Heavy rains delayed his departure with forty-six grenadiers until June 22 or 23. By July 5, he had reached Lafourche des Chetimachas, and on July 20 he was at the Tunica Indian village. Sickness among the rowers and midsummer heat slowed his progress. He arrived in Natchez on July 23, four days ahead of his troops. By then, new developments had occurred in the district.[12]

Green continued to behave outrageously, and reports alleged that his party was stealing slaves and horses. Fearing arrest, he fled from the district after receiving Miró's letter of June 19, which rejected his claims to

10. Bernardo de Gálvez to Miró, Havana, May 6, 1785, in AGI, PC, leg. 11; Vilemont to Miró, Balize, October 10, 1783, and Arturo O'Neill to Miró, Pensacola, November 20, 1783, both *ibid.,* leg. 9B; Piernas to Miró, Pensacola, March 31, 1785, *ibid.,* leg. 11. The first ship from Mexico, the *San Francisco,* arrived at Balize in September, but not until November did the frigate *El Venturoso,* having hit a hurricane, come (Petely to Miró, Balize, [September] 8, 1785, and statement of Joséf Rey[es], Balize, November 4, 1785, both *ibid.,* leg. 11).

11. Miró instructions to Treviño, New Orleans, June 16, 1785, *ibid.,* leg. 2360; Burnett, ed., "Bourbon County," 77, 90–91.

12. Bouligny to Miró, [Lafourche des Chetimachas], July 5, 6, Tonica Village, July 20, and Fort Panmure de Natchez, July 24, 1785, all in AGI, PC, leg. 11. In addition to Bouligny's official letters, he wrote several private letters; Miró wrote almost as many in reply.

Natchez. Meanwhile, William Davenport and his party arrived about June 23 by barge, which, following normal procedure, Treviño ordered quarantined. After several days, he permitted the Davenport family to come ashore but kept the adult men and slaves on board. When the commissioner angrily threatened to use force to free them, Treviño seized the arms on the barge and marched the men off to jail. But of greater concern was a social gathering at Job Curry's house, approximately July 8, where Davenport spoke of seizing Fort Panmure by force and those present concurred. He also called Natchez "American territory." When questioned about his statements, the commissioner dismissed them as having been made frivolously. Although Treviño believed that Davenport deserved to be arrested, he refrained from doing so out of fear of upsetting the district's tranquillity; he would act cautiously until Bouligny arrived. But overall, few residents exhibited animosity toward the Spaniards.[13]

By the time Bouligny reached Natchez, Governor Miró had dispatched new instructions. The commandant was to collect the arms of persons suspected of treacherous behavior, investigate the events at Curry's house, and gather information. If the residents were now behaving well, Bouligny should employ his best judgment; but Davenport was to be arrested if he was guilty of sedition. Bouligny was also to determine if an invasion was imminent. Perplexed about how to treat the commissioners, Miró permitted them to remain in Natchez until he received new orders, but their conduct needed to be impeccable.[14]

Bouligny took possession of Fort Panmure and the district on July 24. Although relieved of command and stricken with fever, Treviño asked to remain in Natchez to serve under Bouligny. Since it was his first time in Natchez, the new commandant learned what he could about the district. A month later he sent a description of it to the governor. Most of the inhabitants were Americans, a few British loyalists or French, and rarely a Spaniard. They engaged in agriculture and lived scattered about the countryside, mainly at three settlements: St. Catherine Bayou, at one league; Second Creek, five leagues; and Cole's Creek, twelve leagues. Bouligny estimated the population at eleven hundred whites and nine hundred slaves. They produced tobacco, cotton, corn, vegetables, lumber, and livestock. Vagabonds easily entered and departed from the dis-

13. Burnett, ed., "Bourbon County," 90–91, 98–100.
14. Bouligny to Miró, Fort Panmure, July 27, 1785, in AGI, PC, leg. 11; Miró to Bouligny, New Orleans, July 19, 1785, ibid., leg. 3B.

trict, often going to the Choctaw and Chickasaw villages ten to twelve days away. Former commandants (Piernas and Treviño) had attempted to eradicate the vagabonds but without success. Travel in the district was by horseback, which greatly inconvenienced the Spaniards, since they lacked horses. Bouligny claimed that litigation and drinking were commonplace among the residents.[15]

Shortly after arriving, the commandant released the jailed Davenport party, except for the abusive John Woods, and set about obtaining information on the extent of the unrest and on Gaillard, Ellis, and Banks. His effort to arrest the three men netted only Banks, since the other two had fled. Benjamin Farrar of Pointe Coupee, one of the richest men in Louisiana, soon appeared to express his mortification over the conduct of his father-in-law, Gaillard, and to give information about the American West. He pledged his complete cooperation and later kept the commandant supplied with news concerning American frontier settlements. John Ellis also visited Bouligny, to deplore his father's conduct. Both Farrar and the younger Ellis persuaded the two fugitives to return, and Bouligny placed them under house arrest, because of their advanced age and sickly condition. On July 29, the commandant issued the governor's proclamation that Natchez was Spanish territory.[16]

In the investigation of Gaillard, Ellis, and Banks, Bouligny considered them guilty only of writing a letter that discussed the fate of Natchez; evidence of sedition was lacking. He dispatched his report to Miró on August 4 for a final judgment but kept Gaillard and Ellis in Natchez so as not to jeopardize their health in a summer journey to the capital. Bouligny also suggested placing a detachment of soldiers at the Cherokee River to learn the accuracy of attacks rather than sending spies each time a rumor cropped up. A recent rumor had alleged that the Americans had attempted to enlist Chickasaw support to seize Natchez but were rebuffed.[17]

As for Davenport, Bouligny spoke to him on July 25 and obtained a negative impression. He was of poor conduct, fond of alcohol, and

15. Bouligny to Miró, Fort Panmure, July 25, 1785, *ibid.,* leg. 11; Bouligny to Miró, Fort Panmure, August 22, 1785, in *SMV,* Pt. 2, pp. 136–39.

16. Bouligny to Miró, Fort Panmure, July 25, 27, 30, 1785, all in AGI, PC, leg. 11. See also Burnett, ed., "Bourbon County," 319–22.

17. Bouligny to Miró, Fort Panmure, three letters of August 4, 1785, all in AGI, PC, leg. 11.

seditious. Davenport informed him of Georgia's creation of Bourbon County, his authority, and the expected arrival of Long and Christmas. Bouligny, however, dismissed the validity of Davenport's documents and proceeded to recount that Spain held West Florida under Governor Miró by right of conquest. He marveled that Georgia could proceed with measuring the boundary at the thirty-first parallel without first contacting Spanish representatives. When Bouligny suggested that Davenport consult Governor Miró, who alone possessed authority to discuss affairs, the commissioner professed to have power only to determine the boundary and preferred to await further instructions in Natchez. Davenport's arguments exasperated Bouligny, who described them as lacking reason, and he was tempted to ship him forcibly to New Orleans. The commissioner, however, refused to budge, and he blamed Green and Gaillard for the district's unrest. He had advised the residents to remain at work and peaceful. As Bouligny considered expelling Davenport, the latter reported that Long and Christmas had arrived. Davenport requested time for them to rest, consult with the commandant, and then journey together to New Orleans.[18]

In early August, Bouligny described the district as calm. He terminated the investigation into Davenport's sedition, since it seemed unimportant. Bouligny decided against seizing the weapons of suspects, which might only disturb the tranquillity of the residents, who needed arms to ward off wild beasts. He sent his findings about Gaillard, Ellis, and Banks to Miró for his judgment. He learned that the mercurial Green, writing from the Indian country, had urged his sons to quit the district rather than pledge fidelity to the Spanish crown. His children, however, showed the letter to Bouligny, which probably led him to recommend officer posts in the militia for several of the younger Greens.[19]

In New Orleans, using Bouligny's evidence, the government lawyer Juan del Postigo gave his judgment against the Natchez dissidents on August 20. He sentenced Gaillard to exile for refusing to take an oath of loyalty, fined Ellis fifty pesos, and gave Banks a fifty-peso fine and three months of imprisonment from the day of his arrest. The sentences, however, were not to be imposed until Gálvez had approved them. The Natchez problem seemed to be subsiding, but an attack against the prov-

18. Burnett, ed., "Bourbon County," 299–303, 304–305, 307–308, 308–309.
19. Bouligny to Miró, Fort Panmure, August 9 and 10, 1785, both in AGI, PC, leg. 11.

ince was still possible. Foreign newspapers that arrived in Louisiana reported U.S. determination to obtain navigation of the Mississippi. While Miró did not raise the Natchez garrison to three hundred, as Bouligny urged, in a display of power he kept soldiers shuttling back and forth on the Mississippi.[20]

In late summer, 1785, Bouligny continued to send information to New Orleans on the Anglo-American West. Treviño had sent a spy, Stephen Hayward, to the United States before Bouligny arrived, and the new commandant later dispatched Louis Chacharet to verify reports of an impending invasion. But contrary to rumors, all the news seemed to emphasize the dishonesty of the commissioners and that no attack was coming. By mid-August, Bouligny realized that Davenport had not been candid with him about the arrival of Long and Christmas. On August 16, the commissioner admitted that they were only then leaving the Indian nations, with Green expected to join them. After waiting several days, on August 24 an irritated Bouligny gave the commissioner the choice of going to New Orleans or quitting Spanish territory in seventy-two hours.[21]

But the arrival of Long and Christmas spared Davenport from choosing. The three commissioners informed Bouligny on August 27 that they would communicate with him shortly. They set up a room, dubbed "Amity Hall," in a Natchez house to correspond with the commandant. Green, who argued even with his cohorts, stayed away on his plantation. Only the young and moderate Long impressed Bouligny as he expressed regret over the rumors and assured the Spaniard that the United States would not seize the district. Bouligny met socially with the commissioners, even paying for a dinner with them out of his own pocket. But their arguments failed to sway him, and he suspected that their true purpose was to win over the population without compromising themselves.[22]

On August 29, Bouligny told the three Americans that he had a bateau ready to convey them to New Orleans to present their documents

20. Juan del Póstigo to [Miró], New Orleans, August 20, 1785, and endorsed by Miró on August 21, 1785, in AGI, PC, leg. 3B.

21. Burnett, ed., "Bourbon County," 324–26; Bouligny to Miró, Fort Panmure, August 24, 1785, in AGI, PC, leg. 11.

22. Bouligny to Miró, Fort Panmure, August 28, 1785, in *SMV*, Pt. 2, pp. 143–45; and Miró's reply to him, New Orleans, September 9, 1785, in AGI, PC, leg. 9B.

and confer with the governor. But rather than do that, they submitted a copy of their authority to Bouligny, claimed all the territory down to the thirty-first parallel, and asked for immediate possession of Bourbon County. Their message thoroughly exasperated Bouligny. He merely acknowledged the receipt of their letter and transmitted it to the governor. This ploy lengthened the commissioners' stay in Natchez—and the crisis. But Green soon panicked again and fled for the Indian country with his son Isaac and three slaves.[23]

In New Orleans, Miró too was disgusted with the commissioners. He had no orders to surrender territory or a fort. He repeated Spanish claims to the Mississippi's left bank as far north as the Ohio River, stated that a government envoy was in the United States to discuss issues in dispute, and complained of Georgia's irregular method of operation, which caused the Spanish government needless expense. Part of that expense consisted of the supply ships Gálvez had sent from Mexico in August with war materials and 200,000 pesos; the viceroy had declined to dispatch soldiers. But since three months had elapsed since the first rumors of invasion surfaced, Miró felt more confident. The commissioners too had failed to gain support in Natchez.[24]

By September 22, after assessing later reports, Gálvez had dismissed the possibility of an American attack and reproached the Louisiana authorities for their lenient treatment of the Georgians. They were not to be regarded as ambassadors, since their credentials were obviously false. Green, the other commissioners, and any residents guilty of misconduct or sedition were to be prosecuted. Gálvez waited for news from the Spanish minister in the United States. He had sent the *Galveztown,* the same brigantine that Miró had hurriedly dispatched to Veracruz in June, for a report of Gardoqui's negotiations with the United States.[25]

Gardoqui had arrived in the United States in May and despite newspaper reports of Georgia's creation of Bourbon County, was ignorant of events on the Mississippi. In September, after receiving Gálvez's inquiry, he contacted John Jay, the American foreign secretary, about Spain's rights to the Mississippi's left bank by virtue of conquest and occupation. He recounted to Jay the behavior of the Georgia justices of the peace,

23. Bouligny to Miró, Fort Panmure, August 28, September 1, 14, 1785, all in AGI, PC, leg. 11; Burnett ed., to "Bourbon County," 329–30, 330, 331, 331–32.

24. Burnett, ed., "Bourbon County," 333–34, 339–40.

25. *Ibid.*, 337–39.

particularly Green. He trusted in an amicable resolution to problems between the two nations and asked for a rapid reply. On October 13, the U.S. Congress reiterated its faith in the 1783 treaty with Britain. But it deplored the conduct of any American who disturbed harmonious relations with Spain and it disavowed the actions of Georgia. The congressional resolution ended the crisis but left unresolved the problems of international boundaries and navigation of the Mississippi. More than two months elapsed before news of the congressional decision reached Louisiana.[26]

Meanwhile, in October, Bouligny had Miró's reply to the commissioners that he would not surrender territory. Long, recognizing the futility of the mission and disagreeing with Davenport and Christmas, asked the commandant for a passport to the Cumberland and departed. The other two commissioners pressed on with their case. Engaging in another fabrication, they declared their expectation that Spanish officials would honor a treaty their king had ratified. They also voiced Georgia's objection to the increase in Spanish defenses in Natchez—Brevet Lieutenant Colonel Grand-Pré had recently brought the 1st Grenadier Company to reinforce Fort Panmure—and their rejection of any suggestion that they be charged for causing Spain expenses.[27]

Bouligny dutifully sent the latest messages down to Miró, who was not amused by them. The Natchez commandant confirmed that the western American settlements were quiet and without signs of preparing for invasion. Moreover, the governor had recently received Gálvez's stinging letter of September 22, reproving him. That, coupled with the commissioners' impolite letter, disinclined Miró to be accommodating. He censured Davenport and Christmas for their arrogance and for treating Spanish-held lands as Georgian. He gave them the ultimate insult by doubting that they were commissioners and ordered them out of Natchez in fifteen days. He instructed Bouligny to arrest them if they had not departed in that time and to investigate Davenport's behavior at Curry's house in July. After Miró had been rebuked by Gálvez, Bou-

26. Diego Gardoqui to [John Jay], New York, September 23, 1785, in AHN, Est., leg. 3893; Jay to Gardoqui, [New York], October 14, 1785, *ibid.*, leg. 3885bis, exped. 6; the congressional resolution is *ibid.*, leg. 3893.

27. Miró to Nicholas Long, Nathaniel Christmas, and William Davenport, New Orleans, September 7, 1785, in AGI, PC, leg. 3B; Bouligny to Miró, Fort Panmure, October 6, 17, 1785, *ibid.*, leg. 11.

ligny's failure to follow orders to investigate Davenport had greatly rankled the governor.[28]

Bouligny had Miró's instructions by early December, and he proceeded to carry them out. The commandant gave the two remaining commissioners the governor's ultimatum, which resulted in their departure on December 11. Davenport obtained Bouligny's permission to leave his pregnant wife and young brother in Natchez. Before he left, the commandant held an inquiry into Davenport's conduct but decided against prosecuting him for criminal outbursts at Curry's house. More than a dozen witnesses failed to yield sufficient incriminating evidence, and his expulsion seemed preferable. In response to Miró's chastisement about Davenport, Bouligny reminded the governor of his earlier approval to drop the Davenport investigation. From the Indian country, Green made an abortive effort to return to Natchez but stopped when he learned that Davenport and Christmas had been expelled. Bouligny tried to capture Gaillard, who had refused to descend to Pointe Coupee to stay with his married daughter. He remained lurking about the fringes of the district. Rumors claimed that he would depart with Davenport and Christmas, but he did not. Only in January, 1786, after Bouligny sent a detachment of soldiers to apprehend him, was it learned that he had left for the Indian nations. These events terminated the commissioners' efforts to create Bourbon County, but they alerted the Spaniards to problems with the new United States.[29]

Before February 17, 1786, Bouligny received word from Miró that the U.S. Congress had disavowed the actions of Georgia and the commissioners. He then proclaimed the news in Natchez, which the inhabitants accepted without murmur. Bouligny also had Miró's orders to relinquish command of Natchez to Grand-Pré, which he did on either February 25 or 26. Grand-Pré would remain in charge until mid-1789. As his duties as commandant of Natchez ended, Bouligny thanked the governor "for

28. Burnett, ed., "Bourbon County," 342–43. Miró sent a copy of this letter to Bernardo de Gálvez; see Miró's letter to Gálvez of the same day, *ibid.*, 343. See also Miró to Bouligny, New Orleans, November 10, 1785, *ibid.*, 346–47.

29. Bouligny to Miró, Fort Panmure, November 30, 1785, in AGI, PC, leg. 11. Bouligny's letters to Miró dealing with a variety of topics are in AGI, PC, legs. 11, 12. Bouligny to Miró, Fort Panmure, December 13, 1785, January 14, 1786, *ibid.*, legs. 11, 12, respectively. "Investigation of Davenport at Job Curry's house," enclosed in Bouligny to Miró, December 6, 1785, ibid., leg. 11. Thirteen people testified.

[his] kindness which dissimulates the faults and errors that I might have incurred during the time I have been in command." About early March, he departed, having successfully accomplished his mission.[30]

While Bouligny was in Natchez, his activities involved much more than negotiating with the Georgia commissioners. He assisted in rebuilding Fort Panmure; administered military justice as, among other things, he participated in a council that investigated a fight between soldiers—Domingo Trujillo had wounded Juan Fondevila after losing to him in card games—and sentenced Trujillo to ten years' imprisonment; and arranged for a resident named Perry to mark a route by land from Natchez to Baton Rouge. As civil commandant, on January 27, 1786, he initiated proceedings against William Duet (Ducett) for inducing slaves to run away from their masters. Miró sentenced Duet to four years of labor on public works.[31]

Moreover, in a report of August, 1785, Bouligny recommended the establishment of mounted militia companies in the three settlements; the selection of company captains from the "decent" monied class, who knew all the inhabitants and their customs; and the expulsion of persons dissatisfied with Spanish government. He noted that many of the district residents were content with Spanish rule and that they would contribute to the maintenance of peace and order. He believed that disputes should be handled locally in the settlements, which would spare the commandant from involvement and keep the residents at work on their lands. Bouligny's recommendations for company officers included persons involved in the recent unrest or their sons. It showed that by August, 1785, conditions had greatly quieted down. Among those recommended were Parker Caradine, Cato West, and William Brokas (Broccus) for leading officer posts and the sons of Thomas Green, Richard Ellis, and James Elliot for subaltern positions.[32]

In his recommendations, Bouligny displayed an evenhandedness to the overwhelming majority of the foreigners in Natchez, since he believed in their loyalty. His administration demonstrated to the residents

30. Bouligny to Miró, Fort Panmure, February 17 and 18, 1786, ibid., leg. 12; [Miró] to Grand-Pré, New Orleans, January 26, 1786, ibid., leg. 117B; Grand-Pré to Miró, Fort Panmure, February 26, 1786, ibid., leg. 14.

31. Bouligny to Miró, Fort Panmure, December 13, 1785, January 14, 1786, ibid., legs. 11, 12, respectively.

32. Bouligny to Miró, Fort Panmure, August 22, 1785, in SMV, Pt. 2, pp. 139–42.

the mildness of Spanish rule. Hotheads like Green and Gaillard were impossible to win over, despite Spanish tolerance, but they were the exceptions. The Spaniards nevertheless permitted even these two to slink back to Natchez. Gaillard, after spending a few months in the Indian country, returned in July and died on November 8, 1786. His son Isaac came back too. The firebrand Green also swallowed his pride and returned in late 1789 to bedevil the authorities for many years. Others, however, who in 1785 had shown disloyalty to the Spaniards subsequently lived quiet lives in West Florida. Davenport was killed in the Indian country in 1787, but his wife remained in Natchez, even receiving a land grant from the Spaniards. Bouligny's work in the district contributed significantly to its general calm. He moved easily among the inhabitants with his knowledge of the languages spoken there—English, French, and Spanish.[33]

Miró too assumed a charitable attitude toward the Americans in the postwar era. He, like Bouligny, became convinced that those settled in West Florida constituted no threat, could be assimilated and even made into a buffer against their kind in the United States. Moreover, they could contribute to the economic development and defense of the colony. Miró suggested to the government that they be allowed to remain in West Florida. In Spain, the council of state discussed the Anglo-American families of West Florida on March 14, 1786, and consented to their remaining if they took oaths of fidelity. A search began in Spain for Irish priests who would volunteer to work at converting the Protestant settlers, and several were located. These were the opening steps by which Spain later permitted American Protestants to settle on its soil. The court also created a governorship for the Natchez district and appointed Bvt. Lt. Col. Manuel Gayoso de Lamos to work under the orders of the now governor-general of Louisiana.[34]

33. Grand-Pré to Miró, Natchez, March 18, 1786, in AGI, PC, leg. 14; Norman E. Gillis, *Early Inhabitants of the Natchez District* (Baton Rouge, 1963), 13, 17–18; R. S. Cotterill, *The Southern Indians: The Story of the Civilized Tribes Before Removal* (Norman, Okla., 1954), 75; Holmes, *Gayoso*, 187, 257.

34. On foreign immigration to Louisiana, see three articles by Gilbert C. Din: "The Immigration Policy of Governor Esteban Miró in Spanish Louisiana," *Southwestern Historical Quarterly*, LXXIII (1969), 155–75; "The Irish Mission to West Florida," *Louisiana History*, XII (1971), 315–34; and "Pierre Wouves d'Argès in North America: Spanish Commissioner, Adventurer, or French Spy?" *Louisiana Studies*, XII (1973), 354–75.

Governor Miró was well pleased with Bouligny's administration of Natchez and the settlement of the Bourbon County dispute. Recognizing that his friend had fared badly in Gálvez's recommendation of only a few months before, Miró attempted to make amends. On January 1, 1786, he informed the viceroy that the commotion produced by the Georgia commissioners had ended successfully, in good measure because of Bouligny. The governor wrote: "Don Francisco Bouligny has fulfilled that command [Natchez] with ability, having conducted himself well with the Georgia commissioners. He has administered justice to the satisfaction of the inhabitants, [and has] put the Fort in the state of defense possible according to my instructions. All of which I inform you if it is your pleasure to manifest your benevolence to him."[35]

But Gálvez failed to display his benevolence. No letter of thanks or recommendation was forthcoming from him. Moreover, about early fall, 1786, Gálvez in Mexico must have received from his uncle José Bouligny's petition of July, 1784, for promotion to colonel. Gálvez's recommendation was needed, since he had resumed the post of inspector general of the infantry. And in Mexico the petition's journey reached its final destination not long before the death of the viceroy. To the end of his life, Gálvez preserved his truculent attitude toward Bouligny.[36]

35. Miró to the conde de Gálvez, New Orleans, January 1, 1786, in AGI, PC, leg. 3B.
36. Sonora to the conde de Gálvez, Aranjuez, May 13, 1786, with enclosure of Bouligny's petition of July 26, 1784, *ibid.*, leg. 1375.

F OLLOWING HIS RETURN from Natchez, Bouligny never
again ventured far from New Orleans. The successful completion of his command at Natchez
and his friendship with Governor Miró and the other senior officers were
pleasing to him. Miró reflected that satisfaction when he wrote in Bouligny's service record in December, 1786: "Good in his post, with a disposition to command." As Bouligny celebrated his fiftieth birthday that
year, his career appeared to be progressing as well as might be expected
in a small Spanish colony with limited opportunities for advancement.
In the next five years, as his career reached its pinnacle, he experienced
serious financial difficulties. However, he had his family to comfort him.[1]

Close to Bouligny and important to him was his growing brood. A
third son, who survived and grew to manhood, Luis Mauricio, was born
on September 22, 1782. The Boulignys' last child, Celeste María, followed
on December 29, 1784. She lived only until the summer of 1787, perhaps
dying of smallpox prevalent that year, and was buried on July 16.
Mme Vilemont, Bouligny's mother-in-law, continued to share the large
household at this time. Her modest pension of 375 pesos per year did not
permit the luxury of her own residence. But there was no reason for her
to live apart, since she was a welcome addition to help with the children.
Her older son, Capt. Carlos de Vilemont, probably also stayed with the
Boulignys when he was in New Orleans. As a member of the 2nd Battalion, he was away at Pensacola from October, 1783, to at least July, 1785,
and possibly 1787 before his unit transferred back. The younger Vilemont
son, Luis, spent much of his youth with his paternal aunt, Mlle de Vilemont, in Seigneure d'Ully, near Sedan, France, first studying and later as

1. Bouligny service sheet, December, 1786, AGI, SD, leg. 2657.

a cavalry officer. After a lengthy absence, he returned to New Orleans on an extended leave in October, 1788, less than a year before the outbreak of the French Revolution.[2]

Shortly after the war against Britain, Bouligny's younger brother Lorenzo arrived in Louisiana, the only member of his family to visit him there. Lorenzo had been in Mexico in the Flanders regiment since at least 1769, first as a cadet and by 1783 as a lieutenant. When he visited his older brother Frasquito, Lorenzo appears to have been returning to Spain after a fourteen-year absence. He reached Balize on August 17, 1783, on board the *Margarita,* which brought forty Canary Islander families from Havana. By the end of the month, he was in New Orleans, where he began a six-month visit. He must have experienced unusual weather when residents reportedly donned winter clothing in July and August, witnessed frost in September, and shivered from the intense cold in mid-November. Lorenzo undoubtedly stayed at Bouligny's imposing riverfront house staffed by numerous slaves. He observed firsthand how well his brother lived. Both the army and the New World had been good to Frasquito. By 1783, his brother's roots in Louisiana were well established. Although scheduled to depart in early February, 1784, continued cold weather that brought large blocks of ice floating down the Mississippi past New Orleans delayed Lorenzo's leaving. Not until mid-March did he sail for Havana on board the *Santa Teresa.* He was the last Bouligny brother to see Francisco.[3]

When Bouligny's daughter Pepa was barely fifteen, she married Pierre de La Roche, inspector (*vista*) of the Royal Customs, on August 7, 1786. (Most young women in Louisiana married between the ages of fifteen and nineteen.) Possibly following a convention of that time, Bouligny and his wife arranged the match. La Roche had arrived in Lou-

2. Martin, *Bouligny Family,* 181–83; *Asiento* of military pension of Francisca Petit de Coulange, widow of Vilemont, AGI, PC, leg. 538B. She received 300 pesos yearly as of July 18, 1772, and 375 pesos from May 21, 1777. Rental agreement fragment, M. de Vilemont and Juan Rodulfo de Briou [?], AGI, PC, leg. 117B; Ignacio Balderas, "Relation of the Passengers that the Brigantine *La Thetis* brings from La Rochelle," Paso de la Lutre, October 22, 1788, AGI, PC, leg. 16; Bouligny to Pierre Harley de Milleville, New Orleans, October 24, 1789, in DB, HNOC.

3. Juan Bouligny to Francisco Bouligny, [n.p.], December 19, 1769, September 7, 1771, in DB, HNOC; José Petely to Martín Navarro, Balize, August 17, 1783, in AGI, PC, leg. 608B; Miró to Ezpeleta, New Orleans, March 13, 1784, in AGI, PC, leg. 1394; Gayarré, *History,* III, 163.

isiana only two years before, at about age twenty-five. He was born on December 8, 1758, in Hagetaubin, in the department of Basses-Pyrenées, France, although he claimed the nearby town of Sauveterre. That created the erroneous assumption that he was from the Spanish town of Salvatierra in the Basque country. Two children, Céleste (perhaps named for her young aunt who died in 1787) and an unknown child, who apparently died young, came to the marriage by 1789. Doubtless their grandparents, Bouligny and his wife, delighted in the children. Pepa's offspring, these and several more born later (the twins María Josefa Cecilia and Alberto Pedro José in 1793, Adelaida in 1794, María Josefa in 1796, José Fernando Pedro in 1798, and María Justina in 1800), were the only grandchildren that Bouligny knew.[4]

Bouligny was probably close to his son-in-law and his only surviving daughter. When La Roche suffered from poor health in 1789, Bouligny testified on July 28 to his illness, which resulted from a blockage in the liver that interrupted blood circulation and the free and easy secretion of bile and caused poor and laborious digestion of food. The medical doctors Joseph Montegut, Robert Dow, and Etienne Fouignet, among the best in New Orleans, declared that La Roche should leave immediately for Europe to reestablish his health. They recommended that he submit to hot baths to increase the circulation of his blood. Three days later, Governor Miró granted him permission to depart, and he appears to have sailed on board Pablo Segond's frigate, which departed for Cádiz in August. He was absent from his family and Louisiana until about November, 1791, and returned to work in December of that year. But bouts of ill health continued to trouble him throughout the 1790s.[5]

Beginning in the 1780s, as they neared their teens, Bouligny's sons embarked on military careers. The sons of officers could enter the army at a young age. For Carlos de Vilemont, who received special permission because of his father's service, the age was eight. Bouligny's oldest son, Domingo, became a cadet in the Louisiana regiment about March 1, 1786, at age twelve, and was educated in the regimental cadet school when it opened. Possibly he and his brothers also attended the Spanish school in

4. Martin, *Bouligny Family*, 195–98. For the ages at which young Louisiana women married, see Antonio Acosta Rodríguez, *La población de la Luisiana española (1763–1803)* (Madrid, 1979), 289.

5. Pedro de La Roche petition, New Orleans, August 3, 1791, LHC, Spanish File 197; Miró to Antonio Hoa, New Orleans, December 1, 1791, in AGI, PC, leg. 2343.

New Orleans that had been established in 1771. All the Bouligny children grew up bilingual, in Spanish and French. Domingo was a cadet for only a brief time (one year and seven and a half months), to October 18, 1787, which was probably due more to influence than exceptional ability. He achieved his first officer rank of sublieutenant at the age of fourteen. Ursino entered the regiment as a cadet at age twelve in November, 1790. Bouligny's youngest son, Luis, followed the well-trodden path on his twelfth birthday in 1793.[6]

That his sons chose their father's career was not surprising. Bouligny was dedicated to army service, and Louisiana offered few occupations or professions for his sons to enter. In tiny New Orleans, schools for training were similarly absent. Moreover, the sons of Louisiana's regular army officers usually followed in their fathers' footsteps, which resulted in the establishment of a regimental school for cadets in the 1780s. Bouligny carefully guided his sons to begin their careers as soon as they were eligible, since seniority was an important principle in the army.[7]

Despite problems, Louisiana appeared to enter a dynamic era after the war. Its population rose from 32,115 in 1785 (14,217 white, 3,477 in West Florida) to 42,611 in 1788 (19,445 white, 6,376 in West Florida). New Orleans had 4,880 residents in the first census and 5,338 in the second, approximately half of whom were blacks. The increased economic activity of the 1780s brought additional people to New Orleans—sailors, merchants, and tradesmen among others—and the city's taverns, cabarets, billiard parlors, and boardinghouses grew in proportion.[8]

6. Service sheets for Domingo, Ursino, and Luis Bouligny are in AGI, PC, leg. 161A. On the New Orleans Spanish school, see David K. Bjork, ed. and trans., "Documents Relating to the Establishment of Schools in Louisiana, 1771," *Mississippi Valley Historical Review,* XI (1925), 561–69. A December, 1786, service sheet for Domingo Bouligny listed his qualities as valor—assumed; application and capacity—average; conduct—good. Governor Miró, as inspector general added, "Good to continue his merit" (AGI, SD, leg. 2657).

7. Little exists on the training of army cadets; Jack D. L. Holmes has a brief account in his *Honor and Fidelity: The Louisiana Infantry Regiment and the Louisiana Militia Companies, 1766–1821* (Birmingham, Ala., 1965), 77.

8. Gayarré (*History,* III, 170, 215) gives population figures as 31,433 and 42,346 for 1785 and 1788, respectively. The 1788 census is in AGI, PC, leg. 1425. Coutts, "Martín Navarro," I, 243, 270–77; Arthur P. Whitaker, "The Commerce of Louisiana and the Floridas at the End of the Eighteenth Century," *Hispanic America Historical Review,* VIII (1928), 193, 196–97, 197*n.* The illicit trade is mentioned in documents in AHN, Est., leg. 3893bis. In 1788, Louisiana exports and imports amounted to 660,000 and 1,200,000 pesos, respec-

In 1782, the crown extended the colony's trading privileges to include France and the French West Indies, in effect tolerating the same trade advantages that Gilbert Antoine de St. Maxent had gained for himself the year before. Moreover, while some restrictions in trade continued, enforcement was generally lax. The 1780s also witnessed the opening of indirect trade with the United States, via the French West Indies, which grew with the years. The greatest trade in 1783 to 1785 was between New Orleans and Santo Domingo in lumber and foodstuffs. The New Orleans fire of March 21, 1788, which destroyed 856 buildings, including the city's main stores, St. Louis Church, the Cabildo building, the Capuchin convent, the prison, the arsenal, and numerous private dwellings, produced damages amounting to $2,595,561. More important, it accelerated contact with the United States. Since the fire caused a serious food shortage and required extensive rebuilding, Governor Miró distributed tents and rice to the needy residents and sent ships with $24,000 to Philadelphia for the purchase of three thousand barrels of flour. It initiated a direct and lasting trade with Philadelphia and other American cities.[9]

To a large degree, by the 1780s the depressed economic conditions of the past were mostly forgotten. Only an acute shortage of specie and the presence of depreciated paper money, first issued in 1780 during the war, hindered a more rapid development. The crown permitted the duty-free importation of slaves, and they came into the colony faster than whites, further attesting to economic expansion. Spain, however, did not benefit appreciably, since Louisiana's economy continued to be controlled almost exclusively by non-Spaniards.[10]

Furthermore, the cost of Louisiana to the crown kept rising. Now there was more territory to protect and a greater danger, from the United

---

tively, and constantly involved 25 ships. See also John G. Clark, *New Orleans, 1718–1812, An Economic History* (Baton Rouge, 1970), 224–33.

9. Miró to Ezpeleta, New Orleans, April 1, 1788, in AGI, PC, leg. 1394; see also Lauro A. DeRojas, "The Great Fire of 1788 in New Orleans," *Louisiana Historical Quarterly,* XX (1937), 578–81; Walter Prichard, "An Account of the Conflagration, 1788," *Louisiana Historical Quarterly,* XX (1937), 582–89. A contract between Miró and Ebenezer Rees to bring five hundred barrels of flour at eight pesos each is in AGI, PC, leg. 1394. Clark, *New Orleans,* 233; Arthur P. Whitaker, "Reed and Forde: Merchant Adventurers of Philadelphia," *Pennsylvania Magazine of History and Biography,* LXI (1937), 237–62.

10. Clark (*New Orleans,* 202–49) discusses Spain's last twenty years in Louisiana. See also Whitaker, "Commerce of Louisiana," 190–203.

States. O'Reilly had set Louisiana's budget at 115,322 pesos; and except for extraordinary funds such as the 40,000 pesos that Bouligny obtained for immigration, Indians, and commerce, that sum remained fixed until 1779, when it was raised to 315,000 pesos because of the war. By 1785, the budget had climbed to 489,385 pesos for Louisiana and 47,896 pesos for West Florida. Although this amount remained static until 1802, the budget was frequently augmented by special expenditures. The bulk of the regular funds was spent for the military; two infantry battalions alone cost 300,838 pesos in 1785. Moreover, the colony often received additional sums for the construction of fortifications, which continually deteriorated.[11]

The sums spent in Louisiana were vital, since they infused hard currency, *pesos fuertes,* as opposed to inflated paper money, and helped to stimulate the economy. Since the colony had a deficit trade, however, hard money kept leaving the province despite government attempts to prevent it. Louisiana needed exports to pay for imported manufactured goods, clothing, slaves, alcoholic beverages, and foodstuffs that could not be grown locally. Furs, skins, lumber, staves, indigo, rice, and tobacco did not leave in sufficient quantities to offset imports. From 1787 to 1791, however, tobacco shipped to Spain and Mexico briefly constituted Louisiana's principal export. Its collapse, due to overproduction, poor packing and shipping, and lack of consumer acceptance, hurt many Louisiana planters and merchants. Cotton and sugar, two new export crops, would not be grown in large amounts until the 1790s.[12]

Almost as soon as he arrived in Louisiana in 1769, Bouligny embarked on economic activities designed to establish his financial well-being. Despite its limited trade, Louisiana offered some opportunities. Since he had no money other than his salary and, after his marriage, his wife's dowry, he sought the best prices possible, often buying at auctions. Although short of capital, his fortune seems to have had a reasonably good start. Unfortunately, there are few documents regarding Bouligny's

11. Coutts, "Martín Navarro," II, 393–421; on p. 421, Coutts states that Louisiana's trade increased by more than 700 percent in the 1780s.

12. On paper money in Louisiana, see *ibid.,* I, 270–85, 291–99. From 1787 to 1791, Louisiana exported 8,128,052 Spanish pounds of tobacco (Coutts, "Boom and Bust," 304–309). A royal order of November 25, 1787, called for Mexico to send Pensacola 200,000 pesos for defense needs, 50,000 in 1789, and 37,500 in each of the next four years (Conde de Revillagigedo to the governor of Pensacola, Mexico City, July 27, 1790, in AGI, PC, leg. 16, with enclosures).

business dealings for the 1770s and the 1780s. Nevertheless, enough survives from the latter decade to outline what he did economically.

At the center of Bouligny's holdings were his plantation outside New Orleans and his slaves. For twenty years the plantation produced lumber and staves and grew crops such as tobacco and rice. Bouligny also owned a large number of slaves, who worked on the land and at his residence and represented a substantial investment. Typical of other well-to-do Louisiana residents, he employed as many as a dozen slaves as household servants in New Orleans.

In the mid-1780s, despite Louisiana's economic growth, Bouligny's fortunes began to decline when he had difficulty meeting his obligations. Several years before, in 1779, he acknowledged a debt of 14,000 pesos, which he expected to liquidate in part that year. However, it did not happen. Instead, the debt grew as he probably assumed responsibility for much or all of the 4,000 pesos required to purchase a captaincy for Vilemont in 1780 and he repaired the considerable hurricane damage to his house. Moreover, he seems to have paid the costs to maintain the younger Vilemont, Luis, in France. That same year, Bouligny suffered a pecuniary setback as he lost his extra pay as lieutenant governor. A part of his indebtedness, at least to 1779, resulted from his plantation overseer's faulty management and his own poor business judgments. In 1784, for example, he cosigned a note for 3,400 pesos for slaves Juan Bautista Cola bought from James Kirk, but Cola failed to pay. In June, 1788, Bouligny satisfied that debt.[13]

Bouligny's last acquisition of business property occurred on March 7, 1785, when he and his brother-in-law Carlos, then stationed in Pensacola, who probably recommended the acquisition, purchased four lots with houses and warehouses from the British merchant David Hodge in that town. They paid 2,100 *pesos fuertes* for them, a large and risky sum in a town that was stagnant in growth. Bouligny apparently believed the investment wise. Unfortunately, little is known about what happened to these lots. Vilemont, however, seems to have retained an interest in them, claiming these abandoned properties as his in 1806.[14]

13. See Chapter 6. Rafael Perdomo Acts, Vol. XII, June 9–December 30, 1788, fols. 284v–285, NONA.

14. Perdomo Acts, Vol. V, January–May 6, 1785, fols. 186–88; Morales to Vicente Folch, Pensacola, July 22, 1806, in AGI, PC, leg. 98A. The lots and slaves had been sold as belonging to the royal treasury, and Vilemont protested.

At the same time that he acquired the Pensacola lots, Bouligny's financial difficulties escalated, in part because of his business dealings with Cuba. He had sent at least two shipments of lumber to Havana in 1784, for which he was not paid. On March 1, 1785, he gave a power of attorney to Capt. Pedro Rousseau of the royal brigantine *Galveztown*, who was sailing to Havana, to take the necessary legal steps in order to collect the compensation due him. But Rousseau appears not to have recovered the money, since Bouligny continued to appoint agents in Havana to represent him. For example, in 1789 he gave a power of attorney to Francisco Carpentier to collect payments for commodities sent to Josef Rafael Catalá in Havana. Earlier, however, in late 1787, Bouligny's financial situation had worsened as his creditors hounded him for payment. These actions led to the sale of his house.[15]

Bouligny's residence already had a mortgage of 6,000 *pesos fuertes* held by Pierre Henri Derneville. It was an obligation that dated from October 31, 1781, when the Boulignys promised to repay the loan within six years, with interest at 5 percent per annum. Possibly Bouligny had obtained the funds to repay Bernardo de Gálvez the 3,000 pesos he owed him. The governor had insisted upon repayment when he departed definitively from Louisiana. Then Bouligny's trading ventures with Havana failed to yield the means to repay Derneville, not even all the interest due. When the six years had elapsed, Derneville sued Bouligny and his wife in November, 1787, for 6,325 pesos. On December 11, 1787, Miró ordered the *aguacil mayor* to carry out the judgment that Bouligny must pay Derneville.[16]

Confronted with no alternatives, the lieutenant colonel settled with his creditors between January and March, 1788, by selling his house to Pablo Segond, a successful New Orleans merchant, on April 5, for 21,000 paper pesos. He also transferred the Derneville mortgage of 6,000 pesos to his plantation, thus giving Segond clear title to the dwelling. Derneville attempted to prevent the transfer, but Miró judged in Bouligny's favor. Bouligny had already received 5,000 pesos at the time of the sale, and two payments of 8,000 pesos each were to come at the end of 1788

---

15. Perdomo Acts, Vol. V, January–May 6, 1785, fols. 165–66, Vol. XIV, May–December, 1789, fols. 414–15.

16. Leonardo Mazange Acts, Vol. IV, July–December, 1781, fols. 871–73; Perdomo Acts, Vol. XI, January–June, 1788, fols. 35–37, 196–98; LHC, Spanish Judicial Records, Doc. 1766, File 54, November 28, 1787. On Segond, see Coutts, "Martín Navarro," II, 438–41.

and in mid-1789. Included in the sale agreement was Segond's permission to allow Bouligny, a close friend, to rent the house, which he did until 1792 when he found a new residence to purchase. Segond, however, seriously hurt by the 1788 New Orleans fire, was slow in paying. His first payment came on March 5, 1789, and in the second Bouligny received only 1,933 pesos and 5 reales. The remainder went to satisfy another creditor.[17]

Since Bouligny still needed money, he attempted to sell the Manchac lands of 640 superficial arpents that Governor Unzaga had granted him in 1771. Bouligny had increased the size by adding 10 arpents of riverfront by 40 deep purchased from Joseph Pauli, the militia commandant of Galveztown, for a total of 1,040 superficial arpents. In 1788 Bouligny sought government permission to dispose of the property to Daniel Clark, Jr., since he claimed that his documents had been destroyed in the recent conflagration. Although the government approved his petition on July 16, Bouligny did not complete the sale. He never attempted to develop the Manchac holding, probably retaining it only for speculation. In 1792 Manchac residents complained in a memorial to the governor about absentee landowners, including Bouligny, who failed to maintain their levees, which harmed their properties. Governor Carondelet gave the absentee owners instructions to repair the levees by November or face a one-hundred-peso fine. At the turn of the century, documents described Bouligny as still owning abandoned lands in Manchac.[18]

Perhaps tied to the Manchac property was a 1788 business transaction that remains a mystery. On September 23, Bouligny purchased a fifteen-hundred-arpent plantation in Pointe Coupee from Daniel Clark, Jr., for 1,000 *pesos fuertes*. He borrowed 400 *pesos fuertes* from Clark, which he pledged to repay in four years and he did on July 19, 1793. But he kept the plantation only briefly, until March 27, 1789, when he sold it to the wealthy Dr. Benjamin Farrar of Pointe Coupee for the exact amount that he had paid. Possibly the transaction was in reality a loan to Bouligny for allowing one American to transfer property to another.[19]

17. LHC, Spanish Judicial Records, Doc. 1766, File 54, November 28, 1787.

18. LHC, Spanish Judicial Records, Spanish File 68, July 16, 1788. A document in this file states that Boligny received the land grant from Unzaga on August 24, 1771. Carondelet to Nicolas Verbois, New Orleans, July 1, 1792, in AGI, PC, leg. 215A; Perdomo Acts, Vol. XI, January–June, 1788, fols. 196–97; LHC, Doc. 1766, File 55, April 3, 1788.

19. Perdomo Acts, Vol. XII, July–December, 1788, fols. 411–12, 412–12v, Vol. XIII, January–June, 1789, fols. 142v–143, 148v–149.

Despite the proceeds from the sale of his house, Bouligny continued to suffer from a shortage of funds. He consequently borrowed 9,000 paper pesos from Capt. Francisco Collell on November 9, 1789, money that belonged to the minor children of the deceased Lt. Col. Francisco Cruzat, commandant of the 3rd Battalion in Pensacola at the time of his death on July 5, 1789. He pledged his plantation outside New Orleans for the loan, which he would repay in 1793 and 1794. His plantation, however, was already mortgaged to Derneville for 3,500 *pesos fuertes* by an agreement negotiated on January 24, 1788. The eight-hundred-arpent plantation contained a large house, two mills for cutting boards, slave cabins, and thirty-five bondsmen. The debt to Collell remained partially unpaid until 1802.[20]

Bouligny's need for money remained pressing, even after the Collell loan. On May 6, 1790, he mortgaged eight more slaves for a two-thousand-peso loan from James Kirk, which he promised to pay on March 10, 1791. To repay the loans, Bouligny entrusted a power of attorney to Manuel García to collect sums owed him in Havana for 3,800 boards for boxes that had been sent to Joseph Pontalba as well as other sums. Carpentier had failed to collect these debts earlier. Bouligny did not know how much he could expect to receive, since the Havana judges would render a decision in June. That he probably did not recover his money should not be surprising. In 1785 Diego Gardoqui described Havana merchants in less than glowing terms, even as corrupt. Finally, on February 27, 1790, Bouligny and his wife granted a power of attorney to Luis de Vilemont, Marie Louise's half brother, who was returning to France, to collect her inheritance. The dangers of the French Revolution were not then evident, since they had not yet reached their deadly heights.[21]

20. Perdomo Acts, Vol. XIV, July–December, 1789, fols. 509v–511v; Jacobo Dubreuil to Miró, Pensacola, July 5, 1789, in AGI, PC, leg. 15B. To replace the deceased Cruzat, Miró appointed Enrique White, the regimental sergeant major, as interim commandant of the third battalion ([Miró] to Jacobo Dubreuil, New Orleans, July 17, 1789, in AGI, PC, leg. 15B).

21. Gardoqui to the conde de Floridablanca, reserved, Havana, January 13, 1785, in AHN, Est., leg. 3893. The Bolignys' power of attorney to Vilemont is in Pedro Pedesclaux Acts, Vol. IX, January–March, 1790, fols. 156–57, NONA. Bouligny power of attorney to Manuel García, Pedesclaux Acts, Vol. X, March–May, 1790, fols. 303–304. A letter fragment without signature or date but written by Luis de Vilemont to his sister is in BB, HNOC. Vilemont arrived in Brest, France, where he witnessed a bloody uprising. He then

On returning from Natchez in 1786, Bouligny resumed his duties as the regimental lieutenant colonel or second in command. There was much to be done as activity grew with the formation of the regiment's 3rd Battalion. Newly arrived officers and soldiers from Havana were sent to Pensacola, where the 3rd Battalion was to be quartered. Meanwhile, the 2nd Battalion was gradually withdrawn to New Orleans. The additional troops on the Mississippi were welcomed as the threat from the United States continued to escalate, particularly as new American projects appeared for settlements on lands that Spain held or claimed on the river's east bank. Although Bouligny was not directly involved in running the colony or establishing policy, as a leading military officer, he was well aware of the problems and dangers that confronted Louisiana.[22]

Many of the threats to the colony resulted from the failure of the Spanish minister in New York, Gardoqui, to secure a settlement with the United States in 1786 over the boundary and the Mississippi River. That would have eased tension between the two nations. Instead Gardoqui sent warnings to Louisiana the next year about hostile American designs, for which the Spanish government counseled making military preparations—placing additional gunboats on the Mississippi and improving fortifications in Pensacola. Governor Miró complained repeatedly from 1787 about the ease with which Americans could invade the province with their growing population in the trans-Allegheny West. The only Spanish fortification strong enough to resist them on the Mississippi was at Natchez, but Louisiana's able-bodied soldiers continued to decline in

---

journeyed to Nantes, and concluded most of his business with M. Deseigne. Outstanding problems, however, remained.

22. Miró to Ezpeleta, New Orleans, August 27, December 20, 1787; Miró to [?], New Orleans, January 28, 1788, February 12, 1789, all in AGI, PC, leg. 1394. In February, 1788, fearing an attack down the Mississippi, Miró sent two gunboats, a galiot, the galley from Balize, and an unspecified number of pirogues with troops to Natchez. The vessels and men stayed until Miró ordered their return on June 1, 1788 (Grand-Pré to Miró, Fort Panmure, July 5, 1788, ibid., leg. 14). Miró had acted in response to the warning sent by Antonio Valdés, now minister of the Indies, in late 1787, which Captain General Ezpeleta forwarded to the governors of Louisiana and Florida ([Ezpeleta] to the governors of Louisiana and Florida, [Havana], January 11, 1788, ibid., leg. 1394). Four shipments totaling 613 recruits entered the first and second battalions of the Louisiana regiment by September 20, 1787; the fifth and sixth shipments went to the third battalion in Pensacola. The regiment then had only 859 effective men (Francisco Collell and Piernas, "Statement that manifests the shipments of Recruits . . . ," New Orleans, September 20, 1787, ibid., leg. 1397).

number. On October 25, 1787, the regiment was short 422 men; by July 15, 1788, the number had risen to 476 of the 1,856 troops authorized for the colony; and by February 12, 1789, the figure was 603, approximately the size of a battalion. Recruits never seemed to come to the province quickly enough.[23]

Louisiana also needed the full amount of the Mexican subsidy. Mexico and Havana frequently reduced the colony's financial assistance. For example, in late 1787 and early 1788, funds for the colony amounted to only 106,606 pesos. In Veracruz, that was reduced to 88,132 pesos. By the time Havana finished with the subsidy, only 70,090 pesos remained for Louisiana of the original 537,281 pesos. Also in 1788, an extraordinary 200,000 pesos designated to redeem paper money in the colony were reduced to 30,000 pesos as the other 170,000 went for the private use of Bernardo de Gálvez's widow, then living in Madrid. Governor Miró did not welcome the reductions, and on June 30, 1788, he objected vehemently to the 100,000 pesos that the Havana intendant would withhold that year; 174,669 pesos were already either in arrears or owed to Louisiana. The colony needed funds badly to alleviate distressing conditions due to the fire and wind and flood damages to agriculture. In August the governor pleaded that he required the 100,000 pesos to retire paper money and to pay the troops, because they suffered a 70 percent loss when they received depreciated paper money. The captain general replied that he would try to send the funds.[24]

With only limited resources available, Governor Miró improvised ways to protect the provinces in his charge. In the summer of 1787, James Wilkinson of Kentucky arrived in New Orleans, ostensibly to trade but in reality bearing a secret proposal to separate the American West from the United States. Many westerners were dissatisfied with their government's failure to persuade the Spaniards to open the Mississippi to their shipping. Miró welcomed the Wilkinson proposal and advised his government to accept it. But he used the opportunity to insert a plan that was purely his own: to allow Americans, most of whom were Protestants, to settle in West Florida where their countercolonization would be useful in protecting and developing Louisiana. Free land in proportion

23. Miró to Ezpeleta, New Orleans, June 30, August 16, 1788, with a draft attached to the latter; [Ezpeleta] to the governor of Louisiana, Havana, October 25, 1788, all *ibid.*, leg. 1394.

24. Coutts, "Martín Navarro," I, 297–98; Miró to Ezpeleta, New Orleans, June 30, 1788, in AGI, PC, leg. 1394.

to the size of their families and slaves were to be the major inducements for settling on Spanish soil. Miró also advised the government to send English-speaking Irish priests who would work to convert the Protestant immigrants to Catholicism and thus speed their assimilation. Several Irish priests were already journeying to Louisiana to work at converting the Natchez Anglo-Americans inherited from the late war. Although the Spanish government refrained from entering an agreement with the western American settlements until they had separated from the United States, by a decree of December 1, 1788, it allowed American Protestants to settle in West Florida, sent Irish missionaries, and opened the Mississippi to trade subject to a 15 percent tariff. The government nonetheless also attempted to improve Louisiana's military defenses.[25]

In 1789, the Spaniards found that a new government had taken charge in the United States. The government soon proved that it was more efficient than the previous one under the Articles of Confederation. The new federal government acquired authority over the western lands except for North Carolina, which ceded them in 1790, and Georgia, which refused to do so until 1802. Greed led the Georgia legislature to sell 25 million acres on December 21, 1789, to three speculation companies. The most important was the South Carolina Yazoo Company, with Dr. James O'Fallon as its general agent. It proposed to establish a sizable colony on the Yazoo River adjacent to the Spanish-held Natchez district. The settlement of a large and potentially hostile population in close proximity frightened the Spaniards and made them realize that they needed to bolster their defenses. O'Fallon made that fear real when in July, 1790, he threatened Governor Miró with invasion of Louisiana unless his company could carry out its colonization scheme without Spanish objection. The increased threat from the United States became more apparent each year that the boundary question and navigation of the Mississippi remained unresolved.[26]

After the Bourbon County episode, tension continued on the Mississippi. In 1786, George Rogers Clark seized Spanish goods at Vincennes on the upper Mississippi in retaliation for the Spanish capture of American property on the river. Gardoqui quickly sent word to Miró via Ha-

25. On immigration, see Din, "Immigration Policy," 155–75, and "Irish Mission," 315–34.

26. John Carl Parish, "The Intrigues of Doctor John O'Fallon," *Mississippi Valley Historical Review*, XVII (1930), 230–63. See also Ray Allen Billington, *Westward Expansion: A History of the American Frontier* (4th ed.; New York, 1974), 228–31.

vana to be vigilant. The Louisiana governor wrote to Minister of the Indies Gálvez on January 17, 1787, about the problems of frontier defense. He asked that the crown authorize posting six men one hundred leagues above Natchez to act as a lookout and stationing a galley, three gunboats, and two canoes at Natchez. While the government permitted Natchez to have the ships, Miró did not send them because he was desperately short of money. But new warnings from Gardoqui and Captain General José de Ezpeleta in Havana reached New Orleans by February, 1788. This time Miró acted. He ordered one galliot and two gunboats, all with eighteen-pound cannon, and the heavier galley from Balize to go upriver under Bvt. Lt. Col. Alejandro de Boulliers. By June 1, however, the possibility of invasion that year had receded, and Miró withdrew the vessels to New Orleans. But to bolster the garrison at Fort Panmure, he instructed Commandant Grand-Pré at Natchez in May, 1788, to form the civilian population into four infantry companies and one cavalry company.[27]

Meanwhile, Miró was having problems using the Southern Indians as effective allies in keeping the United States as distant from Spanish territory as possible. The Indians needed arms and munitions to stop the Americans from encroaching on their lands, and only with difficulty did the Spaniards supply them. By the mid-1780s, warfare had flared up on the Anglo-American frontier. To avoid complications, Governor Miró and the Spanish government urged Alexander McGillivray, leader of the Creeks, to make peace with the United States. From 1788 to 1789, Miró, following court orders, cut off supplying munitions to force a halt to their war against Georgia. McGillivray then entered into negotiations with the United States, and the Treaty of New York was signed on August 7, 1790. It gave the United States sovereignty over Creek towns within its territorial jurisdiction, the right to license traders to those lands, and a provision for the Creeks to obtain trade goods through the United States, a precaution in case Spain and Britain went to war. While Miró mistrusted McGillivray and assigned an agent to watch him, he raised the chief's pension from six hundred to two thousand pesos yearly.[28]

27. Miró to Ezpeleta, New Orleans, February 20, 1788, in AGI, PC, leg. 1394; Miró instructions to Alejandro de Boulliers, New Orleans, February 24, 1788, AGI, PC, leg. 5; *SMV*, Pt. 2, pp. xviii–xx. See also Nasatir, ed., *Spanish War Vessels*, 24–27.

28. Coker and Watson, *Indian Traders*, 112–47; see also John Walton Caughey, ed., *McGillivray of the Creeks* (Norman, Okla., 1938).

But Louisiana's Indian problem was not the only one confronting the Spaniards in 1790. Spain experienced reverses following the death of the able Carlos III in December, 1788. He and his ministers had endeavored to carry out modernizing reforms and to invigorate the economy in Spain and the American colonies. His son and successor, Carlos IV, who was mediocre at best, had to cope with the radical ideas unleashed by revolutionary France. The French Revolution jolted the Spaniards from reform to reaction, and that produced dissatisfaction in the colonies, which favored more change. Moreover, the Spanish seizure of British ships and crews at Nootka Sound in 1789 brought the threat of war unless Spain apologized and withdrew from the Pacific Northwest Coast. Abandoned by revolutionary France, Spain dared not risk war against Britain alone. More discretion was needed in steering the course of empire. Louisiana, exposed and vulnerable, also appeared as a problem child for Spain. By 1790, threats of invasion surfaced yearly, and defenses remained minimal. Louisiana's problems in the final decade of the eighteenth century escalated. Ideas on what course of action to follow took divergent paths in Spain and Louisiana.[29]

While Bouligny was active in bolstering the province's strength—training recruits, dispatching soldiers to the detachments, improving New Orleans' defenses—most of his activities during this time were not recorded. One commission he undertook as regimental lieutenant colonel was the investigation of a four-thousand-reales (five-hundred-pesos) voucher (*libranza*) that had been falsified into forty thousand reales. In January, 1790, Commandant Piernas placed him in charge of determining who was responsible for the crime. Bouligny investigated the trustee captains (*capitanes depositarios*) who had charge of the 1st Battalion's funds from the time the voucher came into army possession. In March, 1784, Intendant Martín Navarro ordered a check on the credit certificates that had been issued because several had already been falsified. At that time the New Orleans merchant Francisco Braquier held the voucher, numbered 112, which was in good condition. What happened to it after it left Braquier's ownership was not known. Since it came into army possession, that meant questioning the trustee captains from that time: Manuel Pérez for 1784 and 1786, José de la Peña for 1785, Felipe Treviño for 1787,

29. Herr, *Eighteenth-Century Revolution*, 239–68; Guillermo Céspedes del Castillo, *América hispánica (1492–1898)* (Barcelona, 1983), 317–18. See also Warren L. Cook, *Flood Tide of Empire: Spain and the Pacific Northwest, 1543–1819* (New Haven, 1973), 146–99.

Manuel Lanzos for 1788, and Zenon Trudeau for 1789. Boulingy questioned the last three men in New Orleans and sent a questionnaire to St. Louis, where Pérez was lieutenant governor; de la Peña had gone to Cuba to help with recruits destined for Louisiana.[30]

Pérez provided the most information about his duties as trustee captain, although he did not solve the mystery. He had handled regimental funds for such diverse purposes as gratuities for services, recruiting costs, sums left by deserters, and money given to presidios where prisoners had been sent. But whenever the cash box was opened to receive or disburse funds, it was done in the presence of superior officers. On concluding his investigation on April 29, 1790, Bouligny felt obliged to suspend his work "due to not having found in the declarations . . . the least clue to pursue." In relating the affair to acting Captain General Domingo Cabello in August, Governor Miró stated that Commandant Piernas and the other regimental officers were extremely scrupulous in handling funds and that it was impossible to impugn their honor. The Spanish government, however, ordered the investigation to remain open.[31]

In 1789, four years after their last promotions, both Bouligny and Piernas requested advancement in rank. Their requests were spurred by the arrival in New Orleans of Bvt. Lt. Col. Manuel Gayoso de Lemos on April 12 to become the governor of the Natchez district, where the Anglo-American immigrants were to settle. Governor Miró had served with Gayoso in Spain in the Lisbon regiment for four years and at that time thought favorably of him. Since Natchez constituted the first line of defense on the Mississippi, Miró confided to Gayoso details about the Wilkinson intrigue and problems related to defense, Indians, and immigration. Although the Spanish government had originally not regarded the post of Natchez governor as significant (it believed that it was beneath Enrique White, then sergeant major of the Louisiana regiment), Miró recommended that Gayoso be promoted to colonel to command

30. There are many letters on Bouligny's investigation; see Piernas to Bouligny, New Orleans, January 16, 17, 20, 1790, with enclosures, and Bouligny's questionnaire to Pérez, New Orleans, January 17, 1790, with Pérez's replies, St. Louis, April 6, 1790, all in AGI, PC, leg. 170A. On the issue of *libranzas* and their falsification, see Coutts, "Martín Navarro," I, 275–85.

31. Pérez, St. Louis, April 6, 1790, and Bouligny to Pérez, New Orleans, April 29, 1790, both in AGI, PC, leg. 170A; Miró to Domingo Cabello, New Orleans, August 10, 1790, *ibid.,* leg. 1425.

more respect from the Anglo-Americans with whom he would be dealing. On May 20, 1789, Miró solicited the promotion, which the Supreme
Council of State approved on October 12, with a dispatch issued to
Gayoso for brevet colonel on October 25. Miró retained seniority in rank,
since he and Arturo O'Neill, governor of Pensacola, had been promoted
to brigadier general in January, 1789.[32]

Since Miró probably informed the senior officers in New Orleans
about his decision to seek a colonelcy for Gayoso, their petitions for
promotion were soon forthcoming. Gayoso was years younger than
Bouligny or Piernas and had been a cadet when they were captains. On
May 24, Piernas as commandant endorsed Bouligny's request for advancement to colonel, testifying that he had "employed valor and activity,
and was constantly fulfilling [his duties] with exactitude, and to the satisfaction of his chiefs, for all of which I consider him meritorious of the
grace he solicits." The coolness with which the government had earlier
received Bouligny's petitions for promotion was gone, as were the Gál-
vezes; Minister of the Indies José de Gálvez had died in June, 1787. Bouligny gained his new rank on August 24, 1789. By December 31, he had
learned of his advancement to brevet colonel; he enjoyed two months of
seniority over Gayoso. Piernas, however, was not as fortunate; his request for promotion to brigadier was denied.[33]

Piernas would never achieve that rank. His successful career in Louisiana, which began with his arrival in the colony with Governor Ulloa
in 1766 as a lieutenant, terminated on March 28, 1791, when he died.
Consequently, Bouligny, as the next ranking officer, took charge as acting
commandant of the Louisiana regiment. He also received Governor
Miró's endorsement for promotion to commandant of the regiment with
the rank of permanent colonel. In Spain, army headquarters concurred

32. Miró to Antonio Valdés, reserved, New Orleans, May 20, 1789, with enclosures,
and dispatch of Gayoso's promotion to the governor of Louisiana, San Lorenzo, October 25, 1789, both in AHN, Est., leg. 3901, exped. 3; Miró to Cabello, New Orleans,
March 10, 1790, in AGI, PC, leg. 1425; Royal order to the governor of Louisiana, San
Lorenzo, November 3, 1787, AHN, Est., leg. 3889, exped. 5.

33. Bouligny petition for promotion, New Orleans, May 26, 1789, AGS, GM,
leg. 6919; Piernas, "Report for Lt. Col. Francisco Bouligny," New Orleans, May 24, 1789,
KCTU; Bouligny's promotion dispatch, Madrid, August 24, 1789, AGI, PC, leg. 570A;
Miró to Cabello, New Orleans, December 31, 1789, in AGI, PC, leg. 1425. Piernas' petition
for promotion and its rejection are in AGS, GM, leg. 6915.

on September 4, 1791. Thus, after twenty-two years in Louisiana, Bouligny had reached the top military post in the colony. He must have bristled with enormous pride and satisfaction on achieving this distinction, particularly after enduring years of slow advancement. A discordant note, however, was Gayoso's promotion to full colonel on October 21, 1790, nearly a year before Bouligny's attainment of that rank. In the next six years the regimental commandant never regained the preeminence that he had briefly enjoyed.[34]

Perhaps in a modest way, Bouligny's brother Juan helped in gaining his new post. On February 1, 1790, he had written to Francisco from Constantinople, where he was Spain's minister to the Ottoman court, that he had learned that Luis de Las Casas had been appointed captain general of Cuba, Louisiana, and Florida (which again had been united into one jurisdiction). Since Juan had met Las Casas and the latter's brother Simón de Las Casas, Spain's ambassador to Venice, was his friend, he took it upon himself to write to the new captain general to congratulate him on his appointment and to recommend Francisco to his benevolence.[35]

But among his brothers, Bouligny confided more in his oldest brother, José, about his hopes and ambitions in Louisiana. While Bouligny's letters are now lost, an important letter from José reveals much about what Francisco was thinking regarding the advice his brother gave him. Upon learning in Madrid of Francisco's promotion to proprietary colonel of the Louisiana regiment, José soon wrote on September 28, 1791, congratulating him. José also recognized the king's devotion in rewarding Francisco for his services, without anyone else intervening on his behalf, except perhaps the governor, "who did it out of a sense of justice."[36]

34. Valdés to the captain general of Louisiana and Florida, Madrid, January 24, 1789, in *SMV,* Pt. 2, P. 266. Piernas' last will, dictated on March 14, 1791, is in Carlos Ximénes Acts, Vol. I, January–December, 1791, fols. 128–46v, NONA, and in AGI, PC, leg. 170A. Miró recommendation on Piernas (probably for his widow and children), New Orleans, January 29, 179[2], AGI, PC, leg. 122A. Piernas, an uncomplicated man, requested a simple funeral, having present only the governor and four gentlemen. Possibly Bouligny, a close friend, was one of the gentlemen. Gayoso patent of promotion, San Lorenzo, October 21, 1790, AGI, PC, leg. 570A.

35. Juan Bouligny to Francisco Bouligny, Constantinople, February 1, 1790, in DB, HNOC.

36. José Bouligny to Francisco Bouligny, Azcovaya, Spain, September 28, 1791, *ibid.*

José was filled with happiness for Francisco:

It should calm all your anxieties, precisely those which make you forget your own well-being. Yes, my Frasquito, they caused me to see by the expressions of your letters the unrest of your soul, born in the truth of your point of honor on considering yourself held back and injured; your spirit tormented, . . . [but] which you yourself could have corrected with a bit more suffering. But, finally, all was resolved. For your part, you owe it to yourself to calm your soul in order not to return to seeing yourself surrounded by emotions that torment and shorten your days. If my advice as an older brother and godfather can induce you to achieve the true happiness that I wish, receive with fraternal affection that which I shall dictate.[37]

José went on to state that Francisco's promotion should incline him more to fidelity for the king and a willingness to shed his last drop of blood in royal service: "Never does our blood glow more than when it is spilt for Religion, for the King, and for our Fatherhood." By doing this, learned and generous men had raised up their lineages; they had enlightened and ennobled their families, filling them with honor. José admitted that his advice was not necessary, since Francisco had displayed his courage at Pensacola. But José continued: "Give a truce to your noble ambition, since as noble as it is, prudence should limit it. Oh, dear Frasquito, how many anxieties would you free yourself from if you only did that!" He added that Francisco should not refuse promotions if he received them but that he should not solicit them and should wait for what God had in store for him. He counseled his younger brother to pardon his opponents generously and to oblige them through kindnesses to like him. He should be generous with his friends and avoid the anger that sprang from ingratitude. For those who had been indifferent to him, repay them in kind, but never harm them in order not to stain his soul.[38]

José's letter revealed several sentiments that were then common, and Bouligny, at least in part, shared them. First and foremost were loyalty to the crown, which meant the Spanish nation, and faith in the Catholic religion. José, much more stoic than Francisco, also believed that one's service would eventually receive its just recognition. José, however, had spent his life in commerce and in Alicante, far removed from and ignorant of the ways of bureaucracy. He similarly lacked the driving ambition,

37. *Ibid.*
38. *Ibid.*

which his brother possessed, that was so often necessary in order to succeed in a hierarchical system. How José's advice affected Francisco is not known, but becoming regimental commandant no doubt increased his confidence and well-being. In the next nine years, as the unit's colonel, Bouligny displayed the talent and ability that had been formed during the previous two decades. It would be a glorious time for him. But having once been lieutenant governor and near the preeminent administrative post in the colony, he still harbored thoughts of becoming governor of Louisiana, since he was now the colony's senior official in longevity and experience.

But as Miró's tenure as governor approached its conclusion, it seemed not the most propitious time for Boulingy to seek that post. Nor was there support from Miró. In Octrober, 1790, Miró, governor of Louisiana and West Florida since 1782 and intendant since 1788, when Navarro retired, requested his return to Spain and a post as aide to the minister of war. For his replacement, Miró advanced Gayoso's name, stating that he possessed both experience and talent. On March 20, 1791, the governor added that Gayoso was already acquainted with confidential matters (the secret correspondence with Americans, who for economic reasons favored a connection with Spain). But the government dismissed his suggestion and selected an outsider as the new governor and intendant of Louisiana.[39]

A royal order of March 9, 1791, instructed Miró to return to Spain, and another of March 18 appointed Francisco Luis Héctor, fifteenth barón de Carondelet, then governor and intendant of El Salvador in Central America, as the governor. Carondelet, a Fleming from northern France born about July, 1747, had entered the Spanish military at sixteen. His family, like many other Flemings, had a tradition of service to Spain. Through his years in the army, Carondelet had climbed to colonel and had seen military action at the beach in Algiers with O'Reilly in 1775 and at Pensacola with Gálvez in 1781. On February 23, 1788, the crown appointed him to govern El Salvador, an office he exercised for three years, encouraging economic development and founding new settlements. The crown thought well enough of his work to promote him to the more exacting task of protecting and developing Louisiana. Carondelet de-

39. Miró to the conde de Campo de Alange, New Orleans, October 12, 1790, in BN, DL; Miró to Antonio Portlier, New Orleans, March 20, 1791, in AGI, SD, leg. 2588; Gayoso to Floridablanca, New Orleans, October 12, 1790, AHN, Est., leg. 3902, exped. 6.

parted from Central America in October, 1791, and stopped in Havana to visit his brother-in-law Captain General Luis de Las Casas. Having a friendly and supportive superior in Cuba was advantageous for the Louisiana governor. Not until year's end did he reach New Orleans, where he took the oath of office as governor and intendant on December 30, 1791.[40]

No doubt Colonel Bouligny and other leading Spanish officials attended the ceremony in the Cabildo, which ushered in a new era. Many Louisianians regretted Miró's departure. He probably enjoyed greater popularity among his men and the provincial residents than any other Spanish governor, including Gálvez. Miró had sought to reconcile different factions in the colony and to employ impartially the talents of the officers and men who served under him. In spite of having arrived in Louisiana in 1778 as an outsider to the regiment, Miró adroitly gained the respect and love of his soldiers and the colony's inhabitants. Only a tiny faction in the New Orleans bureaucracy, headed by the accountant José de Orue y Gorvea, who was involved in illegal activities, represented any opposition. Because of inadequate budgets, a surge in foreign dangers in the late 1780s, and the absense of a patron in Spain, the task of guiding Louisiana through turbulent waters had not been easy for Miró. But Madrid appreciated his efforts and recalled him to Spain upon the completion of his term as governor, a favor that it extended to no other governor of Spanish Louisiana. While his *residencia* (investigation into his conduct while in office) generated tremendous paperwork, dragging on beyond Miró's premature death on June 4, 1795, it ended successfully. Bouligny, who had established a warm and cordial relationship with Miró, would miss him. But Bouligny's career had not yet concluded, and as regimental commandant, he still looked forward to performing his duties and achieving new honors and rewards.[41]

40. On Carondelet, see Thomas Marc Fiehrer, "The Baron de Carondelet as Agent of Bourbon Reform: A Study of Spanish Colonial Administration in the Years of the French Revolution" (Ph.D. dissertation, Tulane University, 1977).

41. Burson, *Miró*, 283; see also the dispatch of the governorship and intendancy of Louisiana to Carondelet and Miró's transfer to Madrid, both in AGS, GM, leg. 6929.

10 COMMANDANT OF THE FIXED LOUISIANA REGIMENT

1791–1797

THE SIX YEARS BETWEEN 1791 and 1797 in Bouligny's life as commandant of the Fixed Louisiana Regiment were filled with constant activity as Louisiana suffered from numerous external and internal threats. To counteract the dangers, Governor Miró started construction of forts at Nogales, at the mouth of the Yazoo River, and at Plaquemines, twelve leagues above the entrance to the Mississippi. Although the possibility of conflict between Spain and Britain over Nootka evaporated in 1791, Spain soon entered into new wars. The first, as a member of a coalition of monarchies, was against republican France (1793 to 1795), and it ended in disaster. Once defeated, Spain entered an alliance with its erstwhile enemy. While the alliance realigned the Iberian nation with its traditional eighteenth-century ally, France, it alienated Great Britain, and war quickly ensued (1796 to 1808). The wartime dangers to Louisiana kept activity there at fever pitch even when measures to fortify the *barreda,* the protective barrier that Louisiana constituted for rich Mexico, were only partially taken. Moreover, Jacobins created by the French Revolution sought the province's return to Gallic rule. They spoke of liberty, equality, and fraternity even for slaves, a proposition that rocked the tranquillity of the province and created the specter of a black insurrection. The grim example of Haiti's 1791 slave rebellion terrified many of the colony's inhabitants, since blacks outnumbered the white population. Coupled to the dangers, a new governor arrived whose experiences in Central America had not prepared him for the complexities of the problems.

1. Gayarré, *History,* III, 312–85; Whitaker, *Spanish American Frontier,* 153–216, and *The Mississippi Question, 1795–1803: A Study in Trade, Politics, and Diplomacy* (1934; rpr. Glouster, Mass., 1962), 51–78; and Fiehrer, "Carondelet."

As governor, the baron de Carondelet has often been depicted by modern writers as overreacting to the many perils that Louisiana faced. In fairness, however, he inherited a situation far different from the one that confronted Miró ten years earlier. The baron nevertheless worked indefatigably to increase the colony's strength, using the resources available to him: the Indians, although frequently unreliable; the Wilkinson conspiracy, which had languished at the end of Miró's tenure; European as opposed to American immigration; and additional troops and several new forts. Carondelet kept advocating massive expenditures for military defenses. While this was done in part, the Spanish government, represented by Secretary of State Manuel Godoy, came to view it as futile. After Britain settled its differences with the United States in the 1794 Jay's Treaty, Godoy sought to avert an American attack on Louisiana through negotiations. In the Treaty of San Lorenzo of October 27, 1795, he capitulated to American demands for territory that Spain had held since 1779 and navigation of the Mississippi to buy goodwill. The new boundary at the thirty-first parallel on the Mississippi's east bank undermined Spanish defenses and greatly extended American influence in Louisiana. It had already been increasing; large numbers of ships from the United States ladened with merchandise visited New Orleans yearly, and they provided many of the colony's needs, particularly foodstuffs.[2]

Becoming colonel and commandant of the Fixed Louisiana Regiment in 1791 was, with one exception, the last important duty that Francisco Bouligny discharged. As commandant, his post, at army headquarters in New Orleans, involved processing massive amounts of paperwork. He no longer participated on commissions such as establishing New Iberia or commanding Natchez in a period of crisis. But at age fifty-five,

---

2. On trade, see Whitaker, *Spanish American Frontier*, 175–76, and *Documents*, xlvii–li; and C. Richard Arena, "Philadelphia–Spanish New Orleans Trade in the 1790's," *Louisiana History*, II (1961), 429–45; on diplomacy, Bemis, *Pinckney's Treaty*; on Indian policy, Coker and Watson, *Indian Traders*, 157–211; on immigration, Din, "Spain's Immigration Policy in Louisiana and the American Penetration, 1792–1803," *Southwestern Historical Quarterly*, LXXVI (1973), 255–76.

A royal order of May 24, 1793, wanted to know the military expenditures required by Louisiana. Carondelet answered that new forts at New Madrid, Nogales, and Plaquemines had increased expenses and that two more forts, at Barrancas de Margot (Chickasaw Bluffs) and Tombigbee, were needed. He believed that Louisiana required a minimum of four battalions and a squadron of galleys, all at a cost of 629,855 pesos per year (Carondelet to Las Casas, New Orleans, September 30, 1793, in AGI, PC, leg. 1442).

physical afflictions, about which we know little, started to trouble him, and his more sedentary life added girth to his physique. His preoccupations now revolved about maintaining the regiment's manpower and an adequate supply of arms and munitions, keeping a full complement of soldiers at the many detachments, corresponding with the outposts (he wrote 185 letters to Pensacola alone in the first fifteen months he was commandant), presiding over courts-martial, training recruits, assigning chaplains to the battalions, recommending personnel for promotion and explaining why others were passed over (*postergados*), and countless other tasks necessary in administering a regiment.[3]

Alarmed by the many dangers, the Carondelet administration labored assiduously to improve defenses, duties that involved the regimental commandant. No sooner did the baron arrive than Miró, Gayoso, and Bouligny alerted him to the problems that disturbed the colony. Carondelet immediately notified his brother-in-law in Havana and the government in Spain. While Gayoso, as head of the Natchez district, became a close adviser to the governor-general in affairs related to Indians, immigration, and the United States, Bouligny kept Carondelet apprised of the status of the regiment, arms, and fortifications. And he did more. In the spring of 1792, since Carondelet was first on horseback in the morning riding out to inspect the improvements in the city's defenses, Bouligny also "bec[a]me a cavalier," procuring a saddle horse and riding about New Orleans attending to his duties. Joseph Xavier de Pontalba informed his uncle Esteban Miró in Spain: "Bouligny is always up in the air, he has hardly finished one job than the Baron gives him another; besides this, he is sent to the [military] works several times a day. All of this lends an air of activity that resembles a time of war."[4]

3. Bouligny to Carondelet, New Orleans, August 2, 1792, enclosed in Carondelet to Las Casas, New Orleans, July 31, 1792, in AGI, PC, leg. 1441. Important matters that involved Bouligny are in the governor's letters to the captain generals as enclosures. Bouligny's correspondence with the post commandants is very scattered; see Roscoe Hill, *Descriptive Catalogue of the Documents Relating to the History of the United States in the Papeles Procedentes de Cuba Deposited in the Archivo General de Indias at Seville* (1916; rpr. New York, 1965), 505.

4. There are many letters with enclosures from Carondelet to officials in Spain in early 1792; see in particular Carondelet to Floridablanca, reserved, New Orleans, January 13, 1792, in AHN, Est., leg. 3898 (with a copy in AGI, PC, leg. 25A); Carondelet to Floridablanca, New Orleans, January 18, 1792, in AHN, Est., leg. 3898. Carondelet wrote to Captain General Las Casas on the same day on the same topic (Carondelet to Las Casas, New Orleans, January 18, 1792, in AGI, PC, leg. 1441, with a copy in AGS, GM, leg. 6925). Miró

For relaxation, Bouligny played cards with Nicolas D'Aunoy, Peytavin, Juan Prieto, Miguel(?) Fortier, and Pedro Rousseau, probably in Government House, where they shared confidences, the latest news, and gossip. Bouligny also developed a close and comfortable relationship with Governor Carondelet. Bouligny kept busy in numerous other matters, some of which dated back to the Miró administration.[5]

An early problem Bouligny encountered was reopening the regimental school of cadets, which Piernas had closed by 1789 because no officer volunteered to teach the youth. Its closure bothered Captain General Las Casas, who in early 1791 raised the question of reopening it, since the regiment needed officers. Governor Miró handed the matter to Bouligny. He found only Captain Francisco Montreuill, then in Pensacola with the 3rd Battalion, willing to teach; he had to be brought back to New Orleans. For books to be used in instruction, Bouligny requested from Havana the most essential volumes: eighty copies of the army ordinances and thirty copies of Félix Colón's *Juzgados militares de España y sus Indias*. These books were useful teaching tools for the cadets and handy reference works for the regimental officers and sergeants.[6]

The location of the cadet school in New Orleans created a problem for the sons of Capts. Diego de Vegas and Francisco Deverges, whose fathers were stationed in Pensacola and could not afford to keep them in New Orleans. Bouligny permitted the boys to remain in Pensacola, attending an elementary school and journeying to New Orleans twice yearly to take the cadet examinations. Las Casas temporarily approved of the arrangement, and it lasted until 1798 when the governor-general ordered the cadets to New Orleans.[7]

---

departed from New Orleans to Havana in February, 1792, and from there to Cádiz on April 24, 1792 (Burson, *Miró*, 284; Heloise H. Cruzat, ed., "Letters in Journal Form, Written to Don Estevan Miró, Ex-Governor of Louisiana by Don Joseph Xavier de Pontalba in 1792," *Louisiana Historical Quarterly*, II [1919] 401–402).

5. Cruzat, ed., "Letters," 409, 411. Carondelet reflected his favorable opinion of Bouligny in the latter's service sheet of June, 1793: "He has talent, much zeal, and accurateness in command" (AGI, PC, leg. 161A). In a private note to Bouligny on a dinner invitation, Carondelet stated he would accept only if it was "a friendly invitation and within the family" (Carondelet to Bouligny, February 19, [no year], in BB, HNOC).

6. Miró to Las Casas, New Orleans, May 22, June 28, 1791, with enclosures of Bouligny to Miró, New Orleans, May 21, June 1, 1791, all in AGI, PC, leg. 1440A.

7. Carondelet to Las Casas, New Orleans, February 7, 1793, with enclosures; Bouligny to Carondelet, New Orleans, January 12, 1793; Petitions of Diego de Vegas and Fran-

The age at which boys could be admitted to the cadet school was another issue Bouligny had to address. Originally, enrollment was limited to boys aged sixteen and older, but Piernas had admitted twelve-year-olds: sons of all army officers, government officials, and nearly everyone else of the right social standing. Miró also permitted the sons of retired French officers to enroll, a policy initiated by Gálvez to engender goodwill. In the fifteen months since Bouligny had assumed command (to mid-1792), he had admitted six boys, four of them sixteen or older, one twelve-year-old (his son Ursino), and the thirteen-year-old son of a lieutenant who had been proposed for promotion to captain. Thus it appears that Bouligny reinstituted the royal ordinances for admitting sons of subalterns and nonmilitary personnel at sixteen or older.[8]

While there is no evidence that he went about looking for quarrels, Bouligny did not run away from them. A tempest in a teapot erupted on May 10, 1791, when the querulous Juan Ventura Morales, then *alcalde* (magistrate) of the first vote on the Cabildo, ordered Bouligny to send the regimental surgeon José Fernández to testify the next day before Morales' tribunal on the wounds suffered by Francisco Mayor. An irritated Bouligny immediately shot back that he would do so upon receiving the governor's orders and suggested that Morales address his request to Miró. After receiving another message the next day questioning Bouligny's motives for refusing, the colonel answered Morales by giving Fernández permission to testify because the governor had consented, but Bouligny refused to explain his conduct. He told the *alcalde* that he would take the matter up with the governor to avoid useless disputes that stole time from the fulfillment of their respective duties.[9]

In not allowing anyone from the regiment to testify before a tribunal

---

cisco Deverges; [Las Casas] to the governor of Louisiana, Havana, March 9, 1793; all *ibid.,* leg. 1442; Vicente Folch to Manuel Gayoso, Pensacola, December 3, 1798, *ibid.,* leg. 53.

8. Miró to Las Casas, New Orleans, June 10, 1791, with enclosure of Bouligny to Miró, New Orleans, June 4, 1791, *ibid.,* leg. 1440A. In June, 1792, Bouligny provided additional information on the cadets, their ages, seniority, and regulations (see Bouligny to Las Casas, New Orleans, June 19, 1792, with enclosures, all attached to Carondelet to Las Casas, June 20, 1792, *ibid.,* leg. 1441). Ursino Bouligny was admitted as a cadet on November 8, 1790 (*oficio* of Bouligny enclosed in Carondelet to Las Casas, New Orleans, June 20, 1792, *ibid.,* leg. 1441).

9. Morales to Bouligny, New Orleans, May 10, 11, 1791; Bouligny to Morales, New Orleans, May 10, 11, all enclosed in Miró to Las Casas, New Orleans, July 27, 1791, *ibid.,* leg. 1440B.

without Miró's express permission, Bouligny had followed orders. He blamed Morales' high-handed behavior for his intransigence in replying to the *alcalde*. He felt that Morales had damaged his esteem and character, and he recommended that the magistrate's wretched conduct be brought to the attention of the captain general. In writing to Las Casas, Miró upheld Bouligny as having acted in accordance with established custom in New Orleans.[10]

Another serious matter Bouligny dealt with was explaining to the captain general the method of trials for soldiers accused of crimes at distant outposts. The usual procedure was to take testimony from witnesses and the accused. If the offense was serious, the written testimony and the accused were sent to New Orleans. Army officers sitting in a council of war examined the testimony and, if they found the accused guilty, imposed a sentence. The sentences for serious crimes were next forwarded to Havana for review by an appellate court. The problem at the outposts concerned adequate defense for the accused. The Supreme Council of War in Havana had recently reduced the death sentence imposed on Pvt. Juan Esgilencia to ten years' imprisonment because he had not had the benefit of counsel when the witnesses were questioned.

Bouligny stated that it was impossible to carry out trials at the outposts in conformance with army ordinances. He argued that the distances to the outposts from New Orleans; the cost and difficulty of sending counsel, usually an officer, for each trial; the small size of the garrisons, with their few officers; and the impracticality of keeping witnesses (often hunters and traders) waiting made fulfilling the ordinances unfeasible. Thus as imperfect as the system appeared, it was necessary. The captain general agreed. He replied on August 27, 1791, that in situations that made it impossible to comply fully with the ordinances, the judge advocate was to be consulted on legal procedure.[11]

In August, 1791, Bouligny first confronted the problem of handling Lt. Antonio Palao, whose intractable behavior had plagued his superiors for years. Palao arrived in Louisiana in 1778 from the Canary Islands,

10. Bouligny to Miró, New Orleans, May 12, 1791, and Miró to Las Casas, New Orleans, July 27, 1791, *ibid.*

11. Miró to Las Casas, New Orleans, July 23, 1791, with enclosure of Bouligny to Las Casas, New Orleans, July 19, 1792; [Las Casas] to the governor of Louisiana, [Havana], August 27, 1791, with an attached *minuta,* all *ibid.* The system for courts-martial in New Orleans differed from that in the outposts because more officers were present. A brief but not completely accurate description of New Orleans courts-martial is in Burson, *Miró,* 44.

where his father, Sublt. Martín Terry Palao, had been stationed. The entire family emigrated at that time, going with the Canary Islanders who had been recruited for Louisiana, with Martín in charge of one shipload of Isleños, and Antonio, soon to become a cadet in Louisiana, in charge of another. During the siege of Pensacola in the war against Britain, Palao and two other cadets, Carlos de Ville Goutin and Ignacio de Acosta, were in Bouligny's grenadier command, and they had been found cowering when they should have assaulted a British position. Although Bouligny reported their misconduct, it did not interfere with their subsequent careers, and it might have contributed to Palao's cynical attitude toward the army. In the 1780s, Commandant Piernas had had his share of difficulty dealing with Palao. More recently, on August 8, 1791, a council of war met until 3 A.M. the next day to consider Palao's accusations against Cpl2c. Pablo Mayor and Pvt. José Domínguez. The council, however, refused to believe his testimony and ordered his arrest.[12]

The next day, Judge Advocate Nicolás María Vidal, a recent arrival in Louisiana who sought to increase his influence in government, disapproved of the arrest because the governor had not consented. But Palao soon showed more disrespect when a soldier inadvertently gave him a Bouligny letter intended for Governor Miró, then refused to surrender it to an aide, to Bouligny (who borrowed the governor's two-wheeled calash for the trip to the guardhouse, since he was suffering from a leg infection), and to Sergeant Major Gilberto Guillemard, sent by Miró. Palao, however, denied being disrespectful and described himself as an unfortunate subject burdened with numerous children. In explaining the affair to the captain general, the governor ignored Vidal and declared that Palao had insulted both Bouligny and himself. Captain General Las Casas, in mid-1792, while consulting Spain on what to do about Palao, ordered his continued detention.[13]

12. [Las Casas] to the governor of Louisiana, [Havana], July 28, 1792; Carondelet to Las Casas, New Orleans, October 1, 1792, both in AGI, PC, leg. 1441. Antonio Palao was born about 1761 in Cataluña, Spain. He was a "distinguished" soldier at age twelve, a cadet on July 16, 1778, a sublieutenant on May 12, 1781, as a reward for participating in the Mobile campaign, a sublieutenant of grenadiers on October 8, 1787, and a lieutenant on March 18, 1789 (Palao's service sheet, December, 1800, *ibid.*, leg. 161B). On the Palao family going to Louisiana, see Din, *Canary Islanders*, 18–19, 213, 217.

13. [Las Casas] to the governor of Louisiana, [Havana], July 28, 1792; Carondelet to Las Casas, New Orleans, October 1, 1792, both in AGI, PC, leg. 1441.

After his arrival in New Orleans, Governor Carondelet also refused to be swayed by the lieutenant. On November 18, 1792, he sent the captain general more documents on the undisciplined Palao. He wrote: "Your Excellency should bear in mind all the trouble caused by Lieutenant Antonio Palao with his plotting. Having this in mind, it seems unnecessary to add new censures, when the simple reading of the documents . . . is enough to form a judgment and to dictate the proper measures."[14]

Bouligny's views about Palao remained unchanged. When Palao petitioned to become adjutant major, the colonel wrote on February 5, 1793: "The conduct of this officer has been consistently bad and reprehensible. . . . He is today under arrest due to serious matters pending at superior headquarters, and despite this [he shows] little disposition to improve." The captain general replied the next month that with royal acceptance, Palao would not be promoted until he had demonstrated improved conduct over a lengthy period. The crown confirmed his arrest for one year at half pay.[15]

Palao spent much of his time "under arrest" at Fort San Felipe, assisting in its construction. By August, 1794, he was at Fort Confederación above Mobile, improving the stockade. In March, 1795, he took command of Fort San Esteban on the Tombigbee River, established in 1789 to protect Mobile, with instructions the next month to build a new fort. It proved to be an unfortunate assignment; controversy and error followed him there. He soon asked to be relieved, pleading poverty, and requested discharge with the rank of captain. Several months earlier, the captain general had warned him that unless he improved his conduct, he would be cashiered from the army. But wars and the shortage of officers

14. [Las Casas] to the governor of Louisiana, Havana, in answer to Carondelet's July 28, 1792, letter to him; Carondelet to Las Casas, New Orleans, November 18, 1792, contains the quotation, all *ibid*. Soon after arriving in Louisiana, Carondelet sent documents on Palao to the captain general in order for him to judge the lieutenant's conduct (Carondelet to Las Casas, New Orleans, February 12, 1792, *ibid*.). Carondelet, however, supported Palao's petition to the king to shorten his imprisonment (see Carondelet to Las Casas, New Orleans, June 10, 1793, *ibid.*, leg. 1442, with Palao's petition enclosed).

15. Bouligny to [Carondelet], New Orleans, February 5, 1793; [Las Casas] to [Bouligny], Havana, March 11, 1793; Las Casas to the governor of Louisiana, Havana, June 3, 1793, all attached to [Gayoso] to the conde de Santa Clara, [n.p.], April 20, 1799, *ibid.*, leg. 154B. See Salcedo to Someruelos, New Orleans, two letters of September 9, one of November 11, 1803, with enclosures, all *ibid.*, leg. 1556.

in Louisiana kept him in uniform. In 1797, he was teaching the cadets of the 3rd Battalion in Pensacola, where he spent the years 1796 to 1800. In 1803, he was still a lieutenant and again under arrest for insubordination and lack of respect. He left the army that year under a cloud.[16]

If Palao's outrageous demeanor generated a negative impression in Bouligny and other officers, that did not extend to all the young subalterns who misbehaved. This can be seen in Bouligny's judgment of Lt. José Le Blanc, whom Piernas (as commandant in 1788) had charged with lack of application and poor conduct. The year after becoming commandant, Bouligny revised his opinion in a report to the governor that revealed his thinking. He explained Le Blanc's bad behavior as proof of "a lively and courageous spirit" for which the lieutenant had suffered three months of house arrest. The colonel believed that Le Blanc's high spirits could be beneficial to the king's service. His "libertinism" was being overcome with age and experience, and Bouligny had advised him that only by study, application, and moderate habits could he win promotion. The lieutenant had reputedly taken this advice to heart.[17]

Bouligny now recommended that Le Blanc be appointed adjutant.

16. Las Casas to the governor of Louisiana, Havana, June 3, 1793, January 27, March 11, 1795; Bouligny to [Carondelet?], New Orleans, October 15, 1795, all attached to [Gayoso] to Santa Clara, [n.p.], April 20, 1799, *ibid.*, leg. 154B; Palao to Manuel Lanzos, San Esteban, March 30, May 4, 1795, both *ibid.*, leg. 67. See also Manuel de Salcedo to Someruelos, New Orleans, October 30, 1801; Palao to Someruelos, New Orleans, October 21, 1801, with attachment of Carlos Howard on passing over Palao for promotion, New Orleans, August 31, 1801, all *ibid.*, leg. 1552. Howard reported that Palao treated as an enemy anyone who did not agree with him. By the mid-1790s, Palao had contracted syphilis (Jack D. L. Holmes, "Spanish Military Commanders in Colonial Alabama," *Journal of the Alabama Academy of Science*, XXXVII [1966], 63–65). Palao's licentious life with a mulatto prostitute, Pognon, caused his wife to complain to an ecclesiastical court.

17. Bouligny to Carondelet, New Orleans, April 23, 1792, in AGI, PC, leg. 1441. Bouligny seemed inclined to give cadets who misbehaved and later repented an opportunity for advancement. This was true for Cayetano Fajardo de Cobarrubias, who was sentenced to eight years in the third battalion. In July, 1792, Bouligny wrote: "Our Benign Sovereign, in imitation of Our Divine Lord, takes pleasure in pardoning those who commit faults if their contrition is sincere and constant" (Bouligny to Carondelet, New Orleans, July 21, 1792, *ibid.*). Despite his improved conduct and being at the head of his class, Fajardo was not treated well (see his petition to Las Casas, New Orleans, November 9, 1792, enclosed in Carondelet to Las Casas, New Orleans, November 18, 1792, *ibid.*). Bouligny blamed the city's unwillingness to forgive for Fajardo's failure to be promoted (see Fajardo's service record of June 30, 1793, *ibid.*, leg. 161A).

That official needed to be acquainted with all the individuals in the regiment—sergeants, corporals, and soldiers—and to know as much as possible about their temper, character, and circumstances to fulfill his duties properly. Bouligny concluded that the regiment would benefit by giving the post to "an up-to-date" officer [Le Blanc] instead of a senior lieutenant, who would look upon it with indifference and as an added burden, since it would not help him become captain. Perhaps Bouligny's treatment of Le Blanc was influenced by the fact that his father (Paul Le Blanc de Villeneufve) was a close friend. Several years later, Domingo Bouligny married into the Le Blanc family.[18]

Bouligny also believed in creating opportunity for soldiers of ability who had risen from the lower classes. One example was Matías Hernández, a sergeant first class who had served in the army for more than twenty-four years, beginning as a nineteen-year-old private. In proposing Hernández's promotion to sublieutenant in the 3rd Battalion, Bouligny wrote: "Sergeant Matías Hernández . . . has proved to be of regular and decent birth, which because of its kind does not lessen his merit to be promoted to the rank of officer." The commandant's recommendation for Hernández was approved on May 20, 1792.[19]

The regimental colonel expected officers to protect rather than exploit the soldiers in their charge. In May, 1791, Bouligny learned that former Arkansas Post commandant Joseph Valliere had been making loans to soldiers who were already in debt. The colonel advised the new commandant, Ignacio Delinó, against this nefarious practice: "You cannot ignore that the soldiers' limited salary is unable to sustain exorbitant charges and that their officer's principal concern should be to free them from debt and even to liquidate it entirely."[20]

In September, 1792, Bouligny tried to capture the crown's attention to reward the officers in his command for their many years of service

18. Bouligny to Carondelet, New Orleans, April 23, 1792, enclosed in Carondelet to Las Casas, New Orleans, April 26, 1792, *ibid.*, leg. 1441; Martin, *Bouligny Family,* 208.

19. Bouligny to Carondelet, New Orleans, February 1, 1792, enclosed in Carondelet to Las Casas, February 24, 1792, in AGI, PC, leg. 1441; Hernández service sheet, June 30, 1793, *ibid.*, leg. 161A.

20. Bouligny to Ignacio Delinó, New Orleans, May 23, 1791, *ibid.*, leg. 122A. Valliere served at Arkansas Post from March, 1787, to July, 1790, where he did not make himself loved by the inhabitants (see Gilbert C. Din, "The Spanish Fort on the Arkansas, 1763–1803," *Arkansas Historical Quarterly,* XLII (1983), 281–83).

with inadequate compensation. Two-thirds (sixty of ninety-four) of the officers served in outposts exposed to numerous hazards, hardships, and expense. He compared their duty to wartime service. Only five men remained of the officers present when the Fixed Louisiana Battalion had been formed in 1769. Bouligny stated that most of the officers and cadets were of superior stature (five feet, six inches or more) and accustomed to Louisiana's harsh terrain. Despite Bouligny's glowing recommendation, Captain General Las Casas disagreed; many army units labored with meager rewards. Moreover, he observed a "spirit of insubordination" among the Louisiana officers, with a tendency to make representations for the slightest cause.[21]

As regimental commandant, Colonel Bouligny was immediately under the governor. But no sooner did the new judge advocate, Vidal, arrive in the colony on March 17, 1791, than he began grabbing at power to enhance his status, and that led to a clash with Bouligny. Vidal, a fifty-one-year-old native of Colombia and a holder of a doctorate in canon and civil law, had held several governmental legal posts in Cartagena de Indias, where he had served for more than twenty years. Initially, the problem concerned how much authority Vidal possessed, but it soon became a question of whether he or Bouligny merited greater prominence in Louisiana. Unfortunately, much of the knowledge about the affair comes from Vidal, who stated only his side of the quarrel.[22]

The colonel had arrested three cadets for an altercation, then released one of them, allegedly his kinsman, which angered the fathers of the other two cadets. Later, in Government House, the father of one of the cadets, Esteban Lalande Dalcourt, passed by Bouligny without removing his hat. The colonel, Vidal claimed, fired off a volley of invectives while pursuing Dalcourt up the stairs to Governor Miró's office. Miró feigned deafness and exhorted the men to a reconciliation. Bouligny, however, wrote a representation to the governor, asserting that Dalcourt had undermined his character and authority. Miró sent the complaint to

21. Bouligny to Carondelet, September 29, 1792, and [Las Casas] *minuta*, [Havana], [n.d.], both attached to Carondelet to Las Casas, New Orleans, October 1, 1792, in AGI, PC, leg. 1441.

22. "Services of Nicolás María Vidal, Lieutenant Governor of Louisiana," January 25, 1800, BN, CDF. Jack D. L. Holmes's sketch of Vidal in *Dramatis Personae*," 152–55, does not examine his role in Louisiana critically. French writers do not treat Vidal well; see James A. Robertson, ed., *Louisiana Under the Rule of Spain, France, and the United States* (1910–11; rpr. New York, 1969), I, 207, and Villiers du Terrage, *Last Years*, 277–78n.

Vidal, who accused Bouligny of exceeding his authority in trying to arrest Dalcourt. The colonel contended that in the governor's absence, he could arrest anyone, since he was New Orleans' second military chief; furthermore, he considered himself as the king's lieutenant, since the city lacked one. Vidal, however, answered that Bouligny did not have a royal appointment and that until the Cabildo recognized him as interim governor, he lacked the power to arrest civilians.[23]

Toward the end of 1791, Vidal received a patent as lieutenant governor in addition to his post as judge advocate. He believed that his authority had been greatly augmented. Bouligny, however, allegedly greeted the news by telling Vidal that he [Bouligny] still held the post immediately beneath the governor. Vidal stated that his position as lieutenant governor and judge gave him preference and that he intended to defend his prerogatives. That led to a fight in November, 1792, over a decision rendered by a military council of war.[24]

After the council of war, over which Bouligny had presided, imposed a sentence on the soldier Julián Saliberry, Vidal reviewed the trial record, disapproved of the sentence, and ordered a new trial. He also complained that an army adjutant had drawn up the *proceso* (trial record), alleging that the sergeant major should have done it. Bouligny defended the action, explaining that it was in reality a *sumaria* (indictment), that superior officers could authorize an adjutant to draw up the *proceso*, and that the sergeant major was already burdened with four criminal proceedings that could merit the death penalty and with numerous other matters. Bouligny resented the intrusion by Vidal, a civilian asserting power over army officers in a council of war. The judge advocate's only authority was deciding if a sentence was appropriate and pointing out errors in the trial proceedings. Rather than do that, Vidal had arrogated to himself the right to impose punishment and dictate to the council president (Bouligny). If Vidal seized this power, he could then foist his decisions on army colonels, presidents, and members of councils of war; determine errors in points of law and interpret the law; and impose punishment. Bouligny requested an immediate definition of Vidal's powers from the governor or the captain general.[25]

23. Vidal to Las Casas, New Orleans, January 23, 1793, enclosed in Carondelet to Las Casas, New Orleans, January 10, 1793, in AGI, PC, leg. 1442.

24. *Ibid.*

25. Bouligny to Carondelet, New Orleans, December 7, 1792, enclosed in Carondelet to Las Casas, December 24, 1792, *ibid.*, leg. 1441.

Aware that Carondelet had sent documents on the dispute to Captain General Las Casas and that he was on tremulous ground, Vidal offered only a tepid defense. A busy schedule in several criminal cases, he alleged, did not afford him time to defend himself. He was satisfied with the governor's rectitude, and he asked Las Casas to suspend judgment until he could clarify his position.[26]

Las Casas, however, sidestepped the issue of authority. He believed that the Louisiana governor should make the decision. He returned all the documents to Carondelet "in order that you may determine what is most just." Back in New Orleans, Carondelet, a military man, upheld Bouligny's points.[27]

The Bouligny-Vidal dispute was still unresolved when the judge advocate threw additional fuel on the fire. On December 16, 1792, the Louisiana regiment held a celebration in honor of its patroness, Our Lady of the Immaculate Conception, in the army barracks that served as a temporary chapel while the reconstruction of the burned-out St. Louis Church went on. Candles were given to the governor, the auxiliary bishop, and Bouligny as the regimental commandant. The use of candles at funerals, obsequies, and anniversaries was then customary in New Orleans. After Mass, bread was consecrated and given first to the three officials.[28]

The following day a ceremony was held for deceased military personnel, and Vidal, presiding in the absence of the governor, received a greater snub. Candles were given to those present, the bishop and Bouligny receiving the same size, while everyone else received smaller candles. Angered, Vidal accused Bouligny of altering the ceremonies to give himself greater prestige and to slight the royal judges. Vidal argued that as a judge, he merited greater recognition than Bouligny, who as a military man should occupy a secondary position. He claimed, and not impartially, that in lieu of a king's lieutenant in New Orleans, the sergeant major should exercise that office, not the colonel. He also claimed that in the death or absence of the governor, the highest-ranking officer

26. Vidal to Las Casas, New Orleans, December 21, 1792, enclosed in Carondelet to Las Casas, December 24, 1792, *ibid.*

27. [Las Casas] to the governor of Louisiana, Havana, [n.d.], attached to Carondelet to Las Casas, December 24, 1792, *ibid.*

28. Vidal to Las Casas, New Orleans, January 23, 1793, enclosed in Carondelet to Las Casas, New Orleans, January 10, 1793, *ibid.*, leg. 1442.

to replace the governor was Brigadier O'Neill of Pensacola, not Colonel Bouligny. He argued that Louisiana had not had a lieutenant governor for eleven years until he was appointed and that his office as *auditor de guerra* was equivalent to that of judge.[29]

And there was more. On Christmas Day, 1792, as Governor Carondelet held a reception at Government House after Mass for army officers, government employees, and local notables, Bouligny and Vidal clashed physically. Both alleged that they were already standing at the governor's side when the other tried to wrest away that position of honor. Vidal provided the most information about the incident. He asserted that he was at the left of the governor when the latter moved away. As Vidal was about to recover his position, the colonel rushed to seize it. Vidal wrote, "[Bouligny] suddenly took two long and oblique strides to stop me, approaching the governor with such haste, that, because I was so close and the colonel was so very heavy and corpulent, he gave me a shove with his body that forced me to fall back. Startled, I lifted my head to see him, and I noted that he glared at me with an insulting and provocative air, as if preparing to strike a greater blow, if it were necessary."[30] In early 1793, Vidal sent the captain general a fifty-four-page vindication of his role in the clashes with Bouligny.

News of the affair, however, astonished Las Casas, who believed that Bouligny and Vidal should serve as models for the other officials and not engage in minutiae (*pequeñeces*). He declared that where a seating arrangement did not exist, the more political official [Vidal] should yield. The captain general declined to send the documentation to the crown, and he hoped that Carondelet would stop other cases of this nature. He advised his brother-in-law to stop anyone who rudely attempted to interpose himself next to the governor and anyone from claiming a designated place, a practice he had never observed anywhere else. Governor Carondelet probably spoke vigorously to both men and thus quieted the affair. Vidal, however, would remember the episode.[31]

Far more important than Vidal's squabbling were the foreign dangers that Miró had warned Carondelet about in January, 1792, and that led him to take immediate defensive measures. He needed more soldiers.

29. *Ibid.*

30. *Ibid.*

31. [Las Casas] to the governor of Louisiana, [Havana], March 6, 1793, enclosed in Carondelet to Las Casas, New Orleans, January 10, 1793, *ibid.*

Bouligny had reported in September, 1791, that the Louisiana regiment was short 511 men, a figure that was expected to rise to 927 by the end of 1792. Las Casas thereafter supplied him with troops: initially three companies of the Fixed Light Infantry of Havana and 200 men from the other two regiments stationed in Havana. Carondelet also reorganized the Louisiana militia and by the end of May, 1792, claimed that it consisted of 3,379 infantry and 240 cavalry. But with the outbreak of war against France, recruits stopped arriving from the Iberian peninsula. Many of those who had come lately were undesirables. In January, 1794, Bouligny described the 400 recruits sent recently as "the most depraved people that it is possible to assemble." The next month, he asked to establish a recruiting team in Mexico, but instead Louisiana received four companies of the Infantry Regiment of Mexico under Col. Francisco Villalba. In 1796, a recruiting team for Louisiana was set up in Cádiz under Capt. Manuel Román.[32]

Because of the war with France, Governor Carondelet asked for more guns, munitions, and sabers. He published the court proclamation of war and the cessation of trade with France in New Orleans on June 21, 1793, an act that caused French loyalists to grumble. The governor soon expelled unemployed and propertyless Frenchmen. He protested the withdrawal of the Havana troops and the captain general's orders for him to retreat to Mobile if attacked by a superior force. Carondelet pointed out that the many rivers, bayous, swamps, and lakes between New Orleans and Mobile would make the retreat impossible, and said that he preferred to die fighting in the five forts he had built to gird New Orleans. To back up the governor's arguments, Bouligny sent a memorial to the king that by the end of the year, the regiment would be short more

32. Carondelet to Las Casas, New Orleans, May 16, 1792, attached to "Mixed Royal Legion of the Disciplined Provincial Militias of the Mississippi," New Orleans, May 31, 1792, *ibid.*, leg. 1441; Carondelet to Las Casas, New Orleans, May 3, 1792, *ibid.;* Bouligny, "Statement of the Effective Force," New Orleans, September 21, 1791, and [Las Casas] to Carondelet, Havana, February 15, 1792, both *ibid.*, leg. 1446; Carondelet to Las Casas, New Orleans, August 20, 1792, with enclosures, *ibid.*, leg. 1441; Carondelet to Las Casas, New Orleans, February 24, 1794, with enclosures, *ibid.*, leg. 1443A. Many documents on Carondelet's 1792 effort to build up defenses are in AGI, PC, leg. 25A. Carondelet stated that two-thirds of the regimental soldiers should be imprisoned for their delinquencies, but because of the French Revolution, he dared not punish them (Ernest R. Liljegren, "Jacobinism in Spanish Louisiana, 1792–1797," *Louisiana Historical Quarterly*, XXII [1939], 19*n*).

than three hundred men. Several months later, troops from Mexico were rushed to Louisiana because of the Genet-Clark expedition then being recruited in Kentucky to invade the province. It produced a serious scare in Louisiana before Spanish officials learned that the organizers' effort had misfired. Nevertheless, in 1794 Carondelet employed galleys, galiots, and gunboats on the upper Mississippi for the first time, and they remained in service until 1797. Although these war vessels never saw action, their presence bolstered Spanish defenses, as did the construction of Fort San Fernando de las Barrancas in 1795 on the Mississippi's east bank at Chickasaw Bluffs (modern Memphis).[33]

Coupled with the external French threat of invasion was that of the local Jacobins, spawned by the revolution, who might incite an insurrection of slaves. In 1792, the Cabildo asked the crown to halt the importation of bondsmen from the French Caribbean, and the crown agreed on January 1, 1793. Carondelet also demanded that persons who had arrived in Louisiana since 1790 and those who owned no property take an oath of allegiance. Dissenters had to quit the colony, and a number of them left. Subversive elements, however, remained, and in November, 1793, the governor sent an appeal for loyal militiamen from the upriver settlements to descend on New Orleans. Their prompt response quelled the ardor of the would-be revolutionaries. A year and a half later, a slave uprising that involved whites was nipped in the bud in Pointe Coupee with the execution of twenty-three slave ringleaders and the sentencing of twenty-two others to ten years of hard labor. Two whites received six years' imprisonment and one white, two free blacks, and one slave were ex-

33. Carondelet to Las Casas, New Orleans, June 21, 1793, AGI, PC, leg. 1442; Carondelet *bando,* New Orleans, September 29, 1793, *ibid.,* leg. 215; Carondelet to Las Casas, New Orleans, May 9, 1794, *ibid.,* leg. 1443A. See printed circular by Carondelet to the inhabitants of Louisiana, dated February 12, 1794, warning them of a possible invasion (*ibid.,* leg. 209).

On Genet, see Harry Ammon, *The Genet Mission* (New York, 1973); F. R. Hall, "Genet's Western Intrigue, 1793–1794," *Journal of the Illinois Historical Society,* XXI (1928), 359–81; Frederick Jackson Turner, "The Origin of Genet's Projected Attack on Louisiana and the Floridas," *American Historical Review,* III (1898), 650–71; Richard Lowitt, "Activities of Citizen Genet in Kentucky, 1793–1794," *Filson Club Historical Quarterly,* XXII (1948), 252–67. Carondelet's explanation for sending the galleys upriver in 1794 is in Carondelet to Las Casas, New Orleans, March 20, 1794, with the enclosure of Gayoso to Carondelet, Natchez, March 13, 1794, both in AGI, PC, leg. 1443A. For a study of the galleys, see Nasatir, ed., *Spanish War Vessels,* 36–54.

pelled from the province. After the Pointe Coupee conspiracy, Carondelet issued a decree on June 1, 1795, for improved police and public order.
It created syndics in rural areas to assist district commandants, required
passes for peddlers and travellers, and regulated the maintenance of
bridges, roads, and causeys. New measures were needed as New Orleans
witnessed the setting of fires and the appearance of anonymous pamphlets critical of the authorities, one of which labeled Carondelet a *cochon
du lait*.[34]

Almost immediately on the heels of the Pointe Coupee conspiracy
came news of a plot among soldiers of Bouligny's regiment. On May 26,
1795, Carondelet ordered the colonel to investigate. In the presence of
two captains, he heard evidence presented by Charles Joseph Lange
(d'Ange), a member of the colored militia and resident of the First German Coast (above New Orleans). Lange had become friendly with a
soldier named Joseph Roland, a Frenchman, in the 1793 expedition to
Fort San Felipe, a friendship that he renewed later in New Orleans.
There, Roland and two other Frenchmen drank and talked of destroying
the Spaniards. The investigation revealed that the plotting consisted
largely of loose talk induced by excessive drinking. Nevertheless, the authorities quickly apprehended Roland, found him guilty of conspiracy,
and transferred him to Pensacola for punishment. These events unhinged
many of the inhabitants, and the Cabildo petitioned the governor to halt
the importation of all slaves. Carondelet issued a temporary decree to
this effect while waiting for royal confirmation.[35]

November, 1793, was a serious time in Louisiana's history. Spain
was at war against revolutionary France, and rumors circulated about a

34. Gayarré, *History,* III, 327–28; Liljegren, "Jacobinism," 6–14; [Carondelet] to the
commandants of lower Louisiana above New Orleans (Judice, Verbois, Cantrelle, Verret,
Andry, Devilliers, and Massicot), New Orleans, October 31, 1793, in AGI, PC, leg. 207B;
Carondelet *bando,* New Orleans, September 29, 1793, AGI, PC, leg. 215; Carondelet to
Las Casas, New Orleans, June 16, 1795, in AGI, PC, leg. 1443B. See also James A. Padgett,
ed., "A Decree for Louisiana Issued by the Baron of Carondelet, June 1, 1795," *Louisiana
Historical Quarterly,* XX (1937), 590–605, and Jack D. L. Holmes, "The Abortive Slave Re-
volt at Pointe Coupée, Louisiana, 1795," *Louisiana Historical Quarterly,* XI (1970), 341–62.

35. Gayarré, *History,* III, 354–56; Roland C. McConnel, *Negro Troops of Antebellum
Louisiana: A History of the Battalion of Free Men of Color* (Baton Rouge, 1968), 27–28. See
Carondelet proclamation of February 19, 1796, against importing slaves in Guillermo Náñez
Falcón, ed., *The Favrot Family Papers: A Documentary Chronicle of Early Louisiana* ([New
Orleans], 1988), II, 184.

French naval invasion of the province. Governor Carondelet secretly absented himself from New Orleans, dropping down to Fort San Felipe de Plaqueminas for four days to inspect defenses. Before doing so, on November 20 he instructed Bouligny, who temporarily replaced him in New Orleans, that if an invasion occurred, he should send the veteran soldiers from Natchez, Baton Rouge, and Galveztown, a detachment from the German Coast, and two galleys from the English Turn to Fort San Felipe; reinforce the New Orleans forts with additional men and gunpowder; and take other defensive measures. But those November days with Bouligny briefly in charge passed peacefully, as the French failed to appear. On several other occasions when the baron was absent from New Orleans, Bouligny assumed command.[36]

In February, 1794, in the midst of the Genet-Clark threat to Louisiana, Governor Carondelet again took measures in which Bouligny played a prominent role. Carondelet issued a circular letter to the inhabitants warning them against involvement with Genet, who sought recruits from the Louisiana populace. The governor also decreed that if he was absent from New Orleans because of a military crisis, Bouligny was to assume command of the city's defenses. That order must have pleased him enormously; it vindicated his status as second in command in the colony.[37]

While involved in many important duties when war threatened, Bouligny also had problems not of his making that took time and generated paperwork. One such incident occurred in the summer of 1796 with his sergeant major, Juan Gautier. On June 23, Gautier uncovered a

36. Carondelet's instructions to Bouligny, New Orleans, November 20, 1793, KCTU. Carondelet was in Balize in April, 1795 (see Carondelet to Bouligny, Balize, April 10, 1795, in BB, HNOC). The only attack on Louisiana in the French war was the seizure of Balize by a French corsair, *La Parisienne,* and the destruction of its swivel guns (Carondelet to Las Casas, New Orleans, October 23, 1795, in AGI, PC, leg. 1443B). The corsair also seized the Spanish ship carrying the news that the war had ended. By November 14, 1795, Carondelet had learned of the peace (Carondelet to Las Casas, New Orleans, two letters of November 14, 1795, both in AGI, PC, leg. 1443B).

37. Carondelet to Bouligny, [New Orleans], February 10, [1794]; [Carondelet] to the inhabitants of Louisiana, [New Orleans], February 12, 1794, both in KCTU, with the latter document published in *SMV,* Pt. 3, pp. 255–57. Carondelet told Bouligny on February 1, 1794, that the Spanish officials in Philadelphia had informed him that Genet had lost credibility and that his mission was failing (New Orleans, BB, HNOC). Carondelet notified Bouligny on July 5, 1796, that if the governor died, was sick or absent, Bouligny would assume power (Bouligny to Carondelet, New Orleans, July 7, 1796, in AGI, PC, leg. 34).

shortage of 1,230 pesos and 5 reales in the accounts of the 2nd Battalion that implicated two officers, José Le Blanc and Tomás de Acosta. Gautier demanded that the commandant make a sworn deposition about the shortage. Miffed by the demand, Bouligny answered testily that he would defer to Judge Advocate Vidal's decision on the matter. At that point, Gautier appealed to Governor Carondelet, accusing Bouligny of showing lack of respect, impugning his honor, and humiliating him. Gautier claimed that differences already existed between the two men because of his zeal. The next day, Carondelet referred the affair to Vidal. On August 11, the judge advocate advised the governor to show Bouligny Gautier's complaints in order for him to reply to them, and Carondelet approved. After seeing the charges, the commandant wrote a defense.[38]

Bouligny dismissed Gautier's charges as lacking in foundation. His resentment stemmed from the sergeant major's lack of respect for him, particularly attempting to force him to make a declaration when he had already agreed to do so. He disagreed with Gautier's investigation and believed that Le Blanc should reimburse the money to the battalion, then claim it from Acosta. Gautier, he charged, had not examined all the evidence or questioned the truthfulness of the declarations he had taken. Bouligny, however, harbored no ill will and had even recommended Gautier for promotion to lieutenant colonel. Carondelet again referred the matter to Vidal, who rendered a judgment on August 23.[39]

Vidal failed to find any basis for the sergeant major's allegations, as Bouligny had contended, and believed that the Le Blanc–Acosta dispute should be regarded as private. The judge advocate suggested closing the matter, and Carondelet agreed five days later. In exonerating Bouligny, Vidal showed that he could behave in a professional and friendly manner, at least in this matter. But Bouligny must have realized the strength of his position, since Gautier's charges had not overly perturbed him. Gautier remained in Louisiana until July, 1799, when he departed for service in Puerto Rico. The adjutant major, Lt. Juan Caso y Luengo, then took over as aide to Bouligny.[40]

38. Juan Gautier to Carondelet, New Orleans, August 8, 1796; Bouligny to Gautier, [New Orleans], June 23, 1796; and Vidal to Carondelet, New Orleans, August 11, 1796, all in KCTU.

39. Bouligny to Carondelet, New Orleans, August 20, 1796, *ibid.*

40. Vidal to Carondelet, New Orleans, August 23, 1796, *ibid.;* Council of War, New Orleans, February, 1797, AGI, PC, leg. 584A; Gautier to Manuel Lanzos, New Orleans, July 16, 1799, in AGI, PC, leg. 68. On August 18 or 19, 1796, Vidal wrote to Bouligny: "My

Bouligny's private life experienced changes during these years. On February 18, 1792, he purchased a new home in New Orleans, the residence of his predecessor as commandant of the Louisiana regiment, Pedro Piernas. The lot measured 65 French feet on Condé (now Chartres) Street by 100 feet (or more) on Dumaine Street (the southeast corner of the intersection). A smaller lot of 20 feet by 20 feet adjoined the larger lot. The residence, measuring 55 feet by 55 feet, faced Condé Street, while another building behind it housed the slaves and horses. The house contained 7 principal and 4 private rooms, 6 chimneys, and 2 balconies, one overlooking Condé Street, another in the rear. In the 1795 New Orleans census, thirteen persons lived there—four whites (Bouligny, his wife, and two sons) and nine blacks. Missing from the census was Mme Vilemont, who usually resided with the Boulignys. The colonel lived out the last years of his life in this house.[41]

The acquisition of his new residence was tied to the sale of his plantation of nearly twenty years, which he sold on March 20, 1792, to Francisco Mayronne and Juan Bautista Degruis for 100,000 pesos. He probably divested himself of the plantation to satisfy debts and to acquire the New Orleans house. With his advance in years, financial setbacks, and more time devoted to fulfilling the duties of regimental commandant, his interest in being a planter had diminished considerably. Debts nevertheless continued to plague Bouligny during these years. The purchasers of his plantation failed to pay him as scheduled.[42]

Bouligny and his family appear to have escaped the calamities that occurred in Louisiana during these years. A major hurricane struck on August 18 and 19, 1793, causing considerable damage from the Mississippi's mouth nearly as far north as Baton Rouge. Ships and boats on the

---

esteemed Friend and Sir: I write this hurriedly and return your papers. You did not tell me why you sent them. I told you yesterday that your paper looked good. I have nothing to add, except [for you] to revise the crossed out lines. Do not add anything" (KCTU).

41. Din, "Death and Succession," 310–11; *Bouligny Foundation Newsletter,* no. 7. The 1795 New Orleans census of the first quarter, which included Bouligny's residence, is in AGI, PC, leg. 211A

42. Din, "Death and Succession," 311. Joseph Xavier de Pontalba wrote in an April 26, 1792, letter to his uncle Miró, almost at the same time that Bouligny sold his plantation: "A [military] officer can have no occupation but his profession" (Cruzat, ed., "Letters," 401). Bouligny owed two thousand pesos to Pierre-Joseph Favrot, which he intended to repay in 1793 but was unable to (see several Bouligny letters in Náñez Falcón, ed., *Favrot Papers,* II, 140, 143, 155–56).

river suffered, as did lower Louisiana's corn and rice crops. Fort San Felipe sustained considerable damage and several deaths, including that of Capt. Luis de Bertucat, in charge of construction there. The next year, on August 10, another hurricane hit the same area, inflicting additional damage to plantations and to craft on the river. But more serious that year was a new conflagration in New Orleans on December 8 that consumed 212 buildings, including royal storehouses, government structures, barracks, stores, and numerous private residences. Among those who lost their homes was Juan Tala, Bouligny's nephew. The 1794 blaze was more costly than the fire of six years earlier, but it too spared Bouligny's home.[43]

Specific information about the private life of the Bouligny family written by third persons is rare. However, Joseph Xavier de Pontalba left two brief remarks about him and his wife in letters to Pontalba's wife in France. On March 14, 1796, Pontalba spent the day at the Bouligny household on Condé Street, where Bouligny's mother-in-law and daughter were also present. He wrote about Marie Louise: "I had never before been the object of so many attentions and courtesies as at that moment on the part of this lady."[44]

Less than two months later, Pontalba told his wife about Bouligny's purchase of two of his slaves, Zamore and Noël. The colonel paid him for them a day ahead of time, informing Pontalba, who was journeying to France, that if he returned to Louisiana, he would gladly sell them back at the same price he had paid, a gesture that did not meet with Marie Louise's approval. Pontalba noted that Bouligny had recently been sick with a leg affliction caused by a pimple that became infected under his cotton stocking and forced him to take to his bed. His convalescence took all of May, 1796, and perhaps longer.[45]

43. Carondelet to Las Casas, August 17, 1793, with enclosures, in AGI, PC, leg. 1442. The governor stated that deaths numbered twenty-two, but they were probably higher (Carondelet to Las Casas, New Orleans, August 31, 1794, with enclosures, *ibid.*, leg. 1443A; Carondelet to Las Casas, New Orleans, December 10, 1794, in AHN, Est., leg. 3899, with an enclosure of the buildings destroyed; Carondelet to Las Casas, New Orleans, December 28, 1794, in AGI, PC, leg. 1443A). See also Jack D. L. Holmes, "The 1794 New Orleans Fire: A Case Study of Spanish *Noblesse Oblige*," *Louisiana Studies*, XV (1976), 21–43.

44. Pontalba to his wife, New Orleans, March 14, 1796, in Pontalba Papers, Special Collections, Howard-Tilton Memorial Library, Tulane University.

45. Pontalba to his wife, New Orleans, May 5, 1796, *ibid*. Pontalba petitioned to go to Spain to assist his aunt, Miró's widow, arrange her affairs (Carondelet to Las Casas, New

The Boulignys were also involved in New Orleans' first theater, renting a box for 250 to 300 pesos per year. The theater opened its doors on October 4, 1794, on the uptown side of St. Peter's Street between Royal and Bourbon streets, probably to the relief of many inhabitants who craved entertainment. Housed in a small building measuring only 31 feet wide by 128 feet deep, it contained an amphitheater, a pit, a gallery, and twelve boxes. The Boulignys were probably among the first patrons. It is known that in 1796 Mme Bouligny was a stockholder in the theater along with other prominent women (St. Maxent, Dow, Montegut, Guillemard, and Almonester) and men (Marigny, Ramos, Macarty, De la Chaisse, Collell, and Fouignet). Performances began at 5:30 P.M. until 1795 when they commenced at 7:30 P.M. Its productions are unknown until 1796 when they included *La Pere de Famille* and *Silvan*.[46]

The theater, however, had financial problems from the outset. Eighteen months after opening, it was incorporated with approximately forty shares selling at 200 pesos each. Pecuniary problems nevertheless continued, and on April 23, 1798, it received permission to run a lotto to help defray expenses.[47]

But a more formidable obstacle than money was Judge Advocate Vidal. A theater box had been partitioned to seat the Cabildo members on one side and the governor and his family on the other side. In September, 1797, the Cabildo doubled the number of its councilmen from six to twelve, and they could no longer fit in their side of the box. Although no change occurred at that time, on July 27, 1799, Acting Civil Governor Vidal decreed that military governors (Bouligny was then acting military governor) were not entitled to a separate box and ordered the theater management to remove the partition. That probably did not upset Bouligny, since he was then sick, but Vidal no doubt intended the move to humiliate him, perhaps in belated revenge for their confrontations in 1792. Vidal played this mischievous game until the interim governor, the marqués de Casa Calvo, appeared in New Orleans on September 13, 1799. He refused to permit the insult to his position and dignity. Vidal, afraid to confront

---

Orleans, September 11, 1795, with Pontalba's petition of September 8, 1795, in AGI, PC, leg. 1443B).

46. René J. Le Gardneur, Jr., *The First New Orleans Theatre, 1792–1803* (New Orleans, 1963), 7–8.

47. *Ibid.*, 16–18.

Casa Calvo directly but fired by spite, shut down the theater on February 8, 1800. It remained closed until the last Spanish governor, Manuel Juan de Salcedo, arrived in mid-1801.[48]

Bouligny, despite being the regimental commandant, or perhaps because he was, sought to further his sons' careers in the army. In 1792, he proposed Ursino, then thirteen and a half and a cadet for eighteen months, for promotion to sublieutenant. He cited the boy's seniority in rank and his application. Although Carondelet approved, Ursino was not promoted until February 25, 1794, after he had turned fifteen. Within a few years, the boy received commissions that temporarily took him out of New Orleans and the parental home.[49]

One such commission occurred in November, 1796, when Ursino was assigned to Plaquemines, taking with him the confiscated papers of the French republican general Georges Victor Collot. The general had conducted a reconnaissance trip down the Mississippi Valley that summer for the French government. It incited rumors of Spanish retrocession of Louisiana to France, and indeed the Spanish government was then contemplating taking that step. When Collot arrived in New Orleans, he warned the baron about the possibility of a British attack on upper Louisiana from Canada and an American plan, the Blount conspiracy, to support it. A now suspicious Governor Carondelet seized Collot's personal papers to examine them, and he soon sent the general to Balize. Ursino descended the river to return the papers to Collot, who was leaving Louisiana. Commandant Pedro Favrot at Plaquemines reported that the sublieutenant obtained the general's signature to the inventory, which Collot at first refused to give because "he was somewhat angry" that Carondelet had not returned all of his papers. Ursino remained in Plaquemines until January 4, 1797, when Sublt. Vicente Bór-

48. *Ibid.,* 18; Casa Calvo to Someruelos, New Orleans, December 27, 1799, in AGI, PC, leg. 1550. See also the *expediente* "The Cabildo and the Theater Box in the Casa de Comedias," February 24, 1802, enclosed in Salcedo to Someruelos, New Orleans, March 2, 1802, AGI, PC, leg. 1553.

49. Bouligny *oficio* in Carondelet to Las Casas, New Orleans, June 20, 1792, and Bouligny to Las Casas, New Orleans, June 19, 1792, with enclosures on the cadets, attached to Carondelet to Las Casas, New Orleans, June 20, 1792; Francisco Paula Morales, "Relation of the cadets . . . ," New Orleans, July 3, 1792, enclosed in Carondelet to Las Casas, New Orleans, August 20, 1792, all in AGI, PC, leg. 1441. Ursino's service sheet of 1809 is in AGI, PC, leg. 161B.

quez relieved him. Mme Bouligny personally wrote a thank-you note to Mme Favrot at Plaquemines for the kindness extended to her son.[50]

Bouligny's youngest son, Luis, a cadet, saw less service. In April, 1797, the baron contemplated putting several of the most suitable cadets on board a frigate and a galley for a short stint. Luis urged the governor to let him go, but the latter felt that at fifteen the lad was too young. Carondelet, however, deferred to the boy's father. Bouligny appointed Luis to one of the ships in order "for him to become acquainted . . . with the din of cannon blasts." The boy served on the *Luisiana* in May and June, 1797.[51]

Far more active in the army than either Ursino or Luis was their older brother, Domingo. After war was declared against France, he saw duty on *La Fina* in the Gulf of Mexico as a sublieutenant (naval duty for army officers in Louisiana was common). Domingo earned the experience necessary for service on the vessels of the Mississippi squadron, where he was assigned in early 1794 because of the Genet-Clark threat. He received command of the land troops on the boats sent to New Madrid that year, perhaps with his father's assistance, and command of the galley *La Castilla*. Once in upper Louisiana, he was temporarily in command of the galiot *La Flecha,* second in command at Fort Celeste in New Madrid, and in charge of the galley *La Felipa* on the descent downriver to Nogales in June. He returned to New Orleans with the troops in July. In 1795, Domingo again had command of the soldiers on the vessels that

---

50. Pedro Favrot to Carondelet, Plaquemines, November 25, 28, 1796, with the quotation in the second letter, both in AGI, PC, leg. 34; Favrot to Carondelet, Plaquemines, January 6, 1797; Marie Louise Le Sénéchal to Marie-Françoise Gérald, New Orleans, December 27, 1796, both in Náñez Falcón, ed., *Favrot Papers,* II, 268–69. On Collot, see Heloise H. Cruzat, "General Collot's Reconnoitering Trip Down the Mississippi and His Arrest in New Orleans in 1796, by Order of the Baron de Carondelet, Governor of Louisiana," *Louisiana Historical Quarterly,* I (1918), 303–20, and Cruzat, trans., "Translation of Some Documents bearing on General Collot's Arrest," *Louisiana Historical Quarterly,* I (1918), 321–26; Durand Echeverria, "General Collot's Plan for a Reconnaissance of the Ohio and Mississippi Valley, 1796," *William and Mary Quarterly,* 3rd ser., IX (1952), 512–20; Georges-Victor Collot, *A Journey in North America* (Paris, 1826); George W. Kyte, "A Spy on the Western Waters: The Military Intelligence Mission of General Collot in 1796," *Mississippi Valley Historical Review,* XXXIV (1947), 427–42.

51. Luis Bouligny service sheets of December 31, 1793, AGI, PC, leg. 161A, and AGS, GM, leg. 7292; Carondelet to Bouligny, [New Orleans], April 6, 1797, with Bouligny's marginal notation of April 7, 1797, in BB, HNOC.

ascended to Ecores de Margot to establish Fort San Fernando de las Barrancas. There, he took charge of *La Felipa*. In December he commanded *La Flecha* on its return voyage. Although Carondelet recommended him for promotion to lieutenant in February, 1796, Domingo had already been advanced to that rank in Spain on December 20, 1795. His lengthiest service with the vessels and upriver posts came between 1796 and 1798 when he participated in Lt. Col. Carlos Howard's expedition to upper Louisiana to bolster defenses. In 1797, Domingo was in Fort Panmure when angry Americans living in Natchez threatened to besiege it. While he gained considerable experience in command and sailing, it failed to earn him promotion to captain.[52]

Domingo, however, was not the only Bouligny desiring a promotion. In January, 1794, three years after his last advancement, Francisco Bouligny requested the rank of brigadier. Governor Carondelet, as Louisiana's inspector of the army, forwarded the petition to the captain general without recommendation. Bouligny wrote directly to Las Casas, imploring him to understand "the notorious and authentic malevolence of the deceased Conde de Gálvez, and that reason and justice could not overcome the channels by which my complaints and representations should have reached the Crown." Las Casas replied to the colonel, "I . . . send [the petition] to His Majesty with the hope of satisfaction."[53]

The crown, however, belatedly answered on December 29, 1794, stating that because many promotions had recently been granted, it was postponing consideration of his request until war's end. Bouligny waited obediently, if not anxiously, as Carondelet attained the rank of brigadier general on March 5, 1794. In 1795, the colonel expected the government

52. Domingo Bouligny petition for captain to the king, New Orleans, February 5, 1796, with a marginal notation by his father, enclosed in Bouligny to Carondelet, New Orleans, February 5, 1796, AGI, PC, leg. 33; Carondelet to Bouligny, New Orleans, January 17, 1794, in BB, HNOC. See also Nasatir's sketch of Domingo in *Spanish War Vessels*, 257n. While his father was acting military governor, on September 8, 1799, Domingo saw action against the British warship *Hero*. See also Ernest R. Liljegren, "The Commission of Lieutenant Colonel Carlos Howard to Defend the Upper Mississippi Valley Against the English" (Senior thesis, San Diego State College, 1936).

53. Bouligny to Las Casas, New Orleans, January 7, 1794, with attached draft [Las Casas] to Bouligny, Havana, March 20, 1794, in AGI, PC, leg. 1396; Bouligny's petition to the king, enclosed in Bouligny to Someruelos, New Orleans, August 8, 1799, AGI, PC, leg. 1550; Carondelet to Las Casas, New Orleans, January 24, May 9, 1794, both in AGI, PC, leg. 1443A.

to act as the war with France ended that summer. Perhaps recognizing that a new promotion in Louisiana might be difficult, in July, 1795, Bouligny asked the crown for the governorship of Panama "or any other [governorship] that is proportional to my rank and services." But he heard nothing about his requests. Then early the next year, he learned of Gayoso's advancement to brigadier on September 4, 1795, and his exclusion in the promotion lists published at the end of the war. That news must have revived his earlier despondent feelings that the government had forsaken him again. But he resiliently submitted a new petition for promotion in February, 1796. On this occasion, Carondelet endorsed the request, writing to the captain general: "Attending to the nearly thirty-eight years of service that he has, I consider him worthy of the grace of brigadier that he solicits."[54]

Not hearing on his petition for promotion, however, in August, 1796, Bouligny asked the crown for a year's leave to travel to Spain to arrange family affairs. Perhaps he wished to present his next request in person, since Carondelet was in his last year as governor. It was widely known in Louisiana that he disliked his assignment in the colony and would not attempt to prolong it. Bouligny and Gayoso, the two officials in the province with the greatest prospect of replacing him, submitted their petitions for his post. Carondelet forwarded Gayoso's request for the governorship on March 30, 1796. Bouligny probably recalled that on two earlier occasions, the head of the Louisiana regiment, Gálvez and

54. Bouligny petition for promotion, New Orleans, February 2, 1796, AGI, PC, leg. 1443B; [Carondelet's] endorsement of Bouligny's petition, made on February 6, 1796, is detached and in AGI, PC, leg. 130. Las Casas forwarded it to the conde de Campo de Alange, the secretary of War, Havana, April 2, 1796 (AGI, SD, leg. 2565). On Panama, see Carondelet to Las Casas, New Orleans, July 4, 1796, in AGI, PC, leg. 1443A. Carondelet's quotation is in his letter to [Las Casas], New Orleans, February 6, 1796, in AGI, PC, leg. 130. Gayoso's request for promotion to brigadier is enclosed in Carondelet to Las Casas, New Orleans, July 15, 1795, in AGI, PC, leg. 1443A.

In 1795, a Madrid lawyer, Juan Antonio García, informed Bouligny that a royal decree of October, 1795, had named him military and political governor of Louisiana and Florida. But García added that the appointment was stalled because no one had paid the fees for the titles, approximately 375 pesos. The letter seems to have been the work of an unscrupulous lawyer willing to defraud an unsuspecting colonial office seeker. Bouligny did not fall for the ruse (Juan Antonio García to Bouligny, Madrid, November 25, 1795; and "Relation of the Merits and Services of don Francisco Bouligny," Madrid, November 19, 1795, both in BB, HNOC).

Miró, had been selected. But that did not happen now. Bouligny, who used his brother-in-law Luis, now in Madrid, as his agent, never learned that his petition for the governorship had arrived at the Ministry of War after Gayoso's appointment had been made. But even had it arrived in time, he might not have won the coveted office, because the post of Natchez district governor was similar to and a better training ground for the provincial governorship than the post of regimental commandant.[55]

When word reached New Orleans of Gayoso's promotion in July, 1797, gloom enveloped Bouligny. He had failed in what appeared to be his last opportunity to gain the governorship. Taking pen in hand, he wrote a letter to the new governor-general of Louisiana, who was in Natchez, that revealed his crushed sentiments:

A thousand times congratulations. Your promotion to this governorship has been completely verified. In the midst of the cruel bitterness that results from the court's oblivion and silence to my requests, what serves as a consolation is having as an immediate superior a person who has knowledge of my services and conduct for many years. I trust that you will not abandon me to the cruel fate that pursues me. The baron made the kindest offers to direct and support my petitions, to which there were no replies. It leads me to conclude that they were not sent on, either due to the bad will of the accusations [against me] or due to other motives that I do not want to explore. My wish now is to present myself before the king. I trust that you will facilitate [my trip] with your assistance. Toward this end, I implore your justice and I claim the old friendship with which you have always favored me. For my part, there has never been the least doubt nor shall I ever fail in the gratitude and friendship that men of justice mutually owe each other. Count on it. I shall serve you with my lifelong honorable conduct as my bond.[56]

With difficulty Bouligny accepted his failure to become governor. A proud man who possessed confidence in his ability, he could not comprehend the government's repeatedly passing him over in favor of younger men with lesser experience. He had also expected Carondelet to do more to help him obtain that office.

On August 5, 1797, Gayoso took the oath of office as civil and military

55. Carondelet to Las Casas, New Orleans, March 30, August 23, 1796, both in AGI, PC, leg. 1444; Bouligny to Carondelet, New Orleans, August 22, 1796, *ibid.*, leg. 34. Gayoso asked for the governorship of Louisiana in his petition of March 30, 1796 (*ibid.*, leg. 1444).

56. Bouligny to Gayoso, New Orleans, July 13, 1797, *ibid.*, leg. 48.

governor of Louisiana and West Florida before local officials and the military corps. Bouligny was there and signed documents as a witness. By then, he had made a fresh attempt to achieve the rank of brigadier. On July 15, he composed a new and lengthier petition to the crown, explaining his past efforts and disappointments to attain that rank. He had fallen behind officers junior to him in seniority as colonel and in service. Basing himself on the royal order of December 29, 1794, which stated that the government would attend to him after the war with France ended, Bouligny requested that he be given the promotion dated September 4, 1795. Gayoso endorsed the petition on August 18, 1797, noting that Bouligny had applied three times under Governor Carondelet. Gayoso expressed his wish that the colonel receive what he wanted. That same day, Gayoso forwarded Bouligny's request of July 21 for a year's leave, which he had renewed.[57] Perhaps with the new governor's assistance, Bouligny might yet achieve a satisfaction that had eluded him under Carondelet.

57. Gayoso to Santa Clara, New Orleans, August 5, 1797; Bouligny to the king, New Orleans, July 15, 1797, enclosed in Gayoso to Santa Clara, New Orleans, August 18, 1797; Bouligny to the king, New Orleans, July 21, 1797, enclosed in Gayoso to Santa Clara, New Orleans, August 18, 1797, all *ibid.*, leg. 1500).

II   THE FINAL YEARS

1797–1800

I N THE LAST three years of his life, Bouligny saw limited professional activity as his health declined precipitously. His 1796 illness served as prelude; he was often sick from 1798 to his death in 1800. His lingering malady proved unfortunate because it came at a time when he might have become governor of Louisiana. The province required a vigorous leader who could confront the threat of invasion at the same time that its defenses, weakened by territorial losses, needed restructuring. Three nations, Britain, France, and the United States, all sought to acquire Louisiana. Spain, moreover, under the guidance of Manuel Godoy as first secretary, failing to derive guarantees of territorial integrity for Louisiana from the United States, seemed desirous of ridding itself of an expensive colony that might embroil the nation in new diplomatic entanglements.[1]

Louisiana officials, meanwhile, worked to the limit of their resources to preserve the province and were disappointed in the decisions made in Spain. They had emphatically disagreed with Godoy's 1795 Treaty of San Lorenzo, and Governor Carondelet had refused to evacuate the lands ceded to the United States. These lands included forts vital to protecting Louisiana and West Florida. It proved to be only a temporary delay, and by 1798, the Spaniards, acceding to new orders from Madrid, had withdrawn from all the forts on the Mississippi (San Fernando de las Barran-

---

1. Alexander DeConde, *This Affair of Louisiana* (New York, 1976), 80–97; Lyon, *French Diplomacy*, 79–126; Mildred S. Fletcher, "Louisiana as a Factor in French Diplomacy, from 1763 to 1800," *Mississippi Valley Historical Review*, XVII (1930), 367–76; J. Leitch Wright, *Anglo-Spanish Rivalry in North America* (Athens, Ga., 1971); Arthur P. Whitaker, "The Retrocession of Louisiana in Spanish Policy," *American Historical Review*, XXXIX (1934), 454–76.

cas, Nogales, and Natchez) and the Tombigbee (Confederación and San Esteban). Their loss substantially weakened Spanish strength in Louisiana and what remained of West Florida (the region east of the Mississippi between the thirty-first parallel and Bayou Manchac). Nevertheless, Spanish officials in Louisiana resumed their efforts at building defenses on the Mississippi's west bank, at Baton Rouge in West Florida, and on the river. American penetration of Spanish possessions in commerce and immigration continued to escalate.[2]

For nearly a year, Gayoso attempted to build up Louisiana before he made a major plea for assistance to the Prince of the Peace, the title Godoy received for negotiating the 1795 treaty with France in which he ceded Santo Domingo, Spain's oldest possession in the New World, to the French. On July 30, 1798, Gayoso feared that the United States, then waging an undeclared naval war with France, might attack Spain and its possessions, since it was a French ally. In a war council held on July 6, which Bouligny did not attend because of illness, the consensus was that Louisiana needed 300,000 pesos urgently to build defenses and six hundred troops just to bring the Louisiana regiment to full strength. But Gayoso believed that the province required much more: a thousand soldiers and nine river galleys for Spanish Illinois (Missouri); a thousand troops and a division of ships for Baton Rouge, now Louisiana's main defense; and a thousand men between New Orleans and Balize, plus a third division of vessels. In addition, he wanted two companies of mounted foresters, a new company of artillerymen and officers, and additional extraordinary funds for militia costs. He speculated that if the United States declared war against France, it would expel the émigrés, many of whom would seek refuge in Louisiana. While they would help defend the province, their presence would create a food shortage. He wanted ten thousand fusils to arm these refugees when they arrived.[3]

Using the engineers in the province, Juan María Perchet and Joaquín

2. Holmes, *Gayoso,* 174–99.

3. Council of War, New Orleans, July 6, 1798, enclosed in Gayoso to the Prince of the Peace, reserved, New Orleans, July 30, 1790, in AHN, Est., leg. 3900, exped. 4. In November, 1798, Gayoso recommended that the Spanish government negotiate a treaty with the English that would keep them east of Great Slave Lake and the Mackenzie River in Canada (Gayoso to Francisco Saavedra, reserved, New Orleans, November 22, 1798, *ibid.*). Gayoso had made an earlier outline of Louisiana's defense needs in his letter to the Prince of the Peace, reserved, New Orleans, April 19, 1798 (*ibid.*). See also Holmes, *Gayoso,* 237–39.

de la Torre, Gayoso began a program of renovating the forts in Gal-veztown, Arkansas Post, and St. Louis, and building armed observation posts opposite Natchez (Concordia) and Chickasaw Bluffs (Campo de la Esperanza). Influenced by the Natchez rebellion of the Anglo-Americans, Gayoso now advocated admitting select immigrants, prefer-ring only useful and trustworthy persons. Religious tolerance (which meant not having to become Catholic, not freedom of religion) would be permitted merely for the present generation. Gayoso maintained this attitude until his death, stating a few days before he died that no new settlements would be made until peace came. The belief that Anglo-Americans could be assimilated and would defend Louisiana was fading in the late 1790s. Gayoso counseled caution and opted for reliance on a larger military establishment to safeguard both Louisiana and Mexico.[4]

One area where renewed strength appeared was in the war vessels on the Mississippi. By June, 1799, four galleys, *La Leal, La Luisiana, Ven-ganza,* and *Phelipa,* were operational, with varying numbers of cannon and swivel guns. Three were stationed in New Orleans; *La Luisiana* served on Lakes Pontchartrain and Borgne and communicated with Mo-bile and Pensacola. In addition, there were three gunboats, three galiots, and one mortar ship (*bombardera*) that mounted two mortars. Most of these vessels served in lower Louisiana. Although not as domineering on the river as they had been, they still commanded respect.[5]

Little is known of Bouligny in the first few months of Gayoso's ad-ministration. No doubt he tried to better the province's defenses, but with the subsidy coming in irregularly because of the war and the Cuban captain general's penchant for seizing Louisiana's funds, there had to be other ways of safeguarding the province. Bouligny soon revealed his thoughts about what was happening in the Mississippi Valley. He began to compose a plan of action that the government in Spain could imple-ment to protect the province. He envisioned a new memoir, which he would submit to First Secretary Godoy. In early 1798, as Spanish forces evacuated fortresses on the east bank of the Mississippi, Bouligny initi-ated his task. He entitled his ambitious project "Agricultural, Commer-

4. Holmes, *Gayoso,* 237–38, 239–40, 242–44; Din, "Spain's Immigration Policy," 270–73.

5. Gayoso, "Statement which manifests the Force of the Squadron of Galleys of the Mississippi," New Orleans, June 10, 1799, attached to Gayoso to Saavedra, New Orleans, June 9, 1799, AHN, Est., leg. 3901, exped. 1.

cial, and Defensive Settlement Plan of the Province of Louisiana." Unfortunately, he never completed the document and perhaps not all of what he wrote has survived. But from what remains, it is apparent that he had in mind a lengthy memoir on how the Spanish government might best protect and develop Louisiana. Bouligny's project was perhaps an outgrowth of Luis de Vilemont's 1795 failed colonization scheme for upper Louisiana, as the colonel probably helped him formulate it.[6]

Only three fragments of the document survive. The first is an introduction that outlined his project. Chapter 1 would contain a geographical description of Louisiana, its rivers, climate, products, and distances. Chapter 2 was to be on the importance of the province, particularly as a bulwark for safeguarding Mexico. Chapters 3, 4, and 5 were to cover the white, black, and Indian populations. Chapter 6 concerned education for the three racial groups in the province, and chapter 7 focused on the troops needed at the mouth of each river to protect the Indians who resided upstream. Bouligny intended first to emphasize the importance of Louisiana; second, to discuss the neighboring Americans, English, and Indians; and third, to explain the powerful reasons for preserving the province. He also planned to discuss where European agricultural settlements could be placed and the Indians relocated.[7]

Reminiscent of his memoir of 1776, he proposed the creation of a lieutenant governor to assist the governor general in emphasizing the role of commerce in the province. All goods imported or exported were to be recorded and yearly summaries sent to Spain. Information on prices, shipping costs, origin of goods, and quality was to be kept. He advocated the establishment of factories in Spain to produce the goods the colony consumed, although no appreciable headway had been made since Martín Navarro had suggested this on his return to Spain in 1788. Tobacco was again to be an important Louisiana export, despite its decline in the early 1790s when Spain and Mexico could no longer absorb the colony's exports. The lieutenant governor, as in 1776, was to be in charge of this crop.[8]

Central in his projected memoir, and its most original part, was a

6. [Francisco Bouligny] to the Prince of the Peace, "Agricultural, Commercial, and Defensive Settlement Plan of the Province of Louisiana," [New Orleans, 1798], KCTU.

7. [Bouligny], "Plan for Trade Policies to Encourage the Growth of Commerce in the Province of Louisiana," [New Orleans, 1798], KCTU.

8. *Ibid.*; Coutts, "Boom and Bust," 306–309.

plan of defense that incorporated the Indians. While other Louisiana officials had suggested using the natives, his plan was more comprehensive. Bouligny saw the major threat to Louisiana coming from the trans-Allegheny West, where Americans had increased in population to 500,000 or 600,000 settlers. They had become so numerous that the Indians of that region could no longer resist them; moreover, internecine quarrels and the lack of arms weakened the natives. A secondary threat came from the English in Canada, who were penetrating the upper reaches of Louisiana to obtain furs and skins. He urged the court to act to stop these intruders. He proposed a method of defense based on increasing the colony's population while conserving the royal treasury. Troops and forts alone could not protect it.[9]

Bouligny advocated reserving for Indians an area in Louisiana bounded by rivers: the Mississippi on the east, the Missouri on the north, the Osage on the west, and the Red on the south. Bouligny believed that only two thousand warriors of the Arkansas (Quapaw), Caddo, Osage, and Chaguano (possibly the Chavuesnon or Shawnee) tribes then inhabited those lands. East-bank tribes (Chickasaw, Choctaw, Creek, and Cherokee), living under American control, could no longer hunt on their lands, but friendly tribes on the Mississippi's west bank allowed them to hunt there. Bouligny said that the United States and Spain had agreed in their 1795 treaty to contain the natives on their respective lands. But he saw the agreement as illusory, since it was impossible to prevent the east-bank natives from crossing into Spanish territory. He estimated that their warriors [hunters] numbered six thousand in a population of thirty thousand. West-bank Indians, meanwhile, had four thousand warriors or twenty thousand people in all. Bouligny thought that the Indians from the United States would soon beg Spain for admittance, and he favored it. The fifty thousand natives from both sides of the Mississippi could fit into the region he described, with room for white settlements along the fringes, particularly the lower reaches of the rivers. White settlements should not be built closer than fifty leagues from the natives.[10]

The tribes needed to learn to cooperate. Whites living in their vi-

9. [Bouligny], "Plan of the Defense of the Province of Louisiana," [New Orleans, 1798], KCTU.

10. *Ibid.* Din and Nasatir, *Imperial Osages*, contains discussions of east-bank Indians entering Spanish lands to hunt.

cinity would trade with them and act as their protectors, stopping other Indians or white hunters from disturbing them. Within their lands, the natives could devote themselves to growing corn and rice, tending livestock, and hunting seasonally. A number of eighteen- to twenty-year-old Creoles from the Louisiana regiment could spend four or five years living among the tribes, learning the indigenous style of life and selecting natives suitable for a European education. Bouligny here showed ignorance of the west-bank Indians, particularly the bellicose Osages, who had repeatedly warred on the Quapaw and Caddo tribes. Although they had been quiet between 1794 and 1797 when the St. Louis merchants Auguste and Pierre Chouteau controlled them through Fort Carondelet, the Osages soon embarked on a new wave of depredations.[11]

Bouligny's last effort at securing the crown's attention for the protection of Louisiana remained unfinished. Ill health probably forced him to put aside the new memoir and he never resumed his task. Had Bouligny completed it, however, it was unlikely that the Spanish government, under the guidance of Godoy, would have made an effort to protect Louisiana. Renewed warfare with Britain in late 1796 and the loss of income from the Spanish-American silver mines due to British domination of the Atlantic disinclined Spain from making expenditures in Louisiana. The colony produced no meaningful income to offset its costs, and it remained heavily dependent on the subsidy from Mexico.[12]

A glimpse of Bouligny is seen in early 1798 when European royalty arrived in New Orleans and thoughts shifted from dreary military and political concerns to the social graces. On February 19, 1798, excitement gripped New Orleans when the dukes of Orleans, Montpensier, and Beaujolois, who were brothers and members of the French royal family, descended the Mississippi to the Crescent City. Gayoso put them up in his household and lavished entertainment upon them. They witnessed the last days of carnival (Mardi Gras) that year. The governor took them on an excursion by boat through the Carondelet Canal, built between 1794 and 1796, which ran from the city to Bayou St. John and down to Lake Pontchartrain. Possibly Bouligny enjoyed the outing with them. Besides the many small gatherings held for the dukes, Bouligny organized the largest feast of all. As Gayoso described it: "The fiesta of 25th

11. [Bouligny], "Plan of the Defense." On the Chouteaus, see William E. Foley and C. David Rice, *The First Chouteaus, River Barons of Early St. Louis* (Urbana, 1983).

12. Whitaker, *Mississippi Question*, 183, 185.

last, given by the Louisiana Regimental Colonel and his officers has appeared to delight them due to the number of persons of both sexes who
attended. They stayed for fifteen hours with the greatest cordiality and
good harmony at a dinner-dance with 360 place settings." Doubtless the
entire Bouligny family, with four men in the regiment, attended the
festivity and enjoyed the occasion. During the dukes' thirty-three-day
residence in New Orleans, many citizens spent extravagantly. Gayoso
claimed to have poured out 4,300 pesos of his own money on them,
adding to his mountain of debt.[13]

In 1798, responding to a royal decree for financial assistance, the men
of the Fixed Louisiana Regiment made contributions to the war effort.
Amounts were assigned on the basis of rank and salary. Bouligny contributed 200 pesos as a colonel, Domingo 40 as a lieutenant, and Ursino
30 as a sublieutenant. The entire regiment was expected to open their
purses to support the crown. Even the debt-ridden common soldiers
were urged to donate 2 pesos; corporals, 10 and 12 pesos; and sergeants,
14 and 16 pesos. The regiment, which probably included only those soldiers in lower Louisiana, raised 2,063 pesos.[14]

Not long after the French dukes departed, an undefined malady
struck Bouligny again (he had been ill in late 1797), so that from at least
May 2, 1798, he was unable to perform his duties. His indisposition continued on September 21 when the regiment's lieutenant colonel, Carlos
Howard, who returned to New Orleans from Pensacola, received Governor Gayoso's orders to take charge of the corps. Howard remained in
command in January, 1799, and perhaps longer. In the interludes when
Bouligny was well enough to handle affairs, much of the paperwork was
carried out in his home where his aide, Lieutenant Caso y Luengo, assisted him. News of Bouligny's lingering illness led the new captain general, Juan Bassecourt, conde de Santa Clara, who replaced Las Casas in
late 1796, to urge him to retire, a suggestion the colonel rejected. The
army was his life and like Piernas, he expected to die in uniform.[15]

13. Gayoso to the Prince of the Peace, February 24, two letters of March 1, April 18,
1798, all reserved and in AHN, Est., leg. 3900, exped. 4.

14. "Offerings that the Officers of the [Louisiana] Regiment make in Virtue of the
Royal Decree of May 27, 1798," [n.p.], [1798], AGI, PC, leg. 160A.

15. Gautier to Carlos Howard, New Orleans, September 21, 1798, *ibid.*, leg. 215A;
Howard to Gayoso, New Orleans, October 6, 1798, enclosed in [Gayoso] to the conde de
Santa Clara, reserved, New Orleans, April 30, 1798, *ibid.*, leg. 154B; Howard to Salcedo,
New Orleans, March 23, 1803, *ibid.*, leg. 1556; Antonio de Soto y Vaillant to Casa Calvo,

Before that happened, Governor Gayoso succumbed to yellow fever on July 18, 1799. Although Bouligny had substituted for the ailing governor in March and April, no one had expected Gayoso to die. The event, however, revitalized Bouligny as it thrust him into the post of acting military governor and rekindled the hope that he might yet achieve the office of governor. Four days after Gayoso's demise, Bouligny began drafting a petition for the governorship of Louisiana and West Florida and renewed his request for the rank of brigadier general. But because of his troublesome illness, the next day, July 23, he temporarily surrendered his duties to the commander of the provincial artillery company, Colonel Nicolas D'Aunoy, until August 6 when he resumed command. Two days later, he sent a packet to the new captain general of Cuba, Salvador de Muro, marqués de Someruelos, containing his request to be named the proprietary governor of Louisiana. He cited his lengthy residence in the colony and the commands and commissions that he had discharged through thirty years, which had given him considerable knowledge. Bouligny enclosed a copy of his January, 1794, request for promotion that detailed his services.[16]

In a personal letter of the same day, the colonel asked Someruelos to reflect on his situation and said he would be hurt if he did not become governor—that coupled to his many delays in winning promotion. He acknowledged his subservient position to the captain general and promised to serve him unflinchingly. The meaning of Bouligny's entreaty was that he looked to Someruelos to assist him as a protector, since he had been without one for years. Carondelet had disillusioned him when he revealed his preference for Gayoso as governor.[17]

Life, however, was never easy for the colonel, and within two weeks after becoming acting governor, two subordinates rose to challenge his

New Orleans, April 9, 1800, *ibid.*, leg. 217A. By May 14, 1799, Santa Clara had been relieved by Someruelos (see the latter's letter to the governor of Louisiana, Havana, May 14, 1799, *ibid.*, leg. 154B).

16. Bouligny to the marqués de Someruelos, August 8, 1799, *ibid.*, leg. 154B; Nicolas d'Aunoy to Manuel Lanzos, New Orleans, July 23, 1799, *ibid.*, leg. 68; Vidal to Bouligny, New Orleans, August 6, 1799, *ibid.*, leg. 134B. Someruelos sent Bouligny's request for the governorship to the crown on September 5, 1799 (Someruelos to the interim military governor of Louisiana, Havana, September 5, 1799, *ibid.*, leg. 154B). On Bouligny's interim governorship under Gayoso, see [Bouligny] to Santa Clara, New Orleans, March 31, 1799, and his other letters to the captain general, all *ibid.*, leg. 1502A.

17. Bouligny to Someruelos, New Orleans, August 8, 1799, *ibid.*, leg. 1550.

authority. One was his longtime friend Carlos de Grand-Pré, who claimed that he should be the acting governor and that Bouligny's power was limited to New Orleans. Over the years, Grand-Pré had risen to brevet colonel and held several important posts, enjoying a position not far behind the regimental commandant. Grand-Pré based his July 25 claim to the governorship on a royal order that had named Gayoso, then the governor of Natchez, as the successor of the governor-general if the latter was absent. Bouligny, however, retorted that the February 22, 1790, royal order had been only for Governor Miró's journey to Havana (which he never made) to instruct the new captain general, Luis de Las Casas. Furthermore, Grand-Pré was not then governor of Natchez and had never assumed that post. Bouligny was certain that the governorship belonged to him.[18]

In addition to Grand-Pré, Lt. Col. Vicente Folch y Juan, governor of Pensacola, disclaimed a subordinate position to the governor-general of Louisiana and said he held an independent command directly under the captain general. Moreover, on August 1, Folch submitted his petition to Captain General Someruelos for the governorship of Louisiana and West Florida, based on twenty-eight years in the army, eighteen of them in the colonies. He claimed a profound knowledge of the province and familiarity with English and French, languages necessary to be governor. He asked for the governorship of the two provinces with the intendancy, since the post's four-thousand-peso salary was insufficient for all the expenditures required of him.[19]

18. Grand-Pré service sheet, December, 1801, AGI, PC, leg. 155A. He had replaced Bouligny as commandant of Natchez in 1786 and remained there until Gayoso arrived as the governor of the district in 1789. He had also served as commandant when Gayoso was temporarily absent. In June, 1796, Governor Carondelet named Grand-Pré lieutenant governor for the new district of Natchitoches, Rapides, Opelousas, and Avoyelles. His chief duty was to keep peace among the natives. The post, however, was not viable. In 1797, when Gayoso became governor of Louisiana, Grand-Pré received the appointment of governor of Natchez, which he never assumed because it was ceded to the United States and evacuated in 1798. Instead he was named commandant of Baton Rouge with authority over the adjacent districts of Feliciana, Manchac, and Galveztown. He was promoted to brevet colonel on September 4, 1795 (Grand-Pré petition to the king and Grand-Pré to Bouligny, Baton Rouge, August 13, 1799; [Bouligny] to Someruelos, New Orleans, August 23, 1799; all enclosed in [Bouligny] to Someruelos, New Orleans, August 28, 1799, and all *ibid.*, leg. 154B).

19. Folch petition, Pensacola, July 29, 1799, enclosed in Folch to Someruelos, Pensacola, August 1, 1799, *ibid.*, leg. 1550; Miró recommendation for Folch, New Orleans, December 28, 1791, *ibid.* Folch's services included the siege of Melilla, the 1775 expedition to

In early August, 1799, Folch wrote to Bouligny stating his position. He alleged that because of earlier instructions, any successor to Gayoso would not have command of Pensacola. Without a royal declaration giving him jurisdiction, Bouligny had charge only of the regiment. Meanwhile, Folch had a royal order naming him governor of West Florida, and he considered himself independent of Bouligny until the crown decided on this issue. The same applied to all the posts dependent on Pensacola (Mobile and San Marcos de Apalache), which would now communicate with him on military issues; civil authority, however, remained unchanged.[20]

Bouligny answered Folch on August 19 that his authority was the same as Gayoso's in military matters. He pointed out to Folch that he was not the governor of West Florida but only of the *plaza* (post) of Pensacola. To support his argument, Bouligny cited the royal order of September 21, 1795, which named Folch to Pensacola alone, not Mobile and not Apalache, much less the province of West Florida. Bouligny also cited additional orders and instructions. He accepted Folch's command of Pensacola but nothing more: "For the good of the Service I require that you, in the name of the King, not innovate anything until the captain general, whom I have consulted today, decides." He added that Mobile had always depended entirely on Louisiana.[21]

Algiers, the 1780 blockade of Gibraltar, and the expedition to America that year under Victorio de Navia. In Louisiana he had commanded Balize and Mobile. In 1793 he made a reconnaissance of Tampa Bay, and in 1794–95 commanded the ship *La Leal,* cruising in the Gulf of Mexico. Carondelet named him to build the fort at San Fernando de las Barrancas in 1795, which he did. In 1796 he was the governor of Pensacola, which he asserted lacked defenses when the war against England began. He alleged to have remedied that in three months, but Folch's claim can be questioned. A 1797 council of war rejected his pleas for major repairs because of a shortage of money (see Council of War, New Orleans, February 8, 1797, enclosed in [Carondelet] to Diego Gardoqui, New Orleans, March 3, 1797, *ibid.,* leg. 584A). On Folch, see David Hart White, *Vicente Folch, Governor in Spanish Florida, 1787–1811* (Washington, D.C., 1981), and Jack D. L. Holmes, "Three Early Memphis Commandants: Beauregard, Deville DeGoutin, and Folch," *West Tennessee Historical Society Papers,* XVIII (1964), 5–38.

20. Folch to Bouligny, Pensacola, August [no day], 1799, enclosed in Bouligny to Someruelos, New Orleans, August 13, 1799, in AGI, PC, leg. 1550. On Folch's character, see Gayoso to Folch, New Orleans, March 21, 1798, *ibid.,* leg. 57.

21. Bouligny to Folch, New Orleans, August 19, 1799, enclosed in Bouligny to Someruelos, New Orleans, August 13, 1799, *ibid.,* leg. 1550. This legajo contains copies of many Bouligny documents, with the originals in AGI, PC, leg. 154B.

The absurdity of Folch's position is easily seen. Pensacola had always been financially dependent on New Orleans. The 3rd Battalion, which was in Pensacola and its dependencies, was part of the Louisiana regiment, and Bouligny was its commandant. Virtually all of its needs had routinely come from New Orleans, not from Havana. Folch's growing ambition and querulous nature, which he had exhibited in the past, must have been responsible for his claim of independence.

By September 3, Captain General Someruelos had Bouligny's correspondence. About the challenges of Grand-Pré and Folch, he replied, "I have no doubt that the said [governorship] corresponds to you, as a result of what was prepared in the royal order of March 23, 1796." He therefore rejected the assertions of both Grand-Pré and Folch. But on Bouligny's request to be governor, Someruelos added: "Taking into consideration how broken your health is, the reason for you having left the command of the regiment from the start of last year (1798), and because the military command of those provinces should fall on a robust individual, I have judged convenient that Brigadier Marqués de Casa Calvo take charge of the command there."[22]

While Someruelos forwarded Bouligny's request for the governorship to the crown, it appeared unlikely that he would be named. But equally as devastating was losing the opportunity of serving as interim governor, since the captain general was sending a replacement. But until Casa Calvo arrived in New Orleans, Bouligny remained acting military governor, and from August 6, it was a busy time for him.

An important event during his short tenure was the arrival of the convoy from Veracruz. Its destination was Havana, but off the Florida coast Comdt. Juan Jabat learned that the port was under an English blockade. Since the convoy had money and goods valued at 8 million pesos, including at least 710,000 pesos in royal funds, he decided to seek the safety of New Orleans until he received further orders. On reaching the southwest pass into the Mississippi, Jabat observed three enemy corsairs lurking about to pick off an easy prey. After chasing them off, he hurriedly unloaded the royal funds onto small boats to send them to the safety of the river; several ships of the convoy, including his own *El Saeta,* drew too much water to cross there, and he sought a deeper pass. On

22. Someruelos to the military governor of Louisiana, Havana, September 3, 5, 1799; Someruelos to Folch, Havana, September 5, 1799, all *ibid.,* leg. 154B.

July 3, the skiff from the *Carlota* arrived at New Orleans with 260,000 pesos. Soon three schooners, *Providencia, María Josefa,* and *Isabela,* brought 150,000 pesos each.[23]

While because of his illness, Bouligny did little when the ships entered the Mississippi, he was active at the time of their departure. On August 8, Bouligny reported to Captain General Someruelos that two royal ships were leaving for Havana: the corvet *Diligencia,* which had been sent from Havana with urgent orders to bring funds, and the brigantine *El Saeta,* which carried 500,000 pesos. The ships also took Bouligny's correspondence, including his request for the governorship. Part of the convoy's funds, however, was retained in New Orleans for use in Louisiana and West Florida. It was not until mid-September that the remainder of the convoy finally cleared the Mississippi. Not all the ships arrived safely; a corsair seized the brigantine *Los Dos Amigos.*[24]

As military governor, Bouligny possessed more authority than the civil governor. He needed greater power to make decisions involving defense, commerce, Indians, and much more, including disputes between officials. Quarrels between rivals, perhaps typical of any bureaucratic organization, were frequent in Louisiana. One such dispute going on when Bouligny took charge was between Manuel García, commandant of the Louisiana river vessels, and Juan Ronquillo, pilot major at Balize. The colonel reprimanded García by letter, telling him to avoid falsehoods and stories, and emphasized that he and Ronquillo should reach an understanding "for the good of the service." Unwilling to accept any blame, García countered that Ronquillo was a villainous man of lies and mischief.[25]

23. Juan Jabat to Gayoso, on board *El Saeta* at the Southwest Pass, June 25, 1799; Gayoso to Jabat, New Orleans, July 3, 1799, both *ibid.,* leg. 134B; Gayoso to Mariano Luis de Urquijo, New Orleans, July 8, 1799, in AHN, Est., leg. 3901, exped. 1.

24. Bouligny to Someruelos, New Orleans, August 8, 1799, in AGI, PC, leg. 1550; [Bouligny] to Jabat [New Orleans], August 9, 1799, and Bouligny to Joaquin de Osorno, New Orleans, September 17, 1799, both *ibid.,* leg. 134B; [d'Aunoy] to Folch, New Orleans, July 30, 1799, *ibid.,* leg. 57; Someruelos to the interim military governor of Louisiana, [Havana], September 7, 1799, *ibid.,* leg. 154B. Holmes (*Gayoso,* 214) states that two ships in April brought 484,239 pesos for use in Louisiana; see also Gayoso to Someruelos, New Orleans, April 21, 1799, in AHN, Est., leg. 3901.

25. [Bouligny] to García, New Orleans, September 11, 1799; García to Bouligny [n.p.], September 17, 1799, both in AGI, PC, leg, 134B. Additional documents on Bouligny as acting governor are in AGI, PC, legs. 134AB, 1502A.

Among the matters that caught Bouligny's attention in the summer of 1799 were health concerns. He tried to remedy abuses that existed in the administration of New Orleans' Charity Hospital, stressing to its director that its purpose was the welfare of humanity. On August 29, because of the continued presence of yellow fever, Bouligny employed a technique tried in various European cities. He used outdated army gunpowder to fire several cannon blasts at the mouth of New Orleans streets, after first alerting the citizenry, to "rarify the air." Bouligny was also involved in quarantining ships that arrived in New Orleans. They had to stop before the redoubt of San Carlos to be inspected. Those ships free from disease could proceed to the city's main wharves.[26]

Bouligny also met with two medal chiefs of the Quapaw (Arkansas) nation, Tas-con-quidiguides and Hua-jubequin, who with a notable and thirty-one warriors had gone to New Orleans to renew their request for a gunsmith to repair their weapons. He explained to them that a gunsmith had not yet been found who was willing to live in Arkansas Post, but he promised to send one as soon as a volunteer appeared.[27]

A more important task was Bouligny's rejection of Evan Jones as the U.S. consul in New Orleans. He marveled at how Jones, bearing his commission from President John Adams, had appeared before him in his Spanish militia captain's uniform. He objected because Jones had taken an oath of loyalty to the Spanish government, was a militia captain in the provincial regiment of the German and Acadian coasts, and had been commandant at Lafourche de Chetimachas. Nevertheless, he accepted Jones's resignation from the militia and thanked him for his services. But in writing to the captain general, he disapproved of Jones's character, which he described as haughty and little inclined toward conciliation; he would be difficult to deal with. Captain General Someruelos agreed and sent his approval. However, he also ordered Jones's arrest and shipment to Havana for accepting an appointment as U.S. consul while still a Spanish subject and militia officer. But Casa Calvo chose not to arrest

26. [Bouligny] to [?], New Orleans, August 22, 1799; [Bouligny] to d'Aunoy, New Orleans, August 29, 1799; Bouligny to Osorno, New Orleans, August 19, 1799, all in AGI, PC, leg. 134A. See also Stella O'Connor, "The Charity Hospital of Louisiana at New Orleans: An Administrative and Financial History, 1736–1936," *Louisiana Historical Quarterly*, XXXI (1948), 5–108.

27. Bouligny to Carlos de Vilemont, New Orleans, September 6, 1799, in AGI, PC, leg. 134A.

Jones, since it would alienate the Americans in the colony. Jones acted informally as consul for a year and a half.[28]

Bouligny also corresponded with many of the post commandants, often giving them advice on local problems. Among the commandants in the outlying districts was his brother-in-law Carlos de Vilemont, who had charge of Arkansas Post and its district from 1794 to 1802.[29]

One post commandant who consulted Bouligny, Martin Duralde of Opelousas, complained about the misconduct of José Piernas, son of the deceased commandant of the Louisiana regiment. Young Piernas had left the army in the 1780s, lived in many places in the province, and dedicated himself to dissipation. Bouligny advised Duralde to inform Piernas to cease his lies and captious conduct and to pay his debts; he should look to his honest birth and the memory of his father.[30]

Perhaps the most serious problem during Bouligny's tenure as acting military governor first reared its head when he was sick in July. D'Aunoy, who acted in his stead, convened a meeting of the leading officials to read letters from the Spanish minister in Philadelphia, Carlos Martínez de Irujo, and Folch, warning them about the malevolent intentions of William Augustus Bowles. An adventurer, commercial agent, and self-professed friend of the Creeks, he had been a menace to Spanish control over the Southern Indians for years. In 1792, Carondelet enticed him to New Orleans with a safe conduct pass and arrested him. He spent the next seven years in prisons in Havana, Spain, and the Philippines. In 1799, Bowles escaped and soon appeared in the Caribbean in Indian dress, ready to resume command over the Creeks. He would cause much mischief for the Spaniards between 1799 and 1803.[31]

28. Bouligny to Someruelos, reserved, August 8, 1799, *ibid.*, leg. 1550; Someruelos to the interim military governor of Louisiana, reserved, Havana, September 3, 1799, *ibid.*, leg. 154B. See also "Despatches of the United States Consulate in New Orleans, 1801–1803, I," *American Historical Review*, XXXII (1927), 805–807, 812.

29. Many Bouligny letters to post commandants are in AGI, PC, leg. 134AB. On Vilemont at Arkansas Post, see Din, "Spanish Fort," 288–92, and Din and Nasatir, *Imperial Osages*.

30. Bouligny to Martin Duralde, New Orleans, August 19, 1799, in AGI, PC, leg. 134A; see also Jack D. L. Holmes, "Joseph Piernas and the Nascent Cattle Industry of Southwest Louisiana," *McNeese Review*, XVII (1966), 13–26.

31. Council of War, New Orleans, July 28, 1799, AHN, EST., leg, 3888. In 1798, Louisiana exceeded its budget by 328,908 pesos (see Gilberto Leonard, "Relation that the Principal Accounting Office of the Army of this Province Forms on Extraordinary Expenses in

At the July 28 council of war, the regimental lieutenant colonel, Carlos Howard, suggested that Panton's schooner be sent to New Providence in the Bahamas, where the Spaniards believed Bowles to be, to investigate. Panton had an interest in Bowles because the latter was trying to destroy his trade with the Southern Indians under Spanish control. Howard also proposed a thousand-pound-sterling reward (4,500 pesos) to the person who apprehended him. Because of the shortage of resources, the council deferred sending aid to Folch until he actually needed it.[32]

When Bouligny had recovered, he wrote to Someruelos on August 12 about the Bowles problem and what measures had been taken thus far, particularly the reward. The captain general approved all these precautions on September 7. Earlier, on August 18, Bouligny had informed Morales of his decision to advance Panton 15,000 pounds of gunpowder, 30,000 pounds of ball, and 20,000 flintstones, materials that might help to maintain the loyalty of the Creeks. But this in turn caused concern in the acting intendant. Because the threat from Bowles became more serious with the arrival of new warnings on September 5, Bouligny called a council of war.[33]

At the meeting, Bouligny had two recent letters from Folch read in which he asked for forty to fifty soldiers, money for extraordinary expenses, and ships for protection against Bowles. A discussion lasting three hours ensued in light of the small number of Spanish soldiers available and the lack of funds. The council members felt it too risky to send

---

1798," New Orleans, February 22, 1798, AGI, PC, leg. 134B). On Bowles, see Whitaker, *Mississippi Question*, 162–65; and J. Leitch Wright, Jr., *William Augustus Bowles, Director General of the Creek Nation* (Athens, Ga., 1967), which is favorable toward him. Spanish efforts against Bowles are in White, *Vicente Folch*, 47–67, "The Spaniards and William Augustus Bowles in Florida, 1799–1803," *Florida Historical Quarterly*, LIV (1975), 144–55, and Lawrence Kinnaird, "The Significance of William Augustus Bowles' Seizure of Panton's Apalachee Store in 1792," *Florida Historical Quarterly*, IX (1931), 156–92.

32. Council of War, New Orleans, July 28, 1799, AHN, Est., leg. 3888; [d'Aunoy] to Folch, reserved, New Orleans, July 29, 1799, in AGI, PC, leg. 54B. Whitaker (*Mississippi Question*, 172–73) erroneously believes that the reward for Bowles originated outside of Louisiana and West Florida; however, it began in this council of war.

33. Bouligny to Someruelos, reserved, New Orleans, August 12, 1799, in AHN, Est., leg. 3889bis, exped. 10; Someruelos to the military governor of Louisiana, Havana, September 7, 1799, and Morales to Bouligny, New Orleans, August 19, 1799, both *ibid.*, leg. 3888.

galleys, and they preferred that Capt. Tomás Portell, commandant of Fort San Marcos, hire twenty armed men from Panton, Leslie and Company and station them in locations where they might apprehend Bowles and his supporters.[34]

On September 9, Someruelos warned Bouligny that Bowles was returning to seek vengeance on the Spaniards and was taking a large quantity of arms to the Creeks. The next day, Someruelos advised that Bowles had not yet left New Providence but was preparing to return to Apalache. Folch would need boats, such as those on the Mississippi, to navigate the shallow waters around San Marcos de Apalache. The captain general approved his use of *El Havanero,* a Havana-based ship then in Pensacola.[35]

Bouligny never saw the end of the Bowles affair as acting military governor. On the night of September 17, the marqués de Casa Calvo (Sebastián Calvo de la Puerta y O'Farrill) reached New Orleans and took charge the next day as interim military governor. In that way Bouligny learned that he was being replaced and that his request to become proprietary governor had no chance of success. He seems to have accepted losing out again with equanimity. Although his administration as governor was too brief to begin new initiatives, it revealed once more his ability to govern as well as any of the men who had held that post, and in the case of the last governor of Spanish Louisiana, Manuel Juan de Salcedo, much better.[36]

With Casa Calvo's assumption of command, Bouligny faded into the background, where he remained for most of his last year of life. But on one additional occasion he replaced Casa Calvo as acting governor. In December, 1799, a report reached New Orleans that an English frigate of thirty-eight cannon was at the Mississippi's mouth. Casa Calvo personally conducted the mortar ship and a galiot to reinforce the vessels at Balize; he also dispatched two galleys and two gunboats to Pensacola to

34. Council of War, New Orleans, September 5, 1799, *ibid.,* leg. 3888.

35. Someruelos to the interim military governor of Louisiana, Havana, September 9, 10, 1799, both *ibid.*

36. Casa Calvo to Someruelos, New Orleans, September 20, 1799, in AGI, PC, leg. 1550. Casa Calvo reported in this letter many corsairs in the Gulf of Mexico. Creek Indians arrested Bowles on May 27, 1803, and took him to New Orleans. He was imprisoned in Morro Castle, Havana, and died in a military hospital on December 23, 1805 (Whitaker, *Mississippi Question,* 174; Wright, *Bowles,* 171).

safeguard the small ships that often fell prey to marauders of this kind. The marqués left Bouligny in charge in New Orleans for the six to eight days that he was gone. By December 11, the interim military governor was back, reporting that there were two English frigates at the mouth of the river. Perhaps the vessels Casa Calvo took helped a five-ship convoy from Havana arrive safely on December 18.[37]

While the documentation is mainly silent, the relationship between Bouligny and Casa Calvo was probably more formal than close. Prior to his assignment in Louisiana, the marqués had been only the lieutenant colonel of the Fixed Havana Regiment despite his rank of brigadier, which illustrates the weight of a noble title. He arrived in Louisiana never having commanded a regiment and never having been acting governor, duties that Bouligny had discharged for many years. Moreover, the foreign character of Louisiana disturbed Casa Calvo, particularly the non-Spanish composition of its inhabitants and many of the officers in the regiment. More than once he informed Captain General Someruelos of the need for Spanish-born officers. Casa Calvo also disagreed with Bouligny on who should succeed Gautier, who had left for Puerto Rico, as sergeant major. Bouligny recommended Lt. Col. Jacobo Dubreuil, and the marqués put forward the names of Ignacio Delinó and Pedro Olivier. The question remained unresolved at the time of Bouligny's death. Casa Calvo also complained that discipline (training) in the regiment had suffered because of Bouligny's illness. But more certain than these allegations was the continuing decline in the regiment's strength, down to 851 men by October, 1799, a loss of nearly half its soldiers. Furthermore, few replacements reached Louisiana. Because of a widespread shortage of soldiers, Someruelos advised against discharging able-bodied men and even the unfit; the latter could be used as hospital orderlies and honor and barracks guards, thus freeing the able-bodied to carry out more rigorous duties.[38]

37. [Bouligny] to Folch, New Orleans, December 5, 1799, and [Casa Calvo] to Folch, New Orleans, December 11, 1799, both in AGI, PC, leg. 57; Casa Calvo to Someruelos, New Orleans, December 26, 1799, *ibid.,* leg. 1550. AGI, PC, leg. 67, has Bouligny letters to Manuel Lanzos at Mobile, which make it clear that he was in charge in New Orleans in December. See also Vidal to Casa Calvo, New Orleans, December 4, 1799, *ibid.,* leg. 71A.

38. Casa Calvo to Someruelos, New Orleans, October 22, 1799, *ibid.,* leg, 1550; Casa Calvo to Someruelos, New Orleans, October 12, 1800, *ibid.,* leg. 1551; "General Statement of the Corps," enclosed in Casa Calvo to Someruelos, New Orleans, October 22, 1799, *ibid.,*

Bouligny was not ill through all of 1800. Part of the time he was able to sign regimental documents and dictate letters. However, he appears not to have been active when Bowles precipitated a crisis in West Florida by seizing the Spanish fort of San Marcos de Apalache on May 19, 1800, and holding it for several days. That same month Casa Calvo wrote to Captain General Someruelos about Bouligny's declining health and advocated his retirement for the good of the service, with a promotion to brigadier to soften his transition to inactivity. Perhaps officials in Spain recognized that the colonel, who had petitioned for promotion on several occasions, might be induced to step down if he achieved one of his last ambitions in life. At last, on September 4, 1800, on Bouligny's sixty-fourth birthday, a patent of promotion was issued to him for the rank of brigadier. But because of slow travel, it arrived in New Orleans after his lingering illness had claimed him. The promotion was his government's last token of appreciation for a lifetime of service that had spanned 42 years, 8 months, and 6 days.[39]

On November 25, 1800, after an illness of at least two and a half years and having received the last rites of the Catholic Church, Francisco Bouligny died. Casa Calvo left the only known description of his death. In a letter to the captain general, he wrote: "The continuing decline of the health of the colonel of the Louisiana regiment ended with an apoplectic accident." Thus a stroke terminated Bouligny's life, although Casa Calvo's description failed to explain the nature of the sickness that had marred his final years. The marqués had stated in May that Bouligny's faculties were diminishing gradually, yet the colonel remained active as late as November 20. To verify the news of his demise, the royal notary Carlos Ximénes, on the morning of November 25, personally visited Bouligny's residence to view the body before issuing a death certificate. He also obtained the keys to desks, chests, and cabinets containing important papers and placed seals on them. However, Lieutenant Caso y

---

leg. 1550; [Someruelos] to Casa Calvo, [Havana], November 7, 1799, *ibid.,* leg. 154B. On wanting more Spanish officers, see Casa Calvo to Someruelos, New Orleans, May 21, 1800, in AHN, Est., leg. 3901, exped. 2.

39. Casa Calvo to Someruelos, New Orleans, May 21, 1800, in AHN, Est., leg. 3901, exped. 2; Casa Calvo to Antonio Coronel, New Orleans, October 15, 1799, AGS, GM, leg. 6920. Bouligny's patent of promotion is in BB, HNOC; his widow did not receive it until June, 1802 (see Manuel Juan de Salcedo to Someruelos, New Orleans, July 1, 1802, AGI, PC, leg. 1554A).

Luengo, Bouligny's aide, objected, claiming that many documents belonged to the regiment. Consequently, the two men sorted out the military papers, which the lieutenant removed.[40]

Because Bouligny failed to make a will despite his lengthy illness, there were no written provisions for a funeral. Perhaps oral arrangements had been made in advance, since the family must have known that the end was approaching. Since he had been a senior official in the colony where he had resided for thirty-one years and had maintained close ties to the church in New Orleans, the family received permission to bury him in the St. Louis Cathedral. In the afternoon or evening of the day he died, and with full military honors, the family, the regiment, and New Orleans society laid Francisco Bouligny to rest in the floor of the cathedral within the altar railing. He was the only layman to be thus honored. Father José Asencio de Agustín de Briones, a regimental chaplain, presided.[41]

Bouligny's life and career spanned most of the Spanish era in Louisiana. He had arrived in the province with O'Reilly in 1769 when Spanish rule effectively began, and his life ended in the year that Spain agreed to retrocede Louisiana to France, an act not implemented until 1803. Bouligny had served under every governor, excluding Ulloa, who preceded his arrival, and Salcedo, who served after his death. Bouligny had personally known O'Reilly, Unzaga, Gálvez, Miró, Carondelet, and Gayoso. And with the exception of Gálvez, he had enjoyed cordial relations with all of them; certainly they had not shared Gálvez's opinion of him, particularly Miró, who had been an eyewitness of the sordid affair with the governor. Bouligny long believed that his embroilment with Gálvez had been responsible for his slow promotions, and he might have been correct.

Bouligny's greatest contribution to Spanish Louisiana was his *Me-*

40. Carlos Ximénes' statements of November 25 and 26, 1800, Bouligny Succession Papers; Casa Calvo to Someruelos, New Orleans, May 21, 1800, AHN, Est., leg. 3901, exped. 2. A burial certificate by José Agustín Briones, November 25, 1800, is in AGI, PC, leg. 155A, attached to Casa Calvo to Someruelos, New Orleans, June 30, 1801.

41. Martin, *Bouligny Family,* 183. When the cathedral was rebuilt in the nineteenth century, the interred bodies were removed, and it is not known if they were returned to their original graves. Nothing today notes where Bouligny was buried (*ibid.*). See also Samuel Wilson, Jr., "Almonester: Philanthropist and Builder in New Orleans," in *The Spanish in the Mississippi Valley, 1762–1804,* ed. John Francis McDermott (Chicago, 1974), 245.

moria of 1776. In it he made important commercial recommendations, which when adopted represented the first major changes in Louisiana after the Spanish takeover. Based on reality, they rejected many of the regulations that the myopic O'Reilly had imposed. Furthermore, most of Minister of the Indies José de Gálvez's instructions to his nephew Bernardo as governor of Louisiana originated with Bouligny. When Bernardo de Gálvez began implementing them, he did not act on his own initiative, as has often been believed, but on orders based on Bouligny's recommendations. Bouligny's success in personally advising José de Gálvez in Spain must have rankled the new governor, who preferred to have subservient subordinates. Governor Gálvez also sought to promote the commercial interests of his merchant father-in-law, Gilbert Antoine de St. Maxent. Both of these factors contributed to Gálvez's stripping Bouligny of his post as lieutenant governor. Instead of the lieutenant governorship serving as a springboard to the higher ranks of officialdom, as Bouligny had expected, his career languished for many years.

Nevertheless, his position near the top in Louisiana's hierarchical command could not be denied him. Even Gálvez recognized that he had to tread carefully in his accusations against Bouligny. That enabled Bouligny to found New Iberia, a settlement that has survived to the present. His war record was also excellent, although Gálvez's pettiness denied him promotion. In the postwar era, Governor Miró found him useful to command New Orleans during his absences, and Bouligny on one occasion launched the expeditions that netted the San Malo gang and many other fugitives. Bouligny also dealt successfully with the Georgia commissioners in Natchez. Moreover, his nine years as commandant of the Fixed Louisiana Regiment in a time of repeated threats to the colony appear to have been handled competently; certainly Miró, Carondelet, and Gayoso registered no complaints against him. As for personal clashes, an endemic nuisance in Spanish Louisiana, Bouligny emerged from them with the support of his superiors, which signified that he had acted correctly. In 1793, Carondelet wrote in Bouligny's service sheet, "He has talent, much zeal, and accurateness in command."[42] That succinctly stated Bouligny's strengths. Thus it was truly unfortunate that with the exception of the

---

42. Bouligny service sheet, June, 1793, AGI, PC, leg. 161A. Under notes, Carondelet wrote: "Valor—known, Application—much, Capacity—good, Conduct—Excellent" (*ibid.*).

occasions when he briefly replaced the governor in New Orleans, Bouligny never exercised the governorship in his own right. Despite this, by his *Memoria* of 1776 and its recommendations, his accomplishments in carrying out his official duties over thirty-one years, and the descendants he left in Louisiana, Francisco Bouligny created an imprint more indelible than that of most governors.

EPILOGUE: THE BOULIGNY

FAMILY REMAINS IN LOUISIANA

Francisco Bouligny's thirty-one years in Louisiana were the beginning of the presence of the Bouligny family there. At his death he left a wife; a daughter, Josefina, or Pepa; and three sons, Domingo, Ursino, and Luis, all members of the Fixed Louisiana Regiment. Because the fate of Louisiana was uncertain at that time, his sons first thought of continuing to serve the Spanish crown. When it became clear that Spain had given up Louisiana, the family began to rethink its options. They could stay or leave, and in the end they stayed. The Bouligny ties to Spain, however, did not vanish immediately, and only with the passage of time did the family become rooted in Louisiana.

Bouligny's heirs had to settle the estate. To make certain that a will did not exist, the New Orleans notaries testified that they had no record of such a document. According to Spanish law, when a married person died intestate, the surviving spouse received half of the community property, and the children inherited the other half. Prior to a division of assets, a complete inventory of Bouligny's property had to be taken. The two Bouligny children under twenty-five, Ursino (twenty-two) and Luis (nineteen), needed to appoint a guardian to represent them; they chose their older brother, Domingo. Pepa was represented by her husband, Pedro de La Roche.[1]

The inventory of the Bouligny holdings began on January 14, 1801, after the holiday season ended. His papers were examined first. They included the letters of Luis de Vilemont to the colonel; letters from vari-

1. Carlos Ximénes' statements of November 25 and 26, December 16, 1800; Statements of Luis and Ursino Bouligny, December 19, 1800; Statement by Domingo Bouligny, December 22, 1800, all in Bouligny Succession Papers. See also Din, "Death and Succession," 308, and Martin, *Bouligny Family,* 188.

ous individuals to him and drafts of his replies; his correspondence with Pedro Piernas, the regimental commandant; royal dispatches of his promotions and orders to him; and many legal documents. Unfortunately, not all of these papers were preserved, and doubtless they would have shed more light on Bouligny's life, particularly his correspondence with Luis de Vilemont in the 1790s.[2]

On January 15, an inventory was taken of his books. It listed 48 titles in 146 volumes. Only 5 titles were in Spanish (representing 15 volumes); the rest were in French. The few books in Spanish probably meant that Louisiana's limited demand for them did not make them readily available. The most popular topics, no doubt reflecting Bouligny's preference, were history and geography, which made up more than 25 percent of the titles. Commerce, economics, literature, and religion came next in interest. Agriculture, natural history, education, and physics had fewer titles. Overall, however, the inventory revealed that Bouligny was fairly well read for a man of the eighteenth century. The histories covered most of the major countries and areas (England, Holland, Russia, the American Revolution, the Western Hemisphere, and ancient history). The library disclosed that he was familiar with the economic and commercial thought of his times; read at least some of the significant literature of his age; exhibited an interest in pious works; and knew something about education, physics, and natural history. Moreover, he probably read other books besides those he owned. His personal collection of books showed that while living in a small city in a remote province, Bouligny had made a good effort to keep abreast of the currents of his time.[3]

The inventory also included the slaves, the house, and its furnishings. The Bouligny family owned a remarkable number of slaves—thirty (thirty-one when a female slave gave birth to a child), all domestics. Many of the slaves were women with children, some of whom were mulattoes. The women were all unmarried, and the inventory was silent about who the fathers of the children might be. The adult male slaves

2. Statement by Ximénes, January 14, 1801, Bouligny Succession Papers.

3. Inventory of January 16, 1801, *ibid.;* Din, "Death and Succession," 314–15. A comparison of Bouligny's books can be made with those of Gayoso; see Irving A. Leonard, "A Frontier Library, 1799," *Hispanic American Historical Review,* XXIII (1943), 21–51. See also two articles by Roger Philip McCutcheon, "Libraries in New Orleans, 1771–1833," and "Books and Booksellers in New Orleans, 1730–1830," *Louisiana Historical Review,* XX (1937), 152–58 and 606–18, respectively.

were cobblers, barbers, coachmen, and carpenters. The slaves were appraised at 21,275 pesos. They represented a value several times that of the Bouligny residence at the corner of Condé (Chartres) and Dumaine streets, which was appraised at 6,000 pesos. The inventory contained household furniture, two horses and a carriage, Bouligny's clothing, and additional household items (crockery, silver, wine, and sundries). The value of the slaves, the house, its furnishings, and other items was placed at 29,038 pesos, 5 reales. While most estate debts were settled privately, on April 10, 1802, the estate acknowledged an obligation to Francisco Collell of 5,468 pesos, 4 reales, of an original debt of 9,000 pesos. Proceeds from the sale of the slaves were used to reimburse Collell.[4]

A major asset of the estate was the unpaid purchase price for Bouligny's plantation and 33 *piezas de esclavos,* which he sold in 1792. The buyers, Francisco Mayronne and Juan Bautista Degruis, had promised to pay 100,000 pesos within a specified period of time but had failed to do so. On February 3, 1800, they pledged to pay Bouligny 45,374 pesos, the sum they still owed, in the next three years.[5]

In October, 1801, the division of the property began when Marie Louise petitioned for the return of her dowry of 10,400 pesos and for 17 slaves (4 adult women, their 11 offspring, and 2 adult men). The rest of the property, the house and other slaves, would be sold at auction. While 12 slaves were sold for 8,700 pesos, the house failed to attract a purchaser willing to pay a reasonable price. Furthermore, one of the slaves Marie Louise chose to keep for herself, Genoveva, filed a claim before a magistrate that she was an Indian, that her daughter and grandson were part Indian, and that they were all entitled to be free because the Spanish government had outlawed Indian slavery. A court upheld her claim. By October, 1802, Marie Louise asked for the 2 slaves who had not been sold and for the house, which she now wanted. Two months later, with the payment of 107 pesos and 7 reales, the settlement of Bouligny's estate was completed. Apart from what Marie Louise obtained, the records do not detail what shares the others received. But it was clear that she retained most of the assets, to which her children apparently

4. Inventory of January 16, 1801; appraisals of July 1, 3, 7, 1801, all in Bouligny Succession Papers; Din, "Death and Succession," 311*n*, 315; Ximénes Acts, Vol. XVIII, January, 1801–November, 1803, fols. 125–29.

5. Statement by notary Pedro Pedesclaux, January 16, 1801, copied from the original agreement of February 3, 1800, Bouligny Succession Papers.

consented. Possibly they received a monetary compensation for their shares.[6]

In addition, as the widow of an army colonel of more than forty-two years' service, Marie Louise was entitled to a pension. In the spring of 1801, she gathered copies of the documents that she needed, and on May 5 Governor Casa Calvo sent them to Vidal, soliciting the pension from the military fund for widows and orphans. On June 30, the governor forwarded the documentation to the captain general in Cuba for him to transmit to Spain. In Spain, the government, acting with its customary lack of speed, agreed on August 8, 1802, to a pension of 500 pesos yearly. The intendancy in New Orleans, however, had anticipated approval and had begun paying her that amount on an interim basis on May 11, 1801. It was made retroactive to the day after Bouligny's death and paid in New Orleans until June 30, 1804, when the accounting office moved to Pensacola. She continued to receive the pension until 1810, although haphazardly. West Florida fared less favorably than Louisiana in receiving the subsidy regularly from Mexico in the early nineteenth century. In June, 1807, Morales, who remained the intendant in Pensacola, complained to Folch, now the governor of West Florida, that 500,000 pesos was owed to widows and retired officers in New Orleans. In 1810, with the Spanish-American colonies, including Mexico, rising in rebellion, payment of the pensions ceased.[7]

Information about Marie Louise in the American period is not extensive. She continued to live in her house at 14 rue de Condé until May 28, 1810, when she sold it at public auction to François Du Suau de la Croix. A fire destroyed it in 1820, and the four houses built on its site have survived to the present. Where Marie Louise lived after selling her

6. Copy of dowry agreement of December 22, 1770, made on October 17, 1801; Petition of María Luisa d'Auberville, October 17, 1801, with approval of Governor Casa Calvo, October 27, 1801; Sale of slaves, December 15, 1801; Statements by notary Luis Liotan, September 18, October 8, and 18, 1802; Statement by Nicolás María Vidal, October 9, 1802; Statement of costs, December 7, 1802; all *ibid.;* Ximénes Acts, Vol. XVIII, January, 1801–November, 1803, fols. 134–35.

7. [Casa Calvo] to Vidal, New Orleans, May 5, 1801, in AGI, PC, leg. 72; Casa Calvo to Someruelos, New Orleans, June 30, 1801, *ibid.,* leg. 1552, with a copy *ibid.,* leg. 155A; Pay record of María Luisa Le Sénéchal d'Auberville to June 30, 1804, *ibid.,* leg. 538B; Morales to Folch, Pensacola, June 16, 1807, *ibid.,* leg. 98A; María Luisa Le Sénéchal d'Auberville petition to the king, New Orleans, June 18, 1824, information provided by Eric Beerman from AHN, Estado.

residence is unknown. Her mother, Mme Vilemont, who usually lived with her, died on October 22, 1812, at eighty. Marie Louise remained close to her offspring. In 1818, she and her children considered moving to Cuba, which showed that their Spanish heritage was not yet forgotten. The three Bouligny brothers and their brother-in-law, now plantation owners and growers of sugarcane, had just experienced a financially devastating year. Since the Spanish government had offered free lands to former subjects as an inducement to settle in Cuba, the Bouligny family investigated the possibility of relocating. Marie Louise wrote to her grandniece, Clementina de Bouligny y Pizarro (the granddaughter of Juan Bouligny, Francisco's brother) in April, 1818. She was married to José García de León y Pizarro, an official in the Spanish government. Marie Louise sought his assistance in transferring family assets to Cuba. Since Louisiana bank notes were valueless in Cuba, the family proposed to liquidate their lands, sugar mills, and other holdings and purchase tools and equipment they would then import into Cuba duty-free. While the family received permission to settle in Cuba, the government kept silent about their duty-free proposal. Unwilling to move without their assets, the family remained in Louisiana. On June 18, 1824, Marie Louise petitioned the king of Spain to resume her pension, which had been suspended in 1810, but it is not likely that it was. Marie Louise, a week short of eighty-four, died in New Orleans on April 23, 1834. She was buried in the tomb that contained her mother and oldest son, Domingo, who had died the year before.[8]

Less is known about Pepa and her husband, Pedro de La Roche, than the other Bouligny children. In the mid-1790s, La Roche seems to have tired of his post as customs inspector. In July and August, 1796, he was at home, sick. In October, he petitioned the king to retire at half pay (350 pesos per year) with the rank of *comisario de guerra*. During his eleven

8. "Directory of Persons Living in New Orleans in 1805," *New Orleans Genesis*, I (1962), 40; Señora Bouligny to Clementina de Bouligny y Pizarro, New Orleans, April 15, 1818; Petition of Domingo, Ursino, and Luis Bouligny to the king, New Orleans, June 25, 1818, both in BB, HNOC. In their petition, the three brothers expressed a desire that Louisiana return to Spanish domination. Copies of the Bouligny family petitions to emigrate to the Spanish government and the government's replies are in AGI, Sección Novena, nos. 1099 and 1102, August 27, 1818, and [1818], respectively. See also Luis de Onís to the marqués de Para Ynife(?), Washington, D.C., January 27, 1819, and María Luisa Le Sénéchal d'Auberville petition to the king, New Orleans, June 15, 1824, information provided by Eric Beerman, from AHN, Estado; Martin, *Bouligny Family*, 188–90, 193–94.

years of employment, he had been sick several times, suffering from "*cóli-cos biliosos*" (a bilious colon), which he attributed to the humidity, and was unable to work regularly. That same year he offered to purchase the office of *alcalde mayor provincial* (provincial justice of the peace); its holder had died without surrendering it. By March, 1797, La Roche had resigned as *vista* without a pension. Morales, the acting intendant, did not believe in his illness, stating that "he was diverting himself constantly, by day and by night, never failing to attend the theater, public dances, and other diversions that the province had to offer, giving proof of not having any legitimate impediments that hindered him in fulfilling the duties of an employee." Morales continued that La Roche was antipathetic and a bad example to the other employees. Morales suspended his salary as of March 9, 1797. How accurate Morales was about La Roche is uncertain; Morales was a cantankerous individual who soon made life miserable for Governor Gayoso.[9]

For nearly a year, La Roche was unemployed. By February 14, 1798, he had attained the office of *alcalde mayor provincial,* and on June 6 of that year Governor Gayoso named him *regidor alférez real* (royal counselor) of the Cabildo with a salary of one hundred pesos per year. An important part of being *alcalde mayor provincial* was apprehending fugitive slaves. On March 10, 1798, La Roche informed Governor Gayoso that many of them infested the New Orleans area and that there was a need to apprehend them. Twenty days later, Gayoso issued his proclamation on slaves and *cimarrones*. During 1798, La Roche sent out *cuadrilleros* (rural guards) to capture them.[10]

With the American takeover, La Roche lost his posts on the Cabildo, and thereafter he became a planter, growing sugarcane. He participated in the Battle of New Orleans, thought of moving to Cuba with the Bou-

9. La Roche petition, New Orleans, July 26, 1792, AGI, PC, leg. 26; Morales to Gardoqui, New Orleans, January 21, 1796; Morales to Joseph Antonio de Hoa, New Orleans, July 28, September 1, 1796; Morales to [Hoa], New Orleans, October 31, 1796; Morales to Gardoqui, New Orleans, January 21, 1797; Morales to [Hoa?], New Orleans, March 31, 1797, all *ibid.*, leg. 2343; [Rendón?] to Gardoqui, New Orleans, October 31, 1796, *ibid.*, leg. 584A.

10. La Roche letters to Gayoso are *ibid.*, legs. 44, 49, 66; see in particular La Roche to Gayoso, New Orleans, March 10, 1798, and Gayoso's proclamation on slaves and *cimarrones,* New Orleans, March 30, 1798, both in leg. 49. See two pay records of La Roche, both dated in New Orleans, January 1, 1802, *ibid.*, leg. 538B.

ligny family, but instead returned in 1820 to France with Pepa and several of their eight children. They settled down in Tarbes, later in Bordeaux. La Roche died sometime after reaching the age of seventy (1828). Pepa was still alive in 1859, at eighty-eight, living in Nantes.[11]

Domingo, the oldest of the Bouligny sons, stayed in the army after his father's death. Earlier, about May 1, 1799, he had requested permission to accompany his father on the latter's journey to Spain. In forwarding the request to the captain general, Bouligny, then acting governor, referred to his own health as "*quebrantado*" (broken). By mid-1803, Domingo and his brother Luis both applied for permission to leave the army, which was granted. His last post in the army was adjutant major at regimental headquarters. Before his discharge, Domingo had already embarked on other activities. In December, 1800, he purchased the Cabildo seat belonging to Gilberto Andry and became a *regidor perpetuo* (perpetual counselor). In July, 1802, Domingo, now twenty-nine, applied for royal permission to marry sixteen-year-old Anne Arthemise Le Blanc, granddaughter of his father's old friend Paul Le Blanc de Villeneufve. His mother gave Domingo her consent on July 12, 1802. Royal permission arrived in May, 1803, and the marriage soon took place.[12]

Unlike his father, who after the sale of his plantation expressed no interest in being a planter, Domingo started to acquire land. He received a Spanish land grant in 1796. In January, 1803, he purchased a half interest in a sugar plantation and soon acquired the other half. He added a sixteen-arpent plantation (by the usual depth of forty) in the Attakapas area that same year. With the American takeover, Dominique (now using the French form of his name) lost his Cabildo seat when that institution was abolished and replaced with an American-style city government. Soon afterward, he became a member of the territorial government. In 1807 he and his brother Luis briefly considered moving to Mexico. In 1808, Dominique was a major in the territorial militia. After Louisiana became a state in 1812, he became a member of the Orleans Parish Police Jury. In

11. Luis Bouligny to Joaquín de Bouligny y Fonseca, New Orleans, November 21, 1859, in BB, HNOC.

12. [Francisco Bouligny] to Santa Clara, [New Orleans], May 1, 1799, in AGI, PC, leg. 154B; Salcedo to Someruelos, New Orleans, July 20, 1802, *ibid.*, leg. 1554A; [Salcedo] to Someruelos, New Orleans, March 31, 1803, *ibid.*, leg, 155B; Salcedo to Someruelos, New Orleans, December 13, 1803, *ibid.*, leg. 1556; Ximénes Acts, Vol. XVIII, January, 1801–November, 1803, fols. 139–40.

early 1815, he, his brothers, and his brother-in-law participated in the defense of New Orleans against the English.[13]

In 1823, Dominique sold a half interest in his plantation for $117,500. The next year, the state legislature chose him to fill the unexpired term of U.S. Sen. Henry Johnson, who had been elected governor of Louisiana. In the Senate, Dominique was a conservative member of the National Republican party, voting for protective tariffs, which southerners abominated. He was not reelected to the Senate. In 1830, he gave up the last of his land holdings in exchange for property in New Orleans, since he intended to retire there. Two years later, he had a house built at 1217 Royal Street, where he died on March 5, 1833, at sixty. His widow also died there fifteen years later. Dominique and his wife had fifteen children, twelve of whom were living in 1833. Many Bouligny descendants today trace their tie to Francisco through Dominique.[14]

Of the Bouligny sons, Ursino wore the uniform of the Spanish army the longest. After it was known that France had acquired Louisiana, Ursino and Luis applied in March, 1803, to transfer to the Royal Corps of Walloon Guards in Spain, retaining their rank and seniority. But approval did not come because the Guards units were being reorganized. Ursino was, however, promoted to lieutenant in April, 1803. Following the transfer to the United States in New Orleans, the Fixed Louisiana Regiment moved to Pensacola, where Ursino served his remaining years in the army. He spent much of his time on the ships the Spaniards used in the Gulf. In May, 1806, he was second in command on the schooner *Favorita,* and by 1808, he commanded the vessel. That year, because of illness, Lt. José Declouet temporarily replaced him. By August, 1808, he had resumed command of the *Favorita.* In 1810 he was the commander of the schooner *La Cometa.*[15]

Because of the tumult in Spain and the empire, Ursino became disenchanted with army life. In 1808 Napoleon took the Spanish royal family captive and placed his brother Joseph on the Spanish throne. Many upper-

13. Martin, *Bouligny Family,* 205–13.

14. *Ibid.,* 215–18.

15. Petitions of Luis and Ursino Bouligny, enclosed in Salcedo to Someruelos, New Orleans, March 31, 1803, in AGI, PC, leg. 1555; Information on the rejection of the Bouligny transfer petitions provided by Eric Beerman; Morales to Folch, Pensacola, May 27, 1806, AGI, PC, leg. 98A; Morales to Folch, Pensacola, August 20, September 5, 1806, both in AGI, PC, leg. 98B; Martin, *Bouligny Family,* 267.

class Spaniards accepted the new king, including Francisco Bouligny's nephew Gen. Juan de Bouligny y Bertholon, son of José, and former governor of Louisiana the marqués de Casa Calvo. The Spanish people, however, refused to accept the "intrusive king," rose up in rebellion, and fought until the French were driven from Spain. The already restless colonies of Spanish America chose that time to declare their independence from the mother country. With the empire in turmoil, the West Florida troops felt abandoned; money, weapons, replacements, and even cloth for uniforms failed to come regularly. Attrition due to death, discharge, and desertion reduced the number of soldiers in the regiment, and eventually it was reorganized as a battalion. Morale in the unit continued to decline. Moreover, in 1810, the United States began seizing the parts of West Florida closest to the Mississippi. About 1811, Ursino concluded that the army was no longer what it had been in his father's day and that he should explore other avenues. A royal dispatch of July 31, 1812, which might have reached Pensacola before the end of the year, authorized his departure.[16]

Actually, Ursino, now known in the documents as "Ursin," probably put army life behind him in 1811. On December 23, 1811, with his brother Louis (whose name also underwent a slight modification), Ursin bought a sugar plantation called La Concession with fourteen slaves six leagues below New Orleans with a frontage on the Mississippi of thirty-four arpents. They soon added more slaves to the work force. In 1814, Ursin was a syndic in Plaquemines Parish, where his plantation was located. Hurt by economic conditions in 1817 and 1818, he and Louis sold a half interest in their plantation, keeping the other half until 1829 when they disposed of it for $100,000. That year the brothers were living in Jefferson Parish. When Ursin first moved to Plaquemines Parish, he began a liaison with Annette Fazende, daughter of Constance Fazende, a free woman of color that lasted until his death. Two sons, Dominique Ursin Gabriel and Louis Ursin Gabriel, were born to them on November 8, 1817, and June 9, 1821, respectively, and possibly there were other chil-

16. Ursino Bouligny service sheets of December, 1800, and January 1, 1808; Luis Piernas, "Relation of the Changes Occurred During the Last Year Among the Officers, First Sergeants, and Cadets of the Louisiana Regiment," Pensacola, January 1, 1813; Francisco Collell, "Statement of the Strength of the Louisiana Regiment," Pensacola, February 1, 1808, stated that there were only 506 men in the regiment, a shortage of 1350, and that the soldiers dressed at their own expense (all in AGI, PC, leg. 161B).

dren. Ursin recognized the two boys as his natural children when they were baptized. He died on October 7, 1842, at the residence of Constance Fazende.[17]

Luis (Louis), the youngest Bouligny to enter the Spanish army, never rose beyond the rank of sublieutenant, which he received on April 8, 1800. The crown transferred him from flag sublieutenant in the 3rd Battalion, which was stationed in Pensacola, to flag sublieutenant in the 8th Company of the 2nd Battalion on April 22, 1803. With Ursino, he thought of remaining in the army and transferring to Spain. He then changed his mind and applied for permission to retire from the army, which he did in 1804. Living in New Orleans, he engaged in political activity, serving as an alderman from 1807 to 1809. Earlier, in August, 1799, when his father was acting governor, the would-be immigration impresario the marquis de Maison Rouge died in Bouligny's house. Before his death, he made a will in which he left a parcel of land to Luis, excepting a five-arpent frontage on the Ouachita River that went to his Irish housekeeper and mistress Mary Fair. In the American era, a lengthy lawsuit took place in which Maison Rouge's natural children and the persons to whom Louis had transferred title tried to obtain possession of it. In the end, the U.S. government rejected all these claimants. When his brother Ursin left the army in 1811, Louis joined him in becoming a planter and moved out of the city.[18]

In 1815, he married Elizabeth Virginie d'Hauterive, who at fifteen was nineteen years his junior. Together they had fourteen children. Little is known about Louis during the next fifteen years aside from his joining in the family's investigation of a possible move to Cuba. In 1829, with Ursin, Louis sold his interest in La Concession, but he had already purchased another plantation from General Wade Hampton, The Cottage, located above New Orleans. He had a one-story house built on it, consisting of 2,376 square feet. Financial difficulties forced him to sell half of his land in 1831. Meanwhile, he moved into politics, and in 1833 he was

17. Martin, *Bouligny Family,* 267–70, has a longer discussion on Ursin Bouligny.

18. *Ibid.,* 271–72; Royal patent to Luis Bouligny, Aranjuez, April 22, 1803, AGI, SD, leg. 2654. The story of the Maison Rouge land grant is told in Jennie O'Kelly Mitchell and Robert Dabney Calhoun, "The Marquis de Maison Rouge, the Baron de Bastrop, and Colonel Abraham Morhouse, Three Ouachita Valley Soldiers of Fortune," and "The Maison Rouge and Bastrop Spanish Land Grants," both in *Louisiana Historical Quarterly,* XX (1937), 289–462.

representing Jefferson Parish, where he resided, in the state legislature. He helped to make it possible to run a railroad line from New Orleans to Carrollton along what is today St. Charles Avenue. In 1834, with the growth of New Orleans, plans were made for subdividing The Cottage. The subdivision was called Faubourg Bouligny and included the portion he had sold. Napoleon Avenue formed the dividing line between the half he kept (West Bouligny) and the half he sold (East Bouligny). Although he disposed of the remaining half of the plantation in 1834, the sale failed to solve his financial problems, and he declared bankruptcy in December, 1834. Louis, who communicated with his Spanish cousins, considered moving to Spain because of hard times in Louisiana in the mid-1830s. Fortunately for the family, however, his wife retained her own property. Louis stayed in the state legislature until the 1840s and held various positions in the Jefferson Parish government in the 1840s and 1850s. His wife passed away in 1849. Louis lived until January 10, 1862, dying at the age of eighty-one, probably the last of the children of Francisco Bouligny to die. His life had spanned an incredible period, from Louisiana under Spain to Louisiana attempting to secede from the United States after nearly six decades in the Union.[19]

Ursino was not the only member of his family to continue to wear a Spanish uniform after 1803. His uncle Carlos de Vilemont also remained in the army. He was commandant of Arkansas Post from 1794 to 1802. While there, he began a liaison with Catalina Bougy, daughter of a prominent merchant at the post, Joseph Bougy. Two children who lived were born to them before Vilemont left Arkansas Post; one other child, Matilde, lived for only nine days in 1798. In 1800, Vilemont took steps to obtain royal permission to marry Catalina and sent documents supporting his request to the governor. His mother gave her consent on September 24, 1799. Casa Calvo enclosed Vilemont's petition in his April 30, 1800, letter to Someruelos. The captain general in Havana approved the marriage, which he had authority to do without writing to Spain. But Vilemont was never notified, and he applied for permission again after returning to New Orleans in late 1802. Approval arrived in May, 1803, and the marriage then took place. That spring, Vilemont also learned

---

19. Meloncy C. Soniat, "The Faubourgs Forming the Upper Section of the City of New Orleans," *Louisiana Historical Quarterly*, XX (1937), 203–204; Martin, *Bouligny Family*, 218, 272–79.

that he had been promoted to brevet lieutenant colonel on October 5, 1802.[20]

On his return to New Orleans, news circulated that Spain had given up Louisiana. It led Vilemont to petition to become the successor to the commandant of the presidio at Bahia in Texas, but he did not obtain it and moved to Pensacola with the Louisiana regiment. In 1806, he sought to recover lots and slaves in Pensacola he claimed had belonged to him and Francisco Bouligny, and he seems to have gained possession of one lot in 1809. He also acquired the post of captain of grenadiers in the regiment on January 22, 1807. In August, 1809, he was still in uniform in Pensacola. But some time in the next few years (possibly he stayed in until Spain transferred West Florida to the United States in 1821), Vilemont left the army and returned to Arkansas. He had received a land grant there in 1795, described as two leagues long and one league deep. A village called Vilemont began in 1822, which possibly coincided with his return. But death soon claimed him at Arkansas Post on August 9, 1823. His heirs failed to establish their claims to his land grant, and it slipped from their grasp.[21]

While Carlos de Vilemont served the Spanish army for forty or more years (his services as a cadet began on November 1, 1770), his brother Luis spent much less time in it. In late 1790, he returned to France to look after his sister's (Marie Louise) inheritance. Encountering legal obstacles and the violence of the French Revolution, he fled to Spain, where he entered the Compañía Americana de Guardias de Corps in the Spanish army and served from 1793 to 1794. Perhaps Bouligny connections eased his way in the army. Marie Louise wrote to Felicité de St. Maxent, Governor Gálvez's widow, then residing in Madrid, on Luis' behalf. The

20. Joseph Bougy gave his daughter consent to marry on September 20, 1799 (Ximénes Acts, Vol. XIV, [1800], fol. 258); see Madame Vilemont's permission for her son Carlos to marry (*ibid.*, fols. 261–62v); [Bouligny?] to Santa Clara, New Orleans, April 29, 1799, in AGI, PC, leg. 154B; Draft by [Someruelos] to the interim governor of Louisiana, Havana, July 3, 1800, AGI, PC, leg. 1551; Salcedo to Someruelos, New Orleans, May 31, 1803, in AGI, PC, leg. 1555; Din, "Spanish Fort," 292; Vilemont service sheet, December, 1808, AGI, PC, leg. 161A. See also Harold R. Ainsworth, "The Ancestry and Some of the Descendants of Charles Petit de Livilliers and His Brother, Pierre Louis Petit, Sieur de Coulanges," *New Orleans Genesis*, XIII (March, 1964), 118.

21. Vilemont petition attached to [Salcedo] to Someruelos, New Orleans, December 20, 1802, AGI, PC, leg. 1554B; Morales to Folch, Pensacola, July 22, 1806, *ibid.*, leg. 98A; Morales to Folch, Pensacola, August 18, 1809, *ibid.*, leg. 98B; Dallas Taber Herndon, ed., *Annals of Arkansas* (Little Rock, Ark., 1947), I, 62.

countess sent a friendly reply that she would do what she could. When Luis left the Guardias de Corps in June, 1794, the Spanish government granted him the rank of brevet captain attached to the Louisiana regiment. The minister of state also gave him a passport to travel through the Spanish dominions in America for three or four years, dedicating himself to the study of natural history.[22]

Luis' travel plans soon changed, and he journeyed at his own expense to Philadelphia to study natural history in the trans-Allegheny West of the United States. That appears to have been a cover story, for he intended to explore upper Louisiana for a settlement project. This was at the height of New Orleans officials receiving proposals for colonizing Louisiana, and perhaps Bouligny alerted him to opportunities in this field. Once in Philadelphia, the Spanish chargé d'affaires, Joséf de Jáudenes, helped Luis obtain a letter of introduction from the American attorney general Edmond Franklin. Soon Luis journeyed through Pennsylvania and Virginia before sailing down the Ohio River to upper Louisiana. He carried out a reconnaissance trip to St. Louis and perhaps to present Iowa. By May, 1795, after stops in New Madrid and Arkansas Post (where he saw his brother Carlos), he reached Natchez. He was soon in New Orleans, undoubtedly staying at Bouligny's house and probably discussing conditions in Louisiana with him. The colonel, knowledgeable about events in the Mississippi Valley, must have helped Luis compose the proposal that the latter soon made to the crown. On July 30, Governor Carondelet issued a passport to Luis for his return to Spain.[23]

He reached Cádiz by October 20 and early in November presented his colonization scheme for upper Louisiana, aimed at safeguarding those lands. But because his proposal involved bringing in refugees at royal expense from France, Germany, and the Low Countries, among

22. El conde de Montarco to Alcudia, San Lorenzo, November 14, 1795, in AHN, Est., leg. 3890, exped. 34; Condesa de Gálvez to Madame Bouligny, Madrid, March 26, 1794, in BB, HNOC.

23. Joséf de Jáudenes to Carondelet, Philadelphia, November 1, 1794; Jáudenes to Alcudia, Philadelphia, October 31, 1795, both in AHN, Est., leg. 3895bis; Carondelet to Alcudia, New Orleans, July 30, 1795, *ibid.*, leg. 3890, exped. 34; Grand-Pré to Carondelet, Natchez, May 8, 1795, in AGI, PC, leg. 15; A. P. Nasatir, ed., *Before Lewis and Clark: Documents Illustrating the History of the Missouri, 1785–1804* (St. Louis, 1952), II, 318*n*. In a letter to Governor Carondelet of March 12, 1795, Lieutenant Governor Zenon Trudeau suggested that Vilemont might have been on a secret mission for the government (Nasatir, ed., *Before Lewis and Clark*, II, 318). It seems more likely, however, that he was learning about conditions in the upper Mississippi Valley for his immigration proposal.

other places, the Spanish court rejected it. First Secretary Godoy had just concluded the Treaty of San Lorenzo, which relinquished claims in the Mississippi Valley that Spain had held since 1783. Godoy also did not want to risk antagonizing the governments where the immigrants would originate.[24]

Luis remained in Spain in the army. For a time, he was in Estremadura as an aide to Field Marshal Benito Pardo de Figueroa. In 1797, he requested to be assigned to an infantry company with the rank of captain *vivo,* a captain in fact rather than his brevet rank. This effort too failed, as did his attempt to transfer as a captain to the Regiment of Volunteer Cavalrymen in February, 1798. Soon after, however, the government gave him a two-year leave to "arrange his affairs and to carry out a secret commission" in Paris. His salary as captain while on leave was to be paid by the Fixed Louisiana Regiment commencing on May 13, 1798. Luis did not remain in the Spanish army much longer. A royal order dated July 14, 1799, gave him an absolute discharge from the army.[25]

In France, Luis was perhaps involved in the negotiations that retroceded Louisiana to France. As the certainty of Louisiana being returned to France grew, he intended to stay there, selling the virtues of the province to Napoleon. From Sedan, on June 6, 1802, he sent a description of conditions in upper Louisiana to the French foreign minister, Charles-Maurice Talleyrand-Périgord, that aroused his interest. On July 3, Luis dispatched more information to Talleyrand on the Indians, their trade, and how they could be controlled through the use of *commissaires.* He praised French efforts in the early eighteenth century in upper Louisiana and condemned the Spaniards, who employed only "rude and inept men" in the Indian trade. Influenced by Luis, Talleyrand thought of In-

24. Luis de Vilemont proposal attached to Carondelet to Alcudia, New Orleans, July 30, 1795; Alcudia to the conde de Montarco, San Lorenzo, November 12, 1795; Montarco to Alcudia, San Lorenzo, November 14, 1795, all in AHN, Est., leg. 3890, exped. 34; see also Din, "Spain's Immigration Policy," 364–65.

25. Alvarez to the Prince of the Peace, New Orleans, October 29, 1797, AHN, Est., leg. 3890, exped. 34; Extract on Vilemont and decree by Godoy, [Madrid], November 2, 1797, *ibid.;* Crown, February 4, 1798, AGS, GM, leg. 6920; Aranjuez, May 8, 1798–July 17, 1798, Palace, AGS, GM, leg. 6920; Morales to Miguel Cayetano Soler, New Orleans, March 31, 1799, in AGI, PC, leg. 2343; Someruelos to the interim governor of Louisiana, Havana, December 14, 1799, in AGI, PC, leg. 154B; Casa Calvo to Someruelos, New Orleans, August 4, 1800, in AGI, PC, leg. 1551. Juan José Andreu Ocariz's article, "El proyecto de Louis de Villemont para la colonización de Luisiana," *Estudios* (University of Zaragoza, Spain) (1976), 41–59, is incomplete and contains errors.

dian alliances as a way of resisting American encroachment. But Napoleon's sale of Louisiana in 1803 eliminated Luis from serving as an adviser to the French. He missed becoming to the French what his father had been to the Spaniards four decades earlier. Luis subsequently disappears from the documents. Possibly he eventually returned to Louisiana.[26]

The only Spanish relative of Francisco Bouligny to settle in Louisiana was his nephew Juan Tala y Bouligny, son of his oldest sister, Inés. They were living in Madrid when Bouligny arrived there in late 1775, and possibly he stayed with them. During the next fourteen months, Bouligny must have spoken frequently of Louisiana and the opportunities that it offered, especially after he became lieutenant governor, and suggested taking Juan there. After her husband's death, Inés was not well off and saw only limited opportunities for her son in Spain. Bouligny probably did not have to persuade the seventeen-year-old boy to accompany him to Louisiana, where they arrived in early April, 1777.[27]

For more than a year, Juan Tala was a house guest of his uncle and without employment. But with Bouligny's expedition to Bayou Teche with the Malagueños to found New Iberia, he was hired on as storekeeper. When war broke out, Tala volunteered to go with Bouligny, who joined Gálvez's army on the Mississippi, and he served in the battles of Manchac and Baton Rouge. On December 1, 1779, he was hired as a scribe by the army accounting office in New Orleans, where he showed his ability and rose in rank. By 1783, he was the second official in the accounting office. That same year, he had seven pesos per month deducted from his salary and paid to his mother in Madrid, who was undergoing hardship. Also in 1783, at twenty-two, he married Charlotte Le Sassier, daughter of Charles Le Sassier, whom the French Creole rebels had sent to France in 1769 and whom the Spaniards had refused to readmit in Louisiana. The marriage forged another tie between the Boulignys and the Petit de Coulange–d'Auberville–Vilemont families, since Tala's wife was a first cousin of Marie Louise's mother, Françoise Petit de Coulange.[28]

26. Vilemont to Talleyrand, Sedan, June 6, July 3, 1802, in Nasatir, ed., *Before Lewis and Clark,* II, 680–87, 690–93, respectively; Lyon, *French Diplomacy,* 115.

27. See Chapter 4.

28. Tala service sheet, New Orleans, December 31, 1793, AGI, SD, leg. 2535; Martín Navarro to José de Gálvez, New Orleans, April 28, 1785, with petition of Juan Tala and royal order to the intendant of Louisiana, Madrid, July 5, 1785, all *ibid.,* leg. 2587; Martin, *Bouligny Family,* 325–26.

Although Tala worked principally in New Orleans, he performed other duties. In 1785, he accompanied Bouligny in his commission to Natchez to deal with Georgia's claim to Bourbon County and presumably returned with him the next year. In June, 1790, he went to Pensacola to replace temporarily the accountant there who was sick. His 1793 service record, made after fourteen years of service, was glowing. In 1804, the Spanish government appointed him as second in command of the boundary commission to determine the dividing line between Spanish Texas and American Louisiana. When that job was finished, he left for Pensacola with the retreating Spaniards. But some time in the next several years, he returned to New Orleans, where he lived out the remainder of his days, dying before 1820.[29]

Four children were born to the Tala–Le Sassier union, one son and three daughters. The only son, Félix, married Louise Euphrosine Rouzier, an emigré from Saint Domingue, and they had three daughters. Félix died in 1833 at forty-five. Thus, after the third generation, the name Tala disappeared from Louisiana.[30]

But this was not the case with the Bouligny name and influence in Louisiana, where they have endured. One salient fact about Francisco Bouligny, however, must be kept in mind. While proud of his ties to France and Italy, he considered himself a Spaniard and like his brothers was completely devoted to the land of his birth. His father, although born in France, conveyed that same dedication to his sons. The documents repeatedly point out where the family's primary allegiance lay. Bouligny's sons in Louisiana also grew up as Spaniards, learning to speak, read, and write Spanish, skills that their father insisted they acquire. Had he lived longer, there is every reason to suggest that Bouligny and his sons would have departed from Louisiana with the other Spaniards. Therefore, his death helped to keep the family in Louisiana. Even then, it took nearly two decades before the Bouligny family accepted Louisiana as its permanent abode.

29. Tala service sheet, New Orleans, December 31, 1793, AGI, SD, leg. 2535; Morales to Casa Calvo, Pensacola, April 9, 1806, AGI, PC, leg. 98A; Charles R. Maduell, Jr., *New Orleans Marriage Contracts, 1804–1820* (New Orleans, 1977), 18.

30. Martin, *Bouligny Family*, 326.

BIBLIOGRAPHY

MANUSCRIPTS, ARCHIVES, AND DOCUMENTARY COLLECTIONS

Archivo General de Indias, Seville

Papeles Procedentes de la Isla de Cuba

Legajos 1, 2, 3AB, 5, 9AB, 10, 11, 12, 14, 15, 15B, 16, 25A, 26, 31, 33, 34, 44, 48, 49, 53, 54B, 57, 66, 67, 68, 71A, 72, 82, 83, 98A, 98B, 116, 117AB, 122A, 126, 130, 134A, 134B, 134AB, 154B, 155A, 155B, 160A, 161AB, 170A, 174AB, 181, 187A, 188A, 190, 191, 192, 193A, 198A, 200, 207B, 209, 211A, 215A, 217A, 538AB, 566, 569, 570A, 576, 584A, 600, 603AB, 606, 608B, 633, 1055, 1145, 1146, 1147, 1232, 1304, 1375, 1377, 1393, 1394, 1396, 1397, 1425, 1440AB, 1441, 1442, 1443AB, 1444, 1446, 1500, 1502A, 1550, 1551, 1552, 1553, 1554A, 1554B, 1555, 1556, 2343, 2351, 2358, 2360, 2535, 2586, 2662

Audiencia de Santo Domingo

Legajos 2534, 2535, 2542, 2543, 2547, 2565, 2586, 2587, 2588, 2595, 2596, 2609, 2633, 2654, 2655, 2656, 2657, 2661, 2662

Archivo Histórico Nacional, Madrid

Sección de Estado

Legajos 84bis, 3883, 3885, 3885bis, 3888, 3889, 3889bis, 3890, 3893, 3893bis, 3894, 3895bis, 3898, 3899, 3900, 3901, 3902

Sección de diversos, títulos y familias, Condado de Priego

Legajo 2270

Universidades [Seminario de Nobles de Madrid]

Legajo 70, 672

Biblioteca Nacional, Madrid

Sección de Manuscritos

Colección de documentos sobre la Luisiana, 1767 a 1792. 3 vols.

Colección de various documentos para la historia de la Florida y tierras adjuntas. 2 vols.

Francisco Bouligny. "Noticia del estado actual del comercio y población de la Nueva Orleans y Luisiana española."

Archivo General de Simancas, near Valladolid

Sección de Guerra Moderna

Legajos 6912, 6915, 6919, 6920, 6925, 6929, 7292

Archivo Militar de Segovia
Colegio de Jesuitas, Málaga, Spain
  Francisco Saavedra Diario
Louisiana Historical Center, New Orleans
  Judicial Records for the Spanish Cabildo
  "Mortuaria de . . . Fran.co Bouligny"
Orleans Parish Civil Courts Building, New Orleans
  Notarial Records
    Andrés Almonester, unnumbered volumes, March, 1770, to December 31, 1778
    Juan B. Garic, Volumes IV, VI, VIII
    Leonardo Mazange Volumes I, IV
    Pedro Pedesclaux, Volumes IX, X
    Rafael Perdomo, Volumes V, XI, XII, XIII, XIV
    Carlos Ximénes, Volumes XIV, XVIII
Historic New Orleans Collection, New Orleans
  Bouligny-Baldwin Family Papers, 1710–1900
  d'Auberville-Bouligny Family Papers, 1618–1873
  Bouligny Foundation Newsletter, 1978–
Howard-Tilton Memorial Library, Tulane University
  Special Collections
    Cruzat Family Papers
    Pontalba Papers
    Rosemonde E. and Emile Kuntz Collection
New Orleans Public Library
  Actas del Cabildo, 1769–1803. 10 vols. Microfilm of WPA transcripts in Spanish.
Mississippi State Department of Archives and History, Jackson, Mississippi
  Mississippi Provincial Archives, Spanish Dominion. 9 vols. In Spanish on microfilm.
Hill Memorial Library, Louisiana State University, Baton Rouge
  WPA transcripts in English
    "Confidential Despatches of Don Bernardo de Galvez, Fourth Spanish Governor of Louisiana."
    "Despatches of the Spanish Governors of Louisiana, 1766–1792." 5 vols.

GUIDES

Bermúdez Plata, Cristóbal. *Catálogo de documentos de la sección novena del Archivo General de Indias.* Tomo I, *Secciones 1 y 2: Santo Domingo, Cuba, Puerto Rico, Louisiana, Florida y México.* Seville, 1949.

Gómez del Campillo. *Relaciones diplomáticas entre España y los Estados Unidos, según los documentos del Archivo Histórico Nacional.* 2 vols. Madrid, 1946.

Hill, Roscoe R. *Descriptive Catalogue of the Documents Relating to the History of the United States in the Papeles Procedentes de Cuba Deposited in the Archivo General de Indias at Seville*. 1916; rpr. New York, 1965.

Holmes, Jack D. L. *A Guide to Spanish Louisiana, 1762–1806*. New Orleans, 1970.

Museo-Biblioteca de Ultramar en Madrid. *Catálogo de la Biblioteca*. Madrid, 1900.

Náñez Falcón, Guillermo, comp. and ed. *The Rosemonde E. and Emile Kuntz Collection . . . : A Catalogue of the Manuscripts and Printed Ephemera*. New Orleans, 1981.

Peña y Cámara, José de la, Ernest J. Burrus, Charles Edwards O'Neill, and María Teresa García Fernández, comps. *Catálogo de documentos del Archivo General de Indias: Sección V, Gobierno, Audiencia de Santo Domingo sobre la época española de Luisiana*. 2 vols. Madrid. 1968.

THESES, DISSERTATIONS, AND REPORTS

Arena, Carmelo Richard. "Philadelphia-Spanish New Orleans Trade: 1789–1803." Ph.D. dissertation, University of Pennsylvania, 1959.

Beerman, Eric. "A Genealogical Portrait of Francisco Bouligny." Copy of typescript in possession of Gilbert C. Din.

Bjork, David K. "The Establishment of Spanish Rule in the Province of Louisiana, 1762–1770." Ph.D. dissertation, University of California, Berkeley, 1932.

Coutts, Brian E. "Martín Navarro: Treasurer, Contador, Intendant, 1766–1788: Politics and Trade in Spanish Louisiana." Ph.D. dissertation, Louisiana State University, 1981.

Cummins, Light Townsend. "Spanish Agents in North America During the Revolution." 2 vols. Ph.D. dissertation, Tulane University, 1977.

Fiehrer, Thomas Marc. "The Baron de Carondelet as Agent of Bourbon Reform: A Study of Spanish Colonial Administration in the Years of the French Revolution." Ph.D. dissertation, Tulane University, 1977.

Liljegren, Ernest R. "The Commission of Lieutenant Colonel Carlos Howard to Defend the Upper Mississippi Valley Against the English." Senior thesis, San Diego State College, 1936.

McGowan, James Thomas. "Creation of a Slave Society: Louisiana Plantations in the Eighteenth Century." Ph.D. dissertation, University of Rochester, 1976.

Morazán, Ronald Rafael. "Letters, Petitions, and Decrees of the Cabildo of New Orleans, 1800–1803: Edited and Translated." Ph.D. dissertation, Louisiana State University, 1972.

Sanders, George Earl. "The Spanish Defense of America, 1700–1776." Ph.D. dissertation, University of Southern California, 1973.

Texada, David Ker. "The Administration of Alejandro O'Reilly as Governor of Louisiana, 1769–1770." Ph.D. dissertation, Louisiana State University, 1968.

Wohl, Michael Stephen. "A Man in Shadow: The Life of Daniel Clark." Ph.D. dissertation, Tulane University, 1984.

BOOKS

Acosta Rodríguez, Antonio. *La población de la Luisiana española (1763–1803)*. Madrid, 1979.

Alcázar, Cayetano. *Las colonias alemanas de Sierra Morena (notas para su estudio)*. Madrid, 1930.

Alden, John Richard. *John Stuart and the Southern Colonial Frontier: A Study of Indian Relations, War, Trade, and Land Problems in the Southern Wilderness, 1754–1775*. Ann Arbor, Mich., 1944.

Ammon, Harry. *The Genet Mission*. New York, 1973.

Andreu Ocariz, Juan José. *Movimientos rebeldes de los esclavos negros durante el dominio español en Luisiana*. Zaragoza, Spain, 1977.

Archer, Christon I. *The Army in Bourbon Mexico, 1760–1810*. Albuquerque, 1977.

Arcila Farías, Eduardo. *El siglo ilustrado en América: Reformas económicas del siglo XVIII en Nueva España*. Caracas, 1955.

Arthur, Stanley Clisby, and George Campbell Huchet de Kernion, eds. *Old Families of Louisiana*. 1931; rpr. Baton Rouge, 1971.

Barbier, Jacques A. *Reform and Politics in Bourbon Chile, 1755–1796*. Ottawa, 1980.

Bemis, Samuel Flagg. *The Diplomacy of the American Revolution*. 1935; rpr. Bloomington, Ind., 1975.

———. *Pinckney's Treaty: America's Advantage from Europe's Distress, 1783–1800*. Rev. ed. New Haven, 1960.

Bergerie, Maurine. *They Tasted Bayou Water: A Brief History of Iberia Parish*. New Orleans, 1962.

Bethancourt Massieu, Antonio. *Patiño en la política internacional de Felipe V*. Valladolid, Spain, 1954.

Billington, Ray Allen. *Westward Expansion: A History of the American Frontier*. 4th ed. New York, 1974.

Boeta, José Rodulfo. *Bernardo de Gálvez*. Madrid, 1977.

Bolton, Herbert Eugene. *Texas in the Middle Eighteenth Century*. Berkeley, Calif., 1915.

Borja Medina Rojas, F. de. *José Ezpeleta, Gobernador de la Mobila, 1780–1781*. Seville, 1980.

Brasseaux, Carl A., ed. *A Comparative View of French Louisiana, 1699 and 1762: The Journals of Pierre Le Moyne d'Iberville and Jean-Jacques-Blaise d'Abbadie*. Lafayette, La., 1979.

———. *Denis-Nicolas Foucault and the New Orleans Rebellion of 1768*. Ruston, La., 1987.

Burson, Caroline Maude. *The Stewardship of Don Esteban Miró.* New Orleans, 1940.

Calderón Quijano, José Antonio, ed. *Los virreyes de Nueva España en el reinado de Carlos III.* 2 vols. Seville, 1972.

Callahan, William J. *Church, Politics, and Society in Spain, 1750–1874.* Cambridge, Mass., 1984.

Campbell, Leon G. *The Military and Society in Colonial Peru, 1750–1810.* Philadelphia, 1978.

Castañeda, Carlos E. *Our Catholic Heritage in Texas, 1519–1936.* 6 vols. Austin, 1936–50.

Caughey, John Walton. *Bernardo de Gálvez in Louisiana, 1776–1783.* Berkeley, Calif., 1934.

———, ed. *McGillivray of the Creeks.* Norman, Okla., 1938.

Céspedes del Castillo, Guillermo. *América hispánica (1492–1898).* Barcelona, 1983.

Chapman, Charles E. *A History of Spain.* New York, 1918.

Clark, John G. *New Orleans, 1718–1812: An Economic History.* Baton Rouge, 1970.

Clonard, Conde de. *Historia Orgánica de las armas de infantería y caballería españolas desde la creación del ejército permanente hasta el día.* 9 vols. Madrid, 1854.

Coker, William S., and Hazel P. Coker. *The Siege of Mobile, 1780, in Maps, with Data on Troop Strength, Military Units, Ships, Casualties, and Prisoners of War including a Brief History of Fort Charlotte (Conde).* Pensacola, Fla., 1982.

———. *The Siege of Pensacola, 1781, in Maps, with Data on Troop Strength, Military Units, Ships, Casualties, and Related Statistics.* Pensacola, Fla., 1981.

Coker, William S., and Thomas D. Watson. *Indian Traders of the Southeastern Spanish Borderlands: Panton, Leslie & Company and John Forbes & Company.* Pensacola, Fla., 1986.

Collot, Georges-Victor. *A Journey in North America.* 2 vols. Paris, 1826.

Comellas, José Luis. *Historia de España moderna y contemporanea (1474–1965).* 2nd ed. Madrid, 1967.

Conrad, Glenn R. *New Iberia: Essays on the Town and Its People.* Lafayette, La., 1979.

Cook, Warren L. *Flood Tide of Empire: Spain and the Pacific Northwest, 1543–1819.* New Haven, 1973.

Córdova-Bello, Eleazar. *Las reformas del despotismo ilustrado en América (siglo XVIII hispano-americano).* Caracas, 1975.

Cotterill, R. S. *The Southern Indians: The Story of the Civilized Tribes Before Removal.* Norman, Okla., 1954.

Dalrymple, Margaret Fisher, ed. *The Merchant of Manchac: The Letterbooks of John Fitzpatrick, 1768–1790.* Baton Rouge, 1978.

DeConde, Alexander. *This Affair of Louisiana.* New York, 1976.

DeVille, Winston, ed. *Yo Solo: The Battle Journal of Bernardo de Gálvez During the American Revolution*. New Orleans, 1978.

Díaz-Plaza, Fernando. *La sociedad española (desde 1500 hasta nuestros días)*. Barcelona, 1968.

————. *La vida española en el siglo XVIII*. Barcelona, 1946.

Din, Gilbert C. *The Canary Islanders of Louisiana*. Baton Rouge, 1988.

————. *Louisiana in 1776: A Memoria of Francisco Bouligny*. New Orleans, 1977.

Din, Gilbert C., and A. P. Nasatir. *The Imperial Osages: Spanish-Indian Diplomacy in the Mississippi Valley*. Norman, Okla., 1983.

Domínguez Ortiz, Antonio. *Hechos y figuras del siglo XVIII español*. Madrid, 1973.

————. *La sociedad española en el siglo XVIII*. Madrid, 1955.

————. *Sociedad y estado en el siglo XVIII español*. Barcelona, 1976.

Dufossat, Guido S. *A Synopsis of the History of Louisiana, from the Founding of the Colony to the End of the Year 1791*. Translated by Charles T. Soniat. New Orleans, 1903.

Dupuy, Trevor N. *The Encyclopedia of Military History, from 3500 B.C. to the Present*. New York, 1970.

Elliott, John Huxtable. *Imperial Spain, 1469–1716*. New York, 1964.

Enciclopedia de la cultura española. Vol. V. Madrid, 1963.

Fabel, Robin F. A. *The Economy of British West Florida, 1763–1783*. Tuscaloosa, Ala., 1988.

Fernández Duro, Cesareo. *La armada española desde la unión de los reinos de Castilla y Aragón*. 8 vols. 1895–1903; rpr. Madrid, 1973.

Ferrer del Río, Antonio. *Historia del reinado de Carlos III en España*. 4 vols. Madrid, 1856.

Figueras Pacheco, Francisco. *Compendio histórico de Alicante*. Alicante, Spain, 1957.

Floyd, Troy S. *The Anglo-Spanish Struggle for Mosquitia*. Albuquerque, 1967.

Foley, William E., and C. David Rice. *The First Chouteaus, River Barons of Early St. Louis*. Urbana, Ill., 1983.

Fortier, Alcée. *A History of Louisiana*. 4 vols. 1904; 2nd ed., Vols. I and II, Baton Rouge, 1966–72.

Gálvez, Bernardo de. *Diario de las operaciones Contra la plaza de Penzacola, 1781*. 2nd ed. Madrid, 1959.

García-Baquero González, Antonio, *Cádiz y el Atlántico (1717–1778): El comercio colonial español bajo el monopolio gaditano*. 2 vols. Seville, 1976.

Gayarré, Charles. *History of Louisiana*. 4 vols. New Orleans, 1885.

Gillis, Norman E. *Early Inhabitants of the Natchez District*. Baton Rouge, 1963.

Giraud, Marcel. *A History of French Louisiana*. 5 vols.

   Vol. I, *The Reign of Louis XIV (1698–1715)*. Translated by Joseph C. Lambert. Baton Rouge, 1974.

Vol. II, *Années de transition (1715–1717)*. Paris, 1958.

Vol. III, *L'Epoque de John Law (1717–1720)*. Paris, 1966.

Vol. IV, *La Louisiane après le système de Law*. Paris, 1978.

Vol. V, *The Company of the Indies, 1723–1731*. Translated by Brian Pearce. Baton Rouge, 1991.

Gold, Robert L. *Borderland Empires in Transition: The Triple Nation Transfer of Florida*. Carbondale, Ill., 1969.

Hamilton, Peter J. *Colonial Mobile: An Historical Study*. Rev. ed. Boston, 1910.

Hargreaves-Mawdsley, W. N. *Eighteenth-Century Spain, 1700–1788: A Political, Diplomatic and Institutional History*. Totowa, N.J., 1979.

———, ed. *Spain Under the Bourbons, 1700–1833: A Collection of Documents*. Columbia, S.C., 1973.

Haring, Clarence H. *The Spanish Empire in America*. New York, 1952.

Haynes, Robert V. *The Natchez District and the American Revolution*. Jackson, Miss., 1976.

Herndon, Dallas Taber, ed. *Annals of Arkansas*. 4 vols. Little Rock, Ark., 1947.

Herr, Richard. *The Eighteenth-Century Revolution in Spain*. Princeton, 1958.

Hoffman, Paul E. *The Spanish Crown and the Defense of the Caribbean, 1535–1585: Precedent, Patrimonialism, and Royal Parsimony*. Baton Rouge, 1980.

Holmes, Jack D. L. *Gayoso: The Life and Times of a Spanish Governor in the Mississippi Valley, 1789–1799*. Baton Rouge, 1965.

———, ed. *Honor and Fidelity: The Louisiana Infantry Regiment and the Louisiana Militia Companies, 1766–1821*. Birmingham, Ala., 1965.

Hull, Anthony H. *Charles III and the Revival of Spain*. Washington, D.C., 1981.

Humboldt, Alexander. *The Island of Cuba*. Translated by J. S. Thrasher. New York, 1969.

Humboldt, Alexander De. *Political Essay on the Kingdom of New Spain*. Translated by John Black. 4 vols. 1811; rpr. New York, 1966.

Hutchins, Thomas. *An Historical Narrative and Topographical Description of Louisiana and West-Florida*. 1784; rpr. Gainesville, Fla., 1969.

Kamen, Henry. *Spain, 1469–1714: A Society of Conflict*. London, 1981.

———. *Spain in the Later Seventeenth Century, 1665–1700*. London, 1980.

———. *The War of the Succession in Spain, 1700–15*. Bloomington, Ind., 1967.

Kany, Charles E. *Life and Manners in Madrid, 1750–1800*. Berkeley, Calif., 1932.

Kennet, Lee. *The French Armies in the Seven Years' War*. Durham, N.C., 1968.

King, Grace. *Creole Families of New Orleans*. 1921; rpr. Baton Rouge, 1971.

Kinnaird, Lawrence, ed. *Spain in the Mississippi Valley, 1765–1794*. 3 parts. Washington, D.C., 1949.

Krousel, Hilda S. *Don Antonio de Ulloa: First Spanish Governor to Louisiana*. Baton Rouge, n.d.

Kuethe, Alan J. *Cuba, 1753–1815: Crown, Military, and Society*. Knoxville, Tenn., 1986.

———. *Military Reform and Society in New Granada, 1773–1803*. Gainesville, Fla., 1978.

Le Gardneur, René J., Jr. *The First New Orleans Theatre, 1773–1803*. New Orleans, 1963.

Liss, Peggy K. *Atlantic Empires: The Network of Trade and Revolution, 1713–1826*. Baltimore, 1983.

Lynch, John. *Spain Under the Habsburgs*. 2 vols. 2nd ed. New York, 1981.

———. *The Spanish American Revolutions, 1808–1826*. New York, 1973.

———. *Spanish Colonial Administration, 1782–1810: The Intendant System in the Viceroyalty of the Rio de la Plata*. New York 1958.

Lyon, E. Wilson. *Louisiana in French Diplomacy, 1759–1804*. 1934; rpr. Norman, Okla., 1974.

McAlister, Lyle N. *The "Fuero Militar" in New Spain, 1764–1800*. Gainesville, Fla., 1957.

McConnel, Roland C. *Negro Troops of Antebellum Louisiana: A History of the Battalion of Free Men of Color*. Baton Rouge, 1968.

Maduell, Charles R., Jr. *New Orleans Marriage Contracts, 1804–1820*. New Orleans, 1977.

March y Labores, José. *Historia de la marina real española, desde el descubrimiento de las Américas hasta el combate de Trafalgar*. 2 vols. Madrid, 1854.

Marchena Fernández, Juan. *La institución militar en Cartagena de Indias, 1700–1810*. Seville, 1982.

———. *Oficiales y soldados en el ejército de América*. Seville, 1982.

Martin, Fontaine. *A History of the Bouligny Family and Allied Families*. Lafayette, La., 1990.

Martin, François-Xavier. *The History of Louisiana, from the Earliest Period*. 1827–29; 3rd ed., Gretna, La., 1963.

Moore, John Preston. *Revolt in Louisiana: The Spanish Occupation, 1766–1770*. Baton Rouge, 1976.

Morner, Magnus, ed. *The Expulsion of the Jesuits from Latin America*. New York, 1965.

Náñez Falcón, Guillermo, ed. *The Favrot Family Papers: A Documentary Chronicle of Early Louisiana*. 3 vols. [New Orleans], 1988.

Nasatir, Abraham P., ed. *Before Lewis and Clark: Documents Illustrating the History of the Missouri, 1785–1804*. 2 vols. St. Louis, 1952.

———, ed. *Spanish War Vessels on the Mississippi, 1792–1796*. New Haven, 1968.

Navarro García, Luis. *José de Gálvez y la Comandancia General de las Provincias Internas*. Seville, 1964.

Parker, David. *The Making of French Absolutism*. New York, 1983.

Petrie, Sir Charles. *King Charles III of Spain: An Enlightened Despot*. New York, 1971.

Pittman, Phillip. *The Present State of European Settlements on the Mississippi.* 1770; rpr. Gainesville, Fla., 1973.

Ponz, Antonio. *Viage de España.* 7 vols. 1772–94; rpr. Madrid, 1972.

Porras Muñoz, Guillermo. *Bernardo de Gálvez.* Madrid, 1952.

Priestley, Herbert Ingram. *José de Gálvez, Visitor-General of New Spain (1765–1771).* Berkeley, Calif., 1915.

Quimby, Robert S. *The Background of Napoleonic Warfare: The Theory of Military Tactics in Eighteenth-Century France.* New York, 1957.

Rashad, Zenab Asmat. *The Peace of Paris, 1763.* London, 1951.

Ringrose, David R. *Transportation and Economic Stagnation in Spain, 1750–1850.* Durham, N.C., 1970.

Robertson, James A., ed. *Louisiana Under the Rule of Spain, France, and the United States.* 2 vols. 1910–11; rpr. New York, 1969.

Rodríguez Casado, Vicente. *La política y los políticos en el reinado de Carlos III.* Madrid, 1962.

———. *Primeros años de la dominación española en la Luisiana.* Madrid, 1942.

Romans, Bernard. *A Concise Natural History of East and West Florida.* 1795; rpr. Gainesville, Fla., 1962.

Serrano y Saenz, Manuel, ed. *Documentos históricos de la Florida y la Luisiana, siglos XVI al XVIII.* Madrid, 1912.

Shafer, R. J. *The Economic Societies in the Spanish World, 1763–1821.* Syracuse, N.Y., 1958.

Starr, J. Barton. *Tories, Dons, and Rebels: The American Revolution in West Florida.* Gainesville, Fla., 1976.

Stradling, R. A. *Europe and the Decline of Spain: A Study of the Spanish System, 1580–1720.* London, 1981.

Swinburne, Henry. *Travels Through Spain in the Years 1775 and 1776.* 2 vols. 2nd ed. London, 1787.

Taylor, Joe Gray. *Negro Slavery in Louisiana.* Baton Rouge, 1963.

Texada, David Ker. *Alejandro O'Reilly and the New Orleans Rebels.* Lafayette, La., 1970.

Thomas, Hugh. *Cuba, The Pursuit of Freedom.* New York, 1971.

Torres Ramírez, Bibiano. *Alejandro O'Reilly en las Indias.* Seville, 1969.

———. *La companía gaditana de negros.* Seville, 1973.

Velázquez, María del Carmen. *El estado de guerra en Nueva España, 1760–1808.* Mexico City, 1950.

Villiers du Terrage, Marc de. *Les dernières années de la Louisiane française.* Paris, 1903.

———. *The Last Years of French Louisiana.* Edited by Carl A. Brasseaux and Glenn R. Conrad. Translated by Hosea Phillips. Lafayette, La., 1982.

Walker, Geoffrey J. *Spanish Politics and Imperial Trade, 1700–1789.* Bloomington, Ind., 1979.

Whitaker, Arthur Preston, ed. and trans. *Documents Relating to the Commercial Policy of Spain in the Floridas, with Incidental Reference to Louisiana.* Deland, Fla., 1931.

―――. *The Mississippi Question, 1795–1803: A Study in Trade, Politics, and Diplomacy.* 1934; rpr. Gloucester, Mass., 1962.

―――. *The Spanish American Frontier: 1783–1795: The Westward Movement and the Spanish Retreat in the Mississippi Valley.* 1927; rpr. Gloucester, Mass., 1962.

White, David Hart. *Vicente Folch, Governor in West Florida, 1787–1811.* Washington, D.C., 1981.

Woods, Earl C., and Charles E. Nolan, eds. *Sacramental Records of the Roman Catholic Church of the Archdiocese of New Orleans.* 4 vols. New Orleans, 1988–89.

Wright, J. Leitch, Jr. *Anglo-Spanish Rivalry in North America.* Athens, Ga., 1971.

―――. *William Augustus Bowles, Director General of the Creek Nation.* Athens, Ga., 1967.

Yela Utrilla, J. F. *España ante la independencia de los Estados Unidos.* 2 vols. Lérida, Spain, 1925.

ARTICLES AND ESSAYS

Ainsworth, Harold R. "The Ancestry and Some of the Descendants of Charles Petit de Levilliers and His Brother, Pierre Louis Petit, Sieur de Coulanges." *New Orleans Gensis,* XIII (March, 1964), 113–20.

Aiton, Arthur S. "Spanish Colonial Reorganization Under the Family Compact." *Hispanic American Historical Review,* XII (1932), 269–80.

Alden, Dauril. "The Undeclared War of 1773–1777: Climax of Luso-Spanish Platine Rivalry." *Hispanic American Historical Review,* XLI (1961), 55–74.

Allain, Mathé. "Bouligny's Account of the Founding of New Iberia." *Attakapas Gazette,* XIV (1979), 79–84, 124–31.

Andreu Ocariz, Juan José. "El proyecto de Louis de Villemont para la colonización de Luisiana." *Estudios* (University of Zaragoza, Spain) (1976), 41–59.

Arena, C. Richard. "Philadelphia–Spanish New Orleans Trade in the 1790's." *Louisiana History,* II (1961), 429–45.

Beer, William, ed. "The Surrender of Fort Charlotte, Mobile, 1780." *American Historical Review,* I (1896), 696–99.

Beerman, Eric. "Arturo O'Neill: First Governor of West Florida During the Second Spanish Period." *Florida Historical Quarterly,* LX (1981), 29–41.

―――. "Un bosquejo biográfico y genealógico del general Alejandro O'Reilly." *Hidalguía: La Revista de genealogía, nobleza, y armas,* XXIV (March–April, 1981), 225–44.

―――. "The French Ancestors of Felicité de St. Maxent." *Revue de Louisiane/Louisiana Review,* VI (1977), 69–75.

Bjork, David K. "Alexander O'Reilly and the Spanish Occupation of Louisiana, 1769–1770." In *New Spain and the Anglo-American West: Historical Contributions Presented to Herbert Eugene Bolton,* edited by George P. Hammond. 2 vols. Los Angeles, 1932.

———, ed. and trans. "Documents Relating to the Establishment of Schools in Louisiana, 1771." *Mississippi Valley Historical Review,* XI (1925), 561–69.

Burnett, Edmund C., ed. "Papers Relating to Bourbon County, Georgia, 1785–1786." *American Historical Review,* XV (1909–10), 66–III, 293–353.

Carr, Raymond. "Spain." In *The European Nobility in the Eighteenth Century,* edited by Albert Goodwin. 2nd ed. London, 1967.

Caughey, John Walton. "Bernardo de Gálvez and the English Smugglers." *Hispanic American Historical Review,* XII (1932), 46–58.

———. "Willing's Expedition Down the Mississippi, 1778." *Louisiana Historical Quarterly,* XV (1932), 5–36.

Chandler, R. E., ed. "Eyewitness History: O'Reilly's Arrival in Louisiana." *Louisiana History,* XX (1979), 317–24.

———, ed. "O'Reilly's Voyage from Havana to the Balize." *Louisiana History,* XXII (1981), 199–207.

Christelow, Allan. "French Interest in the Spanish Empire During the Ministry of the Duc de Choiseul, 1759–1771." *Hispanic American Historical Review,* XXI (1941), 515–37.

Conover, Bettie Jones. "British West Florida's Mississippi Frontier Posts, 1763–1779." *Alabama Review,* XXIX (1976), 177–207.

Conrad, Glenn R. "Some Observations on the Founding of New Iberia." *Attakapas Gazette,* XXII (1987), 41–46.

Corbitt, Duvon Clough. "The Administrative System in the Floridas, 1781–1821." *Tequesta,* I (1942), 41–62.

Coutts, Brian E. "Boom and Bust: The Rise and Fall of the Tobacco Industry in Spanish Louisiana, 1770–1790." *The Americas,* XLII (1985–86), 289–309.

Cruzat, Heloise H. "General Collot's Reconnoitering Trip Down the Mississippi and His Arrest in New Orleans in 1796, by Order of the Baron de Carondelet, Governor of Louisiana." *Louisiana Historical Quarterly,* I (1918), 303–20.

———, trans. "Letters in Journal Form, Written to Don Estevan Miró, Ex-Governor of Louisiana, by Don Joseph Xavier de Pontalba in 1792." *Louisiana Historical Quarterly,* II (1919), 393–417.

———, trans. "Translation of Some Documents Bearing on General Collot's Arrest." *Louisiana Historical Quarterly,* I (1918), 321–26.

Delgado, Jaime. "El Conde de Ricla, Capitan General de Cuba." *Revista de Historia de América* (1963), 41–138.

DeRojas, Lauro A. "The Great Fire of 1788 in New Orleans." *Louisiana Historical Quarterly,* XX (1937), 578–81.

Desdevises du Desert, Georges. "Les institutions de l'Espagne au XVIIIe siècle." *Revue Hispanique*, LXX (1927), 354–99.

"Despatches of the United States Consulate in New Orleans, 1801–1803. I." *American Historical Review*, XXXII (1927), 801–24.

Din, Gilbert C. "Arkansas Post During the American Revolution." *Arkansas Historical Quarterly*, XL (1981), 3–30.

———. "The Canary Islander Settlements of Louisiana: An Overview." *Louisiana History*, XXVII (1986), 353–73.

———. "*Cimarrones* and the San Malo Band in Spanish Louisiana." *Louisiana History*, XXI (1980), 237–62.

———. "The Death and Succession of Francisco Bouligny." *Louisiana History*, XXII (1981), 307–15.

———, ed. "Francisco Bouligny's 1778 Plans for Settlement in Louisiana." *Southern Studies*, XVI (1977), 211–24.

———. "The Immigration Policy of Governor Esteban Miró in Spanish Louisiana." *Southwestern Historical Quarterly*, LXXIII (1969), 155–75.

———. "The Irish Mission to West Florida." *Louisiana History*, XII (1971), 315–34.

———. "Lieutenant Colonel Francisco Bouligny and the Malagueño Settlement at New Iberia, 1779." *Louisiana History*, XVII (1976), 187–202.

———. "Loyalist Resistance After Pensacola: The Case of James Colbert." In *Anglo-Spanish Confrontation on the Gulf Coast During the American Revolution*, edited by William S. Coker and Robert R. Rea. Pensacola, Fla., 1982.

———. "Pierre Wouves d'Argès in North America: Spanish Commissioner, Adventurer, or French Spy?" *Louisiana Studies*, XII (1973), 354–75.

———. "Protecting the '*Barreda*': Spain's Defenses in Louisiana, 1763–1779." *Louisiana History*, XIX (1978), 183–211.

———. "Spain's Immigration Policy in Louisiana and the American Penetration, 1792–1803." *Southwestern Historical Quarterly*, LXXVI (1973), 255–76.

———. "The Spanish Fort on the Arkansas, 1763–1803." *Arkansas Historical Quarterly*, XLII (1983), 271–93.

———. "War Clouds on the Mississippi: Spain's 1785 Crisis in West Florida." *Florida Historical Quarterly*, LX (1981), 51–76.

"Directory of Persons Living in New Orleans in 1805." *New Orleans Genesis*, I (January, 1962), 38–43.

Echeverria, Durand. "General Collot's Plan for a Reconnaissance of the Ohio and Mississippi Valley, 1796." *William and Mary Quarterly*, 3rd ser., IX (1952), 512–20.

Fabel, Robin F. A. "West Florida and British Strategy in the American Revolution." In *Eighteenth Century Florida and the American Revolution*, edited by Samuel Proctor. Gainesville, Fla., 1978.

Faye, Stanley. "British and Spanish Fortifications of Pensacola, 1781–1821." *Florida Historical Quarterly,* XX (1942), 277–92.

Fletcher, Mildred S. "Louisiana as a Factor in French Diplomacy from 1763 to 1800." *Mississippi Valley Historical Review,* XVII (1930), 367–76.

Fortier, Alcée. "Account of the Bouligny Family, Minutes of the Meeting of June 20, 1899." *Publications of Louisiana Historical Society,* II (1900), 16–26.

Gómez Molleda, María Dolores. "El pensamiento de Carvajal y la política internacional española del siglo XVIII." *Hispania,* XV (1955), 117–37.

Haarmann, Albert W. "The Siege of Pensacola: An Order of Battle." *Florida Historical Quarterly,* XLIV (1966), 193–99.

———. "The Spanish Conquest of British West Florida, 1779–1781." *Florida Historical Quarterly,* XXXIX (1960), 107–34.

Hall, F. R. "Genet's Western Intrigue, 1793–1794." *Journal of the Illinois Historical Society,* XXI (1928), 359–81.

Hanger, Kimberly S. "Avenues to Freedom Open to New Orleans' Black Population, 1769–1779." *Louisiana History,* XXXI (1990), 237–64.

Herrero, Juan Manuel. "Notas sobre la idealogía del burgués español del siglo XVIII." *Anuario de estudios americanos,* IX (1952), 297–326.

Holmes, Jack D. L. "The Abortive Slave Revolt at Pointe Coupée, 1795." *Louisiana History,* XI (1970), 341–62.

———. "*Dramatis Personae* in Spanish Louisiana." *Louisiana Studies,* VI (1967), 149–85.

———. "Joseph Piernas and the Nascent Cattle Industry of Southwest Louisiana." *McNeese Review,* XVII (1966), 13–26.

———. "The 1794 New Orleans Fire: A Case Study of Spanish *Noblesse Oblige.*" *Louisiana Studies,* XV (1976), 21–43.

———. "Spanish Military Commanders in Colonial Alabama." *Journal of the Alabama Academy of Science,* XXXVII (1966), 55–67.

———. "Three Early Memphis Commandants: Beauregard, DeVille DeGoutin, and Folch." *West Tennessee Historical Society Papers,* XVIII (1964), 5–38.

Hussey, Roland Dennis. "Spanish Reaction to Foreign Aggression in the Caribbean to About 1680." *Hispanic American Historical Review,* IX (1928), 286–302.

Kamen, Henry. "The Decline of Spain: A Historical Myth?" *Past and Present,* LXXXI (November, 1978), 24–50.

Kinnaird, Lawrence. "The Significance of William Augustus Bowles' Seizure of Panton's Apalachee Store in 1792." *Florida Historical Quarterly,* IX (1931), 156–92.

Kuethe, Allan J. "The Development of the Cuban Military as a Sociopolitical Elite, 1763–1783." *Hispanic American Historical Review,* LXI (1981), 695–704.

———. "Los Llorones Cubanos: The Socio-Military Basis of Commercial Privilege in the American Trade Under Charles IV." In *The North American Role in the Spanish Imperial Economy, 1760–1819,* edited by Jacques Barbier and Allan J. Kuethe. Manchester, Eng., 1984.

Kyte, George W. "A Spy on the Western Waters: The Military Intelligence Mission of General Collot in 1796." *Mississippi Valley Historical Review,* XXXIV (1947), 427–42.

Leonard, Irving A. "A Frontier Library, 1799." *Hispanic American Historical Review,* XXIII (1943), 21–51.

Liljegren, Ernest R. "Jacobinism in Spanish Louisiana, 1792–1797." *Louisiana Historical Quarterly,* XXII (1939), 3–53.

Lowitt, Richard. "Activities of Citizen Genet in Kentucky, 1793–1794." *The Filson Club Historical Quarterly,* XXII (1948), 252–67.

McAlister, Lyle N. "The Reorganization of the Army of New Spain, 1763–1766." *Hispanic American Historical Review,* XXXIII (1953), 1–32.

McCutcheon, Roger Philip. "Books and Booksellers in New Orleans, 1730–1830." *Louisiana Historical Quarterly,* XX (1937), 606–18.

———. "Libraries in New Orleans, 1771–1831." *Louisiana Historical Quarterly,* XX (1937), 152–58.

McDermott, John Francis. "The Myth of the 'Imbecile Governor': Captain Fernando de Leyba and the Defense of St. Louis in 1780." In *The Spanish in the Mississippi Valley, 1762–1804,* edited by John Francis McDermott. Urbana, Ill., 1974.

Martínez-Valverde, C. "Operaciones de ataque y defensa de La Habana en 1762." *Revista general de Marina,* CLXIV (1963), 487–503, 706–27.

Míjares Pérez, Lucio. "Programa político para América del marqués de la Ensenada." *Revista de Historia de América* (January–June, 1976), 82–130.

Mitchell, Jennie O'Kelly, and Robert Dabney Calhoun. "The Maison Rouge and Bastrop Spanish Land Grants." *Louisiana Historical Quarterly,* XX (1937), 369–462.

———. "The Marquis de Maison Rouge, the Baron de Bastrop, and Colonel Abraham Morhouse, Three Ouachita Valley Soldiers of Fortune." *Louisiana Historical Quarterly,* XX (1937), 289–368.

Nachbin, Jac, ed. "Spain's Report of the War with the British in Louisiana." *Louisiana Historical Quarterly,* XV (1932), 468–81.

Nunemaker, J. Horace, ed. "The Bouligny Affair in Louisiana." *Hispanic American Historical Review,* XXV (1945), 339–63.

O'Connor, Stella. "The Charity Hospital of Louisiana at New Orleans: An Administrative and Financial History, 1736–1936." *Louisiana Historical Quarterly,* XXXI (1948), 5–108.

Padgett, James A., ed. "A Decree for Louisiana Issued by the Baron of Carondelet, June 1, 1795." *Louisiana Historical Quarterly,* XX (1937), 590–605.

———, ed. "Bernardo de Gálvez's Siege of Pensacola in 1781 (as Related in Robert Farmer's Journal)." *Louisiana Historical Quarterly,* XXVI (1943), 311–29.

Parish, John Carl. "The Intrigues of Doctor James O'Fallon." *Mississippi Valley Historical Review,* XVII (1930), 230–63.

Porteous, Laura L., trans. and ed. "Index to the Spanish Judicial Records of Louisiana." *Louisiana Historical Quarterly,* VI (1923), 145–63.

———, ed. and trans. "Index to the Spanish Judicial Records of Louisiana." *Louisiana Historical Quarterly,* IX (1926), 321–56.

———, ed. and trans. "Index to the Spanish Judicial Records of Louisiana." *Louisiana Historical Quarterly,* XVII (1935), 727–58.

———, ed. and trans. "Index to the Spanish Judicial Records of Louisiana." *Louisiana Historical Quarterly,* XXVII (1944), 854–927.

Prichard, Walter. "An Account of the Conflagration, 1788." *Louisiana Historical Quarterly,* XX (1937), 582–89.

Rodríguez Casado, Vicente. "La política del reformismo de los primeros borbones en la marina de guerra española." *Anuario de estudios americanos,* XXV (1968), 601–18.

———. "La revolución burguesa del XVIII español." *Arbor* (January, 1951), 5–29.

Scramuzza, V. M. "Galveztown: A Spanish Settlement of Colonial Louisiana." *Louisiana Historical Quarterly,* XIII (1930), 553–609.

Soniat, Meloncy C. "The Faubourgs Forming the Upper Section of the City of New Orleans." *Louisiana Historical Quarterly,* XX (1937), 192–211.

Texada, David Ker, ed. "An Account of Governor Alejandro O'Reilly's Voyage from Havana to New Orleans in July, 1769." *Louisiana History,* X (1969), 370–75.

Turner, Frederick Jackson. "The Origin of Genet's Projected Attack on Louisiana and the Floridas." *American Historical Review,* III (1898), 650–71.

Vázquez de Acuña, Isidoro. "El Ministro de Indias don José de Gálvez, Marqués de Sonora." *Revista de Indias,* XIX (1959), 449–71.

Whitaker, Arthur Preston. "The Commerce of Louisiana and the Floridas at the End of the Eighteenth Century." *Hispanic America Historical Review,* VIII (1928), 190–203.

———. "Reed and Forde: Merchant Adventurers of Philadelphia." *Pennsylvania Magazine of History and Biography,* LXI (1937) 237–62.

———. "The Retrocession of Louisiana in Spanish Policy." *American Historical Review,* XXXIX (1934), 454–76.

White, David Hart. "The Spaniards and William Augustus Bowles in Florida, 1799–1803." *Florida Historical Quarterly,* LIV (1975), 145–55.

Wilkie, Jr., Everett C. "New Light on Gálvez's First Attempt to Attack Pensacola." *Florida Historical Quarterly,* LXII (1983), 194–99.

Wilson, Samuel, Jr. "Almonester: Philanthropist and Builder in New Orleans." In *The Spanish in the Mississippi Valley, 1762–1804,* edited by John Francis McDermott. Urbana, Ill., 1974.

Winston, James. "The Causes and Results of the Revolution of 1768 in Louisiana." *Louisiana Historical Quarterly,* XV (1932), 181–213.

Worcester, Donald E., trans. "Miranda's Diary of the Siege of Pensacola, 1781." *Florida Historical Quarterly,* XXIX (1951), 163–95.

Wortman, Miles. "Bourbon Reforms in Central America, 1750–1786." *The Americas,* XXXII (1975), 222–38.

INDEX